The Secret Code

OF

Destiny

Part 1 (c 1560 – 1899)

Many Mysteries – One Secret Solution

Robert Nield

Preface

Skelton's gematria is the 'golden key' that unlocks many seemingly intractable mysteries: some literary, some historical, some famous, some obscure and some previously unknown, collectively spanning well over four centuries. The first number-letter substitution system in modern English, *Skelton* has been employed as a secret 'cipher' by several well-known individuals including a number of famous writers, viz:

Doctor John Dee, Elizabeth I, *Shake-speare*'s secret author, Isaac Newton, Benjamin Franklin, William Wordsworth, Queen Victoria & Prince Albert, Charles Dickens, Mary Ann Evans/*George Eliot*, Charles Dodgson/*Lewis Carroll*, Thomas Barnardo, Samuel Clemens/*Mark Twain*, Arthur Conan Doyle, Bram Stoker, Edward Elgar, John Buchan, Winston Churchill, T. E. Lawrence, Agatha Christie, J. R. R. Tolkein, Alfred Hitchcock, Eric Blair/*George Orwell,* Orson Welles, Alan Turing, Graham Greene, Ian Fleming, Len Deighton, Kingsley Amis/*Robert Markham*, David Cornwell/*John Le Carre*, Frederick Forsyth, Colin Dexter, Douglas Adams, J. K. Rowling/*Robert Galbraith,* Anthony Horowitz and Stella Rimington.

Skelton's cipher has been used for both 'innocent' and 'nefarious' purposes; examples of the latter include the infamous Victorian serial killer *Jack the Ripper* and the notorious sadistic child-murderers Ian Brady and Myra Hindley. In the US, *Skelton* was used extensively in the famous unsolved *Black Dahlia* and *Zodiac* murders. The cipher has also provided coded 'instructions' for a series of assassinations and murders, including: T. E. Lawrence, Reinhard Heydrich, Alan Turing, Dag Hammarskjold, US President John F. Kennedy, Senator Robert F. Kennedy, Italian PM Aldo Moro, Portuguese PM Francisco de Sa Carniero, Swedish PM Olof Palme, Diana Spencer (Princess of Wales), John Kennedy junior, UK government scientist Dr David Kelly and GCHQ officer Dr Gareth Williams (the 'spy' in a bag).

Characteristics of some that have used *Skelton*'s cipher include, in no special order:

- being a Freemason
- being a professional writer
- being an Oxbridge alumnus
- having a knowledge of cryptography
- having an interest in 'the occult'
- involvement with government intelligence agencies

Part 1 (c 1560 – 1899)

Contents

INTRODUCTION

All is number – Pythagoras (attrib.)

The material comprising *The Secret Code of Destiny* was originally intended for a series of videos on my You Tube channel: *Many Mysteries – One Secret Solution*. However, it soon became apparent that the nature and quantity of subject matter was not suited to exposition by video. It was clear that the only way to do justice to the large 'data-base' of material was to incorporate it in a book, the time-honoured way of presenting information which lends itself to an unhurried perusal of knowledge and ideas. The extensive scope of subject matter meant that one book would not suffice and so *The Secret Code of Destiny* is a trilogy: Part 1 (c 1560 -1899) Part 2 (1900 - 2018) Part 3 (The USA, international assassinations & The Occult).

A technical note - some terminology

Codes and ciphers conceal information intended only for specific recipients. In common use there is little distinction between 'code' and 'cipher'; the terms are often used interchangeably although there is a technical difference. The process of encrypting information is analogous to creating a route between two locations. The start point is the unenciphered 'plain text', the end point is the enciphered text. If the route from plain text to enciphered text is identified by signposts (algorithms) the path can be followed in reverse from enciphered text back to plain text - meaning the cipher is breakable; however, if there is no 'sign-posted route' linking start and finish - meaning encryption is ad hoc - there are no reversible algorithms and the cipher is unbreakable.

Codes operate on *whole* words and expressions. In a code, (*un*coded) plain text is converted to *en*coded text by replacing entire words and/or expressions with a coded version, according to fixed rules (algorithms). This means that coded text is often readable and even intelligible although the true meaning is hidden; for example, a poem might contain encoded information.

Ciphers/cyphers operate at the level of *individual* symbols. Letters of plain text are *replaced* by new letters/symbols according to some rule (algorithm) – a technique called **substitution**. For example, number-letter substitution ciphers replace each letter of plain text with a number, the simplest such key is: A = 1, B = 2, C = 3... Z = 26. Unlike *encoded* text which is readable/intelligible, *enciphered* text is not 'readable/intelligible' as it consists of *seemingly* random numbers, letters or other symbols. For example, using the key above "my name" has the substitution cipher "13 24 14 1 13 5". Without the key the numbers appear random, though one might guess that they correspond with letters of the alphabet. Text can be encoded simply by moving letters around – **transposition** (eg anagrams) Scrambling the numbers (1 5 13 13 14 24) creates an anagram, making the cipher a little harder to solve. Additional layers of complexity can be introduced to generate ciphers of increasing difficulty.

To summarise: *encoded* text is often readable and intelligible; by contrast, *enciphered* text is 'unreadable/unintelligible' because it consists of *apparently* 'meaningless' random symbols. Both systems are breakable or unbreakable dependant on whether the encryption process is reversible.

1. Skelton's Gematria

multum in parvo - much in little

The belief that numbers have magical attributes - occult numerology - has long been held in many cultures. Gematria - number-letter substitution ciphers - were used by the ancient Hebrews, Greeks and Romans for the purpose of divination. For example, it was believed that a person's name contained clues to their fate and that by applying gematria to the name the individual's 'destiny' would be revealed. With the passage of time, awareness of such 'occult methods' has faded so that relatively few people today have even heard of gematria let alone know how to use them. The aphorism, *multum in parvo* which can denote 'many meanings in one' is a precept adopted as the motto for this book. The notion that several *contextually appropriate* code solutions can be hidden as a single word or phrase - an idea current in the Renaissance – plays a key role in *all* of the following.

In 1510 Heinrich Cornelius Agrippa the German polymath and 'magician' completed *Natural Magic,* a work that circulated widely in manuscript and that *might* have inspired John Skelton to devise the first number-letter substitution cipher for use with modern English. However, reasoning and many code solutions (following) indicate that it was almost certainly *not* Skelton who created the cipher named for him; nevertheless, it's helpful to know something of his background if only to see why he was probably not the cipher's true creator.

John Skelton (c 1460 - 1529)

John Skelton (or Shelton) was born at Diss, Norfolk around 1460. He studied at Cambridge and perhaps Oxford and was appointed tutor to the young prince Henry Tudor (later Henry VIII) in the 1490s. On a visit to England in 1500 Erasmus, the famous humanist philosopher referred to Skelton as 'the one light and glory of English letters' but in 1502 Skelton was imprisoned - for reasons unknown - yet two years later he was made Rector of Diss. In the secular world, he gained a reputation as a practical joker and bawdy writer noted especially as a sarcastic wit, *Colin Clout* being his best-known work. In 1512 he moved to London where he *might* have encountered Agrippa's *Natural Magic* in manuscript.

John Skelton died at Westminster on June 21st 1529 and was buried at St Margaret's Church in front of the high altar; however, the grave is lost.

Logic, reasoning and many code solutions (following) provide compelling evidence that Skelton was not the creator of the cipher. In the interests of self-preservation, it would have been prudent if not essential in sixteenth century England for an occult numerologist to adopt a false name so as to obviate accusations of 'calculating' - a 'mystical' activity deemed to have potentially diabolical connotations and certainly not something to which a member of the clergy, like the Rector of Diss, would be expected to attach his name. It's likely that the cipher's true creator used a dead man's name to hide, as the dead cannot be questioned. The chosen name was *Skelton* – chosen perhaps because it related in some way to the cipher-maker's real name.

Skelton's Gematria – a C16 number-letter substitution cipher

***Skelton*'s gematria is a mono-alphabetic cipher which assigns numbers to letters as follows*:**

Vowels: A = 1, E = 2, I = 3, O = 4, U = 5

Consonants: B = 2, C = 3, D = 4, F = 6, G = 7, H = 8, J = 3, K = 10, L = 11, M = 12, N = 13, P = 15, Q = 16, R = 17, S = 18, T = 19, V = 21, W = 22, X = 23, Y = 24, Z = 25

*** *Medusa's Mirrors* Julia M. Walker Associated University Presses ISBN 0-87413-625-3**

'Mystical resonance' and the link with 'Destiny'

According to 'occult' numerology, if the letters of two or more words or phrases are replaced with numbers and each sum to the **same value**, the words / phrases are said to have ***mystical resonance*** and are deemed to be **linked by *destiny***. As indicated previously, a belief long-held was that a person's name contained clues to their fate and so, in that regard, it is apt to examine the name *Skelton*. Substituting numbers for letters and summing:

"Skelton" = 18 + 10 + 2 + 11 + 19 + 4 + 13 = 77   which means '*Skelton*' has gematria number 77

The name is *enciphered* as a string of apparently 'meaningless' numbers.

By trial and error, we find the *contextually appropriate* resonance equations:

1. "Name a cipher" = "Skelton" = 77   a code 'instruction'
2. "Skelton" = "a cipher name" = 77
3. "Skelton" = "hides *The Code*" = 77
4. "Skelton" = "name *hides me*" = 77   suggests 'Skelton' is the creator's alias
5. "Skelton" = "*The* Cipher" = 77

The resonance equations are interpreted to mean that 'Skelton' is *destined* to be the name of *The Cipher*. Next, consider the name *Shakespeare*. Again, substituting numbers for letters and summing:

"Shakespeare" = 18 + 8 + 1 + 10 + 2 + 18 + 15 + 2 + 1+ 17 + 2 = 94   the gematria number is 94

In view of its close association with the bard, we apply *Skelton's* cipher to "Globe Theatre":

"Globe Theatre" = 7 + 11 + 4 + 2 + 2 / + 19 + 8 + 2 + 1+ 19 + 17 + 2 = 94   gematria number 94

We now have the ***resonance equation***: "Shakespeare" = "Globe Theatre" (= 94)

According to 'occult numerology', those words are believed to *mystically* 'resonate' - they are thought to be linked 'mystically'. In other words, the name 'Globe Theatre' is *destined* to be linked with the name 'Shakespeare'.

Crucially, *if the cipher is changed* resonance and the link with 'destiny' is destroyed.

NB: solutions and equations are written inside "   " to distinguish from the text.

For example, using the cipher key: A = 1, B = 2, C = 3... Z = 26

"Shakespeare" = 108 and "Globe Theatre" = 118

Gematria numbers are not equal, meaning no 'mystical resonance' and no 'link with destiny'.

Reversing the cipher key: A = 26, B = 25, C = 24... Z = 1

"Shakespeare" = 189 and "Globe Theatre" = 206

Again, gematria numbers are not equal; therefore, no 'resonance' and no link with 'destiny'.

How has *Skelton's* cipher been used?

The Secret Code of Destiny illustrates the many uses to which the cipher has been put since the sixteenth century; it shows how *Skelton* not only resolves seemingly insoluble *known* mysteries but also how it solves mysteries previously *unknown*. There are no instructions accompanying the cipher and so *Skelton* must be investigated by trial-and-error - many in the past that did so probably used the cipher for amusement only. For example, the famous poet and Dean of St Pauls John Donne (1572-1631) *discovered* the resonance equation: "My name" = "John Donne" = 64. However, in stark contrast to those simply seeking entertainment some individuals, societies and organisations have taken the 'mystical' interpretation of *Skelton* very seriously, believing the cipher to be the basis of a 'supernatural oracle'* and have used it for the darkest purposes including murder and assassination.

***The subject of *The Secret Code of Destiny* part 3 (The Occult)**

Skelton's cipher can transform 'the abstract' into 'the concrete' and visa-versa.

By converting the *abstract* words 'American Independence Day' into a set of gematria numbers (52, 76, 29 respectively) the phrase can be 'encoded' as 'tangible' entities, viz: 'rosebud' + 'pyramid' + 'box' having the same sequence of gematria numbers. Of course, any three 'tangible' objects with gematria numbers 52, 76, 29 in that order could be used to represent 'American Independence Day'. The 'code' is very secure, as only those with a knowledge of *Skelton* would stand any chance of spotting that a rosebud, pyramid and box placed in order means 'American Independence Day' and even then, the 'code' would be very difficult to crack without additional clues.

A secret cipher of the 'elite' – the Freemasons?

Skelton divides the world in two: those who know the cipher - the 'elite' - and those who do not. It seems that long ago the 'elite' decided that the cipher should remain secret, probably reasoning that it could prove dangerous in the 'wrong hands' and perhaps recognising also that sharing power dilutes power. However, the keeping of secrets tends to engender mystery and mystery tends to arouse suspicion in those 'outside the loop'. The Freemasons - The Craft - The Brotherhood are an example of this phenomenon and are known to use gematria. Have they used *Skelton*? The following offers a preliminary answer.

The Capitol in Washington DC, the great 'Masonic City' (Image: Wikipedia commons)

Constructed 1793 – 1866, the Capitol was dedicated in a Masonic ceremony. A Latin motto on the base of *Freedom*, the statue atop the Capitol's rotunda reads: *e pluribus unum* ('out of many, one'). Benjamin Franklin, one of the founders of the Republic and a Freemason helped to choose it. Formerly the *de facto* US national motto, *e pluribus unum* was replaced in 1956 with: 'In God we trust'.

Applying *Skelton*'s cipher to the Latin ("*e pluribus unum*" = 113) we find the following *contextually appropriate* resonance equations referring to cipher/cypher:

1. "e pluribus unum" = "a cypher hint" = 113
2. "e pluribus unum" = "a hint at a cipher" = 113
3. **"e pluribus unum" = "a Masonic motto" = 113**
4. "e pluribus unum" = "cipher in Latin" = 113
5. "e pluribus unum" = "found on statue" = 113
6. "e pluribus unum" = "hid clue as motto" = 113
7. "e pluribus unum" = "hid the cypher" = 113
8. "e pluribus unum" = "is a cipher hint" = 113
9. "e pluribus unum" = "it is a cypher" = 113
10. "e pluribus unum" = "you found cipher" = 113
11. "e pluribus unum" = "you got the clue" = 113

An example of *multum in parvo* - much in little - *many* solutions equating to *one* phrase.

It is unclear how 'code' and 'cipher'/'cypher' were used in the distant past, so resonance equations are split into those referring to cipher/cypher (above) and those referring to code (following).

NB Equations can be reversed, for example: "you found a code hid as" = "e pluribus unum" = 113

And, solutions can be linked to form equations making extended statements, for example:

"A Masonic motto" = "found on statue" = "hid the cypher" = 133 etc.

Contextually appropriate resonance equations referring to 'code':

1. **"e pluribus unum" = "a clue to a Masonic code" = 113**
2. "e pluribus unum" = "a code hidden in Latin" = 113
3. "e pluribus unum" = "a code statue hides" = 113
4. "e pluribus unum" = "a hidden code you found" = 113
5. "e pluribus unum" = "Capitol hid the code" = 113
6. "e pluribus unum" = "code clue statue hid" = 113
7. "e pluribus unum" = "hides code in Latin" = 113
8. "e pluribus unum" = "hides code you found" = 113
9. "e pluribus unum" = "hiding a secret code" = 113
10. "e pluribus unum" = "is code statue hid" = 113
11. "e pluribus unum" = "motto is code clue" = 113
12. "e pluribus unum" = "motto was a code" = 113
13. "e pluribus unum" = "statue's codes" = 113
14. "e pluribus unum" = "was hiding code clue" = 113

Reversed resonance equations:

1. "Mason's code hid as" = "e pluribus unum" = 113
2. "You got code clue in" = "e pluribus unum" = 113

Again, solutions can be linked to make larger contextually appropriate equations:

"Statue hid code clue" = "a clue to a Masonic code" = "a hidden code you found" = 113 etc.

Finally, applying *Skelton* to the English translation 'out of many, one':

1. **"Out of many, one" = "a Freemason's code" = 107**
2. "Out of many, one" = "hiding cypher" = 107
3. "Out of many, one" = "is code on Capitol" = 107
4. "Out of many, one" = "is hiding a hidden code" = 107
5. "Out of many, one" = "is hiding cipher" = 107
6. "Out of many, one" = "the correct code" = 107
7. "Out of many, one" = "you are right" = 107
8. "Out of many, one" = "you found the code" = 107

Again, larger resonance equations can be constructed:

"You are right" = "*out of many, one*" = "is hiding a hidden code" = 107. etc

We note that solutions 7 & 8 above 'talk' to the solver ('you') giving the resonance equations:

"You are right" = "you found the code" = "the correct code" = 107

Reversing the resonance equation:

"Code was hidden *as*" = "out of many, one" = 107

2. The Master Code/Maister Cipher – 'the Golden Key'

The Master Code/Maister Cipher is a vast set of ***contextually appropriate*** solutions, each summing to the 'magic' gematria number **246** using *Skelton's* cipher. The Master Code/Maister Cipher is a sub-set of ***The Code of Destiny***, the latter consisting of ***all contextually appropriate*** **solutions irrespective of gematria number**. Many solutions (following) identify **two-hundred and forty-six** as the most important gematria number associated with *Skelton*'s cipher – the 'magic' number, the key.

Methodology - code solutions and resonance equations

There are no instructions to accompany *Skelton*'s cipher, there is no 'algorithm' or 'formula' by which solutions can be found 'mechanically'; therefore, ***contextually appropriate*** **solutions must be discovered by trial and error guided by experience, intuition, knowledge, logic, grammar and syntax.**

The 'codes' referred to herein are *not* codes in the usual sense - there are very few encoded texts to decipher - rather, the 'codes' are *contextually appropriate* 'solutions' found by applying the cipher in specific contexts. That is to say: **a particular context is chosen and an appropriate solution proposed. The solution is 'tested' by applying the cipher. If the letter-values of the conjectured solution sum to 246 the 'conjecture' is deemed to be a 'Master Code/Maister Cipher' solution.**

An illustration

The context chosen in this case is 'The Code of Destiny' itself; the conjecture is that a Master Code solution tells 'you' (the solver) that 'you' *discovered The Code of Destiny*. All Master Code solutions sum to the 'magic' gematria number **246** and so the conjecture is:

"You *discovered The Code of Destiny*" = 246 using *Skelton*'s cipher.

Letters are replaced with numbers and summed, giving the cipher:

24+4+5/ + 4+3+18+3+4+21+2+17+2+4/ +19+8+2/ +3+4+4+2/+4+6/+4+2+18+19+3+13+24 = **246**

Indeed: **"You discovered *The Code of Destiny*" = 246** using *Skelton*'s cipher.

"You discovered *The Code of Destiny*" is a Master Code/Maister Cipher solution because - as many more solutions indicate - **Master Code/Maister Cipher solutions *always* sum to 246.**

For example, by trial and error we find:

"You have found *The Maister Cipher*" = 246 old spelling of master

Skelton can be used in *two* distinct ways: 'discovery' or 'invention'

1. The code 'solver' can search for *naturally* occurring solutions and equations – that is, solutions and equations that have *not* been constructed or 'engineered' by anyone. The case of John Donne is an example, he found a resonance equation that was 'waiting' to be *discovered*: "John Donne" = "my name" = 64. He didn't 'make' the equation work - it was natural - found by trial and error.

2. By contrast, when writers use *Skelton*'s cipher, they 'engineer' solutions so as to fit a particular context – typically, they use the cipher to link a character's name to the part they play in the story. For instance, in '*A Christmas Carol*' by Charles Dickens we find the Master Code solution:

"*Tiny Tim* was cripple's name" = 246 the solution is an i*nvention* of Dickens

To summarise: the cipher can be used in two distinct ways. Firstly, as a kind of 'oracle' in which the 'solver' looks for naturally occurring solutions and equations using trial and error - the answers are 'discovered'. Secondly, the 'solver' can construct solutions and equations to fit a particular context - which is how writers have used the cipher - the answers are 'invented'.

Nomenclature

Throughout the following '**cipher**' mainly refers to *Skelton*'s number-letter list, '**code**' mainly alludes to solutions and resonance equations and **gematria number** is the sum of letter-values. When *Skelton* was created the word 'code' might not have had its modern usage, at that time what we now call 'code' - meaning encrypted text - might have been referred to as cipher or cypher. In more recent times application of *Skelton* would include the use of 'code' in a modern sense. In any case, those using *Skelton* in times past might not have been too concerned with the technical distinction between code and cipher; therefore, some sets of solutions are split into those that refer to 'cipher/cypher' and those that refer to 'code'. This shows that *both* 'cipher/cypher' *and* 'code' give contextually appropriate solutions.

A summary of the ensuing Master Code solutions

The following examples of the Master Code congratulate the solver ('you') on breaking a very difficult code. Solutions 'tell' the solver that the cipher is *Skelton's* and that 'the code' - *The Code of Destiny* - is 'vast' and 'uncanny'. Solutions also 'tell' the solver that answers are found by trial and error, wit and intuition and indicate several times that the most important gematria number - the special 'magic key' - is **246**. Many solutions show the solver they have the correct key and that *The Master Code* - identified as the 'ultimate cipher' - has been discovered.

NB It is important to remember that <u>none</u> of the lists of solutions or resonance equations in *The Secret Code of Destiny* can be regarded as complete, since it is virtually certain additional solutions/resonance equations will be found in future. Also, it's important to appreciate that nobody 'engineered' the following solutions, they occur naturally – the answers are discoveries.

Applying *Skelton* in the general context of 'the code' and 'you' (the solver).

1. "Clue is correct: *you* have found *The Code*" = 246
2. "Clue is: *you* have found the correct code" = 246
3. "Congratulations on finding *The Code*" = 246
4. "Congratulations: *ye* cracked *The Code*" = 246
5. "Extremely hard code found by *you*" = 246
6. "I congratulate *you* on finding *The Code*" = 246
7. "The code *you* discovered is *uncanny*" = 246
8. "What *you* have found is *The Code Key*" = 246
9. "*Ye* broke extremely difficult code" = 246
10. "*You* are congratulated on cracking code" = 246
11. "*You* are congratulated on finding clue" = 246
12. "*You* are correct: *you* found *The Code* clue" = 246
13. **"*You* are forbidden to reveal this code" = 246**
14. "*You* are right about *Skelton*'s code" = 246
15. "*You* are right: *you* found code numeral" = 246
16. "*You* are right: *you* found secret code" = 246
17. "*You* are right: *you* have found *The Code*" = 246
18. "*You* are the discoverer of *The Code* clue" = 246
19. "*You* are the solver of the code clues" = 246
20. "*You* can be confident this code is true" = 246
21. "*You* cracked extremely hard codes" = 246
22. "*You* discovered a code of *Revelations*" = 246
23. "*You* discovered secret code numeral" = 246
24. "You discovered *Skelton* code. *Bravo*!" = 246
25. "You discovered *The Code* in *Skelton*" = 246
26. "*You* discovered *The Code of Destiny*" = 246
27. "*You* discovered *The Freemasons' Code*" = 246*
28. "You found *Skelton*: the infinite code" = 246
29. "*You* found the secret code's message" = 246
30. "*You* have broken *our* very hard code" = 246
31. "*You* have deciphered the secret codes" = 246
32. "*You* have discovered the code numeral" = 246
33. "*You* have discovered the secret code" = 246
34. "*You* have found answers in *The Code*" = 246
35. "You have found meaning in this code clue" = 246
36. "*You* have hit upon the secret of a code" = 246
37. "*You* have solved the secret codes" = 246
38. "*You* know the secret code numeral" = 246
39. "*You* know the secret of the huge code" = 246
40. "*You* need no help to solve the codes" = 246
41. "*You* use this cipher to solve code" = 246
42. "*Your* wit uncovered the code clues" = 246
43. "*Your* wits have solved the code" = 246
44. "*Your* wits revealed secret code" = 246

Solutions can be reversed with the key (246) first so as to make logical/grammatical sense:

- 246 = "the *Skelton* code key found by *you*"

A sub-set of Master Code solutions referring to 'you' the solver and the '<u>cipher</u>':

1. "Secret cipher discovered by *you*" = 246
2. "The correct cipher-code found by *you*" = 246
3. "Use *your* wit to solve cipher" = 246
4. "Well done! *You* have found the number" = 246
5. "*You* are congratulated on finding clue" = 246
6. "*You* are the seeker after Truth" = 246
7. "*You* found the key to the cipher in" = 246
8. "*You* found extremely hard clues" = 246
9. "*You* found the secret answers" = 246
10. "*You* found the special cipher number" = 246
11. "*You* have found the cypher number" = 246
12. "*You* have found the secret of a cipher" = 246
13. **"*You* have found the *ultimate* cipher" = 246**
14. "*You* have found the vast cipher-code" = 246
15. "*You* have summed letter values" = 246
16. "*You* know how *we* used the cipher" = 246
17. "*You* succeeded in solving the cipher" = 246
18. "*Your* wit has broken the cipher" = 246

Clearly, because all of the solutions sum to the same number, they 'resonate' with each other – the solutions are like the spokes of a wheel with 246 at the hub linking them all together.

Reversed solution

- 246 = "is the cipher number you have found"

The following are Master Code solutions in which the Master Code itself is the context. Again, solutions are found by trial and error, all of them summing to the 'magic' gematria number 246. These solutions refer to 'code':

1. "**2-4-6:** the Master Code number's digits" = 246
2. "All code clues sum to the same number" = 246
3. "All code messages add-up to the number" = 246
4. "All code solutions are *discoveries*" = 246
5. "All codes must sum to the number" = 246
6. "Arithmetic code hid *The Code of Secrets*" = 246
7. "Arithmetic code is very secret" = 246
8. "Arithmetic code of secret knowledge" = 246
9. "Arithmetic code: letters sum to" = 246
10. "Break codes with *Skelton*'s key" = 246
11. "Code number is three even digits" = 246
12. "Code of *Skelton* is very secret" = 246
13. "Extremely difficult secret code" = 246
14. "Here is the key to a great secret" = 246
15. "Here is the most special numeral" = 246
16. "Hid messages as a very clever code" = 246
17. "Letters of code always sum to" = 246
18. "Messages are a proof of the code method" = 246
19. "Messages are left for the future" = 246
20. "Messages in the code are not a coincidence" = 246
21. "Most special number hid secret code" = 246
22. "*Multum in parvo* is THE motto" = 246
23. "*Multum in parvo:* a Latin motto" = 246
24. "Need *Skelton's* key to break our code" = 246
25. "Number-code of gigantic complexity" = 246
26. "Number-code problem solved by you" = 246
27. "Our codes must always sum to" = 246
28. "Same number is always the sum" = 246
29. "Secret codes are not in your mind" = 246
30. "Secret codes in the English language" = 246
31. "*Skelton* code is very hard code indeed" = 246
32. "*Skelton* is name of infinite cipher" = 246
33. "*Skelton* is the code *Merlin* created" = 246 *Merlin* is an alias of *Skelton*'s creator
34. "*Skelton* is the name of an ancient code" = 246
35. "*Skelton* uses trial and error" = 246
36. "*Skelton:* an extremely hard code" = 246
37. "*Skelton:* name of infinite cypher" = 246
38. "*Skelton:* name of *The Code of Secrets*" = 246
39. "*Skelton*'s code key was secret" = 246

40. "*Skelton's* code: ***multum in parvo***" = 246 much in little
41. "***Skelton***'s diabolically difficult code" = 246
42. "***Skelton's*** gematria: an infinite code" = 246
43. "Solve equations to find message" = 246
44. "The answer is hiding in numbers" = 246
45. "The answer is: ***a code having no clues***" = 246 there are no enciphered texts to decrypt
46. "The answer is: secrets hid in code" = 246
47. "The answer is: ***the code fooled many***" = 246
48. "The clue is: trial-and-error method" = 246
49. "The code clues add-up to the same number" = 246
50. "***The Code*** was a great mystery" = 246
51. "The deliberate mistakes are big clues" = 246
52. "The intentional mistakes are code" = 246
53. "The key you found is ***Skelton***'s" = 246
54. "***The Master Code:*** a code of revelations" = 246
55. "The message is proof of code's method" = 246
56. "The motto is: ***multum in parvo***" = 246
57. "The secret about the hidden code is out" = 246
58. "The secret code of Eternal Truth" = 246
59. "The secret gematria number: a clue is" = 246
60. "The secret is: ***The Code of Destiny***" = 246
61. "The secret key is ***this*** number" = 246
62. "The ***Skelton*** code is The Golden Key" = 246
63. "The three digits 2-4-6 are a numeral clue" = 246
64. "***This*** number is hiding ***The Great Code***" = 246
65. "Use code of ***Skelton*** to solve ***The Code***" = 246
66. "Use intuition to solve the codes" = 246
67. "Use ***Skelton*** to break ***invisible*** code" = 246 means no ***explicit*** clues
68. "Very clever code hides messages" = 246

Reversing the order of solutions with key (246) first, so as to make grammatic sense:

- 246 = "is a key that opens the codes"
- 246 = "is a secret number hiding secret code"
- 246 = "is ***Skelton***'s cypher numeral"
- 246 = "is ***The Code***'s most secret number"
- 246 = "is the key to the ***Skelton*** codes"
- 246 = "is the most powerful numeral"
- 246 = "is the secret key to the hidden code"
- 246 = "secret code number of ***The Master Code***"
- 246 = "the all-powerful secret number"
- 246 = "the key opens the code of ***Skelton***"
- 246 = "the most important numeral"
- 246 = "the number hides ***The Code of Secrets***"

- 246 = "was *Skelton*'s secret code key"
- 246 = "was the special key of *Skelton*"
- 246 = "was the very secret number"

The following solutions refer to 'cipher/cypher':

1. "Crack codes using cipher of *Skelton*" = 246
2. "Letters become numbers in cipher" = 246
3. "Secret cipher hidden as a dead man's name" = 246
4. "Secret cipher hides as dead man's name" = 246
5. "*Skelton* is a top-secret cipher" = 246
6. "*Skelton* is name of a secret cipher" = 246
7. "*Skelton* is name of cipher ***not*** man" = 246
8. "*Skelton:* cipher of the Master Code" = 246
9. "*Skelton*: name of cypher ***not*** man" = 246
10. "*Skelton*'s cipher was a secret" = 246
11. "*Skelton*'s cypher is secret" = 246
12. "Solve code with *Skelton* cipher" = 246
13. "The answer is: The Great Cipher" = 246
14. "The cipher of *Skelton* is secret" = 246
15. "The clue is: *Skelton* is *The Cipher*" = 246
16. "The Golden Key's cypher is found" = 246
17. "The secret cypher of *Skelton*" = 246
18. "*This is* The Master Cipher's code" = 246
19. "Use cipher of *Skelton* to break codes" = 246
20. "You have found the cypher number" = 246

Reversed solutions:

- 246 = "a very secret cypher number"
- 246 = "is a very secret cipher number"
- 246 = "is the cipher numeral of *Skelton*"
- 246 = "is *The Master Cipher*'s numeral"
- 246 = "the cypher numeral of *Skelton*"
- 246 = "the numeral of *The Master Cipher*"
- 246 = "was key to *The Master Cipher*"*

*The key is the gematria number 246

Long ago, solutions summing to 246 might have been known as examples of 'The Maister Cipher'; either way, Maister Cipher or Master Code solutions sum to the special gematria number 246 using *Skelton*'s cipher. **As we have seen**:

"You have found *The Maister Cipher*" = 246 and "you discovered" = "the Master Code" = 111

We note also the resonance equations:

"congratulations" = "you are right about" = "the secret cipher' = 138

3. Mathematics, Magic and Mysticism

Whoever created *Skelton*'s gematria would probably have found many of those solutions and a lot more beside. This would have given them confidence that the cipher had a special, even unique significance and that in turn would have stimulated the cipher's application to an expanding range of contexts. However, experimenting with numbers in sixteenth century England - 'calculating' - was viewed with deep suspicion by the authorities as numerals were believed to have magical powers; in particular, it was feared that arithmetic computations might be used to predict or even influence the monarch's death. 'Calculators' and those who devised number-ciphers were potentially risking life and liberty if discovered – it's therefore very likely *Skelton* is a pseudonym. If so, who *really* created the cipher? Someone with a deep understanding of gematria? Someone steeped in the occult? Someone expert at arithmetic? A talented mathematician? A 'magician' perhaps - 'Merlin' at the court?

The contemporary who (probably) answers those questions best is Queen Elizabeth's famous 'philosopher', the secretive polymath Doctor John Dee: mathematician, mystic, alchemist and antiquarian. By contrast with John Skelton, whose biography shows no sign of an interest in or special talent for mathematics, Dee had a professional understanding of the subject and even by his early twenties had given lectures on Euclidean geometry at the University of Paris.

The mysterious Doctor John Dee – 'Merlin' at Queen Elizabeth's court?

C16 portrait – artist unknown (Image: Wikipedia commons)

In that context, we discover the Master Code solution: "Dee is *Merlin* at Elizabeth's court" = 246

John Dee was born 13th July 1527 at Tower Ward, London. His mother Jane Wild was English, his father Roland was of Welsh ancestry. A mercer and gentleman courtier to Henry VIII, Roland fell on hard times and found himself in debtor's prison, a misfortune having long-term consequences for John. The family arrived in the capital with the coronation of Henry VII, Henry Tudor himself a monarch of Welsh lineage. Coincidentally, Dee junior claimed descent from Rhodri the Great, Prince of Wales and he constructed a family history to try and prove it.

After attending Chelmsford Chantry School (1535-42) the youth entered St John's College Cambridge, graduating with a BA in 1544/45. His intellectual abilities were recognised at university and he was made one of the first fellows of Trinity, the famous college founded by Henry VIII. Dee's scholarly reputation and achievements eventually propelled him to the highest echelons of Elizabethan society, as a personal advisor to the Queen and as an associate of the famous chief minister Sir William Cecil (Lord Burghley) and Sir Francis Walsingham, the notorious spy master.

Soon after Elizabeth's coronation in January 1559 her 'philosopher' disappeared from the records for five years, though it's virtually certain he spent the time travelling and studying in Europe. From the perspective of his experiences on the Continent, Dee would have seen that England was a cultural and intellectual backwater and that almost all the leading thinkers and latest ideas were to be found abroad. It was during this period of intellectual exploration and discovery that he became fascinated with gematria, probably through reading works like Agrippa's *Natural Magic*.

Doctor Dee served in the role of advisor to England's voyages of discovery (c 1550-1570s) providing technical aid for navigation as well as political support to create a 'British Empire', a term it seems he was the first to use. In 1577, he published his ideas setting out his vision of a maritime empire, emphasizing the key role of the navy and asserting English territorial claims in the New World.

By the early 1580s Dee was becoming dissatisfied with his progress in learning the secrets of Nature and, at the same time, his influence at court was waning. Failure of his ideas concerning the establishment of overseas colonies and questionable results from the voyages of exploration in North America, nearly ended his hopes of patronage - so, he began to focus on the 'supernatural' as a way of acquiring esoteric knowledge and attempted to contact 'spirits' through a scryer, a 'special' crystal lens that he hoped would act as an interface enabling communication with 'angelic' entities.

In 1582 the Queen's 'philosopher' met Edward Kelly and being impressed with his 'abilities' took him into his service. However, Kelley was a rather dubious character, a plausible con-man who had changed his name to Talbot in an attempt to evade charges of forgery. It was at about this time that Dee was beginning his 'supernatural research', so-called 'spiritual conferences' he was convinced would bring benefits to mankind and in those attempts it seems the charlatan Kelly humored him.

The following year, Dee and Kelly met the Polish nobleman Albert Laski who invited the 'philosopher' and his entourage to accompany him back home. In light of his worsening status at Elizabeth's court Dee accepted; unfortunately, it soon emerged that Laski was bankrupt and so the 'philosopher', Kelley and their respective families began a nomadic life wandering around central Europe.

Many continental scholars regarded Elizabeth's 'philosopher' as a man of profound knowledge - and yet in certain quarters he was viewed with deep suspicion precisely because he was an advisor to the English sovereign; indeed, some were convinced that Dee was a secret agent, an 'intelligencer' spying for the Tudor Queen.

At a 'spiritual conference' in Bohemia in 1587, Kelley told Dee that the angel Uriel had ordered the men to share *all* their possessions - including their wives. A devout Christian, the idea of wife-sharing troubled Dee although he didn't doubt that Uriel's instruction was genuine - but the old man was more interested in communicating with spirits than wife-swopping as he believed the 'angels' would help him solve great scientific mysteries. Soon after receiving the angelic order to commit adultery the spirit conferences ceased and there was a parting of the ways. Dee returned to England with his family while Kelley assumed the role of alchemist at the court of the notorious Holy Roman Emperor Rudolf II, a believer in the occult known as 'Rudolf the mad' for his outrageous and eccentric behaviour.

When Dee returned to Mortlake in 1589 after six years abroad, he found that his house had been ransacked. His magnificent library of 4000 volumes - one of the largest private collections in Europe - was ruined and many of his valuable instruments had been stolen. In desperation he turned to the Queen for support; unfortunately, during his long absence the sovereign's enthusiasm for her 'philosopher' had waned somewhat – probably a case of 'out of sight out of mind'; nevertheless, in 1595 Elizabeth saw fit to appoint him Warden of Christ's College at Manchester where he proceeded to spend ten unhappy years, a decade made miserable by the hostility of colleagues.

Returning to London for the last time in 1605, Dee suffered further misfortune. His wife had just died, his patron the Queen was dead and James I, the new monarch from Scotland, had no time for magick and mystics having written a book dismissing all such as nonsense. So naturally, Elizabeth's venerable 'philosopher' received no help from the Stuart king. A disappointed and disillusioned old man, the erstwhile royal advisor spent his twilight years in poverty and obscurity at Mortlake, selling-off possessions to support himself and his daughter who cared for him until his death at the age of 81.

In view of his interest in and knowledge of gematria, it is appropriate to investigate a possible relationship between Dee and 'Skelton'. First, applying the cipher to 'John Skelton' (= 105), we find the resonance equations:

1. "John Skelton" = "did not fool you" = 105
2. "John Skelton" = "is a dead man's name" = 105
3. "John Skelton" = "the name of a dead man" = 105
4. "*Skelton* name" = "did not fool you" = 105

Preliminary hints which suggest *Skelton* is a pseudonym.

Applying the cipher in the context of John Dee and *Skelton* gives the resonance equations:

1. "John Dee hid by" = "Skelton" = 77
2. "Skelton" = "alias hides Dee" = 77
3. "Skelton" = "be Dee's cover" = 77
4. "Skelton" = "Dee incognito" = 77
5. "Skelton" = "was John Dee" = 77

The resonance equations imply that *Skelton* was *not* the name of the man who created the cipher but that it *was* an alias of John Dee.

Applying the cipher in the context of Doctor Dee and *John Skelton* gives the resonance equations:

1. "John Skelton" = "alias hides John Dee" = 105
2. "John Skelton" = "Doctor Dee's name" = 105
3. "John Skelton" = "hiding name of Dr Dee" = 105
4. "John Skelton" = "is hiding name of Dee" = 105

Finally, applying the Master Code in the context of Dee and *Skelton*'s cipher:

1. "A number substitution cipher of Dee" = 246 gematria are number substitution ciphers
2. "A substitution cipher of Doctor Dee" = 246
3. "Dee named a cipher *Skelton's gematria*" = 246
4. "Doctor Dee is cloaked by *John Skelton*" = 246
5. "Doctor Dee is *Skelton*'s true name" = 246
6. "Doctor Dee uses *Skelton* as a cover" = 246
7. "Doctor Dee: name hides as *John Skelton*" = 246
8. "Doctor John Dee hides as *John Skelton*" = 246
9. "Doctor John Dee hides name as *Skelton*" = 246
10. "Doctor John Dee is cloaked by *Skelton*" = 246
11. "*John Skelton* is hiding John Dee's name" = 246
12. "*John Skelton* was John Dee disguised" = 246
13. "*John Skelton* was masking John Dee" = 246
14. "*John Skelton* was name masking Dee" = 246
15. "*John Skelton* was the alias Dee used" = 246
16. "*John Skelton:* a false name hiding John Dee" = 246
17. "*John Skelton:* hiding the name of John Dee" = 246
18. "*John Skelton:* name was masking Dee" = 246
19. "*John Skelton:* secret alias hiding Dee" = 246
20. "*John Skelton:* secret alias of John Dee" = 246
21. "*John Skelton:* the false name hiding Dee" = 246
22. "*John Skelton:* the false name of John Dee" = 246
23. "*John Skelton:* the name was a ruse" = 246
24. "*Merlin*: alias hiding Doctor John Dee" = 246
25. "My *Skelton* name did not fool you" = 246
26. "*Skelton* cipher is a work of John Dee" = 246
27. "*Skelton* cipher is the work of Dee" = 246

28. "*Skelton* name was masking Dee name" = 246
29. "*Skelton* was Doctor Dee incognito" = 246
30. "*Skelton* was name masking John Dee" = 246
31. "*Skelton* was the work of John Dee" = 246
32. "The secret cyphers of Doctor Dee" = 246
33. "You discovered Dee's secret cipher" = 246
34. "You found that *Skelton* is John Dee" = 246
35. "You knew Doctor Dee's secret name" = 246
36. "You knew Doctor John Dee's numeral" = 246
37. "You knew Doctor John Dee's secret" = 246
38. "You knew of Doctor John Dee's number" = 246
39. "You were not fooled by *Skelton*" = 246

Reversed solution:

- 246 = "is the secret number of Dee's cipher"
- 246 = "the secret number of Dee's cypher"

And, the resonance equation: "Skelton's gematria" = "was John Dee's gematria" = 157

Those solutions support the conjecture that John Dee was the cipher's true creator and that *Skelton,* the name of a dead man, was an alias he used as cover. It was most probably as a result of discoveries made during his continental travels (1559-1564) from works like Agrippa's *Natural Magic* that the Queen's 'philosopher' was inspired to create *Skelton* - a substitution cipher specifically intended for use with English. In that regard, it is noteworthy that Dee chose to write much of his work in the vernacular rather than Latin - the *lingua franca* of scholars – so that 'ordinary' people could understand it. Dee would have known that gematria might be used either for occult purposes or to encode secret messages and while the former possibilities might have intrigued the Queen, the latter would have been of interest to chief minister Sir William Cecil (Lord Burghley) and chief-spy Sir Francis Walsingham. In that case, it's plausible that Cecil and Walsingham used Dee's *'Skelton'* cipher to encode messages.

To test for Cecil, Dee and Walsingham's use of *Skelton* we apply the Master Code:

1. "A secret cipher of: Cecil - Dee - Walsingham" = 246
2. "Cecil - Dee - Walsingham: a *triumvirate*" = 246
3. "Cecil - Dee - Walsingham: *three wise men*" = 246
4. "Cecil, Dee and Walsingham use *Skelton*" = 246
5. "Cecil, Dee and Walsingham's cipher key" = 246
6. "Queene Elizabeth's wise-men trio" = 246
7. "Trio of wise men of Queen Elizabeth" = 246

Reversed solutions:

- 246 = "a cipher numeral of: Cecil - Dee - Walsingham"
- 246 = "is Cecil - Dee - Walsingham cipher number"

4. The Old Hermit of Prague

In *Shakespeare*'s *Twelfth Night* the fool (*Feste*) refers cryptically to 'the old hermit of Prague' (A4 S2). When Dee visited Prague in 1587 about fourteen years before the play was written he was sixty, 'old' by the standards of the time; therefore, 'old hermit' would have been an appropriate alias for the reclusive mystic. The 'old hermit' alluded to by *Feste* never learned to read or write – which, in this case, is somewhat ironic.

The conjecture that Dee used the cover "old hermit" / "old hermit of Prague" etc is tested by applying *Skelton* in each case.

1. "Name of Dee hid as" = "old hermit" = 80
2. "Old hermit" = "alias hiding Dee" = 80
3. "Old hermit" = "alias of John Dee" = 80
4. "Old hermit" = "be a cloak of John Dee" = 80
5. "Old hermit" = "be the cloak of Dee" = 80
6. "Old hermit" = "is Doctor Dee" = 80
7. "Old hermit" = "the name hid Dee" = 80

Old hermit of Prague:

1. "Doctor Dee is hiding as" = "old hermit of Prague" = 137
2. "Doctor John Dee is the" = "old hermit of Prague" = 137
3. "Old hermit of Prague" = "is cover of Doctor Dee" = 137

The old hermit of Prague:

1. "The old hermit of Prague" = "an intelligencer's name" = 166 a spy/secret agent
2. "The old hermit of Prague" = "cypher of Doctor John Dee" = 166
3. "The old hermit of Prague" = "Doctor Dee's secret name" = 166
4. "The old hermit of Prague" = "is cipher of Doctor John Dee" = 166
5. "The old hermit of Prague" = "name hides secret agent" = 166
6. "The old hermit of Prague" = "the hidden secret agent" = 166
7. "The old hermit of Prague" = "was Doctor Dee's cipher" = 166
8. "The old hermit of Prague" = "was hiding Doctor John Dee" = 166
9. "The old hermit of Prague" = "was name hiding Doctor Dee" = 166
10. "The old hermit of Prague" = "was name of Doctor John Dee" = 166

Finally, applying the Master Code in the context of 'the old hermit of Prague':

1. "*The old hermit of Prague* is Doctor Dee" = 246
2. "*The old hermit of Prague* is mask of Dee" = 246
3. "*The old hermit of Prague*: alias hiding Dee" = 246
4. "*The old hermit of Prague*: alias of John Dee" = 246

As mentioned previously, Elizabeth's 'philosopher' was suspected by some in Europe of being a spy. Applying the Master Code in the context of Dee, espionage and the Queen:

1. "Dee was an intelligencer of the Queen" = 246
2. "Dee was name of Queen's secret agent" = 246
3. "Doctor John Dee: Queen's secret agent" = 246
4. "Intelligencer hid as a *philosopher*" = 246 Dee was nicknamed 'philosopher' by the Queen
5. "*Philosopher* hides intelligencer" = 246
6. "*Philosopher* is an intelligencer" = 246

Those resonance equations and Master Code solutions suggest that Dee *was* a spy working for the Queen and that 'old hermit' / 'old hermit of Prague' etc was his cover at Prague in 1587. It seems that Dee's European 'doubters' - those who suspected him of espionage - were probably right. **If so, how did Shakespeare's author know Dee's code-name – a secret privy to *very* few?**

5. *William Shake-Speare* – what's in a name?

It's likely that a decision was taken long ago to keep *Skelton* hidden from the public, a secret cipher known only to the 'elite'. During the second-half of the sixteenth century many if not most of England's 'elite' would have been at or visitors to Elizabeth's court. It appears from code solutions that the Queen's 'philosopher' - Doctor Dee - was the true creator of *Skelton*'s cipher. In light of the 'old hermit of Prague' quotation is there a connection between *Shakespeare* and Dee?

In the context of *William Shakespeare* and *Skelton's* gematria we find the resonance equations:

1. "William Shakespeare" = "Skelton's gematria" = 157
2. "Skelton's gematria" = "was John Dee's gematria" = 157

Also:

1. "*Shakespeare* cipher hid" = "Skelton's gematria" = 157
2. "*Shakespeare* name hides" = "Skelton's gematria" = 157

Further, applying *Skelton* to the full-name 'William Shakespeare' in the context of a cipher:

1. "William Shakespeare" = "is hiding the cypher" = 157
2. "William Shakespeare" = "is name of the cypher" = 157
3. "William Shakespeare" = "name is hiding a cypher" = 157
4. "William Shakespeare" = "was a name hiding a cipher" = 157
5. "William Shakespeare" = "was the name of a cipher" = 157

And: "Shakespeare" = "cipher's name" = 94

Which implies that 'Shakespeare/William Shakespeare' was a code-name for *Skelton's gematria*. In other words, 'William Shakespeare' was *originally* a cipher name not a person's name.

In the context of 'Shake-speare', Dee and the cipher we find the resonance equations:

1. "Shake-speare" = "cipher hiding Dee" = 94
2. "Shake-speare" = "cipher of John Dee" = 94

Also:

1. "Shake-speare is" = "cypher hiding Dee" = 115
2. "Shake-speare is" = "Dee's secret name" = 115
3. "Shake-speare is" = "hiding Dee incognito" = 115
4. "Shake-speare is" = "John Dee's secret" = 115

Applying the Master Code in the context of Dee and *Shake-speare*:

1. "Dee invented the name of *Shake-speare*" = 246
2. "Doctor John Dee made *Shake-speare* name" = 246
3. "Look for a secret joke *Shake-speare* hid" = 246 puns in the name
4. "*Merlin* was hidden as *Shakespeare*" = 246 Merlin & Shakespeare were Dee's aliases
5. "Shake-speare cloaks Doctor Dee's name" = 246
6. "Shake-speare is a name Doctor Dee uses" = 246
7. "Shake-speare is a secret of Doctor Dee" = 246
8. "Shake-speare is alias hiding Doctor Dee" = 246
9. "Shake-speare is alias of Doctor John Dee" = 246
10. "Shake-speare name hid the secret joke" = 246
11. "Shake-speare name is alias of Doctor Dee" = 246
12. "Shake-speare name was hiding Dee's joke" = 246
13. "Shake-speare was a mask of Doctor Dee" = 246
14. "Shake-speare was a name created by Dee" = 246
15. "Shake-speare was hiding John Dee's joke" = 246
16. "Shake-speare was invented by Dee" = 246
17. "Shake-speare: a name masking Doctor Dee" = 246
18. "Shake-speare: code invented by John Dee" =. 246
19. "Shake-speare: name for '*philosopher*'" = 246 Dee was the Queen's 'philosopher'
20. "Shake-speare: secret name used by Dee" = 246
21. "*Shake-speare:* the name was a joke by Dee" = 246
22. "*William Shake-speare* is called *a straw man*" = 246
23. "*William Shake-speare*: name was a joke" = 246

.

Shake-speare hyphenated

The *hyphenated* name, as it appeared on about half of the earliest published works is a *construct* - a non-existent surname – which means the author's *real* name *cannot* have been 'Shake-speare'.

Applying *Skelton* to Shake-speare in the context of joined (hyphenated) words:

- "Shake-speare" = "joined words" = 94
- "Shake-speare is" = "joyned words" = 115 old spelling

Applying *Skelton* to 'William Shake-speare' in the context of the hyphen, gives the resonance equations:

1. "William Shake-speare" = "clue is in the hyphen" = 157
2. "William Shake-speare" = "hyphen in name is a clue" = 157
3. "William Shake-speare" = "is a *constructed* name" = 157
4. "William Shake-speare" = "joined words is a sign" = 157
5. "William Shake-speare" = "joined words was a clue" = 157

Finally, applying the Master Code in the context of the hyphen:

1. "A clue hidden by *Shake-speare* hyphen" = 246
2. "Clue hides in hyphen of *Shake-speare* = 246
3. "Hid a clue as *Shake-speare* hyphenated" = 246
4. "*Shake-speare* hyphenated: a hidden clue" = 246
5. "*Shake-speare* hyphenated hides clue" = 246

Which implies the hyphen is intentional and therefore significant; as solution (3) above says *William Shake-speare* with hyphen is a *constructed* name, not a *real* name. Moreover, applying *Skelton* to 'Shake-speare' we find **the resonance equation**:

"Shake-speare" = "name hid puns" = 94 an important hint

'Shake-speare' hyphenated is joined words that hide puns in Arabic and Italian, *Sheik* and *spia* respectively. Applying the Master Code in that context:

1. "*Shake-speare* is pun at Sheik-spia" = 246
2. "*Shake-speare* was Sheik-spia pun" = 246
3. "*Shake-speare:* look for *two* puns" = 246
4. "The name *Shake-speare* hid the puns" = 246
5. "Translate puns in Sheik-spia" = 246*
6. "Translate *Shake-speare* puns" = 246

***Translating**: 'Sheik' means '**chief**' in Arabic, 'spia' means '**spy**' in Italian.

So, the Arabic/Italian puns **'Sheik-spia'** translate as **'chief-spy'**.

Applying *Skelton* in the context of 'Shake-speare' and 'chief-spy':

1. "Chief-spie hid as" = "*Shake-speare*" = 94 old spelling
2. "*Shake-speare*" = "hid chief-spy" = 94
3. "*Shake-speare*" = "hidden chief-spie" = 94
4. "*Shake-speare*" = "is chief-spie code" = 94

From 1574 until his death in 1590 Sir Francis Walsingham was the chief-spy, the Queen's famous spy-master. Applying *Skelton* in that context:

1. "Francis Walsingham" = "William Shake-speare" = 157
2. "*Shake-speare* name hides" = "Francis Walsingham" = 157
3. "William Shake-speare" = "hid Walsingham's name" = 157

Applying the Master Code in the context of *Shake-speare,* chief-spy and puns:

1. "An intelligencer called *Shake-speare*" = 246
2. "An Italian pun be *hidden* in *Shake-speare*" = 246
3. "An Italian pun *hides* as *Shake-speare*" = 246
4. "An Italian pun *hiding* in *Shake-speare*" = 246
5. "Arabic-Italian pun *hid* by *Shake-speare*" = 246
6. "Called an intelligencer *Shake-speare*" = 246
7. "*Chief-spy hid* in the *Shake-speare* name" = 246
8. "Moorish and Italian puns was a joke" = 246
9. "Moorish pun hidden as *Shake-speare*" = 246
10. "Moorish-Italian puns hidden in name" = 246
11. "Name of *Shake-speare* hiding pun in Arabic" = 246
12. "Senior spie *hiding* as *Shake-speare*" = 246
13. "*Shake-speare hides* name of *chief-spy*" = 246
14. "*Shake-speare* is joke in Arabic and Italian" = 246
15. "*Shake-speare* is *secret agent* name" = 246
16. "*Shake-speare* was Arabic-Italian pun" = 246
17. "*Shake-speare*: an Arabic and Italian jest" = 246
18. "*Shake-speare: hiding deliberate* puns" = 246
19. "*Shake-speare*: *hiding* senior spy" = 246
20. "*Shake-speare*: intelligencer's name" = 246
21. "*Shake-speare*: intentional puns" = 246
22. "*Shake-speare:* name of *senior spy*" = 246
23. "*Shake-speare:* the senior spie name" = 246
24. "The *Shake-speare* name hid the puns" = 246
25. "The *Shake-speare* name hides Arabic pun" = 246
26. "Ye found puns *Shake-speare* name *hid*" = 246
27. "You found secret puns. Well done!" = 246

In that context, applying *Skelton* we find the resonance equation:

"Moorish-Italian puns" = "are hiding in *Shake-speare*" = 168 ('Arabic' equivalent to 'Moorish')

Elizabeth's ruthless 'chief-spy' - 'Sheik-spia', 'the Moor' - Sir Francis Walsingham (1532-1590)

(Image: Wikipedia commons attr. John de Critz c 1585)

We have seen the preliminary resonance equations:

1. **"Francis Walsingham" = "William Shake-speare" = 157**
2. "*Shake-speare* name *hides*" = "Francis Walsingham" = 157
3. "William Shake-speare" = "*hid* Walsingham's name" = 157

Applying *Skelton* to William Shake-speare and Francis Walsingham, we find also:

1. "*Shake-speare* cipher hid" = "Francis Walsingham" = 157
2. "Walsingham cloaked by" = "William Shake-speare" = 157
3. "William Shake-speare" = "a Walsingham disguise" = 157
4. "William Shake-speare" = "alias for Walsingham" = 157
5. "William Shake-speare" = "maskes Walsingham" = 157

Elizabeth nicknamed Walsingham '**the Moor**(e)', so it would be appropriate if as the chief-spy he was secretly known as ***Sheik***-*Spia* – a private joke.

Applying *Skelton* in the context of *the Moor(e)*:

1. "Name the Moor" = "Shake-speare" = 94 code instruction
2. "Shake-speare" = "name for Moore" = 94

Which again implies *Shake-speare* is code for Francis Walsingham.

Also: "Walsingham is" = "Moorish-Italian" = 117 hinting at the *Sheik-Spia* puns.

Applying *Skelton* in the context of 'William Shake-speare' and 'master-spy', gives the resonance equations:

1. "William Shake-speare" = "a master-spye name" = 157
2. "William Shake-speare" = "a spie-maister's name" = 157
3. "William Shake-speare" = "alias hid chief-spie of Queen" = 157
4. "William Shake-speare" = "alias hides chief-spie name" = 157
5. "William Shake-speare" = "is a master of spies" = 157
6. "William Shake-speare" = "is agent for the Queen" = 157
7. "William Shake-speare" = "is the chief-spy name" = 157
8. "William Shake-speare" = "is the master-spie" = 157
9. "William Shake-speare" = "maister-spy name" = 157
10. "William Shake-speare" = "the chief intelligencer" = 157
11. "William Shake-speare" = "the master-spye" = 157
12. "William Shake-speare" = "was Queen's chief-spie" = 157

Finally, applying the Master Code in the context of Shake-speare, master-spy/intelligencer and Walsingham gives the solutions:

1. "*Shake-speare* is a Walsingham alias" = 246
2. "*Shake-speare* is maister-spye" = 246
3. "*Shake-speare* is secret agent name" = 246
4. "*Shake-speare* is spye maister" = 246
5. "*Shake-speare* mask hid Walsingham" = 246
6. "*Shake-speare* was a maister-spie" = 246
7. "*Shake-speare* was a spie-maister" = 246
8. "*Shake-speare*: a name for Walsingham" = 246
9. "*Shake-speare:* intelligencer's name" = 246

Taking all of the foregoing into account it appears - in one sense at least - that *William Shake-speare* was a secret code name for the chief-spy, used as such long before the name appeared in print.

Chief minister Sir William Cecil, Lord Burghley (1520-1598)

Image: Wikipedia commons attr. Marcus Gheeraerts the younger

Sir William Cecil, created Lord Burghley in 1571 was the most powerful individual in England after the Queen. In modern terms he was roughly the equivalent of Prime Minister, Chancellor, Home Secretary, Foreign Secretary and head of the Civil Service. As chief minister he guided and advised Elizabeth for the first thirty-seven years of her reign.

We have seen the Master Code solutions:

1. "Cecil - Dee - Walsingham: *a triumvirate*" = 246
2. "Cecil - Dee - Walsingham: *three wise men*" = 246
3. "Trio of wise men of Queen Elizabeth" = 246

In the context of three old sages/wise men and 'Shake-speare' we find the resonance equations:

1. "Shake-speare" = "3 wise old men" = 94
2. "Shake-speare" = "*three* old men" = 94
3. "Shake-speare" = "*three* sages" = 94

In the context of the full name *William Shake-speare*:

1. "The *three old men* hid as" = "*William Shake-speare*" = 157
2. "The *three sages* hid as" = "*William Shake-speare*" = 157
3. "*Three old men* hid as a name" = "*William Shake-speare*" = 157
4. "*William Shake-speare*" = "a clue was: *three old men*" = 157
5. "*William Shake-speare*" = "name hides *three old men*" = 157
6. "*William Shake-speare*" = "name hides *three sages*" = 157

Applying the Master Code in the context of Shake-speare and the three (old) men:

1. "Secret is: *Shake-speare* is 3 old men" = 246
2. "*Shake-speare*: cipher of *three* old men" = 246
3. "*Shake-speare*: cipher of *three* sages" = 246
4. "*Three* men are hiding as *Shake-speare*" = 246

The foregoing solutions imply that the third 'wise man', the third 'sage' of 'the triumvirate' was Sir William Cecil, Lord Burghley and in that context, we find the Master Code solutions:

1. "Burghley hid: cloaked by *Shake-speare*" = 246
2. "*Shake-speare* is name for Burghley" = 246
3. "*Shake-speare* is shield of Burghley" = 246
4. "*Shake-speare* mask hides Burghley" = 246
5. "*Shake-speare* was a Burghley alias" = 246
6. "*Shake-speare* was Burghley cloaked" = 246
7. "*Shake-speare*: a cloak of Lord Burghley" = 246
8. "*Shake-speare:* a name hiding William Cecil" = 246
9. "*Shake-speare:* the name of William Cecil" = 246
10. "*Shake-speare's* maske hid Burghley" = 246

Applying *Skelton* in the context of Shake-speare/Cecil (Burghley) we find the resonance equations:

1. "Name of Cecil hid as" = "Shake-speare" = 94
2. "Shake-speare" = "a maske of Cecil's" = 94
3. "Shake-speare" = "a name Cecil uses" = 94
4. "Shake-speare" = "Cecil's cipher" = 94
5. "Shake-speare" = "hid the name Cecil" = 94
6. "Shake-speare" = "is mask of Cecil" = 94
7. "Shake-speare" = "name a Cecil maske" = 94
8. "Shake-speare" = "the Cecil maske" = 94

In the context of the full name 'William Shake-speare' and William Cecil/Lord Burghley we find the resonance equations:

1. "Name of William Cecil hid as" = "William Shake-speare" = 157
2. "Sir William Cecil hid as" = "William Shake-speare" = 157
3. "William Shake-speare" = "'guise of Lord Burghley" = 157
4. "William Shake-speare" = "is Burghley disguise" = 157
5. "William Shake-speare" = "is mask of William Cecil" = 157
6. "William Shake-speare" = "name was Cecil disguise" = 157
7. "William Shake-speare" = "the name hid William Cecil" = 157

It appears that Shake-speare/William Shake-speare was a special name; originally a secret code-name for Cecil, Dee and Walsingham - three old men/wise men/sages - a triumvirate. In that context, we find the resonance equations:

1. "3 old men are hidden by name" = "William Shake-speare" = 157
2. "A trio of wise men hid in" = "William Shake-speare" = 157
3. "Called trio of wise men" = "William Shake-speare" = 157
4. "The *three old men* hid as" = "William Shake-speare" = 157
5. "*Three old men* hid as a name" = "William Shake-speare" = 157
6. "*Three sages* hid as" = "William Shake-speare" = 157
7. "William Shake-speare" = "*hiding* triumvirate" = 157
8. "William Shake-speare" = "name *hides three old men*" = 157
9. "William Shake-speare" = "name *hides three sages*" = 157
10. "William Shake-speare" = "name of triumvirate" = 157
11. "William Shake-speare" = "the Queen's wise men" = 157
12. "William Shake-speare" = "the three *hidden* sages" = 157

The examples show that although 'Shake-speare'/ 'William Shake-speare' sounds like a man's name it was in fact a multi-purpose secret cipher. The hyphen in the early publications of 'Shake-speare' works indicates that the name is a construct. In other words, there was no such name and therefore no such person as *William Shake-speare*.

Summary: it appears that *Shake-speare / William Shake-speare* was:

- A code-name/alias created and used by Doctor Dee long before it appeared in print
- Arabic & Italian puns - an alias for the chief-spy, the 'Moor' Sir Francis Walsingham
- A code *for* the cipher *using* the cipher: "William Shake-speare" = "Skelton's gematria" = 157
- A code for Sir William Cecil, Lord Burghley the chief minister
- A code for Cecil, Dee, Walsingham collectively: *three wise men, triumvirate, three old men, three sages.*
- A code-name used by the ruling elite – including the Queen (see below)
- **The code-name of a *secret* courtier** (see following)

NB Cecil, Dee and Walsingham were alumni of Cambridge University.

Master Code solutions relating the Queen's three wise men, Shake-speare and a code:

1. "Code of Queen Elizabeth's *three* old men" = 246
2. "Code of Queen Elizabeth's *three* sages" = 246
3. "*Shake-speare* alias hides three-in-one" = 246
4. *"Shake-speare:* is the Queen's sages" = 246
5. "*Shake-speare*: Queene's three sages" = 246

In addition, we find Master Code solutions relating 'Shake-speare' and Queen Elizabeth:

1. "*Shake-speare* is the Virgin Queen" = 246
2. "*Shake-speare* was Queen Elizabeth" = 246
3. "*Shake-speare*: a code for Queen Elizabeth" = 246
4. "*Shake-speare*: name for good Queen Bess" = 246

The Queen was known as *Pallas Athena* - goddess of knowledge & wisdom - whose epithet was *hasti-vibrans* - the **spear-shaker** – Elizabeth's link to the special cipher *Shake-speare*.

It follows from the foregoing solutions and resonance equations, that the code-name 'Shake-speare' was used secretly at the highest level many years before it first appeared in print on the poem *Venus & Adonis* (1593). During the 1590s the true author of the works appropriated the name and used it as an especially apt and memorable *nom de plume*. It's therefore highly likely that the real playwright was not an 'ordinary' person but a member of the Elizabethan 'elite', someone *very* close to the seat of power, someone who 'saw' power in action at close quarters, someone who knew of the secret name 'Shake-speare' and its special meanings.

NB The 3 old men/3 sages/ 3 wise men/ triumvirate (ie 'Shake-speare') are *represented* in the famous 'procession' picture of Elizabeth I (Robert Peak c 1600) as the *three* identical old men (in red livery) immediately behind the Queen – in *reality* there would be *two* pairs of distinguishable men, an example of a deliberate mistake.

Applying *Skelton* to *Shake-speare* in the context of poet/bard/name etc, we find the resonance equations:

1. *"Shake-speare"* = "a counterfeit" = 94
2. *"Shake-speare"* = "a poet *unseen*" = 94
3. *"Shake-speare"* = "disguise of bard" = 94
4. *"Shake-speare"* = "*hid* a bard in-hiding" = 94
5. *"Shake-speare"* = "*hid* name of a poet" = 94
6. *"Shake-speare"* = "*hid* unseene bard" = 94
7. *"Shake-speare"* = "*hides* a *hidden* bard" = 94
8. *"Shake-speare"* = "is the actor" = 94
9. *"Shake-speare"* = "is the bald man" = 94 Droeshout engraving in First Folio
10. *"Shake-speare"* = "maske for bard" = 94
11. *"Shake-speare"* = "maske of a poet" = 94
12. *"Shake-speare"* = "name a deception" = 94
13. *"Shake-speare"* = "name fools all" = 94
14. *"Shake-speare"* = "name *hides* codes" = 94
15. *"Shake-speare"* = "name is our joke" = 94
16. *"Shake-speare"* = "name of folly" = 94
17. *"Shake-speare"* = "poet-in-hiding" = 94
18. *"Shake-speare"* = "the bard-mask" = 94
19. *"Shake-speare"* = "THE deception" = 94
20. *"Shake-speare"* = "war-like name" = 94
21. *"Shake-speare"* = "was a trick" = 94

And, reversed resonance equations:

1. "A poet *hidden* as" = *"Shake-speare"* = 94
2. "Called *false* bard" = *"Shake-speare"* = 94
3. "*False* bard named" = *"Shake-speare"* = 94
4. "I am a bard *hidden* as" = *"Shake-speare"* = 94
5. "Poet *hides* as" = *"Shake-speare"* = 94

Applying *Skelton* to the full name 'William Shakespeare' in the context of a writer/bard/poet etc, gives the resonance equations:

1. "William Shakespeare" = "*false* name of a writer" = 157
2. "William Shakespeare" = "*hid* a *secret* writer" = 157
3. "William Shakespeare" = "is falsehood *hiding* poet" = 157
4. "William Shakespeare" = "is *not* the real poet" = 157
5. "William Shakespeare" = "is *not* the true name" = 157
6. "William Shakespeare" = "is the *fraudulent* bard" = 157
7. "William Shakespeare" = "name of poet is *falsehood*" = 157
8. "William Shakespeare" = "**so you got the hint**" = 157
9. "William Shakespeare" = "was a *secret* author" = 157
10. "William Shakespeare" = "was *false* name of poet" = 157
11. "William Shakespeare" = "was *impostor* bard" = 157
12. "William Shakespeare" = "was player's name" = 157

Reversed resonance equations:

- "Bard *hid* by impostor" = "William Shake-speare" = 157
- "*Hoodwinked* by the name" = "William Shake-speare" = 157
- "The true bard *cloaked* by" = "William Shake-speare" = 157
- "True bard *cloaked* by a name" = "William Shake-speare" = 157

The dedication in *Shake-speare's Sonnets* (1609) by Thomas Thorpe identifies 'the only begetter' of the work as '**M**[r] **W. H.**' It is generally agreed that 'only begetter' refers to the poet, the 'father'/ creator of the sonnets which means the real poet's initial was **H** not S*. The true author almost certainly adopted *Shake-speare* because it's an appropriately dramatic and memorable *nom de plume*.

Moreover, in the context of the initials we find the Master Code solution:

"You discovered initials of bard: **WH**" = 246 consistent with the Sonnet dedication

The 'Shake-speare grave' in Holy Trinity Church, Stratford was scanned in 2016 with GPR. The results show a void less than 3 ft deep, 4 ft long and with a transverse wall dividing the space in two. Clearly, there never was a coffin within. The ***nameless*** gravestone - an C18 replacement - is inscribed with a crude verse cursing any that dare disturb the grave's contents. In every respect - inside *and* out - the 'grave' is very odd indeed, almost certainly because it's a folly.

Applying the Master Code in the context of *Shake-speare* and a secret/hidden writer:

1. "A writer court *hid* was secret" = 246
2. "A writer *hid* at court is secret" = 246
3. "Clue is: a secret poet *hidden* at court" = 246
4. "Clue is: secret poet *hides* at court" = 246
5. "*Hidden* poet is *secret* courtier" = 246*
6. "*Hidden* poet shielded by *Shake-speare*" = 246
7. "Poet of *Shake-speare hidden* at court" = 246
8. "Poet of *Shake-speare hiding* in court" = 246
9. "*Secret* courtier *secret* author" = 246
10. "*Secret* playwright of court" = 246
11. "*Shake-speare hid* a bard: hyphen is clue" = 246
12. "*Shake-speare hides* at Tudor court" = 246
13. "*Shake-speare* is a secret bantling" = 246 old English meaning 'bastard'
14. "*Shake-speare* is play writer" = 246
15. "*Shake-speare* is secret courtier" = 246*
16. "*Shake-speare* is shielding a secret" = 246
17. "*Shake-speare* is straw-man name" = 246
18. "*Shake-speare* name hoodwinked many" = 246
19. "*Shake-speare* playwright *hid*" = 246
20. "*Shake-speare*: the silent shadow" = 246
21. "*William Shake-speare* is at court" = 246
22. "*William Shake-speare* is made-up name" = 246
23. "*William Shake-speare* is make-believe" = 246

24. *"William Shake-speare:* it's a cipher" = 246
25. *"William Shake-speare:* secret name" = 246
26. "Writer court *hides* is a secret" = 246

***Linking 5 & 17, we find the Master Code resonance equation:**

"*Hidden* poet is *secret* courtier" = "*secret* courtier is *Shake-speare*" = 246

And, crucially the Master Code solutions:

1. "A playwright son of Elizabeth" = 246
2. "A playwright son of Queen *hides*" = 246
3. "A Prince of Wales *hid* as *Shake-speare*" = 246*
4. "A secret bard *hid* bastard son of Queen" = 246
5. "A Tudor was cloaked by *Shake-speare*" = 246
6. "Bard *hid* the secret Prince of Wales" = 246
7. "Hidden playwright: son of Queene" = 246
8. "I wrote dramas called *Shake-speare*" = 246 implies *Shakespeare* is the name of the works
9. "Playwright son of Queen is *hid*" = 246
10. "Prince is shielded by *Shake-speare*" = 246
11. "Prince wrote *Shake-speare* drama" = 246
12. "Secret poet: bastard son of Queen" = 246
13. "*Shake-speare* clue is: Earl of Chester" = 246
14. "*Shake-speare hides* Prince of Wales" = 246
15. "*Shake-speare* is fictional poet name" = 246
16. "*Shake-speare* is in fact a secret bard" = 246
17. "*Shake-speare* is name of poet-prince" = 246
18. "*Shake-speare* is shielding a secret" = 246
19. "Shake-speare is shielding name of bard" = 246
20. "*Shake-speare* is the Tudor prince" = 246
21. "*Shake-speare* poet: son of the Queen" = 246
22. "*Shake-speare* secret found by you" = 246
23. "*Shake-speare* shields a *hidden* prince" = 246
24. "*Shake-speare* was a secret Tudor" = 246
25. "*Shake-speare*: bantling son of Queen" = 246
26. "*Shake-speare*: *hidden* son of Elizabeth" = 246
27. "*Shake-speare*: *hides* Prince of Wales" = 246
28. "*Shake-speare: hiding* secret prince" = 246
29. "*Shake-speare: hiding* the secret bard" = 246
30. "*Shake-speare:* name of secret prince" = 246
31. "*Shake-speare:* name of the secret bard" = 246
32. "*Shake-speare:* shielding son of Queen" = 246
33. "Son of Queen Elizabeth is bantling" = 246
34. "Wrote drama *hidden* as *Shake-speare*" = 246

*The secret prince, bastard son of the Queen, is the 'unknown' earl/garter knight (in white) in the famous 'procession' picture of Elizabeth I standing next to Gilbert Talbot (in green).

Applying *Skelton* in that context, we find the resonance equations:

1. "*Shake-speare*" = "a poet-prince" = 94
2. "*Shake-speare*" = "courtier-bard" = 94
3. "*Shake-speare*" = "hid a royal bard" = 94
4. "*Shake-speare*" = "royal poet" = 94
5. "*Shake-speare*" = "was prince" = 94

And:

1. "*Shake-speare* is" = "a *secret* prince" = 115
2. "*Shake-speare* is" = "*bastard* prince" = 115
3. "*Shake-speare* is" = "*hidden* royal bard" = 115

And:

1. "*William Shake-speare*" = "cloaks the royal bard" = 157
2. "*William Shake-speare*" = "hid secret royal bard" = 157
3. "*William Shake-speare*" = "Is hidden Tudor prince" = 157
4. "*William Shake-speare*" = "name hides royal poet" = 157
5. "*William Shake-speare*" = "the hidden royal poet" = 157

It seems the author used *Skelton* to link the names of (at least some) characters to their roles:

Henry IV

1. "Davie is name of a" = "servant" = 91
2. "Fang and Snare are" = "the officer names" = 116
3. "Francis Feeble" = "is a souldier" = 86
4. "hostesse was called" = "mistris Quickly" = 162
5. "Raphe Mouldie" = "is souldier name" = 113
6. "Shallow" = "is a Justice" = 75
7. "Sir John Falstaffe" = "is the fat knight" = 136
8. "Tearesheete" = "name of a whore" = 92

Henry V

1. "Captaine Gower" = "is Englishman" = 109
2. "Irish souldier" = "called Makmorrice" = 113
3. "Welch Souldier" = "name is Fluellen" = 110

Measure for Measure

1. "Constable" = "called Elbow" = 73
2. "Froth" = "the fool" = 54

The Two Gentlemen of Verona

1. "Crab is" = "the dog" = 44 the only dog named in *Shake-speare*
2. "Launce is" = "a clowne" = 56
3. "Speed is" = "a jester" = 62

A Midsommer Nights dreame

1. "Bottom is" = "the ass-head" = 81
2. "Oberon is a" = "Faerie King" = 64
3. "Peter Quince is" = "the carpenter" = 118
4. "Puck was" = "sprite" = 74
5. "Snug" = "a joiner" = 43
6. "Titania" = "is Queen" = 59

As You Like It

1. "Audrey name of" = "the goatherd" = 91
2. "Jaques is" = "melancholy" = 89
3. "Touchstone" = "be a wit's name" = 95

Love's Labour's Lost - the longest 'word' in *Shakespeare*

The longest 'word' in English *honorificabilitudinitatibus* (= 195) appears in *Love's Labours' Lost* (A5, S1). It was known long before the play was written. However, applying *Skelton* we find the following contextually appropriate resonance equations:

1. "honorificabilitudinitatibus" = "a code *Loves' Labours' Lost* hid" = 195
2. "honorificabilitudinitatibus" = "code in *Love's Labours' Lost*" = 195
3. "honorificabilitudinitatibus" = "code uses *Skelton* gematria" = 195
4. "honorificabilitudinitatibus" = "is the cipher you have found" = 195
5. "honorificabilitudinitatibus" = "*Shake-speare hid* a secret bard" = 195
6. "honorificabilitudinitatibus" = "*Shake-speare* is code *hiding* a name" = 195
7. "honorificabilitudinitatibus" = "*Shake-speare* was disguise" = 195
8. "honorificabilitudinitatibus" = "*Shake-speare*'s bard is *hiding*" = 195
9. "honorificabilitudinitatibus" = "*Shake-speare's* bard left clue" = 195
10. "honorificabilitudinitatibus" = "very long word *hides* a code" = 195
11. "honorificabilitudinitatibus" = "you have found the cypher" = 195

Twelfth Night

1. "A twin brother" = "name is Sebastian" = 127
2. "Cesario hiding" = "Viola's name" = 86
3. "Duke Orsino" = "of Illyria" = 80
4. "Feste" = "is a fool" = 47
5. "Malvolio is" = "foolish gull" = 88

Cymbeline

1. "Cymbeline is a" = "king of England" = 94
2. "Fidele's name" = "hidd Innogen" = 74

King Lear

1. "Edmund is a" = "bastard" = 62
2. "Smulkin" = "my demon" = 72

Othello

1. "Othello is a" = "jealous Moor" = 81
2. "Othello" = "is a Moor" = 59
3. "Wicked Iago be a" = "souldier" = 64
4. "Othello's wife" = "name is Desdemona" = 110

Much Ado about Nothing

1. "Dogberry" = "is a clowne" = 77
2. "Verges is" = "foolish gull" = 88

Hamlet, Prince of Denmark

1. "Claudius the" = "usurper" = 79
2. "Hamlet's ghost" = "father's ghost" = 127
3. "Hamlet" = "prince" = 53
4. "Laertes" = "a brother" = 70
5. "Polonius" = "the old fool" = 73
6. "Yorick" = "jester" = 61

Romeo & Juliet

1. "Juliet is" = "virgin" = 64
2. "Mercutio" = "is a wit" = 66
3. "nurse" = "an old maide" = 55

The Merchant of Venice

1. "A Jew's name be" = "Shylock" = 78
2. "Old Jew called" = "Shylock" = 78

The Tempest

1. "Caliban's dam is" = "Sycorax" = 90
2. "Prospero" = "olde magician name" = 92
3. "Sycorax" = "is a blue-eyed hag" = 90

Macbeth

1. "I am Lady Macbeth" = "an evil woman" = 103
2. "Scottish King" = "his name is Macbeth" = 125

Summary: The constructed name 'Shake-speare' had two distinct applications; originally as a code-name for Cecil, Dee and Walsingham and later as the pen name adopted by a secret royal writer.

*See ***Breaking the Shakespeare Codes*** ISBN 978-0-949001-34-4 (Robert Nield, 2007) for a preliminary solution of the 'authorship mystery'. A much fuller account will be provided in a forthcoming book: '*Shakespeare's Secret Author – Mr WH*'.

6. Elizabeth I and The Secret Royal Code

The most highly educated woman in England, the intellectually gifted Elizabeth I (1533-1603) loved puzzles and riddles, performing double translations of Latin every day just for mental exercise. Many solutions (following) indicate that she used *Skelton*'s cipher and the Master Code; however, as head of the Church in England it was vital that she was not seen to be involved with 'the occult' - any interest she might have in such 'dark matters' had to be kept strictly secret. In 1577 a great comet appeared in the skies over England, a celestial phenomenon thought to be a harbinger of doom. To see a comet in those days was believed to bring misfortune - to princes especially - so the shutters at Richmond palace where the Queen was resident were closed. In a demonstration of personal courage, Elizabeth promptly opened the windows so as to get a good look at the 'ill-omen'. It seems the Tudor Queen believed in finding things out for herself. Being naturally inquisitive and vain, when investigating *Skelton*'s cipher she would almost certainly have looked for solutions that related to her personally. **Applying knowledge, logic and intuition an attempt is made to find some of the Master Code solutions Elizabeth could have discovered herself:**

1. "A message of Elizabeth Tudor: *I'm Queen*" = 246
2. "Believe ciphers by Queen Elizabeth" = 246
3. "Believe in ciphers of Queen Elizabeth" = 246
4. "Believe the cipher Queen Elizabeth *hid*" = 246
5. "Believe the message *hid* by Elizabeth" = 246
6. "Cipher ye cracked was Elizabeth's" = 246
7. "Elizabeth found the secret number" = 246
8. "Elizabeth *hid* the secret truth" = 246
9. "Elizabeth *hides* the secret cipher" = 246
10. "Elizabeth sent a message for you" = 246
11. "Elizabeth used the *Skelton* oracle" = 246
12. "Elizabeth's cipher broken by you" = 246
13. "*Ever the same:* a motto of Elizabeth" = 246 her Latin motto: *semper eadem*
14. "Few find Elizabeth's cipher number" = 246
15. "Few find Queen Elizabeth's numeral" = 246
16. "Few find Queen Elizabeth's secret" = 246
17. "I'm Elizabeth Tudor: England's Queene" = 246
18. "*I'm Queen* is the message of Elizabeth" = 246
19. "Message of Elizabeth is: I'm the Queen" = 246
20. "Message of Elizabeth Tudor: *I am Queen*" = 246
21. "Messages from Elizabeth to you" = 246
22. "My message is: *I am Queene Elizabeth*" = 246
23. "Queen Elizabeth's Master Cipher" = 246
24. "Queene Elizabeth has The Golden Key" = 246
25. "*Skelton* is an oracle for the Queene" = 246
26. "*Skelton:* Queene Elizabeth's oracle" = 246
27. "The Queen talks to you in cipher" = 246
28. "This is Queen Elizabeth's cipher" = 246
29. "You have got Elizabeth's message" = 246

Reversed solutions:

- 246 = “the Tudor Queen’s secret number”
- 246 = “was secret numeral of Elizabeth”

7. Queen Elizabeth’s M-cipher

In a letter replying to a communication from Doctor Dee, Elizabeth signed herself ‘M’. Presumably, she knew that her ‘philosopher’ would understand the cipher because he (probably) created it.

Applying *Skelton* in that context, we find the resonance equations:

1. “Big **M:** a cipher hiding” = “Queen Elizabeth” = 111
2. “Big **M:** the cipher of” = “Queen Elizabeth” = 111
3. “Capital **M** means” = “Queen Elizabeth” = 111
4. “**M** was cipher of” = “Queen Elizabeth” = 111
5. “**M** was in place of” = “Queen Elizabeth” = 111
6. “Queen Elizabeth” = “is uppercase **M**” = 111
7. “Queen Elizabeth” = “used letter **M**” = 111
8. “The letter **M**” = “Queen Elizabeth” = 111

Applying the Master Code in that context:

1. “An **M:** the monogram of Queen Elizabeth” = 246
2. “An **M:** the sign of Queen Elizabeth” = 246
3. “Initial **M** is Elizabeth’s cypher” = 246
4. “**M** cipher alludes to Queen Elizabeth” = 246
5. “**M** is the cipher-initial of Elizabeth” = 246
6. “**M** is the special cipher of Elizabeth” = 246
7. “**M** represents Queen Elizabeth” = 246
8. “**M:** the secret insignia of Elizabeth” = 246
9. “**M** was a symbol of Queen Elizabeth” = 246
10. “**M** was insignia of Elizabeth Tudor” = 246
11. “Queen Elizabeth signed herself big **M**” = 246
12. “Queen Elizabeth signs herself **M**” = 246
13. “Queen Elizabeth used **M** as her cipher” = 246

In addition, we find the general Master Code solutions:

1. “**M** is letter for the sovereign” = 246
2. “**M** is letter used for the monarch” = 246

8. Nicknames of Elizabeth's courtiers

The Queen gave her courtiers nicknames derived in part from personal attributes; for example, Sir Robert Cecil - son of Lord Burghley and a leading minister from 1591 - was called 'pygmy' because he was dwarfish. However, it seems there was another reason for the handles: it appears that Elizabeth applied *Skelton*'s cipher to courtiers' names so as to derive 'occult' nicknames:

1. "Burghley" = "a spirit" = 76 - Lord Burghley was called 'spirit'
2. "Doctor Dee's name" = "philosopher" = 105 - Elizabeth called Dee 'philosopher'
3. "Doctor Lopez" = "a Jewish doctor" = 108 - A Jewish physician from Portugal
4. "Hatton is" = "a Lord Keeper" = 85 - Hatton was Lord Keeper
5. "Mutton is" = "a Hatton name" = 93 - Christopher Hatton was 'mutton'
6. "Mutton is" = "my lyds" = 93 - Hatton, nicknamed lyds
7. "Robert Cecil" = "a pygmy" = 83 - named 'pygmy' by the Queen
8. "Robert Dudley" = "my horse man" = 111 - Queen's favourite, 'master of horse'
9. "Robert is" = "my eyes" = 82 - Dudley was called 'eyes' by Elizabeth
10. "Thomasina" = "the dwarf" = 79 - The Queen's dwarf, Thomasina
11. "Walsingham" = "is my Moore" = 96 - The spy-master was called 'Moore'
12. "Walter Ralegh" = "is my *water*" = 118 - West Country pronunciation of Walter
13. "William Cecil" = "a Lord Keeper" = 85 - Burghley (WC) was Lord Keeper

Applying *Skelton* to the name and title of Elizabeth:

"Elizabeth Tudor" = "is *Pallas Athena*" = 122 goddess of knowledge & wisdom

"Elizabeth" = "*Gloriana*" = 73 a famous name for the Queen

1. "Queen Elizabeth" = "is called *Astrea*" = 111 virgin goddess of the 'golden age'
2. "Queen Elizabeth" = "the Sun's name" = 111 she was known as 'The Sun'

Appearance and reality: The 'Virgin Queen' - a pseudonym

'Appearance and reality' played a central role in Elizabethan philosophy: the question of how things seem in contrast with how they truly are. In that regard, the 'real' Elizabeth Tudor was hidden by the mask of the 'Virgin Queen', a beguiling image that has proven remarkably durable and almost invulnerable to analysis. A significant consequence of the Reformation in England was that the 'cult of the Virgin Mary' – central in the Roman tradition – was replaced with the 'cult of the Virgin Queen', a 'venerable' icon under which it was hoped a theologically divided nation would unite. In the role of demigoddess, Elizabeth - a consummate actress - assumed the mythic status of 'England's bride' and that meant (in theory) she could not be married and could not have legitimate offspring.

It is therefore especially noteworthy that in 1570 people at Norwich claimed publicly that Elizabeth was, in secret, a mother – unfortunately, they soon found themselves swinging at the end of a rope because the government had declared it treason to claim that the Queen had issue. The executions did not have the desired effect, however - they failed to silence people; the rumour that Elizabeth was a mother 'in secret' continued to circulate for many years, despite the draconian punishments meted out to rumour mongers - often involving the removal of tongues and ears.

The following solutions indicate that the 'Virgin Queen' title was a secret jest - a private joke that was meant to gull a credulous public, an image at once seductive and deceptive that concealed Elizabeth Tudor's true sexual status.

Applying *Skelton* to "Virgin Queen" in that context, we find the resonance equations:

1. "Secret *hid* by" = *"Virgin Queen"* = 102
2. *"Virgin Queen"* = "a conspiracy" = 102
3. *"Virgin Queen"* = "a *giant* falsehood" = 102
4. *"Virgin Queen"* = "a huge *deliberate* lie" = 102
5. *"Virgin Queen"* = "be a private joke" = 102
6. *"Virgin Queen"* = "*cipher* fooled all" = 102
7. *"Virgin Queen"* = "cloak *hides* Queen" = 102
8. *"Virgin Queen"* = "*disguised* Queen" = 102
9. *"Virgin Queen"* = "gulls many" = 102
10. *"Virgin Queen"* = "*hid* huge deception" = 102
11. *"Virgin Queen"* = "*hid* the monarch" = 102
12. *"Virgin Queen"* = "*hid* sovereign" = 102
13. *"Virgin Queen"* = "*hid* Tudor Queen" = 102
14. *"Virgin Queen"* = "*hides* THE Queen" = 102
15. *"Virgin Queen"* = "is a secret joke" = 102
16. *"Virgin Queen"* = "is *hiding* a jest" = 102
17. *"Virgin Queen"* = "is misnomer" = 102
18. *"Virgin Queen"* = "just a folly" = 102
19. *"Virgin Queen"* = "laughable title" = 102
20. *"Virgin Queen"* = "*masking* Queen" = 102
21. *"Virgin Queen"* = "misleads you" = 102
22. *"Virgin Queen"* = "ruse and jest" = 102
23. *"Virgin Queen"* = "the royal lie" = 102
24. *"Virgin Queen"* = "was untrue" = 102

Applying the Master Code in the context of the *Virgin Queen* title:

1. "*The Virgin Queen* is a lie of the Queen" = 246
2. "*The Virgin Queen*: cipher Queen used" = 246
3. "*The Virgin Queene* title is false" = 246
4. "Tudor Queen *hiding* as *Virgin Queen*" = 246
5. "*Virgin Queen:* a *disguise* of Elizabeth" = 246
6. "*Virgin Queen:* name fooled everyone" = 246
7. "*Virgin Queen* was a conspiracy" = 246
8. "*Virgin Queen* was a laughable title" = 246
9. "*Virgin Queen* was secret *jest*" = 246
10. "*Virgin Queen* was secret *ruse*" = 246

Collectively, the resonance equations and Master Code solutions imply that the 'Virgin Queen' title was simply that – merely a title.

9. A SECRET ENCRYPTED PORTRAIT

Attributed to Marcus Gheeraerts the younger (1561-1636)

Image: © the author

The author believes this 'lost' painting to be a secret encrypted portrait of Elizabeth I, a unique picture never intended for public display owing to its occult associations. The sitter is identified, in part, by applying *Skelton*'s cipher and the Master Code to elements in the picture. For example, **excluding the necklace the sitter is wearing 246 individual gems** consisting of pearls, diamonds and rubies - the Master Code key, the 'magic' gematria number 'hidden' as gems. Applying *Skelton* in that context, we find: "gems" = "clues" = 39 which suggests gems in the portrait are clues in a cipher. However, **the entire costume – not just the gems – comprises a set of coded clues that identify the sitter.**

Evidence/reasoning that the portrait is a depiction of Elizabeth I

1. Facial appearance - resembles Elizabeth, though depicted in the 'mask of youth'
2. A very large number of pearls (530+), the gem famously identified with Elizabeth*
3. The silver sleeves - 'hanging' sleeves - referred to in several code solutions
4. Robe of books - design on costume - symbol of Elizabeth's renowned learning
5. Six appears *three* times on the wig: six is the sun's number (see Agrippa's *Natural Magic*)
6. Number of pearls across wig: consistent with Queen's age (60) & regnal year (36) in 1594
7. Brooches on the shoulders represent Moon Carrots ('moon cult' of QE in 1590s)
8. *Moon* carrot (*seseli* libanotis) – pun on Cecil name – so, the flower links the Queen & Cecil
9. Robert Dudley (Leicester) bequeathed Elizabeth a 600-pearl necklace in his will (1588)
10. The wig – in the 1590s the Queen was noted for wearing a dark-red wig

*Pearl relates to Cynthia - the moon goddess - who was pure and virgin and linked to Elizabeth's famous 'moon cult' of the 1590s. The Queen was referred to as 'Cynthia' and **in that context, we find the Master Code solution:** "Cynthia was alias for Elizabeth" = 246.

The Queen was famed for wearing pearls - her 'totemic' gem - pearl was a symbol of 'purity' and 'virginity'. There are over 500 pearls in the picture, a plethora even by Elizabeth's opulent standards; few if any of her portraits have comparable abundance. In 1588 the Earl of Leicester, Robert Dudley, Elizabeth's favourite left her a 600-pearl necklace in his will - over 400 pearls can be counted in the visible part of the portrait's necklace. No aristocratic lady living in England at the time would dare 'out-do' or 'up-stage' the Queen with her famous 'trade-mark' pearls – especially in something explicit and permanent like a portrait; so, the sheer number of pearls alone is a very strong indication that the sitter is Elizabeth I and, **in that context, we find the Master Code resonance equation**:

"Pearls are sign of Queen Elizabeth" = "Queen Elizabeth's favourite gems" = 246

The significance of the *silver* sleeves. Like pearl, silver was traditionally associated with the moon, the goddess Artemis and the Queen. Two very prominent elements in the portrait - pearls and silver sleeves - are both linked to the moon and to the Elizabeth's 'moon cult' at its height in the 1590s. By symbolic association with the moon those significant elements - pearl and silver - help to identify the sitter as the Queen.

A gift to the Queen from William & Robert Cecil

Many Master Code solutions (following) indicate that the painting was a gift from Sir William Cecil (Lord Burghley) and his son Robert, celebrating Elizabeth's thirty-six years as monarch when she was sixty years old - the special occasion: Accession Day, 17th November 1594. The Cecils were the leading ministers during the last decade of Elizabeth's reign. Sir William Cecil, had been chief minister for thirty-seven years until his son Robert assumed the role in 1596. Wily, cunning and clever the Cecils knew that the Queen possessed some of the finest and most expensive jewellery, so rather than presenting her with yet more costly but 'soon-to-be-forgotten' gems to commemorate the special Accession Day in 1594, they commissioned a coded 'puzzle-portrait' that *displayed* a lot of very expensive jewels. A highly cost-effective gift and the ideal present for a woman who loved the intellectual challenge and stimulation of puzzles and riddles.

The sitter's age & regnal years

Elizabeth Tudor was sixty years old in 1593/94. The sitter's face, depicted as the so-called 'mask of youth', disguised the Queen's true appearance - a legal requirement for portraits made from 1594 onwards. Sixty pearls are arrayed in an arc across the top of the sitter's head, which is interpreted to mean that there are sixty years 'on her head' consistent with the Queen's age in 1593/94 *and* her thirty-sixth regnal year. Thirty-six was a special number in occult numerology, a secondary 'Sun number' (36 = 6 x 6) the Sun's primary number six (Agrippa, *Natural Magic*). Elizabeth was known as 'the Sun' so she was associated with six and thirty-six. Six rings, each of six pearls are displayed across the front of the wig - an allusion to the Queen's 36 regnal years in 1594 - and there are also six lozenge brooches on the wig. So, in total there are '*three* lots of six' on the wig.

***Six* appears *three* times on the wig – what does it signify?**

To summarise: there are six rings of pearl, six pearls in each ring and six lozenge brooches on the wig. According to occult numerology six and thirty-six - 'sun' numbers - are linked to the Queen since she was known as 'The Sun'. **We recall the equation**: "Queen Elizabeth" = "the Sun's name" = 111

Applying *Skelton* in the context of 'three' sixes and Queen Elizabeth:

- "Six-six-six" = "is Queen Elizabeth" = 132 666 - no wonder the portrait was secret!
- "*Triple six*" = "Queen Elizabeth" = 111

Applying the Master Code in that context:

1. "A *trio* of *sixes* on Queen Elizabeth" = 246
2. "Elizabeth was *six-six-six*" = 246
3. "Hid *treble six* on the Queen's wig" = 246
4. "Look for *three sixes* on the wig" = 246
5. "Queen Elizabeth's *trio* of *sixes*" = 246
6. "*Six* is a cipher of Elizabeth Tudor" = 246
7. "*Six*: a cypher of Elizabeth Tudor" = 246
8. "*Three sixes* on the Queen's wig" = 246

The repeated occurrence of 'six' on the wig - the Sun's primary 'occult' number - helps to identify the sitter as 'the Sun', in other words: Elizabeth I.

The costume – in particular the robe of books – is also highly significant.

Applying *Skelton*: "Robe of books" = "Elizabeth" = 73*

And, the resonance equations: "Robe of books" = "hides name of" = "Elizabeth" = 73

Also, in that context:

1. "A robe of bookes hides" = "Queen Elizabeth" = 111 old spelling
2. "Queen Elizabeth" = "is in a robe of books" = 111
3. "Robe of books hiding" = "Queen Elizabeth" = 111

*An example of *Skelton* being used to transform the abstract into the tangible: 'Elizabeth' (abstract) equates to 'robe of books' (tangible).

The sitter wears a robe depicting many books arranged on shelves - like the wall of a library - symbolising the Queen's famed erudition. Elizabeth was known as *Pallas Athena,* goddess of knowledge and wisdom – *hasti-vibrans* the **spear shaker**.

The painting would have been a *surprise* gift and that means it was a *construction* - Elizabeth didn't sit for the portrait. Style and period (1590s) suggest it's likely the artist was Marcus Gheeraerts the younger, an identification consistent with some of the (following) code solutions. The pair of identical brooches, at the sitter's shoulders, are identified as representations of *moon carrots* (*seseli libanotis*). The central brooch is possibly a sun symbol - 'the sun in splendour'? – that too would be an important emblem identified with the Queen. Thus, some emblems in the portrait connect the sitter with the moon while other icons link the sitter to the sun. It is noteworthy that throughout English history, *only* Elizabeth I was simultaneously associated with sun and moon and that was during the 1590s.

Reversed solutions:

- 246 = "her Majesty's secret numeral"
- 246 = "is *hiding* as Queen Elizabeth's gems"
- 246 = "is the cipher number of the monarch"
- 246 = "the cypher number of the monarch"
- 246 = "the sovereign's secret number"

Combining the solutions gives the resonance equations:

1. "Her Majesty's secret numeral" = "is *hiding* as Queen Elizabeth's gems" = 246
2. "The sovereign's secret number" = "is *hiding* as Queen Elizabeth's gems" = 246

Reversed solutions:

- 246 = "a cipher numeral in Queen's picture"
- 246 = "a number *hid* as gems of Queen Elizabeth"
- 246 = "a number Tudor Queen's painting *hid*"
- 246 = "a numeral *hidd* in the Queen's picture"
- 246 = "a numeral *hiding* in Elizabeth's gems"
- 246 = "a numeral Tudor Queen's picture *hid*"
- 246 = "find number in Queene's portrait"
- 246 = "*hid* in painting of the *Virgin Queen*"
- 246 = "*hid* in portrait Cecil gave the Queen"
- 246 = "*hid* in *Virgin Queen*'s portrait"
- 246 = "*hides* as Queen Elizabeth's costume"
- 246 = "*hides* in painting of Queen Elizabeth"
- 246 = "in costume in Queen's portrait"
- 246 = "in Tudor Queen's secret picture"

- 246 = “is a numeral hidden in a picture of Queen”
- 246 = “is a numeral the Queen’s costume hid”
- 246 = “is clue hidden as Queen’s portrait”
- 246 = “is *hid* in *Virgin Queen*’s painting”
- 246 = “is *hiding* as Queen Elizabeth’s gems”
- 246 = “is number *hid* in portrait of Queen”
- 246 = “is numeral *hid* as Elizabeth’s gems”
- 246 = “is numeral in the Queen’s costume”
- 246 = “is numeral the Queen’s picture *hid*”
- 246 = “number *hid* by Elizabeth’s costume”
- 246 = “number *hides* in a portrait of Queen”
- 246 = “number in Tudor Queen’s painting”
- 246 = “number of gems in Queen’s painting”
- 246 = “numeral hid as Queen’s portrait”
- 246 = “numeral in Tudor Queen’s picture”
- 246 = “the number Queen’s portrait hid”
- 246 = “was *hiding* in Queen’s portrait

A large set of additional Master Code solutions relate to the portrait

The number of gems on the sitter, excluding the necklace, is 246. Code solutions above tell us that 246 is the secret cipher numeral of the monarch/sovereign. Hence, the sitter is Elizabeth I.

1. "A cipher is in an image of Queen Elizabeth" = 246
2. **"A clue is: *silver sleev'd* Elizabeth" = 246**
3. "A cypher in an image of Queen Elizabeth" = 246
4. "**A *hidden* silver sleeves picture**" = 246
5. "A huge pearl necklace is in portrait" = 246
6. "A necklace from Dudley is in painting" = 246 — bequeathed in his will, 1588
7. "A necklace in picture of Queen Elizabeth" = 246
8. "A necklace of pearl signals Elizabeth" = 246
9. **"A painting of Queen *hid* Skelton's code" = 246**
10. "A pearl necklace in portrait is huge" = 246
11. "A picture *hid* necklace of Robert Dudley" = 246
12. "A picture *hid* Tudor Queen's numeral" = 246
13. **"A picture of a *silver-sleeved* Queen" = 246**
14. "A picture of the Queen be *hiding* a secret" = 246
15. "A picture of the Queene *was* secret" = 246
16. "A portrait *hid* face of Queene Elizabeth" = 246 — hidden as the 'mask of youth'
17. "A portrait in an oval window *hid*" = 246
18. "A portrait in the oval window" = 246
19. "A portrait of Elizabeth the Queen" = 246
20. "A portrait of Queen was *secret*" = 246
21. "A portrait of the Queen is an enigma" = 246
22. "A riddle *hidden* as Queen's portrait" = 246
23. "A riddle painting *hid* is for the Queen" = 246
24. "A ring in Queene Elizabeth's left ear" = 246
25. "A ring of pearls: a signal of the Queen" = 246
26. "A secret cipher in Queen's picture" = 246
27. "A secret clue *hidden* in a picture of Queen" = 246
28. "A secret costume of Queen Elizabeth" = 246
29. "A secret *hidd* in the Queen's picture" = 246
30. "A secret is *hidden* in a picture of Queen" = 246
31. "A secret number be in a picture of Queen" = 246
32. "A secret number clue in a portrait" = 246
33. "A secret picture *hid* necklace of Dudley" = 246
34. "A secret picture of the Queen is a clue" = 246
35. **"A silver sleeved picture hides a code" = 246**
36. "Age of Queen Elizabeth *hidden* in a picture" = 246
37. "Age of Queen Elizabeth *hides* in picture" = 246
38. "Age of Queen Elizabeth in gems: 60" = 246 — 60 pearls across top of wig
39. "An image of Queen Elizabeth *hid* hard riddle" = 246
40. "An image of Queen Elizabeth *hiding* cipher" = 246
41. "Apparel of Queen Elizabeth *hid* cipher" = 246
42. "Blood moons *hidden* in Queen's picture" = 246
43. "Books are Queen Elizabeth's dress" = 246
44. "Burghley's gift to Queene *hid* clues" = 246
45. "Cecil gave the painting to the Queen" = 246
46. "Cecil gave the Queene the portrait" = 246
47. "Cecil's gift for the Queen *hides* a riddle" = 246

48. "Cecil's gift *hides* a riddle for the Queen" = 246
49. "Cecil's *secret* portrait of Queene" = 246
50. "Cipher *hidden* as portrait of Queene" = 246
51. "Cipher *hides* as a portrait of Queen" = 246
52. "Cipher in image of Queen Elizabeth is hid" = 246
53. "Cipher in the Queene's portrait" = 246
54. **"Cipher of Dee is in portrait of Queen" = 246**
55. "Cipher-portrait of Queen is *hidden*" = 246
56. "Clue is: count gems of Queen Elizabeth" = 246
57. "Clue is: Elizabeth Tudor's picture" = 246
58. "Clue is: Queen's special portrait" = 246
59. "Clue *hides* in a *secret* picture of Queen" = 246
60. "Clues are *hidden* as portrait gems" = 246
61. "Clues *hiding* in portrait as gems" = 246
62. **"Code of the silver sleev'd picture" = 246**
63. "Code-portrait of Queen as Cynthia" = 246
64. "Costume painting is of Queen Bess" = 246
65. "Costume portrait of Queen Bess" = 246
66. "Count gems of Queene's portrait" = 246
67. "Count the gems of the portrait" = 246
68. **"Cypher of Dee in portrait of Queen" = 246**
69. "Cyphers in portrait of Queen" = 246
70. **"Dee's code *hid* as a portrait of the Queen" = 246**
71. **"Doctor Dee *hid* code in portrait of Queen" = 246**
72. "Dudley's necklace be in a picture of Queen" = 246
73. "Dudley's necklace is in a portrait" = 246
74. **"Elizabeth: a silver sleeved lady" = 246**
75. "**Elizabeth has silver sleeves**" **= 246**
76. "Elizabeth in a *secret* portrait" = 246
77. "**Elizabeth Tudor is wearing books**" = 246
78. **"Elizabeth was silver sleeved" = 246**
79. "Elizabeth wears Dudley's necklace" = 246
80. "Elizabeth wears small earring" = 246
81. "Elizabeth's initial on the sleeve" = 246
82. "Elizabeth's name *hides* as: *robe of books*" = 246 "robe of books" = "Elizabeth" = 73
83. "Elizabeth's picture found by you" = 246
84. "Elizabeth's robe of books is secret" = 246
85. "Elliptical window picture is a code" = 246
86. "Examine picture of Queen: look for a clue" = 246
87. "Examine portrait of Queen: find clue" = 246
88. "Examine Queen Elizabeth's attire" = 246
89. "Examine Queene Elizabeth's dress" = 246
90. "Face in the portrait is Elizabeth" = 246
91. "Find a number Queene's portrait hid" = 246
92. "Find hundreds of riddles in picture" = 246
93. "Find number in Queene's portrait" = 246
94. **"Find picture of silver sleeves" = 246**
95. **"Find 'silver sleeves' painting" = 246**
96. "Gems are clues in Queene's painting" = 246

97. "Gems in image of Tudor Queen are a cipher" = 246
98. "Gems in picture of Queen hide a secret" = 246
99. "Gems in Queene's painting are clues" = 246
100. **"Gheeraerts *hid* a cipher in image of Queen" = 246**
101. **"Gheeraerts *hides* royal numeral" = 246**
102. **"Gheeraerts is the hired painter" = 246**
103. **"Gheeraerts made a cypher picture" = 246**
104. **"Gheeraerts painted a portrait" = 246**
105. "Gift of Cecil to the Queen *hiding* number" = 246
106. "Gold ring is in the Queen's left ear" = 246
107. **"Hanging silver sleeves of Queen" = 246**
108. "Head and shoulders of the Tudor Queen" = 246
109. "*Hid* a hard riddle in portrait of Queen" = 246
110. "*Hid* a number as an image of Queen Elizabeth" = 246
111. "*Hid* a number as gems of Queen Elizabeth" = 246
112. "*Hid* a test as Queene's portrait" = 246
113. "*Hid* a wit test in picture of Queen" = 246
114. "*Hid* clue in *Virgin Queen's* painting" = 246
115. "*Hid* clues in picture of *Virgin Queen*" = 246
116. "*Hid* hundreds of clues in portrait" = 246
117. "*Hid* number riddle as Queen's picture" = 246
118. **"*Hid* picture of Queen by Gheeraerts" = 246**
119. "*Hid* secret as Queen's portrait" = 246
120. "*Hid* the Queen in special portrait" = 246
121. "*Hidden* cypher portrait of Queen" = 246
122. "*Hidden* portrait of Queen is cipher" = 246
123. "*Hide* a numeral in Queen's portrait" = 246
124. "*Hide* code in oval window portrait" = 246
125. "*Hide* numeral in portrait's gems" = 246
126. "*Hide* the oval window portrait" = 246
127. "Huge pearl necklace: clue in a portrait" = 246
128. "I am Queen Elizabeth attired in books" = 246
129. "I am Queen Elizabeth dressed in books" = 246
130. "I enchanted portrait of Elizabeth" = 246 'I' is Doctor Dee – he designed portrait
131. "I *hid* a number in an image of Queen Elizabeth" = 246.
132. "I *hid* cipher clue in portrait of Queen" = 246
133. "I *hid* cypher in portrait of Queen" = 246
134. "I *hid* numeral in Queen's portrait" = 246
135. "I *hid* test as Queen's portrait" = 246
136. "I *hide* riddles in Queen's portrait" = 246
137. "I put test in Queen's painting" = 246
138. **"I use *Skelton* code in picture of Queen" = 246**
139. "Inspect a portrait of the Queen" = 246
140. "Jewels are Queen's secret number" = 246
141. "Left a hard riddle in Queen's picture" = 246

142. “Look for a number in Queene’s picture” = 246
143. **“Look for hanging sleeves picture” = 246**
144. **“Look for silver-sleeved Queene” = 246**
145. “Look for the Queene in oval window” = 246
146. “Look for *three sixes* on the wig” = 246
147. “Many books cover Queen Elizabeth” = 246
148. “Many pearls are in a portrait” = 246
149. “Many pearls be in picture of Queen” = 246
150. **“Marcus Gheeraerts painted Queene” = 246**
151. “*Moon carrot* was Queen Elizabeth” = 246
152. **“My silver sleeves picture” = 246**
153. “Necklace of Dudley in secret picture” = 246
154. “Necklace of Robert Dudley in picture” = 246
155. “Number of the sun *hid* on Queen’s wig” = 246
156. “Number of the sun in pearl rings” = 246
157. “Number riddle *hid* as Queen’s picture” = 246
158. “Number riddles in Queen’s picture” = 246
159. “Numeral clue *hid* as Elizabeth’s gems” = 246
160. “Numeral clue *hides* in a picture of Queen” = 246
161. “Numeral clue in the Queen’s costume” = 246
162. “Numeral of sun *hidd* in pearl rings” = 246
163. “Numeral of sun *hidden* on Queen’s wig” = 246
164. “Numeral of sun *hides* in Queen’s wig” = 246
165. “Numerals in Queen’s portrait” = 246
166. “Numerals of sun hide in Queen’s wig” = 246
167. “Occult number clue *hid* as portrait” = 246
168. “Occult number clue in a picture of Queen” = 246
169. “Occult number is in a picture of Queen” = 246
170. “Oval window painting *hid* a number” = 246
171. “Oval window picture *hid* a numeral” = 246
172. “Oval window picture *hid* a secret” = 246
173. “Oval window portrait *hid* codes” = 246
174. “Painting *hid* huge riddle *for* the Queen” = 246
175. “Painting is *hiding* Dudley’s necklace” = 246
176. “Painting of Queen *hid* our puzzle” = 246
177. “Painting of Queen *hidd* sun numbers” = 246
178. “Painting of the Queene is a hard riddle” = 246
179. “Painting was the *Virgin Queen*” = 246
180. “Pearl necklace is portrait’s clue” = 246
181. “Pearl necklace of Dudley be in a painting” = 246
182. “Pearl necklace of Dudley *hid* in picture” = 246
183. “Pearls are sign of Queen Elizabeth” = 246
184. “Pearls in rings is regnal time” = 246
185. “Pearls on Elizabeth’s head are the age” = 246
186. “Pearls: Queen Elizabeth’s signal” = 246
187. **“Picture by Gheeraerts *hid* cipher” = 246**

188. **"Picture Gheeraerts made is a cipher" = 246**
189. "Picture *hid* a riddle test *for* Queene" = 246
190. "Picture is to mark Queen's reign" = 246
191. "Picture of Queen Bess *hid* in costume" = 246
192. **"Picture of Queen by Gheeraerts *hid*" = 246**
193. "Picture of Queen Elizabeth of England" = 246
194. "Picture of Queen *hid* numeral of cipher" = 246
195. "Picture of Queen *hid* the *Skelton* code" = 246
196. "Picture of Queen *hidd* sun's numeral" = 246
197. "Picture of Queen *hiding* occult number" = 246
198. "Picture of Queen is hard puzzle" = 246
199. "Picture of Queene Elizabeth had a necklace" = 246
200. "Picture of Queene *hidd* a secret number" = 246
201. "Picture of Queene *hides* sun numeral" = 246
202. **"Picture of silver-sleeved lady" = 246**
203. **"Picture of silver-sleeved Queene" = 246**
204. **"Picture of the Queen hid Skelton code" = 246**
205. "Picture of *Virgin Queen* is a cipher" = 246
206. "Picture was of the *Virgin Queen*" = 246
207. "Picture-riddles: test for Queen" = 24
208. "Portrait *hid* a riddle *for* the Queen" = 246
209. "Portrait *hid* a very hard riddle" = 246
210. "Portrait *hides* the key number" = 246
211. "Portrait *hiding* a secret number" = 246
212. "Portrait *hiding* Dudley's necklace" = 246
213. "Portrait is a gift for the Queen" = 246
214. "Portrait is gift of Cecil to Queene" = 246
215. "Portrait is of head and shoulders" = 246
216. **"Portrait is silver sleev'd" = 246**
217. "Portrait of Her Majesty *hides*" = 246
218. "Portrait of Queen conceals cipher" = 246
219. **"Portrait of Queen cypher by Dee" = 246**
220. "Portrait of Queen *hid* her secret" = 246
221. "Portrait of Queen *hidd* a puzzle" – 246
222. "Portrait of Queen *hides* Cecil's name" = 246
223. **"Portrait of Queen hid a cypher of Dee" = 246**
224. **"Portrait of Queen is cipher by Dee" = 246**
225. **"Portrait of Queen is code of Doctor Dee" = 246**
226. "Portrait of Queen is *hidden* cipher" = 246
227. "Portrait of the Queen aged 60" = 246
228. "Portrait of the Queen *hid* riddles" = 246
229. **"Portrait of the Queen *hides* Dee's code" = 246**
230. "Portrait of the Queen is special" = 246
231. "Portrait was a secret cipher" = 246
232. "Puzzle be in portrait of Queen" = 246
233. "Puzzle *hid* by painting of Queen" = 246
234. "Queen Bess *hid* in costume painting" = 246
235. "Queen Elizabeth + diamond + ruby + pearl" = 246
236. "Queen Elizabeth adorned with books" = 246
237. "Queen Elizabeth cloaked by a robe of books" = 246
238. "Queen Elizabeth dresses in bookes" = 246

239. “Queen Elizabeth in an oval window” = 246
240. “Queen Elizabeth in gems at 60” = 246
241. “Queen Elizabeth robed in many bookes” = 246
242. “Queen Elizabeth wears her cipher” = 246
243. “Queen Elizabeth wears knowledge” = 246
244. “Queen Elizabeth’s gems are as clues” = 246
245. “Queen Elizabeth’s picture be a cipher” = 246
246. **“Queen had a silver sleev’d picture” = 246**
247. “Queen is attired in a necklace of Dudley” = 246
248. “Queen is dressed in a necklace of Dudley” = 246
249. “Queen is framed by an oval window” = 246
250. “Queen of England’s *hidden* portrait” = 246
251. “Queen of England’s painting is *hidden*” = 246
252. “Queen’s brooches are moon carrots” = 246
253. “Queen’s costume *hid* secret number” = 246
254. **“Queen’s hanging sleeves picture” = 246**
255. “Queen’s hidden secret portrait” = 246
256. “Queen’s image *hid* hard wit-tests” = 246
257. “Queen’s numeral *hid* as portrait” = 246
258. “Queen’s numerals in portrait” = 246
259. “Queen’s painting: a clue is *robe of books*” = 246
260. “Queen’s painting *hid* puzzles” = 246
261. **“Queen’s painting is Dee’s cypher” = 246**
262. “Queen’s picture is huge puzzle” = 246
263. “Queen’s portrait be giant cipher” = 246
264. **“Queen’s portrait: Dee’s cypher” = 246**
265. “Queen’s portrait: gems *hide* clues” = 246
266. “Queen’s portrait *hid* huge test” = 246
267. “Queen’s portrait *hid* the number” = 246
268. “Queen’s portrait *hides* message” = 246
269. **“Queen’s portrait hiding Dee’s codes” = 246**
270. **“Queen’s portrait is Dee’s cipher” = 246**
271. “Queen’s secret *hid* as portrait” = 246
272. “Queen’s secret is in the costume” = 246
273. “Queen’s secret number be in jewels” = 246
274. “Queen’s secret painting is *hidden*” = 246
275. **“Queen’s sleeves are silvery” = 246**
276. “Queen’s wig *hid* secret numeral clue” = 246
277. “Queen’s wig *hides* a secret numeral” = 246
278. “Queen’s wig *hiding* an occult numeral” = 246
279. **“Queene Bess: sleeves are silver” = 246**
280. “Queene Elizabeth dresses in books” = 246
281. “Queene Elizabeth robed in many books” = 246
282. “Queene Elizabeth wore a dark-red wig” = 246
283. “Queene Elizabeth’s jewel of the sun” = 246
284. “Queene had over five hundred pearls” = 246
285. **“Queene in hanging sleeves picture” = 246**
286. “Queene inherited a necklace from Dudley” = 246
287. “Queene is 60 in 15 94” = 246
288. **“Queene wears silver sleeves” = 246**

289. "Queene's numeral is in her costume" = 246
290. "Queene's painting *hid* riddle test" = 246
291. "Queene's picture be head and shoulders" = 246
292. "Queene's picture *hid* secret cipher" = 246
293. "Queene's portrait *hides* test" = 246
294. "Queene's portrait is a hard riddle" = 246
295. "Queene's robe of books be in portrait" = 246
296. "Queene's secret is in her costume" = 246
297. **"Queene's silver sleeves are a clue" = 246**
298. "Riddle for the Queen in portrait" = 246
299. "Riddle *hiding* in Queen's portrait" = 246
300. "Riddle in painting is *for* the Queen" = 246
301. "Riddle in picture is *set for* Queen" = 246
302. "Riddle-test *hid* as a picture of Queen" = 246
303. "Riddle-test in picture *for* Queene" = 246
304. "Riddles are in Queen's portrait" = 246
305. "Riddles *hide* as Queen's portrait" = 246
306. "Rings of pearl: signal of the Queene" = 246
307. **"*Robe of books* has silver sleeves" = 246**
308. "*Robe of books* in a secret portrait" = 246
309. "*Robe of books* was clue in portrait" = 246
310. "Search for a number in image of the Queen" = 246
311. "Secret clue in six pearl rings" = 246
312. "Secret clue in the Queen's costume" = 246
313. "Secret clues *hide* in a picture of Queen" = 246
314. "Secret *hid* as Queen's portrait" = 246
315. "Secret in Tudor Queen's picture" = 246
316. "Secret is in the Queen's costume" = 246
317. "Secret picture in oval window" = 246
318. "Secret picture of Queen Elizabeth" = 246
319. "Secret portrait of Queene Bess" = 246
320. "Secret portrait was a cipher" = 246
321. "Secrets in Queen's portrait" = 246
322. "*Seseli libanotis*: *hid* a wit test" = 246
323. "*Seseli libanotis: hid* Cecil name as a pun" = 246
324. "*Seseli libanotis: hides* Cecil name-pun" = 246
325. "*Seseli libanotis:* pun on Cecil's name" = 246
326. **"Silver sleev'd lady *hiding* Queen" = 246**
327. **"Silver sleev'd picture hiding a code" = 246**
328. **"Silver sleeves picture hid clue" = 246**
329. **"Silver sleeves picture *hides*"** = 246
330. **"Silver sleeves: sign of Tudor" = 246**
331. "Six pearl rings: a Tudor cipher" = 246
332. "Six pearl rings: *hid* a secret clue" = 246
333. "Six pearl rings of a Tudor Queen" = 246
334. "Six pearls are in six rings" = 246
335. **"*Skelton*'s code in painting of Queen" = 246**
336. **"Sleeves of silver are the sign" = 246**
337. **"Sleeves of silver in painting" = 246**
338. **"Sleeves of silver on Elizabeth" = 246**

339. **"Sleeves of silver on *robe of books*" = 246**
340. "Sun numeral in the pearl rings" = 246
341. "Sun's number is in pearl rings" = 246
342. "Test is in Queen's portrait" = 246
343. "The *hidden* portrait of Queen Bess" = 246
344. "The occult portrait of the Queen" = 246
345. "The painting Cecil gave to the Queen" = 246
346. "The painting is Elizabeth Tudor" = 246
347. "The painting of the *Virgin Queene*" = 246
348. "The pearl rings *hid* a sun numeral" = 246
349. "The picture had hundreds of riddles" = 246
350. "The picture is of Elizabeth Tudor" = 24
351. "The picture you found is the Queen" = 246
352. "The picture you have is the Queen" = 246
353. **"The Queen has silvered sleeves" = 246**
354. **"The Queen was wearing a *robe of books*" = 246**
355. "The Queen wearing many pearls" = 246
356. "The Queen's books are on her dress" = 246
357. "The Queen's costume *hid* a secret clue" = 246
358. "The Queen's picture *hides* a secret" = 246
359. "The Queen's portrait hid magical code" = 246
360. "The Queen's portrait is occult" = 246
361. "The Queen's portrait's cipher" = 246
362. **"The Queene has silver'd sleeves" = 246**
363. "The Queene is in *the mask of youth*" = 246
364. "The Queene's portrait *hid* a cipher" = 246
365. "The red wig was a sign of the Queen" = 246
366. **"The *robe of books* signals Elizabeth" = 246**
367. "The six pearl rings are a cipher" = 246
368. "The *Virgin Queene*'s portrait" = 246
369. "The wig of Queen Elizabeth was red" = 246
370. **"Tudor Queen had silver sleeves" = 246**
371. "Tudor Queen's picture *hid* a secret" = 246
372. "Very hard riddle in portrait" = 246
373. "*Virgin Queen* painting is a cipher" = 24
374. "*Virgin Queen*'s costume *hid* cipher" = 246
375. "*Virgin Queen*'s costume was a clue" = 246
376. "Ye counted gems in a picture of Queene" = 246
377. "Ye counted Queene Elizabeth's gems" = 246
378. "Ye possess painting Queen *hid*" = 246
379. "You count gems on Queene Elizabeth" = 246
380. "You examined Queene's portrait" = 246
381. "You have found the Queen's picture" = 246
382. "You possess Queen's picture" = 246

Reversed solutions:

- 246 = "a number hid by Queene's portrait"
- 246 = "a number hidden in a portrait of Queen"
- 246 = "a numeral hid in Queene's portrait"
- 246 = "a numeral Tudor Queen's picture hid"
- 246 = "is cipher number in the Queen's image"
- 246 = "is number hid in portrait of Queen"
- 246 = "is numeral in the Queen's costume"
- **246 = "number Dee hid in code-portrait of Queen"***
- 246 = "number hidden in portrait of Queene"
- 246 = "number hides in a portrait of Queen"
- 246 = "number John Dee has hidden in Queen's image"
- 246 = "number Queene's image *hides* as jewels"
- 246 = "number the Queen's portrait hid"
- 246 = "numeral hid as Queen's portrait"
- 246 = "numeral I hid in Queen's portrait"*

That gives an idea of the size of the puzzle hidden in this secret gift - especially as the list is far from complete. It is doubtful that the Cecils had the time and expertise to create a coded portrait of such complexity. So, who designed the picture? *Logic and code solutions indicate the creator of *Skelton*'s gematria himself – Doctor Dee. It's possible Elizabeth gave him the Manchester College appointment in 1595 as recognition for his work in designing the 1594 occult portrait.

Master Code solutions link the portrait to Accession Day 1594

The Queen's Accession Day - November 17th - was celebrated every year during her reign and for many years after her death. Master Code solutions link the portrait to the special Accession Day in 1594.

1. "36 th Accession Day painting *hid*" = 246
2. "A clue is: Accession Day 15 94" = 246
3. "A portrait for the Accession Day" = 246
4. **"Accession Day picture is gift of Cecil" = 246**
5. **"Accession Day picture is John Dee's code" = 246**
6. "Accession Day picture of Queen Bess" = 246
7. "Accession Day portrait *hid* a riddle" = 246
8. "Accession Day portrait *hides* a clue" = 246
9. "Accession Day portrait is a gift" = 246
10. **"Accession Day portrait is code Dee hid" = 246**
11. "Clue was in Accession Day painting" = 246
12. **"Code by Dee hid in Accession Day painting" = 246**
13. **"Dee hid a cipher in Accession Day picture" = 246**
14. **"John Dee hid clue in Accession Day picture" = 246**
15. "Riddle in Accession Day portrait" = 246
16. "Study Accession Day's picture" = 246
17. "Test be in Accession Day painting" = 246
18. "The Accession Day picture is *hiding*" = 246

Reversed solutions:

- 246 = "a numeral in Accession Day painting"
- 246 = "a *secret* in Accession Day painting"
- 246 = "is clue Accession Day portrait *hid*"

Master Code solutions in the context of the Queen's portrait's date:

1. "Our Queen for XXXVI years" = 246
2. "LX be Queen's age in Roman numerals" = 246 "the age is" = 60 (pearls on top of wig)
3. "The Queen's portrait date is 1 5 9 4" = 246
4. "1 5 9 4: an auspicious year for the Queen" = 246

1594 was the only year Elizabeth organized the Accession Day celebrations herself, presumably *because* it was an auspicious time.

10. The Sun's magic square & Elizabeth's secret portrait date

Magic squares have been known since antiquity; they comprise square arrays of cells each containing a different number such that the sum in each row, each column and both diagonals is the same. A famous example is the 4 x 4 magic square in Albrecht Durer's engraving *Melancholia:* 15 & 14 appear in adjacent cells in the square's bottom row, denoting the engraving's date (1514).

In Agrippa's *Natural Magic* (1510) the astrological significance of certain magic squares is explained. Each of the 'planets', including sun and moon, is associated with a magic square. According to Agrippa, the sun's primary occult number is six, so the magic square of the sun is a 6 x 6 array.

In general, the magic number of an n x n magic square is: $M = n\frac{(n^2+1)}{2}$.

In the Sun's case n = 6 so M = 111. Each row, each column and both diagonals of the Sun's magic square sum to 111. **The numbers in the Sun's magic square sum to the infamous 666 (= 6 x 111). We note that writing 666 in words and applying *Skelton* gives the Master Code solution:**

"Six hundred and sixty-six" = 246.

So, 'six hundred and sixty-six' and 246 are equivalent in *Skelton*'s system.

6	32	3	34	35	1
7	11	27	28	8	30
18	20	22	21	17	13
19	14	16	15	23	24
25	29	10	9	26	12
36	5	33	4	2	31

The Sun's Magic Square with portrait date (1594) in red

The magic number of the Sun's magic square is 111. Applying *Skelton* in the context of 'the Sun' and 'Queen Elizabeth', we find:

"You discovered" = "the Sun's name" = "Queen Elizabeth" = **111**.

So, Elizabeth is linked to 'the Sun' via the magic square and *Skelton*. **If the cipher is changed then, in general, "Queen Elizabeth" $\neq$ 111 and her link to the Sun via the magic square is destroyed.**

Applying *Skelton* "sun" = 36 which is the number of pearls in the rings on the portrait's wig, the number of cells in the sun's magic square and the number of Elizabeth's regnal years in 1594. **A Master Code solution indicates that a secret hides in the sun's magic square:**

- "A secret in the sun's magic square" = 246 a secret is the date 1594

Applying the Master Code in the context of the Sun's magic square and the portrait date:

1. "15 9 4 *hidden* in the sun's magic square" = 246
2. "A magic square *hiding* a portrait date" = 246
3. "A painting's date *hid* in a magick square" = 246
4. "A picture's date hides in a magic square" = 246
5. "Date *hid* in the magic square of the sun" = 246
6. "Date of picture *hidden* in a magick square" = 246
7. "Date of picture *hides* in magick square" = 246
8. "Date of portrait be in magick square" = 246
9. "Elizabeth in *fifteen ninety-four*" = 246
10. "*Fifteen-nine-four* hid in magic square" = 246
11. "Look for picture-date magic square *hid*" = 246
12. "Magic square *hid* Queen's picture date" = 246
13. "Magic square *hides* painting date" = 246
14. "Magick square *hid* a clue: *one five nine four*" = 246
15. "Date of a portrait: *one five nine four*" = 246
16. "*One five nine four*: clue in magick square" = 246
17. "*One five nine four* is date of a painting" = 246
18. "*One five nine four* is in magick square" = 246
19. "Picture date is *hidden* in magic square" = 246

Summary

The enciphered secret portrait was a gift from the Cecils to the Queen on the occasion of her special Accession Day in 1594, celebrating 36 regnal years when she was 60. The picture is a huge puzzle, a suitably demanding challenge for an intellectual sovereign who loved riddles and puzzles, a special gift that would hold far more lasting fascination than any expensive but soon-to-be-forgotten jewel. The portrait displays a subtle allusion to the Queen's favourite Robert Dudley, Earl of Leicester in the form of a huge pearl necklace that he bequeathed her in 1588; however, because the puzzle involves 'occult' numerology - regarded as a form of 'magick' - and since the picture relates to Elizabeth, it had to remain hidden from public view. Several code solutions indicate that Doctor Dee enciphered the portrait – which makes sense because as *Skelton*'s creator he was THE expert at using it. Solutions indicate also that Marcus Gheeraerts the younger was the (probable) artist.

Symbolism plays a key role in identifying the sitter. Both the pearls and the silver sleeves are associated with the Moon, numbers represented by the pearl rings and lozenges on the wig are linked to the Sun (6 and 36) and so, the sitter is associated with *both* Sun *and* Moon. The Sun a masculine symbol, the Moon a feminine symbol. Elizabeth Tudor was the only person in English history simultaneously linked to Sun and Moon. In that context, we recall the resonance equation:

"Queen Elizabeth" = "the Sun's name" = 111

And the Master Code solution:

"Cynthia was alias for Elizabeth" = 246 Cynthia, the moon goddess

***We note also the resonance equation**:

"A secret in the sun's magic square" = "six hundred and sixty-six" = 246

The sum of the numbers in the sun's magic square is 666.

11. Secret ciphers in Oxford University's Motto & Arms

Image: Wiki commons

Dominus Illuminatio Mea – the Lord is my light – Psalm 27

Oxford University's motto appeared in the second half of the sixteenth century, coeval with Elizabeth's reign. Master Code solutions (following) indicate that the Queen gifted the arms/crest to the university and that she hid a code in the motto, intended as a *secret* test of scholar's wits. **Applying the Master Code in that context:**

1. "A test *hidden* as Oxford's motto" = 246
2. "A test *hidden* in a motto at Oxford" = 246
3. "A test *hides* in motto at Oxford" = 246
4. "A test is *hidden* in Oxford motto" = 246
5. "Elizabeth set motto's test" = 246
6. "Elizabeth set Oxford's test" = 246
7. "Find a test in the Oxford motto" = 246
8. "*Hid* a test in the crest of Oxford" = 246
9. "Look for a test Oxford motto *hid*" = 246
10. "Look for test in Oxford motto" = 246
11. "Motto in Oxford is a hidden test" = 246
12. "Motto is the scholar's test" = 246
13. "Oxford crest is the test clue" = 246
14. "Oxford motto is hiding code-test" = 246
15. "Oxford's motto *hid* test's clue" = 246
16. "Queen *hid* test as Oxford motto" = 246
17. "Queen set tests *hid* at Oxford" = 246
18. "Queen set tests motto *hides*" = 246
19. "Queen's test in Oxford motto" = 246
20. "Test clues *hide* in Oxford motto" = 246
21. "Test *hides* as Oxford's motto" = 246
22. "Test *hiding* in Oxford's motto" = 246
23. "Test of scholars *hidden* by Queen" = 246
24. "Tests are in Oxford's motto" = 246
25. "The crest at Oxford is a test" = 246
26. "The Oxford crest was a test" = 246

The following Master Code solutions address the solver (you) in that context:

1. "Use *Skelton* to crack the motto" = 246
2. "You discovered a secret motto hid" = 246
3. "You discovered secret in motto" = 246
4. "You know a secret the motto hid" = 246
5. "You know of secret hid as a motto" = 246
6. "You know of secret hid at Oxford" = 246
7. "You know of secret motto hides" = 246
8. "You know of secret Oxford hides" = 246
9. "You know the secret in Oxford" = 246
10. "You must have found a clue motto hid" = 246
11. "You must have found clue in motto" = 246
12. "You noticed the book of seven seals" = 246
13. "You solved a riddle hidden as motto" = 246
14. "You solved riddle hidden at Oxford" = 246
15. "You solved riddle hiding in motto" = 246
16. "You solved riddle hiding in Oxford" = 246
17. "You solved the motto's cipher" = 246

What do the three gold crowns signify?

Applying *Skelton* in the context of the gold crowns, we find the resonance equations:

1. "3 golden crowns" = "hide the digit clues" = "Two Four Six" = 121
2. "3 golden crowns" = "hiding the digits" = "Two Four Six" = 121

Using *Skelton*, "3 golden crowns" alludes to the three digits of the Master Code "Two Four Six".

Also, in the context of the three crowns we find the resonance equations:

1. "3 crowns are 3 nations" = "England, Ireland and Wales" = 174
2. "*A trio of gold crowns* hide" = "England, Ireland and Wales" = 174
3. "*The three crowns* are" = "a cypher clue of Elizabeth" = 174
4. "*The three crowns* are" = "cipher Queen Elizabeth hid" = 174
5. "*The three crowns* are" = "Elizabeth hid in a cypher" = 174
6. "*The three crowns* are" = "England, Ireland and Wales" = 174
7. "*The three crowns* are" = "Queene Elizabeth's hint" = 174
8. "*The three crowns* are" = "signal of Queen Elizabeth" = 174
9. "*Three* crowned realms" = "England, Ireland and Wales" = 174
10. "You found *three* realms" = "England, Ireland and Wales" = 174

The three gold crowns represent the three realms of Queen Elizabeth: England, Ireland and Wales. The crown beneath the motto - larger than the two above in the crest on a wall at Oxford - probably represents England, largest of the realms. In addition, the three crowns symbolise Elizabeth herself since she was, in effect, thrice-crowned for England, Ireland and Wales. The three crowns also allude to *Skelton* (see 13 following) and the number 246 (see 16 following).

Applying the Master Code in the context of the three crowns:

1. "1 large, 2 small crowns in crest" = 246
2. "*3 crowns* be sign of Queen Elizabeth" = 246
3. "*3 crowns* in Oxford's arms be a clue" = 246
4. "*3 crowns* in the crest at Oxford" = 246
5. "*3 crowns* of England, Ireland, Wales" = 246
6. "*3 gold crowns* in Oxford's arms" = 246
7. "*3 golden crowns* are hiding the Queen" = 246
8. "A *trio of golden crowns* in Oxford" = 246
9. "Cipher hid by a *trio of gold crowns*" = 246
10. "Elizabeth: a *triple* crowned Queene" = 246
11. "Elizabeth Tudor's *3 gold crowns*" = 246
12. "The *3 crowns:* a signal of Elizabeth" = 246
13. "The *three crowns* hid *Skelton*" = 246
14. "The *three gold crowns* hide a cipher" = 246
15. "*Three crowns* of Queen Elizabeth" = 246
16. "*Three gold crowns* hid the number" = 246
17. "Thrice-crowned Queen found by you" = 246

Reversed solutions:

- 246 = "is number hiding as Oxford crest"
- 246 = "is a numeral hiding as Oxford arms"

In summary, the three gold crowns:

- Are a sign of Queen Elizabeth herself - she gave the crest to the university
- Are a representation of the Queen's three 'realms' - England, Ireland and Wales
- Allude to *Skelton* and represent the number 246

The following Master Code solutions indicate that Queen Elizabeth hid a joke in the motto.

1. "Message from Elizabeth in motto" = 246
2. "Motto at Oxford: Elizabeth's joke" = 246
3. "Motto hid a message from Elizabeth" = 246
4. "Motto hid Queene Elizabeth's jest" = 246
5. "Motto in Oxford be Elizabeth's joke" = 246
6. "Motto-code left by Queen Elizabeth" = 246
7. "Queen Elizabeth hid jest as a motto" = 246
8. "Queen Elizabeth hid jest at Oxford" = 246
9. "Queen Elizabeth made Oxford motto" = 246
10. "Queen Elizabeth's jest in a motto" = 246

Inspection of the motto prompts four questions

- Why does a quotation from *Psalms* (OT) appear in a book with seven seals? (the '7-seals' book is in *Revelation* (NT))
- Why is the book open? God closed the book in *Revelation* until Judgement Day.
- Why are the words fragmented? In C16, Biblical quotes were regarded as *sacrosanct* - they could not be modified in any way.
- Why are the words split thus: domi/nus/illu/mina/tio/mea?

As the foregoing solutions suggest, the fragmented motto is a code and a joke. The conjecture is tested by applying *Skelton* to the word-fragments:

DOMI = 23 = ALL

NUS = 36 = IS HID

ILLU = 30 = IN A CODE

MINA = 29 = A CODE HID

TIO = 26 = BY

MEA = 15 = GOD

Which reads: **"ALL IS HID IN A CODE A CODE HID BY GOD"**

No other *contextually appropriate* solution exists using *Skelton*'s cipher. The significance of the 7-seals book is that the solution is a *revelation* - of sorts.

Master Code solutions relating to the motto provide a proof of the code

1. "Cipher of John Dee in motto at Oxford" = 246
2. "Motto at Oxford hid the cipher of Dee" = 246
3. "Look for cipher's proof at Oxford" = 246
4. "Oxford motto hides a cipher of John Dee" = 246
5. "Oxford motto hides the cipher of Dee" = 246
6. "Oxford motto hides proof of Dee's code" = 246
7. "Oxford motto: proof of Dee's cipher" = 246
8. "Oxford's motto hides the cipher" = 246
9. "You found a secret proof motto hid" = 246
10. "You found secret proof in motto" = 246

Oxford University's Motto-Cipher

Applying *Skelton*'s cipher to the fragmented Latin inscription: "Domi/nus/illu/mina/tio/mea" (= 156)

First, we find: "Dominus illuminatio mea" = "look for arithmetic code" = 156

And the following contextually appropriate resonance equations:

1. "Dominus illuminatio mea" = "*bits* of words hide a clue" = 156
2. "Dominus illuminatio mea" = "clue is: an arithmetic code" = 156
3. "Dominus illuminatio mea" = "clue is: motto hid riddle" = 156
4. "Dominus illuminatio mea" = "hid a riddle-clue at Oxford" = 156
5. "Dominus illuminatio mea" = "hid a secret clue ye found" = 156
6. "Dominus illuminatio mea" = "hid cipher by the Queen" = 156
7. "Dominus illuminatio mea" = "is a riddle hid as a motto" = 156
8. "Dominus illuminatio mea" = "is a riddle hid at Oxford" = 156
9. "Dominus illuminatio mea" = "is a riddle motto hides" = 156
10. "Dominus illuminatio mea" = "motto hid puzzle" = 156

Reversed resonance equations:

- "Riddle *hiding* as motto" = "Dominus illuminatio mea" = 156
- "The test is *this*" = "Dominus illuminatio mea" = 156
- "Ye found secret clue *in*" = "Dominus illuminatio mea" = 156

Why use a psalm for the motto? Master Code solutions provide answers:

1. "Use a psalm for motto at Oxford" = 246
2. "Used a psalm for motto in Oxford" = 246

Applying *Skelton* to: "psalm 27" = 84

1. "Psalm 27" = "hid cipher clue" = 84
2. "Psalm 27" = "hid cypher" = 84
3. "Psalm 27" = "hides a cipher" = 84
4. "Psalm 27" = "quotation" = 84

And: "psalm XXVII" = 130

1. "Psalm XXVII" = "an Oxford motto" = 130
2. "Psalm XXVII" = "is secret cipher" = 130
3. "Psalm XXVII" = "secret cypher" = 130
4. "Psalm XXVII" = "the motto is a clue" = 130

And: "psalm twenty-seven" = 212

1. "Oxford motto hid a secret as" = "Psalm twenty-seven" = 212
2. "Psalm twenty-seven" = "hid a motto-message at Oxford" = 212
3. "Psalm twenty-seven" = "is a secret cipher-message clue" = 212
4. "Psalm twenty-seven" = "is a secret cypher-message" = 212
5. "Psalm twenty-seven" = "message in motto at Oxford" = 212
6. "Psalm twenty-seven" = "motto at Oxford hid a message" = 212
7. "Psalm twenty-seven" = "Oxford motto hides a message" = 212

Again, solutions can be linked together to make extended equations:

- "Psalm 27" = "quotation" = "hides a cipher" = 84
- "Psalm XXVII" = "an Oxford motto" = "is secret cipher" = 130

Applying *Skelton* to the English translation - "The Lord is my light" - gives the following *contextually appropriate* resonance equations:

1. "The Lord is my light" = "a cipher of Queen Elizabeth" = 170
2. "The Lord is my light" = "a secret cipher message" = 170
3. "The Lord is my light" = "a secret hidden in motto" = 170
4. "The Lord is my light" = "broken words hid the code" = 170
5. "The Lord is my light" = "hid the cipher in English" = 170
6. "The Lord is my light" = "hid the clue in word-bits" = 170
7. "The Lord is my light" = "hides secret in motto" = 170
8. "The Lord is my light" = "psalm quotation hid a code" = 170
9. "The Lord is my light" = "you found my cipher clue" = 170
10. "The Lord is my light" = "you found my cypher" = 170

A large set of Master Code solutions

Applying the Master Code in the context of Oxford University's motto and details on the arms/crest gives rise to a large set of solutions – the following sub-set excludes the word 'code':

1. "A cipher is hidden by Oxford motto" = 246
2. "A cipher is hidden in motto of Oxford" = 246
3. "A clue at Oxford in psalm XXVII" = 246
4. "A clue is at Oxford University" = 246
5. "A clue is in open book in Oxford crest" = 246
6. "A clue is motto at university" = 246
7. "A cypher hidden by Oxford motto" = 246
8. "A cypher hidden in motto of Oxford" = 246
9. "A deep secret in the Oxford motto" = 246
10. "A motto at Oxford hid a revelation" = 246
11. "A motto at Oxford tests you" = 246
12. "A revelation in motto at Oxford" = 246
13. "A secret hid by Oxford coat-of-arms" = 246
14. "A secret hid in coat-of-arms of Oxford" = 246
15. "A secret hidden by Oxford's arms" = 246
16. "A secret hidden in Oxford's motto" = 246
17. "A secret meaning in bits of words" = 246
18. "A secret message is in the motto" = 246
19. "A test hides in motto at Oxford" = 246
20. "A test is hidden in Oxford motto" = 246
21. "A tome in crest at Oxford is open" = 246
22. "Bits of words hide secret meaning" = 246
23. "Broken motto was clue at Oxford" = 246
24. "Broken psalm quotation hides a clue" = 246
25. "Broken quote in motto at Oxford" = 246
26. "Broken words in Oxford crest" = 246
27. "Broken words of motto hid the clue" = 246
28. "Broken words of motto hide cipher" = 246
29. "Cipher in motto's divided words" = 246
30. "Cipher riddle hid by Oxford motto" = 246

31. "Clue is: deliberately broken motto" = 246
32. "Clue is: look for fragmented words" = 246
33. "Clue is: open tome in Oxford crest" = 246
34. "Clue is: psalm XXVII in Oxford" = 246
35. "Clue is: split words in psalm" = 246
36. "Clue to the secret hidden at Oxford" = 246
37. "Clue to the secret hiding in motto" = 246
38. "Clue was *broken* motto at Oxford" = 246
39. "Clue was hiding in Oxford's open book" = 246
40. "Crest at Oxford hid clue as open book" = 246
41. "Crest at university is clue" = 246
42. "Cypher hid by motto at Oxford" = 246
43. "Cypher hides in motto of Oxford" = 246
44. "*Deliberately* broken motto is clue" = 246
45. "Divided words of Psalm XXVII" = 246
46. "Few find a test Oxford motto hid" = 246
47. "Few find test in Oxford motto" = 246
48. "Find clue in Oxford University" = 246
49. "Find clues in the motto at Oxford" = 246
50. "Find the clue hiding in Oxford motto" = 246
51. "Fragmented words hid a secret clue" = 246
52. "Fragmented words hiding message" = 246
53. "Fragments of words hid a message" = 246
54. "Fragments of words hid secret" = 246
55. "Go to Oxford and find a secret cipher" = 246
56. "Hid a clue as a broken psalm quotation" = 246
57. "Hid a clue in motto of university" = 246
58. "Hid my message as Oxford motto" = 246
59. "Hid secrets in motto at Oxford" = 246
60. "Hid test clue in motto at Oxford" = 246
61. "I hid my message in Oxford motto" = 246
62. "I mutilated words in the psalm" = 246
63. "I quoted psalm as bits of words" = 246
64. "Look for a test Oxford motto hid" = 246
65. "Look for chopped words in motto" = 246
66. "Look for test in Oxford motto" = 246
67. "Look for the puzzle at Oxford" = 246
68. "Message hidden in motto at Oxford" = 246
69. "Message hiding in motto in Oxford" = 246
70. "Message in fragments of words" = 246
71. "Motto at Oxford is cipher-riddle" = 246
72. "Motto at Oxford was cipher clue" = 246

73. “Motto at Oxford was cypher” = 246
74. “Motto at university is a clue” = 246
75. “Motto cipher is solved by you” = 246
76. “Motto hiding the secret message” = 246
77. “Motto in Oxford is in 7 seals book” = 246
78. “Motto in Oxford is revelation” = 246
79. “Motto is a revelation Oxford hid” = 246
80. “Motto is an old riddle hid at Oxford” = 246
81. “Motto is an old riddle Oxford hides” = 246
82. “Motto of Oxford hid a puzzle clue” = 246
83. “Motto of Oxford is by Elizabeth” = 246
84. “Motto of Oxford is *hiding* a message” = 246
85. “Motto’s divided words hid a cipher” = 246
86. “Open book in Oxford crest hiding clue” = 246
87. “Open book was in Oxford’s crest” = 246
88. “Open tome in Oxford crest is clue” = 246
89. “Open tome is in a crest at Oxford” = 246
90. “Oxford cipher is solved by you” = 246
91. “Oxford coat-of-arms is secret clue” = 246
92. “Oxford crest hiding clue in open book” = 246
93. “Oxford motto hid my secrets” = 246
94. “Oxford motto is a cipher message” = 246
95. “Oxford motto is secret cipher” = 246
96. “Oxford motto my test of ye” = 246
97. “Oxford motto was cipher-riddle” = 246
98. “Oxford motto word-puzzle” = 246
99. “Oxford motto: psalm XXVII” = 246
100. “Oxford’s motto hid my secret” = 246
101. “Oxford’s motto hid revelation” = 246
102. “Psalm quote in motto is broken” = 246
103. “Psalm XXVII is a clue Oxford hid” = 246
104. “Puzzle is in motto of Oxford” = 246
105. “Queen Elizabeth’s Oxford crest” = 246
106. “Revelation in a motto at Oxford” = 246
107. “Revelation is in Oxford motto” = 246
108. “Riddle clues are in an Oxford motto” = 246
109. “Riddle clues hidden in Oxford motto” = 246
110. “Secret clue in fragmented words” = 246
111. “Secret hidden in 7-seals book motto” = 246
112. “Secret hidden in Oxford’s crest” = 246
113. “Secret hides in Oxford’s motto” = 246
114. “Secret is in fragmented words” = 246

115. “*Seven seals* book is clue at Oxford” = 246
116. “*Seven seals* book motto was clue” = 246
117. “Test hides in a motto at Oxford” = 246
118. “Test in motto at Oxford is hid” = 246
119. “The 21-letter motto of Oxford” = 246
120. “The book in arms at Oxford is open” = 246
121. “The book in the Oxford crest is gules” = 246
122. “The crest at Oxford is a test” = 246
123. “The motto at Oxford is hiding a clue” = 246
124. “The motto in Oxford is sacrilege” = 246
125. “The motto of Oxford *hid* 11 words” = 246
126. “The motto’s quotation is biblical” = 246
127. “The mutilated psalm hides a cipher” = 246
128. “The mutilated quotation hides a clue” = 246
129. “The Oxford crest was a test” = 246
130. “The Oxford motto is hiding a riddle” = 246
131. “The Oxford motto was hiding a clue” = 246
132. “The Oxford motto: test of you” = 246
133. “The revelation is in the motto” = 246
134. “Tome on crest at Oxford is open” = 246
135. “Translate the Oxford motto” = 246
136. “University crest was clue” = 246
137. “University motto was a clue” = 246
138. “Ye noticed a clue hid as Oxford motto” = 246
139. “Ye noticed clue motto at Oxford hid” = 246
140. “Ye noticed clue Oxford motto hides” = 246

There are many more contextually appropriate solutions that include the word ‘code’.

12. Sir Isaac Newton – the Master Code & Indigo joke

Newton's statue in Trinity College chapel, Cambridge

Mathematician, physicist, occultist and alchemist

Perhaps the most famous of Cambridge alumni, Sir Isaac Newton (1642-1727) achieved immortality as a mathematician and natural philosopher, yet he spent far more time researching alchemy and a 'secret code' that he believed God had hidden in the book of *Revelation*.

Newton came from yeoman Lincolnshire stock. A posthumous child, at the age of three he was effectively abandoned by his mother when she re-married. The boy was then left in the care of grandparents at the family home, Woolsthorpe Manor, a farmhouse near Colsterworth. After attending Grantham grammar school, he entered *Trinity College* as one of the older undergraduates in 1661. It seems he was not the most committed of students and nearly failed his degree - said to have been the talk of Cambridge for forty-years.

Obsessively secretive and suspicious of others, Newton was afraid that his precious discoveries might be stolen by unscrupulous contemporaries. He was fearful also that his research into the occult - if made public - would seriously jeopardise his career by bringing him into conflict with the university authorities; that meant he had to adopt a pretence of orthodoxy in order to retain his prestigious academic position, the Lucasian chair in mathematics - awarded when he was just twenty-six.

Newton's most significant contribution in mathematics was a version of the Calculus he called *fluxions,* his secret method for calculating the rate of change of a variable - a technique indispensable for describing many phenomena mathematically. In Natural Philosophy, as physics was then known his most famous discovery was the law of universal gravitation - inspired allegedly by the fall of an apple from a tree in his garden; Newton's first important published works were in optics, including a correct account of the nature of white light and later as every school child knows, he propounded the three laws of classical mechanics.

Much of Newton's greatest work was published in *Mathematical Principles of Natural Philosophy* (1687), usually referred to as *The Principia* and generally regarded as the most significant scientific publication to date because it's effectively a 'blue-print' for the scientific method. In view of his secret interest in The Occult, it's likely that Newton knew of and experimented with *Skelton*'s gematria and being a mathematical genius it's very likely he hit upon the Master Code; if so, he almost certainly discovered what it had to 'say' about him personally. The following solutions are an attempt to 'second-guess' Newton and find some of the answers he would (probably) have found himself:

Master Code solutions, excluding the word 'code':

1. "A secret sent you by Newton" = 246
2. "Believe *hidden* message of Isaac Newton" = 246
3. "Believe in messages of Isaac Newton" = 246
4. "Believe messages by Isaac Newton" = 246
5. "Believe the message Isaac Newton *hid*" = 246
6. "Cipher of Newton is very hard" = 246
7. "Cipher ye cracked was Newton's" = 246
8. "Clue is: *indigo* colour deceived everyone" = 246
9. "Clue is: colour of *indigo* fooled everyone" = 246
10. "Clue is: Isaac Newton's *hidden* joke *indigo*" = 246 "indigo" = "hidden" = 34
11. "Clue is: Newton created *fluxions*" = 246*
12. "Clue was: a *hidden* colour Newton named" = 246
13. "Clue was *indigo:* a colour Newton named" = 246
14. "Few find Newton's cipher number" = 246
15. "*Fluxions* are but secret tools" = 246
16. "*Fluxions* are used to calculate a change" = 246
17. "*Fluxions* be infinitesimal changes" = 246
18. "Force of gravity is universal" = 246
19. "I. Newton's law of gravitation" = 246
20. "I. Newton's theorem of the binomial" = 246 did basic work on binomial theorem
21. "*Indigo* hid Isaac Newton's secret joke" = 246
22. "*Indigo* is a fictional colour of Newton" = 246
23. "*Indigo* is false colour of Isaac Newton" = 246
24. "*Indigo* was Newton's secret joke" = 246
25. "Isaac Newton: a secret occultist" = 246
26. "Isaac Newton *hid* ciphers ye cracked" = 246
27. "Isaac Newton *hides* secret number" = 246
28. "Isaac Newton knew of the numeral" = 246
29. "Isaac Newton knows the number" = 246
30. "Isaac Newton sent a hidden message" = 246
31. "Isaac Newton sent you a secret" = 246
32. "Isaac Newton's apple is a myth" = 246 Newton invented the apple story
33. "Isaac Newton's cypher message" = 246
34. "Isaac Newton's *indigo* was a *hidden* joke" = 246

35. "Messages from Newton to you" = 246
36. "Newton cracked a motto in Oxford" = 246
37. "Newton found a cipher *Skelton* hid" = 246
38. "Newton found the secret number" = 246
39. "Newton has *hidden* secret number" = 246
40. "Newton *hid* a secret discovery" = 246
41. "Newton *hid* secret messages as" = 246
42. "Newton *hid* the secret truth" = 246
43. "Newton hides *multum in parvo*" = 246
44. "Newton *hides* the cipher numeral" = 246
45. "Newton *hides* the secret cipher" = 246
46. "Newton knows The Golden Key" = 246
47. "Newton named a colour *indigo* as a jest" = 246
48. "Newton named the *hidden* colour *indigo*" = 246
49. "Newton sent a message for you" = 246
50. "Newton wrote book on *Opticks*" = 246
51. "Newton's cipher broken by you" = 246
52. "Newton's secret joke hid by *indigo*" = 246
53. "Newton's secret number: a clue is" = 246
54. "Telescope Newton made reflects" = 246 he made the first reflecting telescope
55. "The cipher message of Isaac Newton" = 246
56. "The method of *fluxions* was hidden" = 246
57. "This is Isaac Newton's message" = 246
58. "Very hard cypher of Newton" = 246
59. "*Woolsthorpe:* abode of Isaac Newton" = 246
60. "*Woolsthorpe:* home to Newton" = 246
61. "Ye cracked ciphers hid by Newton" = 246
62. "Ye found Newton's numeral key" = 246
63. "Ye found Newton's secret key" = 246
64. "Ye found secrets of Isaac Newton" = 246
65. "Ye have Newton's key numeral" = 246
66. "Ye have Newton's secret key" = 246
67. "You cracked Newton's *hidden* cipher" = 246
68. "You have found cipher of Newton" = 246
69. "You have found numeral Newton *hid*" = 246
70. "You have found secret Newton *hid*" = 246
71. "You have got Newton's message" = 246
72. "You must have Newton's key" = 246

Reversed solutions:

- 246 = "a secret number *hidden* by Newton"
- 246 = "a secret occult number Newton *hid*"
- 246 = "secret number Isaac Newton *hides*"

Master code solutions that refer to 'code':

1. "A great secret hid as Newton's code" = 246
2. "A message from Isaac Newton *hid* as code" = 246
3. "An occult code *hid* message by Newton" = 246
4. "Cipher you cracked is Newton's code" = 246
5. "Code *hid* by Newton solved by you" = 246
6. "Code *hides* message from Isaac Newton" = 246
7. "Code *hides* the message of Isaac Newton" = 246
8. "Code *hiding* Isaac Newton's messages" = 246
9. "Code Newton discovered is secret" = 246
10. "Codes are *hidden* messages of Newton" = 246
11. "Codes *hidden* by Newton are a secret" = 246
12. "Codes *hide* Newton's great secret" = 246
13. "Few find codes Newton *hid* as a number" = 246
14. "I. Newton discovered secret codes" = 246
15. "I. Newton found a code hid in *Revelation*" = 246
16. "I. Newton *hid* a great secret in codes" = 246
17. "I. Newton *hides* secret code numeral" = 246
18. "I. Newton knows the code numeral" = 246
19. "I. Newton knows the secret code" = 246
20. "I. Newton talked to you via the code" = 246
21. "Isaac Newton believed code of *Skelton*" = 246
22. "Isaac Newton found the clue to the code" = 246
23. "Isaac Newton gave you a hint by code" = 246
24. "Isaac Newton *hid* a code in *The Principia*" = 246
25. "Isaac Newton *hid* an occult code message" = 246
26. "Isaac Newton *hid* code solved by you" = 246
27. "Isaac Newton *hides* secrets as a code" = 246
28. "Isaac Newton kept secret code safe" = 246
29. "Isaac Newton knew arithmetic code" = 246
30. "Isaac Newton knew code of *Skelton*" = 246
31. "Isaac Newton left clues to hidden code" = 246
32. "Isaac Newton left subtle code clues" = 246
33. "Isaac Newton sends message as code" = 246
34. "Isaac Newton sends secret codes" = 246
35. "Isaac Newton used codes of *Skelton*" = 246
36. "Isaac Newton's code *hiding* messages" = 246
37. "Isaac Newton's code-message to you" = 246
38. "Isaac Newton's secret code is *hidden*" = 246
39. "Isaac Newton's secrets *hide* as a code" = 246
40. "Isaac Newton's voice *hiding* in the code" = 246
41. "Look for code discovered by Newton" = 246
42. "Look for code Isaac Newton discovered" = 246

43. “Look for code Isaac Newton sent ye” = 246
44. “Look for code sent ye by Newton” = 246
45. “Message Isaac Newton sent is a code” = 246
46. “Message sent by Newton is a code” = 246
47. “Messages of Newton *hiding* in codes” = 246
48. “Newton believed *Skelton*’s codes” = 246
49. “Newton discovered secret code clue” = 246
50. “Newton found a code hid as *Revelation*” = 246
51. “Newton found code *Revelation* hides” = 246
52. “Newton found The Occult’s code-key” = 246
53. “Newton *hid* great secrets as a code” = 246
54. “Newton *hid* secret of the occult code” = 246
55. “Newton *hid* truth in secret code” = 246
56. “Newton knew *Skelton*’s codes” = 246
57. “Newton made use of the *Skelton* code” = 246
58. “Newton sends messages by a code” = 246
59. “Newton sends ye secret codes” = 246
60. “Newton talks to you in the code” = 246
61. “Newton used *Skelton*’s code key” = 246
62. “Newton’s code *hides* great secret” = 246
63. “Newton’s extremely hard code” = 246
64. “Newton’s message is *hidden* by a code” = 246
65. “Newton’s message is secret code” = 246
66. “Newton’s message to you by code” = 246
67. “Newton’s secret code is for you” = 246
68. “Newton’s very difficult codes” = 246
69. “Newton’s very hard cipher code” = 246
70. “Secret code clues *hidden* by Newton” = 246
71. “Secret code message from Newton” = 246
72. “Secret codes used by Isaac Newton” = 246
73. “Secret occult codes of Isaac Newton” = 246
74. “Secrets of Isaac Newton in the code” = 246
75. “Subtle code clues left by Newton” = 246
76. “The code here is used by Isaac Newton” = 246
77. “The code *hides* message of Isaac Newton” = 246
78. “The codes *hide* Newton’s messages” = 246
79. “The codes of Isaac Newton *hid* a secret” = 246
80. “The message of Isaac Newton *hid* as a code” = 246
81. “The message of Newton in occult code” = 246
82. “The occult code *hid* a message of Newton” = 246
83. “These code clues are by Isaac Newton” = 246
84. “Very difficult code of Isaac Newton” = 246
85. “Ye found secret code *hid* by Newton” = 246
86. “Ye found secret code Isaac Newton *hid*” = 246
87. “Ye have secret code *hid* by Newton” = 246

88. "Ye have secret code Isaac Newton *hid*" = 246
89. "You broke codes of Sir Isaac Newton" = 246
90. "You found Isaac Newton's code number" = 246
91. "You found message Newton *hid* as a code" = 246
92. "You found Newton's clue *hidden* as a code" = 246
93. "You found secret Newton *hid* as code" = 246
94. "You found the code number Newton *hid*" = 246
95. "You have found a clue to Newton's code" = 246
96. "You have found a *hidden* code of Newton" = 246
97. "You have found Newton's occult code" = 246
98. "You have Isaac Newton's code number" = 246
99. "You have the code number Newton *hid*" = 246
100. "You solved code *hid* by Isaac Newton" = 246

Reversed solutions:

- 246 = "is code numeral Newton discovered"
- 246 = "number Newton used as secret code"
- 246 = "was occult number of Isaac Newton"

It is noteworthy that towards the end of his life Newton burned many of his private unpublished papers, probably because they concerned research into the occult and other 'dark matters'. In that context, it is important to recognise that the great scientist was *both* a rigorously logical, rationalist *and* a speculative, intuitive mystic. To understand something of Newton's genius it is necessary to take into account both aspects of his mind.

A link to alchemy

As mentioned previously, Newton spent many years studying alchemy and performing alchemical experiments in his private laboratory at Trinity. In that context, it's possible he might have discovered the following Master Code solutions:

1. "A cypher hid the secret of Alchemy" = 246
2. "Here is the secret Alchemical number" = 246
3. "Isaac Newton found the Alchemical codes" = 246
4. "Isaac Newton *hid* the Alchemical cipher" = 246
5. "Isaac Newton's secret Alchemical code" = 246
6. "Newton *hid* the secret Alchemical code" = 246
7. "*Skelton* is the cipher of Alchemy" = 246
8. "The Alchemical codes found by Newton" = 246
9. "The golden key of Alchemy is a hidden code" = 246
10. "The secret of Alchemy is hidden in a code" = 246
11. "The secret of Alchemy is in cipher" = 246
12. "You discovered the Alchemical number" = 246

Reversed solution:

1. 246 = "the hidden secret number of Alchemy"

Indigo – Newton's 'hidden' joke

In studying the spectrum of white light, Newton claimed to have found a 'new' colour located between blue and violet which he named *indigo* (c 1672). However, the precise location of *indigo* has long been a moot point since there is uncertainty as to exactly what it looks like. The conjecture here is that Newton named a *fictitious* colour '*indigo*' as both a jest and a test - a joke that fooled the credulous but a 'test' that showed those who knew the cipher that the code solutions are intentional (This implies he knew *Skelton* and the Master Code by c 1672).

Firstly, we note the resonance equation: "Indigo" = "hidden" = 34 indigo - a *hidden* colour!

Master Code solutions in the context of 'Newton' and 'indigo':

1. "Clue is: *indigo* is colour Newton named" = 246
2. "Clue was: Newton named a colour *indigo"* = 246
3. "Colour called *indigo*: Isaac Newton's joke" = 246 "indigo" = "hid Joke" = 34
4. "Colour Newton named *indigo* is jest" = 246
5. "Colour of *indigo* is impossible to find" = 246*
6. "*Indigo* colour: Isaac Newton's fiction" = 246
7. "*Indigo* hid Isaac Newton's secret joke" = 246
8. "*Indigo* was hiding Isaac Newton's lie" = 246
9. "*Indigo* was name of a colour Newton hid" = 246
10. "*Indigo* was Newton's secret joke" = 246
11. "*Indigo*: a secret fiction by Newton" = 246
12. "Newton fooled you all with *indigo*" = 246*
13. "Newton named a colour *indigo* as a jest" = 246
14. "Newton named fictional colour *indigo*" = 246
15. "Newton named *indigo* to test ye" = 246
16. "Newton named the *hidden* colour *indigo*" = 246
17. "The colour of *Indigo* does not exist" = 246

13. Newton's tomb-monument by William Kent in Westminster Abbey

The monument was installed in 1731, the ornate surround is a C19 addition

(Image: Wikipedia commons)

Solutions (following) refer to the eight Putti in the frieze on the sarcophagus and their activities as they relate to Newton's work. The *six* known planets (in 1731) are located at the bottom of the frieze in the centre.

William Kent (1685-1748) was an architect, designer, polymath and senior Freemason. The following solutions show that it's very likely he knew *Skelton* and the Master Code/ Maister Cipher:

1. "Kent designed the tomb of Newton" = 246
2. "William Kent made tomb of Newton" = 246

Master Code solutions including the word 'code':

1. "Code *hid* by Kent at Newton's tomb" = 246
2. "Code *hid* by Kent on I. Newton's tomb" = 246
3. "Code hiding at the tomb of Isaac Newton" = 246
4. "Codes by Kent on Newton's tomb" = 246
5. "Kent *hid* code at Isaac Newton's tomb" = 246
6. "Kent *hid* the code on Newton's tomb" = 246
7. "Kent used *Skelton* code on the tomb" = 246
8. "Kent's code on Isaac Newton's tomb" = 246
9. "Monument on tomb of Newton hid a code" = 246
10. "Newton's tomb *hides* code by Kent" = 246
11. "Tomb of Isaac Newton *hid* codes of Kent" = 246

As a senior member of The Craft, Kent probably knew of *Skelton's* cipher and the Master Code through Freemasonry. **In view of those solutions, it's appropriate to apply the Master Code in the context of 'Newton' and details on his tomb-monument. Solutions *excluding* reference to 'code':**

1. "**2** cherubim **4** books **6** planets *hid* the clue" = **246**
2. "**2** cherubs **4** books **6** planets are a sign" = **246**
3. "**2** cherubs **4** books **6** planets: clues to" = **246**
4. "**6** planets are a secret ***digit*** hint" = 24**6**
5. "**6** planets hint at a secret ***digit***" = 24**6**
6. "8 putti found on Newton's tomb" = 246
7. "A clue was *hiding* on Newton's tomb" = 246
8. "A clue was left on Newton's tomb" = 246
9. "A figure of *Astronomy* on the tomb" = 246 goddess Urania
10. "A hint is: **2** cherubim **4** books **6** planets" = 246
11. "A secret clue *hid* at Newton's tomb" = 246
12. "*Astronomy* on tomb monument" = 246 Urania
13. "Cherubim, books and planets are clues" = 246
14. "Cherubim, books and planets *hid* a hint" = 246
15. "Cipher is found on Newton's tomb" = 246
16. "Clue to ***digits*** at Newton's tomb" = 2 4 6
17. "Clue was: **2** cherubs **4** books **6** planets" = 246
18. "***Digit*** clues on Isaac Newton's tomb" = 246
19. "***Digits Two Four Six*** *hide* on tomb" = 246
20. "Find number Isaac Newton's tomb *hid*" = 246
21. "***Four*** big books are Newton's work" = 246

22. "Get hint left on tomb of Newton" = 246
23. "*Hid* a numeral clue at Newton's tomb" = 246
24. "*Hid* a secret clue at Newton's tomb" = 246
25. "*Hid* the ***digits*** at Newton's tomb" = 246
26. "Hint in: cherubim, books and planets" = 246
27. "I hid a numeral clue on Newton's tomb" = 246
28. "I hid cipher key in Newton's tomb" = 246
29. "I hid the ***digits*** on Newton's tomb" = 246
30. "I hid the number at Newton's tomb" = 246
31. "I reclined Newton on a sarcophagus" = 246
32. "Isaac Newton's tomb hiding ***digits***" = 246
33. "Left a sign on the tomb of Newton" = 246
34. "Look for cherubs, books and planets" = 246
35. "Look for ***cipher-digits*** hidden on tomb" = 246
36. "Newton leans on the **four** big books" = 246
37. "Newton lying on a sarcophagus" = 246
38. "Newton rests on **four** big books" = 246
39. "Newton's books are on monument" = 246
40. "Newton's tomb goddess is Urania" = 246*
41. "Newton's tomb *hides* a numeral clue" = 246
42. "Newton's tomb *hides* the *digits*" = 246
43. "Newton's tomb *hiding* the number" = 246
44. "Newton's tomb-monument date 1731" = 246
45. "Newton's tomb-monument hiding" = 246
46. "Newton's tomb's date is 1731 AD" = 246
47. "Number of planets is a cipher ***digit***" = 24**6**
48. "Putti are minting coins on tomb" = 246
49. "Putti looked at telescope on tomb" = 246
50. "Putti on monument mint coins" = 246
51. "Putto in frieze on tomb number 8" = 246
52. "Putto looking through a prism" = 246
53. "Putto using instruments" = 246
54. "Pyramid and star on monument" = 246
55. "Repose Newton on a sarcophagus" = 246
56. "Signs of Zodiac on tomb of Newton" = 246
57. "The cherubim hold a page of *The Principia*" = 246
58. "The tomb of Isaac Newton is the clue" = 246
59. "***Two*** cherubim are clue to a cipher ***digit***" = **2**46
60. "Urania be goddess on Newton's tomb" = 246*
61. "You found: **2** cherubim **4** books **6** planets" = 246
62. "You got hint at tomb of Newton" = 246
63. "You got hint on tomb of I. Newton" = 246
64. "You noticed name on tomb of Newton" = 246 the name is Kent

Reversed solutions:

- 246 = "is a numeral *hid* at Newton's tomb"
- 246 = "is a numeral **I** *hid* on Newton's tomb"
- 246 = "is a numeral Newton's tomb *hides*"
- 246 = "is hid as digits on tomb of Newton"
- 246 = "is *hid* by **2** cherubs **4** books **6** planets"
- 246 = "is the number on Newton's tomb"
- 246 = "the number I *hid* at Newton's tomb"
- 246 = "the numbers at Newton's tomb"

*Urania: goddess of astronomy.

Solutions referring to 'code':

1. "**4** books are the secret clue to a code ***digit***" = 2**4**6
2. "A secret code on Isaac Newton's tomb" = 246
3. "Code clue at Sir Isaac Newton's tomb" = 246
4. "Code clue was on Isaac Newton's tomb" = 246
5. "Code clues *hiding* on Newton's grave" = 246
6. "Code ***digit*** hiding as number of planets" = 24**6**
7. "***Four*** books are a secret clue to a code digit" = 2**4**6
8. "*Hid* a code number on the tomb of Newton" = 246
9. "*Hid* code clue in **2** cherubim **4** books **6** planets" = 246
10. "Isaac Newton's tomb's secret code" = 246
11. "Newton tomb-code solved by you" = 246
12. "Planets on tomb are clue to code ***digit***" = 24**6**
13. "The code clues are on Newton's tomb" = 246
14. "Tomb of Newton hid the code numbers" = 246

Reversed solutions

- 246 = "key to the code on Newton's tomb"

Presumably, Kent was aware that Newton knew *Skelton* and that is why he hid the Master Code key on the great man's tomb monument.

14. CYPHER MYSTERIES AT SHUGBOROUGH HALL

The enigmatic cipher - O.U.O.S.V.A.V.V - inscribed on the base of a folly in the garden at Shugborough Hall is solved by applying *Skelton's* cipher and the Master Code. Commonly known as the 'Shepherds Monument', the folly was erected in the mid-eighteenth century - an era that saw the birth of modern science, the first stirrings of the Industrial Revolution and the establishment of the British Empire. Known as The Enlightenment, it was a time of rapid intellectual development when new societies flourished (Freemasonry for example) and when architectural follies were fashionable on the estates of rich aristocrats like Thomas Anson (1695-1773) Shugborough's owner.

An alumnus of St John's College Oxford, Thomas Anson went on to become a law student at the Inner Temple until his father's death when he gave-up his studies and began the first of several travels in Europe – *de rigueur* for wealthy young gentlemen at the time. In 1732 he and his friend the Earl of Sandwich formed a dining-club - *Society of the Dilettanti* - which among other less 'academic' matters encouraged the study of Greek architecture. As a leading advocate for a return to the classical style, Anson had a significant influence on the development of architecture in eighteenth century Britain.

Shugborough Hall was home to a cornucopia of *objects d'art* during Thomas Anson's stewardship; an eclectic mix of items from a wide range of cultures and periods, collected during his sojourns abroad. In 1762, he inherited a vast fortune in Spanish treasure from his younger brother, Admiral George Anson, which allowed him to indulge his acquisitive zeal to the full. Years later, tales began to circulate that part of the treasure was buried on the Shugborough estate and a few credulous individuals took the stories sufficiently seriously to pursue the legend. As a result, large areas were excavated though nothing of value was found; nonetheless, code solutions indicate that 'treasure' *was* hidden at Shugborough but it was of a kind the bounty hunters never imagined.

The 'Shepherds Monument' at Shugborough

***Et in Arcadia ego* by Nicolas Poussin – (the Louvre, Paris)**

Image: Wiki-commons

A carved relief based on this famous painting by Nicolas Poussin (*et in Arcadia ego*, 1637-38) is set within a shrine-folly in Shugborough's garden. The folly is dedicated to Pan, the god of wild places and shepherds whose homeland was Arcadia. Almost unique among the Greek gods, Pan died. In Poussin's painting three shepherds and a shepherdess discover an inscription on his tomb: *Et in Arcadia ego* the Latin translating literally as *and I am (also) in Arcadia* where 'I' alludes to *Death*, meaning *Death* is everywhere - even Arcadia.

The relief in the shrine is a left-right 'mirror image' version of Poussin's painting (second version)

‘Arcadia’ within Pan’s shrine-folly – aka the ‘Shepherds Monument’ c 1750

Pan’s face is located below the folly’s top lintel, just left of centre; Thomas Anson’s face is at the corresponding position on the right. The tomb’s inscription is in Latin, yet Pan was a Greek god from Arcadia in Greece; the shepherds are Greek and Greek is a classical language - why is the inscription Latin? If the inscription *had* been Greek, it would not be possible to apply *Skelton*’s cipher.

In that context, we note the Master Code solutions (including the word ‘code’):

1. “A secret code hidden in Latin *not* Greek” = 246
2. “Secret code hides in Latin *not* Greek” = 246

Master code solutions including the word ‘cipher’

1. “Latin *not* Greek hid a secret cipher” = 246
2. “Secret cipher in Latin *not* Greek” = 246

Applying the cipher to the Latin, we find the following *contextually appropriate* resonance equations (including ‘code’):

1. *“Et in Arcadia ego”* = “a code clue Arcadia *hid*” = 80
2. ***“Et in Arcadia ego”* = “Anson’s code” = 80**
3. *“Et in Arcadia ego”* = “code clue in Arcadia” = 80
4. *“Et in Arcadia ego”* = “*hid* a hard code clue” = 80
5. *“Et in Arcadia ego”* = “is a clue to a code” = 80
6. *“Et in Arcadia ego”* = “is a code Arcadia *hid*” = 80
7. *“Et in Arcadia ego”* = “is code in Arcadia” = 80
8. *“Et in Arcadia ego”* = “it *hid* hard code” = 80
9. *“Et in Arcadia ego”* = “means code clue” = 80

10. *"Et in Arcadia ego"* = "meant as a code" = 80
11. *"Et in Arcadia ego"* = "was *our* code" = 80 the Anson family code
12. *"Et in Arcadia ego"* = "ye cracked a code" = 80

Solutions excluding the word 'code':

1. ***"Et in Arcadia ego"* = "clue of Anson" = 80**
2. *"Et in Arcadia ego"* = "*hiding* a riddle" = 80
3. *"Et in Arcadia ego"* = "is a test" = 80
4. *"Et in Arcadia ego"* = "is *hiding* clue" = 80
5. *"Et in Arcadia ego"* = "ye found a clue" = 80

The purpose of those equations is to show the 'solver' that *Skelton* is the right cipher - another example of *multum in parvo*. Again, solutions can be linked together to make extended statements:

"Ye found a clue" = *"et in Arcadia ego"* = "is a test" = *"hiding* a riddle" = 80 etc.

Inscriptions on Arcadia's base

O.U.O.S.V.A.V.V

D. **M.**

The inscription is both simple and enigmatic. O.U.O.S.V.A.V.V has been identified* as the acronym for: Orator Ut Omnia Sunt Vanitas Ait Vanitas Vanitatum (*Suggested by Steve Regimbal).

The Latin translates as: *'Vanity of vanities, saith the preacher all is vanity'*. This is taken to mean that life is ultimately pointless because everyone dies. The quotation, from Ecclesiastes (1:2), is consistent in tone with the inscription on Pan's tomb: 'et in Arcadia ego' reminding us that Death is everywhere, even Arcadia.

The 'dots' were a lapidary style common at the time, although here they are part of the code solutions. The very wide spacing of D – M means it's unlikely the letters are initials. The Latin inscribed on the tomb suggests (contextually) that the letters probably represent the Roman numerals 500 and 1000 respectively. We recall that the image on the monument is a *mirror* of Poussin's painting, a hint perhaps that the D - M too should be 'mirrored' left-right to read M-D, 1500 in Roman numerals.

First, applying *Skelton* to: "O.U.O.S.V.A.V.V" (= 95) gives the following *contextually appropriate* resonance equations (excluding 'code'):

1. "O.U.O.S.V.A.V.V" = "7 dots be clues" = 95
2. "O.U.O.S.V.A.V.V" = "a clue is 7 dots" = 95
3. "OUOSVAVV" = "3 shepherds" = 95 — 3 shepherds on the monument
4. "OUOSVAVV" = "a test of ye" = 95
5. "OUOSVAVV" = "acronym clue" = 95 — Ecclesiastes quotation
6. "OUOSVAVV" = "*all is number*" = 95 — a maxim attributed to Pythagoras
7. "OUOSVAVV" = "Anson's name" = 95
8. "OUOSVAVV" = "big puzzle" = 95
9. "OUOSVAVV" = "carved on Arcadia" = 95
10. "OUOSVAVV" = "cipher on Arcadia" = 95
11. "OUOSVAVV" = "clue on a folly" = 95
12. "OUOSVAVV" = "folly's clue" = 95
13. "OUOSVAVV" = "hard clue hid a name" = 95
14. "OUOSVAVV" = "hid huge test" = 95
15. "OUOSVAVV" = "hid the Arcadia clue" = 95
16. "OUOSVAVV" = "hid the hard clue" = 95
17. "OUOSVAVV" = "is acronym" = 95
18. "OUOSVAVV" = "is on a folly" = 95
19. "OUOSVAVV" = "is our cipher" = 95
20. "OUOSVAVV" = "my riddles" = 95
21. "OUOSVAVV" = "name of family" = 95
22. "OUOSVAVV" = "our cypher" = 95
23. "OUOSVAVV" = "Pan's cipher" = 95
24. **"OUOSVAVV" = "reverse D-M" = 95** — M D is 1500 in Roman numerals
25. "OUOSVAVV" = "riddle's key" = 95
26. "OUOSVAVV" = "well done ye!" = 95

Reversed, we find the resonance equations:

- "*Hid* my name in" = "OUOSVAVV" = 95
- "*Hid* secret as" = "OUOSVAVV" = 95
- "I *hid* test as" = "OUOSVAVV" = 95
- "Riddles hide as" = "OUOSVAVV" = 95
- "Riddles are in" = "OUOSVAVV" = 95
- "Test is in" = "OUOSVAVV" = 95
- "Ye found clue in" = "OUOSVAVV" = 95

Resonance equations including 'code':

1. "OUOSVAVV" = "a code hidden on Arcadia" = 95
2. "OUOSVAVV" = "Arcadia's code be hard" = 95
3. "OUOSVAVV" = "be a *Skelton* code" = 95
4. "OUOSVAVV" = "be clue to hidden code" = 95
5. "OUOSVAVV" = "cipher hides code" = 95
6. "OUOSVAVV" = "code clue is cracked" = 95
7. "OUOSVAVV" = "code decoded by you" = 95
8. "OUOSVAVV" = "code found at Arcadia" = 95
9. "OUOSVAVV" = "code hid a saying" = 95
10. "OUOSVAVV" = "code I hid is true" = 95
11. "OUOSVAVV" = "code in Arcadia be found" = 95
12. "OUOSVAVV" = "code of Anson decoded" = 95
13. "OUOSVAVV" = "coded messages" = 95
14. "OUOSVAVV" = "few find our code" = 95
15. "OUOSVAVV" = "hid Anson's code" = 95
16. "OUOSVAVV" = "hid code of family" = 95
17. "OUOSVAVV" = "hides code on Arcadia" = 95
18. "OUOSVAVV" = "hides Pan's code" = 95
19. "OUOSVAVV" = "hides the codes" = 95
20. "OUOSVAVV" = "is a deciphered code" = 95
21. "OUOSVAVV" = "is a difficult code" = 95
22. "OUOSVAVV" = "is a solved code" = 95
23. "OUOSVAVV" = "is secret code" = 95
24. "OUOSVAVV" = "key to a huge code" = 95
25. "OUOSVAVV" = "proof of *our* code" = 95 the Anson family code
26. "OUOSVAVV" = "the code is found" = 95
27. "OUOSVAVV" = "you decoded our code" = 95

Reversed equations

- "Arcadia's code *hid* as" = "OUOSVAVV" = 95
- "Code *hides* name as" = "OUOSVAVV" = 95 the family name, Anson
- "You found a code in" = "OUOSVAVV" = 95

Again, solutions can be strung together to make extended statements:

"Ye found clue in" = "O.U.O.S.V.A.V.V" = "well done ye!" = 95 etc.

Applying the Master Code in the context of O.U.O.S.V.A.V.V (excluding 'code')

1. **"A cipher hid name of Anson: OUOSVAVV" = 246**
2. "A cypher of 8 letters and 7 dots" = 246
3. "A clue was: read the Book of Ecclesiastes" = 246* see interpretation of acronym (above)
4. "An OUOSVAVV clue is 95" = 246 since "OUOSVAVV" = 95
5. "Eight letters and seven dots" = 246*
6. "Find OUOSVAVV on Pan's shrine" = 246
7. "I left OUOSVAVV for the future" = 246
8. "Latin hides as OUOSVAVV cipher" = 246* Latin acronym
9. "Latin hiding in OUOSVAVV cipher" = 246*
10. "Look for OUOSVAVV cipher on Arcadia" = 246
11. "Look for OUOSVAVV hid on base of Arcadia" = 246
12. "Name of Anson in OUOSVAVV cipher" = 246
13. "Nobody cracks OUOSVAVV cipher" = 246
14. "OUOSVAVV in Arcadia at Shugborough" = 246
15. "OUOSVAVV is an uncrackable cipher" = 246
16. "OUOSVAVV is Anson's huge riddle" = 246
17. "OUOSVAVV is eight-letter clue" = 246
18. "OUOSVAVV is insoluble code cipher" = 246
19. "OUOSVAVV is just a cipher key" = 246
20. "OUOSVAVV is nonsense word" = 246
21. "OUOSVAVV sum is 95" = 246 applying *Skelton* to "OUOSVAVV" = 95
22. "OUOSVAVV was a secret cipher" = 246
23. "OUOSVAVV was for the future" = 246
24. "OUOSVAVV was unpronounceable" = 246
25. "OUOSVAVV: 8 Latin words in code" = 246*
26. "OUOSVAVV: a cipher on the folly" = 246
27. "OUOSVAVV: Anson's giant riddle" = 246
28. "OUOSVAVV: be meaningless word" = 246
29. "OUOSVAVV: cipher of Freemasons" = 246
30. "OUOSVAVV: cipher on Arcadia folly" = 246
31. "OUOSVAVV: clue to Latin motto" = 246*
32. "OUOSVAVV: hid a cipher of *Skelton*" = 246
33. "OUOSVAVV: hid the Latin motto" = 246*
34. "OUOSVAVV: hides *many* ciphers" = 246
35. "OUOSVAVV: hides the cipher clues" = 246
36. **"OUOSVAVV: name of Anson in cipher" = 246**
37. "OUOSVAVV: Shugborough's cipher" = 246
38. "Pan's shrine hid Latin acronym" = 246*
39. **"*Skelton* solves OUOSVAVV" = 246**
40. "Solve OUOSVAVV using a cipher" = 246
41. "The 8 letters 7 dots are a cipher" = 246
42. "The cipher is 8 letters 7 dots" = 246
43. "You decoded OUOSVAVV cipher on Arcadia" = 246

Applying the Master Code, we note: "eight letters and seven dots" = 246

So, O.U.O.S.V.A.V.V seen simply as "eight letters and seven dots" encodes the Master Code key, 246, using *Skelton*'s cipher. Clearly, the solution would be true for *any* eight letters in any sequence.

Master Code solutions including the word 'code':

1. "8 letters 7 dots cypher hid a code" = 246
2. "A code of Freemasons hid as OUOSVAVV" = 246
3. "A *Skelton* code solved OUOSVAVV" = 246
4. "A strange code hidden by OUOSVAVV" = 246
5. "Anson's code: 8 letters and 7 dots" = 246
6. "Code is in 8 letters 7 dots cipher" = 246
7. "Code of *Skelton* hides in OUOSVAVV" = 246
8. "Eight letters seven dots be a code" = 246
9. "Few find code OUOSVAVV hides on Arcadia" = 246
10. "Many codes are hidden in OUOSVAVV" = 246
11. "Nobody cracks a code hid as OUOSVAVV" = 246
12. "Nobody cracks a code I hid in OUOSVAVV" = 246
13. "Nobody cracks code OUOSVAVV hides" = 246
14. "OUOSVAVV is a code word of Hiram Abiff" = 246 see 'Freemasons' following
15. "OUOSVAVV is code on shrine of Pan" = 246
16. "OUOSVAVV is the impossible code" = 246
17. "OUOSVAVV is the key to the code" = 246
18. "OUOSVAVV: cipher is code of Hiram Abiff" = 246
19. "OUOSVAVV: code hid Latin acronym" = 246*
20. "OUOSVAVV: hid an impossible code clue" = 246
21. "OUOSVAVV: hid code you decrypted" = 246
22. "OUOSVAVV: hid the very hard code" = 246
23. "OUOSVAVV: hides code of Freemasons" = 246
24. "OUOSVAVV: hides name of Anson in code" = 246
25. "OUOSVAVV: name of Anson hidden in a code" = 246
26. "OUOSVAVV: secret code of Anson's" = 246
27. "OUOSVAVV: the cipher hides our code" = 246
28. "OUOSVAVV: the eight-letter code" = 246
29. "Our OUOSVAVV code solved by ye" = 246
30. "The OUOSVAVV code hides on a folly" = 246
31. "The OUOSVAVV code is an acronym" = 246
32. "The OUOSVAVV code on my folly" = 246
33. "Thou hast cracked code in OUOSVAVV" = 246
34. "You cracked OUOSVAVV: code Arcadia hides" = 246
35. "You deciphered the code in OUOSVAVV" = 246
36. "You solved the code in O.U.O.S.V.A.V.V" = 246

Also, we find the reversed solution:

- 246 = "is the key to the OUOSVAVV code"

Master Code solutions 'tell' the solver ('you') that Shugborough's cipher/code is broken:

1. "Code at Shugborough is broken by you" = 246
2. "Code in Shugborough: ye got it right" = 246
3. "Shugborough code was broken by you" = 246
4. "The code at Shugborough cracked by you" = 246
5. "The Shugborough code solved by you" = 246
6. "Ye are right about a code in Shugborough" = 246
7. "Ye found my code hidden at Shugborough" = 246
8. "Ye unlocked my codes in Shugborough" = 246
9. "You are right about code of Shugborough" = 246
10. "You broke a code hid in Shugborough cipher" = 246
11. "You deciphered a code hidden at Shugborough" = 246
12. "You decoded secret code hid in Shugborough" = 246
13. "You found many codes Shugborough hid" = 246
14. "You found the code hidden at Shugborough" = 246
15. "You have broken code hid at Shugborough" = 246
16. "You have broken code Shugborough hides" = 246
17. "You have cracked Shugborough Arcadia code" = 246
18. "You have found Shugborough code number" = 246
19. "You have found the huge Shugborough code" = 246
20. "You solved a code hidden at Shugborough" = 246
21. "You solved huge code at Shugborough" = 246

Solutions excluding the word 'code':

1. "Ye decoded the cipher hid at Shugborough" = 246
2. "Ye decoded the cipher Shugborough hides" = 246
3. "Ye unlocked cipher hid at Shugborough" = 246
4. "Ye unlocked cipher Shugborough hides" = 246
5. "You broke the cipher in Shugborough" = 246
6. "You cracked cipher of Shugborough Arcadia" = 246
7. "You deciphered cipher at Shugborough" = 246
8. "You found treasure Shugborough hid" = 246 — the treasure is the cipher itself
9. "You have broken Shugborough cipher" = 246
10. "You solved cipher at Shugborough" = 246

Significance of the 3 shepherds in Arcadia, we recall:

1. "OUOSVAVV" = "3 shepherds" = 95
2. "OUOSVAVV" = "Anson's name" = 95
3. "OUOSVAVV" = "*hid* Anson's code" = 95

It follows from the above that:

1. "3 shepherds" = "Anson's name" = 95 converts the 'tangible' to the 'abstract'
2. "3 shepherds" = "*hid* Anson's code" = 95

So, using *Skelton's* cipher '3 shepherds' represents Anson's name *and* his code.

Additional Master Code solutions relating to Shugborough and the cipher (including 'code'):

1. "A code clue on the Shugborough monument" = 246
2. "A code *hid* by Shugborough is hard to break" = 246
3. "A code *hid* in Shugborough fooled everyone" = 246
4. "A code *hides* treasure hid in Shugborough" = 246
5. "A code in Shugborough is insoluble riddle" = 246
6. "A code is on the Shugborough monument" = 246
7. "A secret occult code clue at Shugborough" = 246
8. "A secret occult code is at Shugborough" = 246
9. "A secret Shugborough code has been cracked" = 246
10. "A secret unbreakable code at Shugborough" = 246
11. "A very big secret code of Shugborough" = 246
12. "Cipher of Shugborough is insoluble code" = 246
13. "Clue to the code *hidden* at Shugborough" = 246
14. "Clue to the code *hiding* in Shugborough" = 246
15. "Code at Shugborough fools everyone" = 246
16. "Code clue at Shugborough was unbreakable" = 246
17. "Code *hid* by Shugborough was unbreakable" = 246
18. "Code of Shugborough Hall was unbreakable" = 246
19. "Coded Masonic clues at Shugborough Hall" = 246
20. "Codes *are* the Shugborough treasure" = 246
21. "Codes in Shugborough are very hard" = 246
22. "Cryptic Shugborough cipher *hid* a code" = 246
23. "Few find code numeral hid in Shugborough" = 246
24. "Few find huge Shugborough puzzle" = 246
25. "Few find number *hidden* at Shugborough" = 246
26. "Few find number *hiding* in Shugborough" = 246
27. "Few find proof of my Shugborough code" = 246
28. "Few find secret code clue of Shugborough" = 246
29. "Few find secret code *hid* in Shugborough" = 246
30. "Few find the giant code at Shugborough" = 246
31. "Find the code clues *hidden* at Shugborough" = 246
32. "Find the code proof in Shugborough Hall" = 246
33. "Find the *hidden* code clues at Shugborough" = 246
34. "Freemasons' code *hides* at Shugborough" = 246
35. "Freemasons' codes *hide* at Shugborough" = 246
36. "Go to Shugborough Hall find secret code" = 246

37. "*Hid* a secret code number at Shugborough" = 246
38. "*Hid* an insoluble code at Shugborough Arcadia" = 246
39. "*Hid* code on Shugborough's monuments" = 246
40. "*Hid* code proof as cipher at Shugborough" = 246
41. "*Hid* my strange code at Shugborough" = 246
42. "*Hid* proof of secret code in Shugborough" = 246
43. "*Hid* the cryptic code at Shugborough" = 246
44. "Huge secret occult code at Shugborough" = 246
45. "I *hid* an insoluble code on Shugborough Arcadia" = 246
46. "Incomprehensible code at Shugborough" = 246
47. "Insoluble riddle *hiding* Shugborough code" = 246
48. "Look for secret code *hid* in Shugborough" = 246
49. "Look for the giant code at Shugborough" = 246
50. "Many coded messages in Shugborough" = 246
51. "Many fail to crack code at Shugborough" = 246
52. "Many fail to decipher Shugborough code" = 246
53. "Many failed to break code in Shugborough" = 246
54. "My very hard Shugborough codes" = 246
55. "Nobody cracks the code in Shugborough" = 246
56. "Our code-key *hides* at Shugborough Hall" = 246
57. "Our mysterious Shugborough code" = 246
58. "Proof of code *hidden* on a folly at Shugborough" = 246
59. "Proof of code *hides* on folly at Shugborough" = 246
60. "Proof of code was at Shugborough Hall" = 246
61. "Proof of hidden code *hiding* at Shugborough" = 246
62. "Proof of the giant code at Shugborough" = 246
63. "Secret Shugborough code is unbreakable" = 246
64. "Shrine to Pan at Shugborough *hid* code" = 246
65. "Shrine to Pan *hides* Shugborough code" = 246
66. "Shugborough Arcadia *hides* an insoluble code" = 246
67. "Shugborough cipher *hid* proof of the code" = 246
68. "Shugborough codes are insoluble riddle" = 246
69. "Shugborough Hall cipher *hid* Masonic code" = 246
70. "Shugborough Hall code broken at last" = 246
71. "Shugborough Hall code is the Masonic code" = 246
72. "Shugborough Hall *hides* secret code clue" = 246
73. "Shugborough Hall *hiding* coded Masonic clue" = 246
74. "Shugborough Hall *hiding* secret codes" = 246
75. "Shugborough *hides* my strange code" = 246
76. "Shugborough *hides Skelton* code key" = 246
77. "Shugborough *hides* the cryptic code" = 246
78. "Shugborough *hides* the unbreakable codes" = 246
79. "Shugborough riddle *hid* a huge insoluble code" = 246
80. "*Skelton* code: secret of Shugborough" = 246

81. “*Skelton* code is *hidden* in Shugborough” = 246
82. “The code of Shugborough cracked at last” = 246
83. “*The Code*’s proof *hides* at Shugborough” = 246
84. “The Master Code *hidden* in Shugborough” = 246
85. “The secret at Shugborough is in a code” = 246
86. “The secret in Shugborough was a code” = 246
87. “The secret code *hiding* at Shugborough” = 246
88. “The treasure in Shugborough is a code” = 246
89. “The unbreakable codes *hid* at Shugborough” = 246
90. “The unbreakable codes Shugborough hides” = 246
91. “*This* is the code *hidden* in Shugborough” = 246
92. “Very hard code *hidden* at Shugborough” = 246
93. “Very hard code *hiding* in Shugborough” = 246

Reversed solutions:

- 246 = “a secret code number *hid* at Shugborough”
- 246 = “a secret code number Shugborough *hides*”
- 246 = “cipher numeral found at Shugborough”
- 246 = “is code number at Shugborough few find”
- 246 = “is cypher-number at Shugborough”
- 246 = “is secret number Shugborough *hid*”
- 246 = “the key to the Shugborough Hall code”
- 246 = “the secret number at Shugborough”
- 246 = “the secret numeral of Shugborough”

Solutions excluding ‘code’:

1. “A cipher clue on Shugborough’s folly” = 246
2. “A cipher is on Shugborough’s folly” = 246
3. “A cryptogram is at Shugborough” = 246
4. “A problem in Shugborough is difficult” = 246
5. “A secret hid in cipher at Shugborough” = 246
6. “A secret was *hiding* at Shugborough” = 246
7. “A *Skelton* cipher *hid* at Shugborough” = 246
8. “A treasure is *hiding* at Shugborough” = 246
9. “An insoluble riddle is in Shugborough” = 246
10. “An occult secret is at Shugborough” = 246
11. “Cipher number: clue is at Shugborough” = 246
12. “Clues *hid* at Shugborough Hall folly” = 246
13. “Decrypt the Shugborough cipher” = 246
14. “Difficult problems at Shugborough” = 246
15. “Find treasure *hidden* at Shugborough” = 246
16. “Folly at Shugborough Hall *hid* clues” = 246
17. “Great secret *hidden* at Shugborough” = 246
18. “Great secret *hiding* in Shugborough” = 246

19. *"Hid* a *Skelton* cipher at Shugborough" = 246
20. *"Hid* a strange cipher at Shugborough" = 246
21. *"Hid* clues at Shugborough Hall folly" = 246
22. *"Hid* Roman numerals at Shugborough" = 246
23. "I *hid* difficult problem at Shugborough" = 246
24. "Insoluble riddle *hides* in Shugborough" = 246
25. "Look for huge Shugborough puzzle" = 246
26. "Look for number *hidden* at Shugborough" = 246
27. "Look for number *hiding* in Shugborough" = 246
28. "Look for Shugborough Hall's folly" = 246
29. "My strange Shugborough cipher" = 246
30. "Nobody cracks cipher of Shugborough" = 246
31. "Our Shugborough cipher is unbreakable" = 246
32. "Our treasure *hidden* at Shugborough" = 246
33. "Our treasure *hiding* in Shugborough" = 246
34. "Proof of cipher on folly at Shugborough" = 246
35. "Secret cipher found at Shugborough" = 246
36. "Shrine of Pan was at Shugborough" = 246
37. "Shugborough Arcadia *hid* many ciphers" = 246
38. "Shugborough Arcadia *hid* the cipher of Pan" = 246
39. "Shugborough Hall folly hides clues" = 246
40. "Shugborough Hall *hiding* the number 2-4-6" = 246
41. "Shugborough *hid Skelton's* number" = 246
42. "Shugborough *hides* a *Skelton* cipher" = 246
43. "Shugborough *hides* a strange cipher" = 246
44. "Shugborough *hides* an occult secret" = 246
45. "Shugborough *hides* difficult problem" = 246
46. "Shugborough *hides* Roman numerals" = 246
47. "Shugborough *hiding* difficult problem" = 246
48. "Shugborough is *hiding* the answer" = 246
49. "Shugborough was *hiding* a treasure" = 246
50. "The unbreakable Shugborough ciphers" = 246
51. *"Treasure* of Shugborough *is* a cipher" = 246

Master Code solutions relating to Pan's shrine folly

1. "A secret *hiding* on the shrine of Pan" = 246
2. "A shrine of Pan in Shugborough garden" = 246
3. "Few find Pan on the Shugborough Arcadia" = 246
4. "Few find Pan's grave-cipher on Arcadia" = 246
5. *"Hid* numeral clue at the shrine of Pan" = 246
6. "I used Latin *not* Greek on tomb of Pan" = 246
7. "Inscription on Pan's tomb is code" = 246
8. "Latin *not* Greek hides the secret" = 246
9. "Latin *not* Greek is clue on the tomb" = 246
10. "Latin *not* Greek is secret hint" = 246

11. "Latin code on Pan's grave *not* Greek" = 246
12. "Latin on Pan's tomb is hiding our code" = 246
13. "Look for the code *hid* at shrine to Pan" = 246
14. "Look for the code I *hid* on shrine to Pan" = 246
15. "Look for the code shrine of Pan hides" = 246
16. "Pan's grave in Arcadia at Shugborough" = 246
17. "Pan's shrine is *hiding* secrets" = 246
18. "Roman numerals at shrine of Pan" = 246 D-M / M-D
19. "Secret clue *hid* at the shrine of Pan" = 246
20. "Secret code clues *hide* in shrine of Pan" = 246
21. "Shrine of Pan *hides* The Master Code" = 246
22. "Shrine of Pan *hides* the numeral clue" = 246
23. "Shrine of Pan *hiding* OUOSVAVV code" = 246
24. "Shrine of Pan *hiding* our secret clue" = 246
25. "Shrine of Pan *hiding Skelton*'s code" = 246
26. "Shrine of Pan *hiding* the secrets" = 246
27. "Shrine of Pan is *hiding* our numeral" = 246
28. "Shrine of Pan is *hiding* our secret" = 246

Reversed solutions

- 246 = "a numeral *hiding* on the shrine of Pan"
- 246 = "is numeral *hid* at the shrine of Pan"
- 246 = "is numeral I *hid* on the shrine of Pan"
- 246 = "is numeral the shrine of Pan *hides*"

THE ARCADIA CODES

Arcadia: relief within Pan's shrine-folly

Three shepherds watched by a shepherdess discover an inscription on Pan's tomb:

Although the title 'shepherds' monument' is not strictly accurate - the entire monument is a shrine-folly to the Pan - there are Master Code solutions relating to the shepherds' monument, viz:

1. "Code *hidden* on monument of shepherds" = 246
2. "*Hid* code on the shepherds' monument" = 246
3. "The monument of shepherds *hides*" = 246
4. "The monument of shepherds is a code" = 246

Applying the Master Code specifically to Arcadia and its design:

1. "3 shepherds find an inscription" = 246
2. "3 shepherds in Arcadia at Shugborough" = 246
3. "8 letters 7 dots hiding a code in Arcadia" = 246
4. "8 letters 7 dots hiding code on Arcadia" = 246
5. "8 letters on Arcadia are a secret clue" = 246
6. "8 letters on Shugborough's Arcadia" = 246
7. "A clue in Poussin's painting of Arcadia" = 246
8. "A code Arcadia hid was a very difficult riddle" = 246
9. "A code hid as Poussin's Arcadia painting" = 246
10. "A code hidden at Arcadia is incomprehensible" = 246
11. "A code in Arcadia hides eternal truths" = 246
12. "A code in Arcadia is cryptic and enigmatic" = 246
13. "A cryptic and enigmatic code clue in Arcadia" = 246
14. "A cryptic and enigmatic code is in Arcadia" = 246
15. "A cryptic inscription at Arcadia" = 246
16. "A giant code hidden at Arcadia at Shugborough" = 246
17. "A number problem in Shugborough Arcadia" = 246
18. "A painting of Arcadia by Poussin hid a code" = 246
19. "A secret code's clue on Shugborough Arcadia" = 246
20. "A secret key is on Arcadia monument" = 246
21. "A test at Arcadia hiding cipher-number" = 246
22. "A very difficult riddle hidden in Arcadia" = 246
23. "A very hard problem hiding at Arcadia" = 246
24. "A very hard puzzle is on Arcadia" = 246
25. "An eight-letter cipher hid code on Arcadia" = 246
26. "An eight-letter clue is hidden on Arcadia" = 246
27. "An unbreakable cipher-code is hidden at Arcadia" = 246
28. "An unbreakable cipher-code is hiding in Arcadia" = 246
29. "An unbreakable code is on Shugborough Arcadia" = 246
30. "Anson's code left on Arcadia for future" = 246
31. "Arcadia cipher was incomprehensible" = 246
32. "Arcadia code-problem is solved by you" = 246
33. "Arcadia folly at Shugborough is code clue" = 246
34. "Arcadia folly at Shugborough was a code" = 246

35. “Arcadia hid code clue: you have got the hint” = 246
36. “Arcadia hid extremely hard riddles” = 246
37. “Arcadia hides a code: you have got the hint” = 246
38. “Arcadia hides extremely clever code” = 246
39. “Arcadia hides extremely hard clues” = 246
40. “Arcadia hides the insoluble puzzle” = 246
41. “Arcadia hiding a very hard puzzle” = 246
42. “Arcadia inscription is cryptic” = 246
43. “Arcadia is an extremely clever code” = 246
44. “Arcadia is at the Shugborough estate” = 246
45. “Arcadia is hiding an eight-letter code clue” = 246
46. “Arcadia is hiding cipher-number test” = 246
47. “Arcadia is hiding eight-letter cipher” = 246
48. “Arcadia is hiding very hard problem” = 246
49. “Arcadia is the shrine at Shugborough” = 246
50. “Arcadia monument at Shugborough Hall” = 246
51. “Arcadia monument hides a code of Skelton” = 246
52. “Arcadia monument hiding a numeral key” = 246
53. “Arcadia monument hiding a secret key” = 246
54. “Arcadia problem was solved by ye” = 246
55. “Arcadia was hiding very big secret” = 246
56. “Arcadia was the greatest secret” = 246
57. “Arcadia’s codes: you have got the hint” = 246
58. “Arcadia’s puzzle is very hard” = 246
59. “Arcadia’s test is solved by you” = 246
60. “Arcadia’s very difficult secret code” = 246
61. “Cipher at Arcadia is eight letters” = 246
62. “Cipher at Arcadia is incomprehensible” = 246
63. “Clue at Arcadia hiding very big secret” = 246
64. “Clue at Shugborough Arcadia is insoluble” = 246
65. “Clue at Shugborough Arcadia is proof of code” = 246
66. “Clues in Arcadia folly at Shugborough” = 246
67. “Code in a painting of Arcadia by Poussin” = 246
68. “Code in Arcadia is a very difficult riddle” = 246
69. “Code of Anson hiding in monument of Arcadia” = 246
70. “Code you have found hides secret of Arcadia” = 246
71. “Cryptic and enigmatic code clue on Arcadia” = 246
72. “Cryptic and enigmatic code is on Arcadia” = 246
73. “Cryptic clue hides message in Arcadia” = 246
74. “Cryptic message is hidden on Arcadia” = 246
75. “Decrypt code in Shugborough’s Arcadia” = 246
76. “Eight letters on Arcadia are hiding a code” = 246
77. “Eight-letter cipher is clue on Arcadia” = 246
78. “Eight-letter cypher is on Arcadia” = 246
79. “Eternal truth hidden as a code in Arcadia” = 246

80. "Eternal truth hidden as code on Arcadia" = 246
81. "Eternal truth hidden in code at Arcadia" = 246
82. "Eternal truth hides as code in Arcadia" = 246
83. "Eternal truth hiding in code in Arcadia" = 246
84. "Extremely clever Arcadia cipher" = 246
85. "Extremely clever code hid at Arcadia" = 246
86. "Extremely clever codes on Arcadia" = 246
87. "Extremely hard clues hid at Arcadia" = 246
88. "Extremely hard code riddle at Arcadia" = 246
89. "Faces of Anson and Pan hid on top of Arcadia" = 246
90. "Few find secret code ciphers at Arcadia" = 246
91. "Find clue to secret codes hidden at Arcadia" = 246
92. "Find clue to secret codes hiding in Arcadia" = 246
93. "Find clues to secret code hidden at Arcadia" = 246
94. "Find clues to secret code hiding in Arcadia" = 246
95. "Few find the Shugborough Arcadia proof" = 246
96. "From a picture of Arcadia by Poussin" = 246
97. "Giant code hides at Arcadia at Shugborough" = 246
98. "Giant code hiding on Arcadia at Shugborough" = 246
99. "Giant code is hidden at Shugborough Arcadia" = 246
100. "Giant code is hiding in Shugborough Arcadia" = 246
101. "Hid a clue at Shugborough's Arcadia folly" = 246
102. "Hid a code at Arcadia: you have got the hint "= 246
103. "Hid clue at Shugborough as Arcadia folly" = 246
104. "Hid code at Shugborough Arcadia monument" = 246
105. "Hid code in Shugborough Hall Arcadia folly" = 246
106. "Hid extremely clever code at Arcadia" = 246
107. "Hid extremely hard clues at Arcadia" = 246
108. "I hid a code on Arcadia: you have got the hint "= 246
109. "I hid Arcadia's code: you have got the hint "= 246
110. "I hid eternal truths as code in Arcadia" = 246
111. "I hid extremely clever code on Arcadia" = 246
112. "I hid extremely hard clues on Arcadia" = 246
113. "I hid a code on Arcadia: you have got the hint" = 246
114. "I left a cipher in Arcadia for the future" = 246
115. "I left a code hidden on Arcadia for the future" = 246
116. "I left cipher on Arcadia for the future" = 246"
117. "I used Latin not Greek on tomb of Pan" = 246
118. "Incomprehensible code clues are on Arcadia" = 246
119. "Insoluble cipher puzzle in Arcadia" = 246
120. "Insoluble code puzzle hidden on Arcadia" = 246
121. "Insoluble code puzzles hide in Arcadia" = 246
122. "Left cipher at Arcadia for the future" = 246
123. "Left code hiding on Arcadia for the future" = 246
124. "Look for Arcadia painting of Poussin" = 246

125. “Look for Pan on the Shugborough Arcadia” = 246
126. “Look for Poussin painting of Arcadia” = 246
127. “Look for secret cipher-codes at Arcadia” = 246
128. “Look for secret test clue at Arcadia” = 246
129. “Many fail to solve Arcadia’s cipher” = 246
130. “Many failed to break Arcadia’s ciphers” = 246
131. “Many have failed to break Arcadia’s code clue” = 246
132. “Many have failed to break the code of Arcadia” = 246
133. “Many tried to break codes Arcadia hides” = 246
134. “Many tried to break codes hid at Arcadia” = 246
135. “Many try breaking codes at Arcadia” = 246
136. “Many try to break code clue on Arcadia” = 246
137. “Many try to break codes at Arcadia” = 246
138. “Monument of Arcadia hides the Anson code” = 246
139. “Pan’s face hides on Arcadia at Shugborough” = 246
140. “Problem at Arcadia is solved by ye” = 246
141. “Problem of Arcadia’s code solved by ye” = 246
142. “Reflected Arcadia picture of Poussin” = 246
143. “Rotated Poussin picture of Arcadia” = 246
144. “Secret code number hidden in Arcadia” = 246
145. “Secret key be on Arcadia’s monument” = 246
146. “Shepherd points at *et in Arcadia ego”* = 246
147. “Shepherds find a code hid as *et in Arcadia ego”* = 246
148. “Shepherds find Arcadia’s *et in Arcadia ego”* = 246
149. “Shepherds find code *et in Arcadia ego* hides” = 246
150. “Shepherds found the code *et in Arcadia ego*” = 246
151. “Shugborough Arcadia clue was insoluble” = 246
152. “Shugborough Arcadia faces north-east” = 246
153. “Shugborough Arcadia monument hiding code” = 246
154. “Shugborough’s Arcadia folly hides a clue” = 246
155. “*Skelton* cipher a key to Arcadia’s code” = 246
156. “*Skelton* code is the secret Arcadia hid” = 246
157. “*Skelton* cipher solved Arcadia’s code” = 246
158. “The Arcadia code at Shugborough is broken” = 246
159. “The Arcadia picture is by Poussin” = 246
160. “The cipher at Arcadia deciphered by you” = 246
161. “The clue in Arcadia found by shepherds” = 246
162. “The code is on Arcadia at Shugborough Hall” = 246
163. “The eight letters of code are on Arcadia” = 246
164. “The face of Pan hidden on Shugborough Arcadia” = 246
165. “The faces of Anson and Pan hidden on Arcadia” = 246
166. “The key of *Skelton* unlocks Arcadia” = 246
167. “The secret is at Shugborough Arcadia” = 246
168. “The secret number is hidden at Arcadia” = 246
169. “The secret of Shugborough hid in Arcadia” = 246

170. “The shepherds found the Arcadia code clue” = 246
171. “The very difficult Arcadia problem” = 246
172. “The very difficult code hidden in Arcadia” = 246
173. “This is the code at Shugborough Arcadia” = 246
174. “This was the Shugborough Arcadia code” = 246
175. “Thomas Anson’s Arcadia hides a number” = 246
176. “Three shepherds find *et in Arcadia ego*” = 246
177. “Tomb of Pan is in Shugborough’s Arcadia” = 246
178. “Unbreakable code hides on Shugborough Arcadia” = 246
179. “Unlock Arcadia using a key of *Skelton*” = 246
180. “Used a painting of Arcadia by Poussin” = 246
181. “Used painting of Poussin for Arcadia” = 246
182. “Very big secret is hiding at Arcadia” = 246
183. “Very difficult riddle hidden on Arcadia” = 246
184. “Very difficult riddle hides in Arcadia” = 246
185. “Very difficult riddles hide in Arcadia” = 246
186. “Very difficult to solve Arcadia code” = 246
187. “Very few solved codes hid in Arcadia” = 246
188. “Ye have solved Shugborough Arcadia code” = 246
189. “You broke code hid on Shugborough’s Arcadia” = 246
190. “You broke codes hid on Shugborough Arcadia” = 246
191. “You cracked a code the Shugborough Arcadia hid” = 246
192. “You cracked cipher of Shugborough Arcadia” = 246
193. “You cracked the code in Shugborough Arcadia” − 246
194. “You deciphered a secret Arcadian cipher” = 246
195. “You discovered secret code hid in Arcadia” = 246
196. “You found the key to Arcadia hidden in code” = 246
197. “You found the secret number of Arcadia” = 246
198. “You got the hint hid in *et in Arcadia ego*” = 246
199. “You have found the key to Arcadia’s code” = 246
200. “You have found the secret code in Arcadia” = 246
201. “You have mastered the codes in Arcadia” = 246
202. “You pass the test Arcadia hid in code” = 246
203. “You passed code-test hiding on Arcadia” = 246
204. “You passed the tests at Arcadia” = 246
205. “You solved a hard code problem in Arcadia” = 246
206. “You solved a problem Arcadia is hiding” = 246
207. “You solved a very hard code Arcadia hid” = 246
208. “You solved Arcadia’s hidden code-test” = 246
209. “You solved code hid as Arcadia’s test” = 246
210. “You solved difficult Arcadia problem” = 246
211. “You solved the code Arcadia’s cipher hid” = 246
212. “You solved very hard code in Arcadia” = 246

Reversed solutions, key first:

- 246 = "a number hid at Thomas Anson's Arcadia"
- 246 = "a number Thomas Anson's Arcadia hides"
- 246 = "is number Thomas Anson's Arcadia hid"

Significance of the D - M cipher

As suggested previously, the most likely interpretation of D - M is that the letters are the Roman numerals 500 and 1000 respectively. The image on Arcadia is the 'mirror' of Poussin's picture which suggests the D-M should be M-D; in other words, fifteen hundred in Roman numerals (MD = 1500). Moreover, a resonance equation indicates the reversal of D–M: **"OUOSVAVV" = "reverse D-M" = 95**

Applying the Master Code in that context:

1. "Roman numerals are *hiding* a numeral" = 246
2. "Roman numerals are *hiding* a secret" = 246
3. "Roman numerals *hiding* numeral clue" = 246
4. "The clue was the Roman numerals" = 246

Reversed solutions:

- 246 = "a numeral Roman numerals are *hiding*"
- 246 = "is a number *hid* as Roman numerals code"
- 246 = "number *concealed* by Roman numerals"

And crucially: "Fifteen hundred in Roman numerals" = 246 M-D (fifteen hundred)

Applying the Master Code in that context:

1. "A code number clue *hid* as Roman numerals" = 246
2. "A Roman numeral code in Pan's shrine" = 246
3. "A Roman numeral *hid* Arcadia's code numeral" = 246
4. "Arcadia code numeral *hid* as Roman numeral" = 246
5. "Arcadia's code numeral in Roman numeral" = 246
6. "Arcadia's Roman numerals are a number" = 246
7. "*Hid* code number of Arcadia as Roman numeral" = 246
8. "I *hid* code number of Arcadia in Roman numeral" = 246
9. "Roman numeral: code on Pan's shrine" = 246
10. "Roman numeral is cipher's number" = 246
11. "Roman numerals at Shugborough *hid*" = 246
12. "Shugborough's Roman numerals *hide*" = 246

Applying the Master Code in the context of the D-M cipher:

1. "A code numeral in Arcadia is *hid* by the D and M" = 246
2. "A Roman numeral is *hidden* on Arcadia as D – M" = 246
3. "D and M are a clue on Anson's Arcadia folly" = 246
4. "D and M are not a Shugborough monogram" = 246
5. "D and M cipher *hides* numeral clue on Arcadia" = 246
6. "D and M cipher is a *hidden* numeral on Arcadia" = 246
7. "D and M is clue on Anson's Arcadia folly" = 246
8. "D and M on Arcadia are widely separated" = 246
9. "D and M on Arcadia is a *hidden* cipher-numeral" = 246
10. "D and M on Shugborough Arcadia *hid* a code number" = 246
11. "Roman numeral clues on Arcadia *hide* as D – M" = 246
12. "The code numeral clue on Arcadia *hid* by D and M" = 246
13. "The code numeral on Arcadia is *hid* by D and M" = 246
14. "The D and M on a line below OUOSVAVV" = 246
15. "The D and M on Arcadia are Roman numbers" = 246
16. "The D and M was Thomas Anson's code" = 246
17. "Wide space between D and M on base of Arcadia" = 246
18. "You broke D - M code in Shugborough's Arcadia" = 246
19. "You deciphered D - M code I *hid* on Arcadia" = 246
20. "You deciphered D - M codes on Arcadia" = 246
21. "You have broken a code *hid* as D – M. Well done." = 246
22. "You have broken code D – M *hides.* Well done." = 246
23. "You have cracked a code Arcadia's D - M cipher *hid*" = 246
24. "You have decoded the D - M ciphers on Arcadia" = 246
25. "You have decrypted code D - M *hid* on Arcadia" = 246

Applying *Skelton,* we find a Master Code resonance equation linking O.U.O.S.V.A.V.V and D-M:

"Eight letters and seven dots" = "fifteen hundred in Roman numerals" = 246

And the solutions: "You found *a* key O.U.O.S.V.A.V.V and D-M *hid*" = 246

"You found key in O.U.O.S.V.A.V.V and D-M" = 246

So, both O.U.O.S.V.A.V.V and D-M on the base of the monument represent the special gematria number, the Master Code key 246.

The Cat Monument

Pan's shrine is not the only folly in the Shugborough estate, on a small island opposite stands the monument of a Persian cat and four Corsican goats. The plinth displays a plaque depicting two griffins guarding a chalice. According to Master Code solutions, the chalice represents the 'Holy Grail' - as one might guess - an icon representing *The Code* itself, Shugborough's secret 'treasure'.

The cat monument detail

The detail is a Persian cat lying atop an orb with two of the four Corsican goats below. A pair of griffins are on the plaque below, chimeras with the head and wings of an eagle and the body of a lion.

The plaque displays a chalice 'guarded' by a pair of griffins

With a pair of griffins for protection the chalice is more than simply decorative, it represents something important. As griffins are mythical the chalice probably alludes to the Holy Grail, which in turn stands for *The Code*. **In that context, we find the Master Code solution**:

"*Skelton* code *was* the Holy Grail" = 246

The conjecture is that the animals on the monument are coded emblems. This is tested by applying *Skelton* in the context of the cat, goats and griffins the numbers of which are assumed to be significant. **First, writing the emblems as**: "two griffins and four goats and one cat" = 277

1. "Two griffins and four goats and one cat" = "are code clues on Shugborough cat monument" = 277
2. "Two griffins and four goats and one cat" = "are Thomas Anson's codes you have found" = 277
3. "Two griffins and four goats and one cat" = "is code on cat's monument at Shugborough" = 277
4. "Two griffins and four goats and one cat" = "is a clue on the Shugborough cat monument" = 277
5. "Two griffins and four goats and one cat" = "the animals are *hiding* a secret cypher" = 277
6. "Two griffins and four goats and one cat" = "the secret ciphers of Thomas Anson" = 277
7. "Two griffins and four goats and one cat" = "Thomas Anson's secret cyphers" = 277

Reversed equations:

1. "Code on Shugborough's cat monument hid by" = "Two griffins and four goats and one cat" = 277
2. "Code on Shugborough's cat monument was" = "Two griffins and four goats and one cat" = 277

Writing the emblems as: one cat + two griffins + four goats = 241 (two-four-one)

1. "Two griffins + four goats + one cat" = "a secret on Shugborough monument" = 241
2. "Two griffins + four goats + one cat" = "Holy Grail *hides* on cat monument" = 241
3. "Two griffins + four goats + one cat" = "is a secret cipher you found. *Bravo*!" = 241
4. "Two griffins + four goats + one cat" = "is Anson's cipher at Shugborough" = 241
5. "Two griffins + four goats + one cat" = "Shugborough monument's secret" = 241
6. "Two griffins + four goats + one cat" = "you found a secret cypher. *Bravo*!" = 241

Writing the emblems as: A cat + four goats + two griffins, we find the resonance equations:

1. "A cat + four goats + two griffins" = "animals are emblems of a secret code" = 223
2. "A cat + four goats + two griffins" = "animals on Anson's monument" = 223
3. "A cat + four goats + two griffins" = "Anson hid a secret on monument" = 223
4. "A cat + four goats + two griffins" = "Anson's cipher broken by you" = 223
5. "A cat + four goats + two griffins" = "*hidden* codes have been broken by you" = 223
6. "A cat + four goats + two griffins" = "*hiding* a secret code for the future" = 223
7. "A cat + four goats + two griffins" = "is secret cipher you solved" = 223
8. "A cat + four goats + two griffins" = "is the cipher you have solved" = 223
9. "A cat + four goats + two griffins" = "is the code *hidden* on the monument" = 223
10. "A cat + four goats + two griffins" = "left by Anson for the future" = 223
11. "A cat + four goats + two griffins" = "monument hid Anson's secret" = 223
12. "A cat + four goats + two griffins" = "on Shugborough's cat monument" = 223
13. "A cat + four goats + two griffins" = "the animals are *hiding* the cipher" = 223
14. "A cat + four goats + two griffins" = "well done: you have cracked a cipher" = 223
15. "A cat + four goats + two griffins" = "well done: you have cracked my code" = 223
16. "A cat + four goats + two griffins" = "you have solved the cypher" = 223
17. "A cat + four goats + two griffins" = "you solved secret cypher" = 223

Writing the emblems as: "1 cat and 4 goats and 2 griffins" = 170

1. "1 cat and 4 goats and 2 griffins" = "a cipher of Thomas Anson" = 170
2. "1 cat and 4 goats and 2 griffins" = "a code cat's monument hides" = 170
3. "1 cat and 4 goats and 2 griffins" = "a code *hid* at cat's monument" = 170
4. "1 cat and 4 goats and 2 griffins" = "a code I *hid* on cat's monument" = 170
5. "1 cat and 4 goats and 2 griffins" = "animal monument *hides* a code" = 170
6. "1 cat and 4 goats and 2 griffins" = "animals are the clue for a code" = 170
7. "1 cat and 4 goats and 2 griffins" = "are code by Thomas Anson" = 170
8. "1 cat and 4 goats and 2 griffins" = "*hides* a code of Thomas Anson" = 170
9. "1 cat and 4 goats and 2 griffins" = "you cracked Anson's codes" = 170
10. "1 cat and 4 goats and 2 griffins" = "you solved the cipher" = 170

Writing the emblems as: "1 cat + 4 goats + 2 griffins" = 134

1. "1 cat + 4 goats + 2 griffins" = "a clue *hid* on monument" = 134
2. "1 cat + 4 goats + 2 griffins" = "a secret code of Anson" = 134
3. "1 cat + 4 goats + 2 griffins" = "clue left by Anson" = 134
4. "1 cat + 4 goats + 2 griffins" = "code of Thomas Anson" = 134
5. "1 cat + 4 goats + 2 griffins" = "*hiding* a secret code clue" = 134
6. "1 cat + 4 goats + 2 griffins" = "is cipher you found" = 134
7. "1 cat + 4 goats + 2 griffins" = "is *hiding* a secret code" = 134
8. "1 cat + 4 goats + 2 griffins" = "the animals *hid* codes" = 134

Reversed: "You broke code *hidden* as" = "1 cat + 4 goats + 2 griffins" = 134

Applying the Master Code in the context of the cat's monument, we find the solutions:

1. "**142** cypher *hides*" = 246 — the *number* 142 (**1** cat, **4** goats, **2** griffins)
2. "**142** the cipher for" = 246
3. "**246 is *hiding* as 142 on the cat monument**" = 246 — digits 246 & 142
4. "A cat at Shugborough hiding secrets" = 246
5. "A numeral clue is in Roman numerals" = 246
6. "A Persian cat at Shugborough hides code" = 246
7. "A Persian cat in Shugborough hiding a code" = 246
8. "A Persian cat was lying on an orb" = 246
9. "A secret clue is in Roman numerals" = 246
10. "A treasure is hiding at Shugborough" = 246
11. "Animals are hiding the code of *Skelton*" = 246
12. "Cat at Shugborough hides a secret clue" = 246
13. "Cat monument at Shugborough hiding" = 246
14. "Cat monument hid the *Holy Grail* code" = 246
15. "Cat, goats and griffins hide ciphers" = 246
16. "Cat's monument code solved by ye" = 246
17. "Cat's monument hid the treasure" = 246
18. **"Cat's monument hides the numeral" = 246**

19. "Cat's monument hides the secret" = 246
20. "Clue is: an orb on the cat's monument" = 246
21. "Clue is: Persian cat lying on an orb" = 246
22. "Clue is: two griffins and *The Grail*" = 246
23. "Code for *Holy Grail* hid at Shugborough" = 246
24. "Code hid at cat monument of Shugborough" = 246
25. "Code hidden as monument of cat and goats" = 246
26. "Code hides on a monument of cat and goats" = 246
27. "Code on cat's monument of Shugborough" = 246
28. "Goats from Corsica be at Shugborough" = 246
29. "Goats of Corsica on cat's monument" = 246
30. "Griffins are guardians of secret code" = 246*
31. "Griffins are guarding the code's key" = 246
32. "*Hid* a cipher as cat, goats and griffins" = 246
33. "*Hid* a cipher clue as **142**" = 246
34. "*Hid* a code at Shugborough as a Persian cat" = 246
35. "*Hid* a cypher as **142**" = 246
36. "*Hid* a secret as the cat's monument" = 246
37. "*Hid* code key as cat, goats and griffins" = 246
38. "*Hide* a secret on the cat's monument" = 246
39. "*Holy Grail hides* secret code number" = 246
40. "*Holy Grail* is code clue at Shugborough" = 246
41. "*Holy Grail* is guarded by griffins" = 246
42. "*Holy Grail* is on a cat's monument" = 246
43. "*Holy Grail* on the monument of a cat" = 246
44. "*Holy Grail* represented my code" = 246
45. "*Holy Grail* stands for the codes" = 246
46. "*Holy Grail* symbol *hid* secret code" = 246
47. "*Holy Grail* symbolised a numeral" = 246
48. "*Holy Grail* symbolised a secret" = 246
49. "*Holy Grail* symbolises a *hidden* code" = 246
50. "*Holy Grail* was a code at Shugborough" = 246
51. "I *hid* code on cat monument of Shugborough" = 246
52. "I *hid* numeral on the cat's monument" = 246
53. "I *hid* secret on the cat's monument" = 246
54. "Look for the chalice on monument of cat" = 246
55. "Monument of cat at Shugborough *hid* code" = 246
56. "One-Four-Two are on monument of cat" = 246
57. "Secret *hid* at the cat's monument" = 246
58. "Secrets on the cat's monument" = 246
59. "Shugborough was *hiding* a treasure" = 246
60. "The cat monument *hides* secrets" = 246

61. "The cat's monument is a secret code" = 246
62. "The cat's monument is *hiding* a key" = 246
63. "The cat's monument on the island" = 246
64. "The Persian cat *hides* the numeral" = 246
65. "The Persian cat *hides* the secret" = 246
66. "The Shugborough cat monument *hid* a code" = 246
67. "You found a code 1 cat, 4 goats, 2 griffins *hid*" = 246
68. "You solved a code on a cat's monument" = 246

Reversed solutions:

- 246 = "numeral *hid* at the cat's monument"
- 246 = "numeral I *hid* on the cat's monument"
- 246 = "numeral Shugborough's cat is *hiding*"
- 246 = "numeral two griffins and a chalice *hide*"
- 246 = "secret number *hid* by a Persian cat"

The distance from Shugborough estate's main gate to Land's End

The direct distance from the estate's main gate to Land's End is 246 miles, measured using *Google Earth*. Is that just coincidence? **We recall the Master Code solution**: "Make measurements to find number" = 246

Applying the Master Code in that context:

1. "Distance to Land's End is a number clue" = 246
2. "How far to Land's End? A clue in miles is" = 246
3. "You found the distance to Land's End" = 246
4. "You measured distance to Land's End" = 246

And the reverse solution:

246 = "is the number of miles to Land's End"

Remarkably, the solutions suggest it is not coincidence that the direct distance from Land's End to the gates of Shugborough's estate is 246 miles.

Finally, we recall some of the Master Code solutions concerning a secret number hidden at Shugborough:

- 246 = "a secret code number *hid* at Shugborough"
- 246 = "a secret code number Shugborough *hides*"
- 246 = "Shugborough Hall's secret number"
- 246 = "the secret number at Shugborough"
- 246 = "the secret numeral of Shugborough"

15. Thomas Anson and the Master Code

Thomas Anson (1695-1773) by an unknown artist

(Image: Wikipedia commons)

Master Code solutions relating to Thomas Anson and Shugborough etc:

1. "8 letters and 7 dots: Anson's code" = 246 (O.U.O.S.V.A.V.V)
2. "8 letters and 7 dots: clue of Anson" = 246
3. "A cipher at Shugborough concealed *Anson*" = 246
4. "A clue is: Thomas Anson's secret code" = 246
5. "Anson concealed a cipher at Shugborough" = 246
6. "Anson designed the Shugborough Arcadia" = 246
7. "Anson *hid* secret on Arcadia's folly" = 246
8. "Anson *hid* the cipher at Shugborough" = 246
9. "Anson *hid* treasure in Shugborough" = 246
10. "Anson *hides* code in Shugborough's Arcadia" = 246
11. "Anson *hides* secret number at Arcadia" = 246
12. "Anson *hiding* at the shrine of Pan" = 246
13. "Anson used Poussin's painting" = 246
14. "Anson uses the *Skelton* cipher" = 246
15. "Anson was on the shrine of Pan" = 246
16. "Anson's Arcadia *hid* a secret number clue" = 246
17. "Anson's Arcadia in Shugborough *hides* code" = 246
18. "Anson's cipher in Shugborough Arcadia" = 246
19. "Anson's face is on the shrine of Pan" = 246
20. "Anson's name *hidden* on shrine of Pan" = 246
21. "Anson's secret code at Shugborough" = 246
22. "Arcadia *hiding* Thomas Anson's code key" = 246
23. "Arcadia is *hiding* Thomas Anson's name" = 246
24. "Arcadia proves Thomas Anson *hid* code" = 246
25. "Ciphers of Anson are on Arcadia's folly" = 246
26. "Code you have deciphered was Anson's" = 246
27. "Codes *hid* secrets of Thomas Anson" = 246
28. "Codes on Anson's Arcadia in Shugborough" = 246

29. "Few find Thomas Anson's numeral" = 246
30. "Few find Thomas Anson's secret" = 246
31. "Find Thomas Anson's name *hidden* in code" = 246
32. "Go to Shugborough find the code of Anson" = 246
33. "Hid code at Anson's Arcadia in Shugborough" = 246
34. "Name of Anson *hid* by code of OUOSVAVV" = 246
35. "OUOSVAVV *hid* Anson's name as a clue" = 246
36. "OUOSVAVV is Anson's code at Arcadia" = 246
37. "OUOSVAVV was Anson's Arcadia code" = 246
38. "OUOSVAVV: a code by Thomas Anson" = 246
39. "OUOSVAVV: clue *hides* Anson's name" = 246
40. "OUOSVAVV: code concealed Anson's name" = 246
41. "Proof Thomas Anson knew the code" = 246
42. "Proof Thomas Anson used the codes" = 246
43. "Secret code *hid* Thomas Anson's name" = 246
44. "Secret number is in Anson's Arcadia" = 246
45. "Secret of Anson is at Shugborough" = 246
46. "Secret of Shugborough *hid* by Anson" = 246
47. "Secrets *hide* in code of Thomas Anson" = 246
48. "Shrine of Pan *hid* Thomas Anson's face" = 246
49. "Shrine of Pan *hides* Thomas Anson" = 246
50. "Shugborough Arcadia *hid Anson* as cipher" = 246
51. "Shugborough cypher concealed *Anson*" = 246
52. "Shugborough *hid* Anson's secrets" = 246
53. "Shugborough's Arcadia *hid* Anson's codes" = 246
54. "The code is a secret of Thomas Anson" = 246
55. "The face of Anson on the shrine of Pan" = 246
56. "The shrine of Pan *hiding* Anson's face" = 246
57. "Thomas Anson *hid* a big secret in Arcadia" = 246
58. "Thomas Anson *hid* a secret occult code" = 246
59. "Thomas Anson *hid* secret code in Arcadia" = 246
60. "Thomas Anson knew Freemason code" = 246
61. "Thomas Anson left a code clue *hid* on Arcadia" = 246
62. "Thomas Anson left code clues Arcadia *hid*" = 246
63. "Thomas Anson left the clue on Arcadia" = 246
64. "Thomas Anson made OUOSVAVV clue" = 246
65. "Thomas Anson put a cipher on Arcadia" = 246
66. "Thomas Anson used Freemason's code" = 246
67. "Thomas Anson's code key is on Arcadia" = 246
68. "Thomas Anson's secret code is huge" = 246
69. "Ye are right about Anson's cipher" = 246
70. "Ye discovered Thomas Anson's code" = 246
71. "Ye found Thomas Anson's code in Arcadia" = 246
72. "You discovered a code of Thomas Anson" = 246
73. "You found an Anson family secret" = 246*

74. "You found code of Thomas Anson on Arcadia" = 246
75. "You found the codes of Thomas Anson" = 246
76. "You proved Thomas Anson used a code" = 246
77. "You solved code Anson's cipher *hid*" = 246

Reverse solutions:

- 246 = "cypher number Thomas Anson *hid*"
- 246 = "is a secret number Anson's Arcadia *hid*"
- 246 = "is cipher number Thomas Anson *hid*"
- 246 = "is the key of Tom Anson's cipher"
- 246 = "is the secret number Anson *hides*"
- 246 = "secret code number of Thomas Anson"
- 246 = "was cipher key of Thomas Anson"
- 246 = "was the secret number Anson *hid*"

And finally: "*Skelton* is the Anson family code" = 246

16. FREEMASONRY - 'THE CRAFT' - A SECRET BROTHERHOOD

The Freemasons - also known as The Craft / The Brotherhood - is paradoxically a *famous* secret society, a supposedly clandestine fraternity that emerged in Scotland in the seventeenth century and developed south of the border during the early-mid eighteenth century. The first lodge meeting in England took place in 1717 on 24/6 at London.

The Freemasons took their name from the itinerant craftsmen who built the great cathedrals of medieval Europe, whose work involved specialist knowledge and for whom secrecy was essential in maintaining the integrity of their profession. By contrast, the 'modern' Freemasons are a 'secret' society in as much as their membership, rules, rituals, symbols and *modus operandi* are not open to public scrutiny and so, the question most often asked of a 'brother' is: *why the need for secrecy*?

The medieval masons formed a free union of self-employed skilled craftsmen, an elite fraternity. They used secret signs to recognise one another as 'experts' and to prevent less skilled 'impostors' from infiltrating The Craft. Secrets entrusted to 'Brothers' in the modern Craft similarly confer a sense of belonging to an 'elite' - the 'chosen ones' - those *trusted* to keep the Masonic secrets. As with the masons of old, the honour of being selected to keep secrets is key in forging allegiance to the Fraternity. Secrets therefore play a central role in establishing and maintaining the elite status of the 'Brothers'; and so, an ethos of 'exclusiveness' is fundamental to Freemasonry as not just 'anyone' can become a 'brother'.

In keeping with tradition, membership of The Craft is by invitation following due consideration. The Brothers are careful to choose new members having the 'right' views and attitudes; they select potential members who, like themselves, 'fit' a particular socio-economic profile. Candidates *must* believe in a supreme being and tend to be white middle-class, middle-aged professionals - reflecting the status of the craftsmen that built the cathedrals. Humans impose order on the environment by design, much as God is believed by some to have imposed order on chaos at the Creation. The nature of Masonic mythology, which *a priori* assumes the existence of a Creator means there has always been a strong link between The Craft, architecture and architects to the extent that Freemasons have traditionally identified 'God' as *Great Architect of the Universe.*

Not being a member of The Craft myself, it has been necessary to make 'informed guesses' as to how *Skelton's* cipher and the Master Code has been/might have been used in a Masonic context; that means the following conjectures concerning 'the Brotherhood' arise mainly from a knowledge of the symbols and myths that have found their way into the public domain.

The 'Craft' shares links with the occult through its use of arcane symbolism and 'ancient' myths, exemplified by the Temple of King Solomon. According to tradition *Hiram Abiff,* master-mason of the temple and an important figure in Masonic lore, was accosted by three 'ruffians': *Jubela, Jubelo* and *Jubelum*. *Hiram* was killed by *Jubelum* during an attempt to obtain the secret password for the Temple given to the master mason by Solomon.

Inspired by the legend, it's plausible that *high-level* Freemasons have used *Skelton* and the Master Code for secret passwords, messages and other clandestine purposes. It is public knowledge that number-letter ciphers (gematria), symbols and signs have long been used by Masons to hide 'secrets' in plain sight, unrecognised by the commonality. A member of The Craft - knowing the signs - is able to identify and communicate secretly with a 'brother', among a group of non-masons.

Applying *Skelton* in the context of 'the Freemasons' and 'the ruling elite', we find the resonance equation:

"The Freemasons" = "The ruling elite" = 122

Also: *"The Freemasons' Code" = "The Code of Destiny"* = 135

Applying *Skelton* in the context of Hiram Abiff, Solomon's master-mason and the code:

1. "You discovered" = "the code of Hiram Abiff" = 111
2. "The code of Hiram Abiff" = "the Master Code" = 111

It seems that 'the code of Hiram Abiff' and 'the Master Code' are one and the same.

Preliminary solutions hinting at a Masonic use of the Master Code

G inside compasses and square is a well-known Masonic symbol

Applying the Master Code (the code of Hiram Abiff) in the general context of The Craft and its symbolism:

1. **"A capital letter *G* stands for God" = 246**
2. "A code hidden at King Solomon's Temple" = 246
3. "A code hiding in King Solomon's Temple" = 246
4. "A Freemason's oath is ***a dark saying***" = 246 — see Elgar's *Enigma* following
5. "A Freemason's ritual is a secret code" = 246
6. "A skull is masonic symbol of death" = 246
7. **"*All is number*: a belief of Pythagoras" = 246** — a maxim attributed to Pythagoras
8. "Blue apron, white gloves of a Mason" = 246
9. **"Capital *G* cipher represents God" = 246**
10. "Code hides at King Solomon's Temple" = 246
11. "*Code of Jehovah* hid in Solomon's Temple" = 246
12. "Code of the Freemasons' craft is hidden" = 246
13. "*e pluribus unum:* Freemason motto" = 246 — statue's motto on the Capitol in Washington

14. “*e pluribus unum* is Masonic motto” = 246
15. “Esoteric knowledge of Freemasons” = 246
16. “*Eye of Providence* is a Masonic cipher” = 246
17. “*Eye of Providence*: A Masonic cypher” = 246
18. “Freemason’s Hall in London hid the code” = 246
19. “Freemasons code is the Golden Key code” = 246
20. “Freemasons found *The Code of Secrecy*” = 246
21. “Freemasons hid a secret as a ritual” = 246
22. “Freemasons hid the secret cipher” = 246
23. “Freemasons hide the codes of Solomon” = 246
24. “Freemasons hide the secret craft” = 246
25. “Freemasons made secret society” = 246
26. “Freemasons murder secretly” = 246
27. “Freemasons rule by secret codes” = 246
28. “Freemasons solved the number code” = 246
29. “Freemasons use *Hiram Abiff*’s number” = 246
30. “Freemasons’ ritual hides a secret” = 246
31. “Hid the Key of Solomon in secret code” = 246
32. “*Hiram Abiff* was the Master Mason” = 246
33. “*Hiram Abiff*: grandmaster of Masons” = 246
34. “*Hiram Abiff*: murdered by the ruffians” = 246
35. “*Jubela, Jubelo and Jubelum* are three ruffians” = 246
36. “Killing ritual of Freemasons hid a code” = 246
37. “Look for codes Freemasons have hidden” = 246
38. “Look for Solomon’s Golden Key” = 246
39. “Mason’s code: Doctor John Dee’s gematria” = 246
40. “Masonic brotherhood used secret code” = 246
41. “Masonic brothers hid *Skelton* code” = 246
42. “Masonic message hidden in plain sight” = 246
43. “Masonic motto hid a clue to secret code” = 246
44. “Message at the Temple of Solomon” = 246
45. “Message be in the Temple of Solomon” = 246
46. “Name the Key of Solomon: *Skelton*” = 246
47. “*Skelton* cipher is the Masonic code” = 246
48. “*Skelton* code hid *The Key of Solomon*” = 246
49. “*Skelton* is used by Freemasons” = 246
50. “*Skelton* is used in a Masonic cipher” = 246
51. “*Skelton* was secret Masonic code” = 246
52. “*Skelton:* code of the Master Mason” = 246
53. “*Skelton*’s cipher hides a Masonic code” = 246
54. “*Skelton*’s cypher hid Masonic code” = 246
55. “*Skelton*’s gematria is a Masonic code” = 246
56. “Solomon’s code word was secret” = 246

57. "Solomon's numeral is the number" = 246
58. "Solomon's secret cipher is found" = 246
59. "Temple of King Solomon hid a message" = 246
60. "Temple of King Solomon hid numeral" = 246
61. "Temple of Solomon hid the code number" = 246
62. "The answer is: a hidden Masonic code" = 246
63. "*The Candle*: Masonic symbol of light" = 246
64. "*The Chamber of Reflection* hid Masonic code" = 246
65. **"The cipher of Hiram Abiff hid Masonic codes" = 246**
66. "*The Code* is the Freemasons' secret" = 246
67. "*The code of Hiram Abiff:* Freemason's hidden code" = 246
68. "*The Code of Solomon*: secret Masonic code" = 246
69. "*The Craft* are a secret brotherhood" = 246
70. "The *Eye of Providence*: Masonic sign" = 246
71. **"The Freemason *are* the ruling elite" = 246**
72. "The Freemasons hid secrets in a code" = 246
73. "The Freemasons hid this numeral" = 246
74. **"The Freemasons use the murder code" = 246**
75. "The Freemasons use this number" = 246
76. "The Freemasons' name is *The Craft*" = 246
77. "The Freemasons' plan is hidden in code" = 246
78. "The Freemasons' plans hidden as code" = 246
79. **"The Golden Key:** Freemason's hidden code" = 246
80. "**The Golden Key**: name of Masonic cipher" = 246
81. "**The Golden Key**: Solomon's code is a clue" = 246
82. "*The Great Architect* hid *The Book of Life*" = 246
83. "The *Great Architect* name is *Jehovah*" = 246
84. "*The Great Architect*'s code be secret" = 246
85. "The Key of Solomon was in cipher" = 246
86. "The Masonic brotherhood secret code" = 246
87. "The Masonic secrets are hidden in a code" = 246
88. "The Master Mason was *Hiram Abiff*" = 246
89. "*The mirror* is a Masonic symbol" = 246
90. "The murderer of *Hiram Abiff* called *Jubelum*" = 246
91. "The obelisk was a Masonic symbol" = 246
92. "The secret code is the *Freemasons'*" = 246
93. "The secret code *The Brotherhood* use" = 246
94. "The speculum is Masonic symbol" = 246
95. "The three ruffians killed *Hiram Abiff*" = 246
96. "The twin pillars: *Boaz and Joachim*" = 245
97. "*This* is secret code of Freemasons" = 246
98. "*This* was *The Craft*'s code number" = 246
99. "*This* was the secret Masonic code" = 246

100. "Used *Skelton* in a Masonic cypher" = 246
101. "Ye understand Freemason's codes" = 246
102. "You discovered a secret society" = 246
103. "You discovered the Freemasons' code" = 246
104. "You found a cipher of the Freemasons" = 246
105. "You found King Solomon's code number" = 246
106. "You found number of Solomon's key" = 246
107. "You found secret Masonic ciphers" = 246
108. "You found secret number of *Hiram Abiff*" = 246
109. "You found Solomon's secret key" = 246
110. "You have discovered a Masonic cipher" = 246
111. "You have found the number of *Hiram Abiff*" = 246
112. "You have King Solomon's code number" = 246
113. "You have Solomon's secret key" = 246
114. "You know cipher of Freemason's code" = 246
115. "You know of Freemason's numeral" = 246
116. "You understand the Freemason code" = 246

Reversed solutions:

- 246 = "a number in King Solomon's Temple"
- 246 = "a secret code number for Freemasons"
- 246 = "a secret number the Craft are hiding"
- 246 = "code number in the Temple of Solomon"
- 246 = "code number of the Masonic brotherhood"
- 246 = "code numeral Masonic brotherhood used"
- 246 = "is a code number of *The Great Architect*"
- 246 = "is secret number of a Masonic cipher"
- 246 = "is secret numeral of Freemasons"
- 246 = "is the code number of the Freemasons"
- 246 = "is the Master Mason's numeral" Master Mason, *Hiram Abiff*
- 246 = "is the Master Mason's secret"
- 246 = "is the secret numeral *Hiram Abiff hid*"
- 246 = "number in the secret code of Solomon"
- 246 = "secret number of Freemasons' code"
- 246 = "the great secret of *Hiram Abiff*"
- 246 = "the number is Solomon's numeral"
- 246 = "the number is Solomon's secret"
- 246 = "the numeral of the Master Mason
- 246 = "the secret key to Solomon's code"
- 246 = "the secret number: key of *Hiram Abiff*"
- 246 = "the secret of the master mason"
- 246 = "was Freemason's secret number"
- 246 = "was the secret Masonic numeral"

17. The Ruling Elite and National Secrets

The conjecture is that *Skelton*'s cipher has been used secretly by the ruling class/elite for many years. Applying *Skelton* in the context of the Freemasons and the 'ruling elite' we have seen the resonance equation: "The Freemasons" = "the ruling elite" = 122.

In addition, we find the Master Code solution: "The Freemasons *are* the ruling elite" = 246

Applying the Master Code in the context of the 'ruling class/elite':

1. "A secret cipher ruling class used" = 246
2. "A secret code for national secrets" = 246
3. "Codes hid the secrets of the Nation" = 246
4. "Hidden code is secret of ruling class" = 246
5. "National secrets hidden by the code" = 246
6. "Ruling class hide secret numeral" = 246
7. "Ruling class know of the number" = 246
8. "Ruling class know the cipher code" = 246
9. "Ruling class know the numeral" = 246
10. "Ruling class know the secret" = 246
11. "Ruling class used a secret cipher" = 246
12. "Ruling elite uses a secret cipher" = 246
13. "Secret code of ruling class is hidden" = 246
14. "Secret codes of national secrets" = 246
15. "Secrets of the Nation hide in the code" = 246
16. "*Skelton:* national security code" = 246
17. "*The giant book* of National Secrets" = 246
18. "The Nation's secrets are in codes" = 246
19. "The Nation's secrets hidden as a code" = 246
20. "The Nation's secrets hide as codes" = 246
21. "The Nation's secrets hiding in code" = 246
22. "The ruling class hides a secret code" = 246
23. "The ruling class know this code" = 246
24. "The ruling class used this as a code" = 246
25. "The ruling classes hid a secret code" = 246
26. "The ruling elite knew *Skelton*" = 246
27. "The ruling elites used *Skelton*" = 246
28. "These are codes of the ruling class" = 246
29. "*We the ruling class* use this code" = 246
30. "*We the ruling elite* use *Skelton*" = 246
31. "*We the ruling elite* use the cipher" = 246
32. "Ye found the code of the ruling class" = 246
33. "You discovered code ruling class hid" = 246
34. "You discovered code ruling elite used" = 246

Reverse solutions:

- 246 = "a cipher number of the ruling class"
- 246 = "cypher number ruling class used"
- 246 = "is cipher number ruling class used"
- 246 = "is secret numeral of ruling elite"
- 246 = "is the code number of the ruling elite"
- 246 = "ruling elite's secret code numeral"

18. Chiswick House Garden: William Kent & the Master Code key

Temple, pool and obelisk are Masonic symbols

(Image: Wikipedia commons)

The gardens at Chiswick House in London were designed by William Kent (1729), the designer of Newton's tomb monument. Certain features in the gardens are Masonic symbols; of special note in that context are the Ionic temple, pool and obelisk. The pool's diameter (~ 940 inches, ~ 78.3 ft) measured using *Google Earth*, gives a calculated circumference (c = πd) very close to 246 ft. A second obelisk is located exactly 246 yards from the obelisk in the pool, again measured with *Google Earth*. It appears that Kent deliberately arranged precise measurements in yards - *separation of the obelisks* - and in feet - *circumference of the pool* - to have the same numeric value as the Master Code key.

In that context, we note the Master Code solution:

"Make measurements to find number" = 246

Measurements made at locations identified by the Master Code are demonstrations that the 'magic' gematria number - the key 246 - has been left at specific places to show that it exists *independently* of the solver; in other words, to show that the key is *not* a figment of the solver's imagination. Together with Newton's tomb monument, the garden-features at Chiswick House lend strong support to the conjecture that the architect William Kent, a senior Freemason, used *Skelton's* cipher and the Master Code in some of his designs.

Applying the Master Code in the context of Chiswick House Garden etc:

1. "A number *hides* as pool's circumference" = 246
2. "Chiswick Garden was Kent design" = 246
3. "Chiswick Garden's code-puzzles" = 246
4. "Circumference of pool is the code number" = 246
5. "Clue is: a Masonic code number Chiswick hid" = 246
6. "Clue is: Chiswick *hid* a Masonic code number" = 246
7. "Clue is: Masonic code number in Chiswick" = 246
8. "Clue is: obelisk separation in yards" = 246
9. "Codes *hid* by Kent in Chiswick Garden" = 246
10. "Garden at Chiswick is Kent design" = 246
11. "Garden of Chiswick is design of Kent" = 246
12. "*Hid* codes at the garden at Chiswick House" = 246
13. "*Hid* puzzles in Chiswick Garden" = 246
14. "I *hid* Chiswick Garden's code puzzle" = 246
15. "Kent's code at Chiswick House Garden" = 246
16. "Kent's code be in Chiswick House Garden" = 246
17. "Key to the code hid in Chiswick Garden" = 246
18. "Look for numeral Chiswick Garden *hid*" = 246
19. "Masonic design *hid* in garden at Chiswick" = 246
20. "Masonic design *hides* in Chiswick Garden" = 246
21. "Masonic obelisk, pool and temple *hid* a code" = 246
22. "Obelisk in the pool is a Masonic sign" = 246
23. "Pool's circumference is *hidden* number" = 246
24. "The garden at Chiswick House *hides* codes" = 246
25. "The obelisk was a Masonic symbol" = 246
26. "The obelisks are 246 yards apart" = 246
27. "You found a number Chiswick Garden *hid*" = 246
28. "You found number in Chiswick Garden" = 246

Reversed solutions:

- 246 = "a number *hidden* by Kent at Chiswick"
- 246 = "a secret Masonic code number in Chiswick"
- 246 = "circumference of pool at Chiswick Garden"
- 246 = "is a Masonic code number clue Chiswick *hid"*
- 246 = "is distance from obelisk to obelisk"
- 246 = "is Masonic code number clue in Chiswick"
- 246 = "is number *hid* as pool's circumference"
- 246 = "is numeral *hidden* in Chiswick Garden"
- 246 = "number *hid* as circumference of the pool"
- 246 = "number *hid* by Kent in Chiswick Garden"
- 246 = "number *hidden* at pool as circumference"
- 246 = "number you found in Chiswick Garden"
- 246 = "numeral *hidden* as circumference of pool"
- 246 = "pool's circumference measured in feet"
- 246 = "the secret number Chiswick *hides*"
- 246 = "the secret number *hid* at Chiswick"

William Kent (1685-1748)

Originally from Bridlington on the Yorkshire coast, William Kent was an eminent architect and polymath professionally active c 1718 - 1748. As mentioned previously, he was a senior Freemason and designed the gardens at Chiswick House (1729) and Newton's tomb-monument in Westminster Abbey (1731); he also designed the coded *Shakespeare* statue at Wilton House (1743). Master Code solutions suggest it is very likely William Kent also helped with the design of the ornamental west-gate at *All Souls* College, Oxford.

We recall solutions relating to the design of Chiswick House gardens

1. "Chiswick garden was Kent design" = 246
2. "Code in Chiswick's Garden *hid* by Kent" = 246
3. "Garden at Chiswick is Kent design" = 246
4. "Kent be Chiswick garden's designer" = 246
5. "Kent's code at Chiswick House Garden" = 246
6. "Kent's code be in Chiswick House Garden" = 246

And:

1. "You discovered codes hidden by Kent" = 246
2. "You found numeral of Kent's cipher" = 246
3. "You found secret of Kent's cipher" = 246
4. "You solved codes William Kent hid" = 246
5. "You solved secret code Kent hides" = 246

19. William Kent (1685-1748) *and* Thomas Anson (1695-1773)

In light of the foregoing, it makes sense to look for Master Code solutions linking Thomas Anson and William Kent as they were of the same generation. It's plausible that a partnership developed either through membership of the Freemasons or through a shared interest in architecture and The Occult. If they were inclined so to do, Anson and Kent would have found code solutions such as the following that 'confirm' their professional association and their use of *Skelton*.

1. "A secret code *hidden* by Anson and Kent" = 246
2. "Anson and Kent congratulate you" = 246
3. "Anson and Kent found the secret code" = 246
4. "Anson and Kent *hid* a secret occult code" = 246
5. "Anson and Kent left a code puzzle" = 246
6. "Anson and Kent left code cypher hid" = 246
7. "Anson and Kent spoke to you in a code" = 246
8. "Anson and Kent use a secret cipher" = 246
9. "Anson and Kent use the same cipher" = 246
10. "Anson and Kent's giant secret code" = 246
11. "Anson and Kent's Master Cipher" = 246
12. "Anson and Kent's secret code is huge" = 246
13. "Believe ciphers by Anson and Kent" = 246
14. "Believe in ciphers of Anson and Kent" = 246
15. "Believe the cipher Anson and Kent *hid*" = 246
16. "Code-test left by Anson and Kent" = 246
17. "Codes *hid* secrets of Anson and Kent" = 246
18. "Few find Anson and Kent's numeral" = 246
19. "Few find Anson and Kent's secret" = 246
20. "Messages of Anson and Kent *hide* in a code" = 246
21. "Proof Anson and Kent knew the code" = 246

22. "Proof Anson and Kent used the codes" = 246
23. "*The Code* is a secret of Anson and Kent" = 246
24. "The huge secret code of Anson and Kent" = 246
25. "*The Master Code:* a code of Anson and Kent" = 246
26. "*This* is Anson and Kent's cipher" = 246
27. "Ye discovered Anson and Kent's code" = 246
28. "Ye found the codes Anson and Kent *hide*" = 246
29. "You discovered a code of Anson and Kent" = 246
30. "You found the codes of Anson and Kent" = 246

Reverse solutions:

- 246 = "key to ciphers of Anson and Kent"
- 246 = "secret code number of Anson and Kent"
- 246 = "was cipher key of Anson and Kent"

20. The West Gate at *All Souls College*, Oxford

The most intellectually rarefied of Oxbridge colleges, *All Souls* is graduate-only and has acquired a reputation as one of the world's most elite academic institutions. Few candidates for fellowship - alumni of the university by invitation - pass what is claimed to be the hardest of entrance exams. One suspects that nothing is quite what it seems in this citadel of cerebral brilliance and that subtle complexity is concealed by a façade of deceptive simplicity. Such is the mystique of *All Souls* that the ornamental west gate naturally attracts attention. Installed in 1737, the structure presents the observer with several points of interest; for example, the pair of *dissimilar* gilded faces either side of the gate that probably represent real people - if so, who?

Applying the Master Code in that context:

1. "Faces adjacent to *All Souls* gate *hide* a clue" = 246
2. "Faces adjacent to the gate of *All Souls*" = 246
3. "Faces are either side of *All Souls* gate" = 246
4. "Faces either side of gate at *All Souls*" = 246
5. "Faces on *All Souls* gate found by you" = 246
6. "Faces on the gate at *All Souls* are a clue" = 246
7. "Find *two* faces on gate at *All Souls*" = 246
8. "Go to *All Souls* look for faces on a gate" = 246
9. "Go to *All Souls* look for gate's faces" = 246
10. "*Our* faces be either side *All Souls* gate" = 246
11. "Pair of faces at *All Souls* gate are a clue" = 246
12. "The faces at *All Souls* gate are clues" = 246
13. "The faces on *All Souls* gate are a sign" = 246
14. "You found *our* faces on *All Souls* gate" = 246
15. "You noticed faces on gate of *All Souls*" = 246

The solutions imply that *Skelton's* cipher and the Master Code have been used in the design of *All Souls* gate and that the faces are significant clues. In view of the gate's installation date (1737) the conjecture is that the faces probably represent the men who helped design it, much as Thomas Anson's face appears on Pan's shrine-folly at Shugborough.

Do the faces represent Anson and Kent?

Whereas Thomas Anson was an amateur architect, William Kent was a professional. Although differing in age by ten-years, they were of the same 'cultural' generation. It is clear from the foregoing that both knew *Skelton*'s cipher and the Master Code and so it's plausible that they contributed in some way to the design of *All Souls* west gate - especially as both were professionally active when the gate was installed. **The conjecture is tested by applying the Master Code in the context of Anson, Kent and *All Souls* gate:**

1. "A code by Kent *hiding* in *All Souls* gate" = 246
2. "A code *hidden* by Kent at *All Souls* gate" = 246
3. "A face on *All Souls* gate was Anson's" = 246
4. "A visage at *All Souls* gate is Kent" = 246
5. "*All Souls College* gate *hid* code by Kent" = 246
6. "*All Souls* gate *hid* Kent's numeral" = 246
7. "*All Souls* gate *hid* Kent's secret" = 246
8. "*All Souls* gate design is by Kent" = 246
9. "*All Souls* gate: William Kent's code" = 246
10. "Anson and Kent are the faces by a gate" = 246
11. "Anson and Kent *hid* code numeral on gate" = 246
12. "Anson and Kent *hid* secret code on gate" = 246
13. "Anson and Kent in *All Souls College*" = 246
14. "Anson and Kent on gate of *All Souls*" = 246
15. "Anson is *All Souls* gate's left face" = 246
16. "Anson's face in *All Souls* gate is a clue" = 246
17. "Anson's face is clue on *All Souls* gate" = 246
18. "Clue is: Anson's face on *All Souls* gate" = 246
19. "Code by Kent *hides* at *All Souls* gate" = 246
20. "Code by Kent *hiding* on *All Souls* gate" = 246
21. "Face of Anson on gate of *All Souls* College" = 246
22. "Face of Kent *hidden* on a gate at *All Souls*" = 246
23. "Face of Kent *hides* on gate at *All Souls*" = 246
24. "Face of Kent is *hidden* on *All Souls* gate" = 246
25. "Faces of Anson and Kent in *All Souls*" = 246
26. "Kent *hid* code clues on gate of *All Souls*" = 246
27. "Kent *hid* code on the gate at *All Souls*" = 246
28. "Kent's image *hidden* on *All Souls* gate" = 246
29. "Visage of Anson on gate of *All Souls*" = 246

The solutions suggest that Thomas Anson and William Kent were involved with the design of *All Souls* west gate – hence the pair of dissimilar faces. However, Nicholas Hawksmoor (1661-1736) was the chief architect of the new build at *All Souls*, including the west gate (1737). Like Kent and possibly Anson, Hawksmoor was a Freemason. According to code solutions, the cipher on *All Souls* gate is Masonic. It seems that Isaac Newton used *Skelton*'s cipher and the Master Code - it's plausible Hawksmoor met Newton in London and the latter introduced the former to *Skelton*'s occult cipher.

Applying the Master Code in that context:

1. "17 37 *All Souls College* gate's date" = 246* written 17, 37
2. "A cipher of Newton and Hawksmoor" = 246
3. "*All Souls College:* Hawksmoor's code" = 246
4. "*All Souls*: Hawksmoor is the clue" = 246
5. "*All Souls:* Hawksmoor's work" = 246
6. "Anson and Kent *hid* a code of Hawksmoor" = 246
7. "Anson, Hawksmoor and Kent's clue" = 246
8. "Code by Anson, Hawksmoor and Kent" = 246
9. "Code of Hawksmoor on *All Souls* gate" = 246
10. "Gate in *All Souls* by Hawksmoor" = 246
11. "Hawksmoor left code at *All Souls*" = 246
12. "Hawksmoor: a clue at *All Souls* gate:" = 246
13. "Hawksmoor's gate be at *All Souls*" = 246
14. "Hawksmoor's secret code test" = 246
15. "Newton and Hawksmoor *hide* the code" = 246
16. **"The gate commemorated Hawksmoor" = 246***

*The gate was installed the year *after* Hawksmoor's death.

Applying *Skelton*'s cipher to "*All Souls*" gives the resonance equation:

1. "*All Souls*" = "code clue in gate" = 79
2. "*All Souls*" = "gate *hid* a code clue" = 79
3. "*All Souls*" = "gate *hid* huge code" = 79
4. "*All Souls*" = "name of a college" = 79

Reverse equations:

1. "A code in gate at" = "*All Souls*" = 79
2. "Code on gate at" = "*All Souls*" = 79

Applying *Skelton* to "All Souls College" we find the resonance equations:

- "*All Souls College*" = "gate *hid* a secret code" = 119
- "Secret codes on the gate of" = "*All Souls College Oxford*" = 177

Applying *Skelton* to "*All Souls* gate" gives the resonance equations:

1. "*All Souls* gate" = "*hid* an unbreakable code" = 108
2. "*All Souls* gate" = "*Skelton*'s code" = 108
3. "*All Souls* gate" = "the unbreakable code" = 108

And:

1. "Gate at *All Souls*" = "*hides* an unbreakable code" = 128
2. "I *hid* an unbreakable code on" = "gate at *All Souls*" = 128

Preliminary hints at the use of *Skelton* in the context of the west gate at *All Souls*, the same cipher used for the university crest and motto. Solutions show that the name of the college is encoded as emblems on the gate. **Applying *Skelton* to the gate's emblems:**

1. "*Fleur de lis*" = "*All Souls*" = 79
2. "Gilded lilies" = "*All Souls*" = 79
3. "The shell" = "*All Souls*" = 79

Applying the Master Code in the context of the gate's emblems:

1. "*All Souls*' name *encoded* as gate emblems" = 246
2. "*All Souls'* name *hid* as emblems on gate" = 246
3. "*All Souls*' name *hides* in gate emblems" = 246
4. "Each emblem on gate *hiding All Souls'* name" = 246
5. "Name of *All Souls hid* by gate emblems" = 246

It appears that emblems on the gate encode the college name using *Skelton*'s cipher.

The heraldic shield on *All Souls* gate

Applying *Skelton* in the context of the gate's heraldic shield, we find the resonance equation:

"The heraldic code hidden" = "on *All Souls*' gate" = 125

The full heraldic description equates to 246 using *Skelton*'s cipher which is how the Master Code key is hidden on the shield.

Applying the Master Code to *All Souls* coat of arms:

1. *"A chevron 3 cinquefoils gules field or"* = 246 full heraldic description of the shield
2. "A code clue in blazon at *All Souls College*" = 246
3. "A code *hid* as crest at *All Souls College*" = 246
4. "A code *hides* as *All Souls College* crest" = 246
5. "A code *hiding* in *All Souls College* crest" = 246
6. "A code is in blazon at *All Souls College*" = 246
7. "A code was in *All Souls College* blazon" = 246
8. "A heraldic code is hidden at *All Souls* gate" = 246
9. "A heraldic code is hiding in *All Souls* gate" = 246
10. *"All Souls College* arms *hide* a secret" = 246
11. *"All Souls* heraldic shield *hiding* code clue" = 246
12. *"All Souls* heraldic shield is *hiding* code" = 246
13. *"All Souls* shield is hiding a secret" = 246
14. "Blazon at *All Souls College hiding* code" = 246
15. *"Chevron 3 cinquefoils gules* hides code" = 246
16. *"Chevron and 3 cinquefoils gules hide* code" = 246
17. "Clue is: *All Souls College* coat of arms" = 246
18. "Clues *hide* in coat of arms of *All Souls*" = 246
19. "Coat of arms of *All Souls* is *hiding* code" = 246
20. "Code clue is in *All Souls College* blazon" = 246
21. "Code hid as: *A chevron 3 cinquefoils gules*" = 246
22. "Crest at *All Souls College hides* code" = 246
23. "Crest on *All Souls College hiding* code" = 246
24. "Gate at *All Souls* hiding heraldic codes" = 246
25. "Heraldic code is *hiding* on *All Souls* gate" = 246
26. "Heraldic shield at *All Souls* hiding a code" = 246
27. "Hid code as: *A chevron 3 cinquefoils gules*" = 246* see below
28. "I hid code in: *A chevron 3 cinquefoils gules*" = 246*
29. "The answer is: secret heraldic code" = 246
30. "The secret clue of *All Souls* shield" = 246

***It seems "*A chevron 3 cinquefoils gules*" is code. In that context, we find the resonance equations:**

1. *"A chevron 3 cinquefoils gules"* = "*hiding* a secret at *All Souls*" = 199
2. *"A chevron 3 cinquefoils gules"* = "secret code on *All Souls* gate" = 199
3. *"A chevron 3 cinquefoils gules"* = "you found code of Anson and Kent" = 199
4. *"A chevron 3 cinquefoils gules"* = "you found our cipher-message" = 199
5. *"A chevron 3 cinquefoils gules"* = "you found secret code-message" = 199
6. *"A chevron 3 cinquefoils gules"* = "you have found the big secret" = 199

And, we recall *"A chevron 3 cinquefoils gules field or"* encodes the number 246.

Applying the Master Code in the context of *All Souls College* and the ornamental west gate gives rise to a large set of solutions:

1. "A cipher at *All Souls College* Oxford" = 246
2. "A cipher hidden in the gate of *All Souls*" = 246
3. "A clue hid at west gate at *All Souls*" = 246
4. "A clue hiding on *All Souls* west gate" = 246
5. "A clue is *All Souls* gate heraldic shield" = 246
6. "A clue is *fleur de lis* in *All Souls* gate" = 246
7. "A clue to a code is hiding at *All Souls* gate" = 246
8. "A code hides at *All Souls College* Oxford" = 246
9. "A code hiding in *All Souls College* crest" = 246
10. "A code in decorations at *All Souls* gate" = 246
11. "A code on gate at *All Souls* is unbreakable" = 246
12. "A gate at *All Souls College* hid a numeral" = 246
13. "A gate at *All Souls College* hid a secret" = 246
14. "A gate at *All Souls College* hid heraldic code" = 246
15. "A gate at *All Souls College* is ornate" = 246
16. "A gilded shell on the gate of *All Souls*" = 246
17. "A proof of *Skelton* code at *All Souls*" = 246
18. "A puzzle be hidden in *All Souls* gate" = 246
19. "A puzzle hidden at *All Souls* gate" = 246
20. "A puzzle hiding in *All Souls* gate" = 246
21. "A secret clue hides at *All Souls* gate" = 246
22. "A secret clue in the gate of *All Souls*" = 246
23. "A secret code hides on a gate of *All Souls*" = 246
24. "A secret code in the west gate is hid" = 246
25. "A secret is hiding on *All Souls* gate" = 246
26. "A secret riddle hid at *All Souls* gate" = 246
27. "*All Souls* at Oxford hid secret code" = 246
28. "*All Souls* cipher solved by you" = 246
29. "*All Souls College* at Oxford hides a code" = 246
30. "*All Souls College* gate hides the code clue" = 246
31. "*All Souls College Oxford* hiding codes" = 246
32. "*All Souls* gate hid a secret numeral" = 246
33. "*All Souls* gate hid same code as motto" = 246
34. "*All Souls* gate hides a secret riddle" = 246
35. "*All Souls* gate hides insoluble code clue" = 246
36. "*All Souls* gate hides Masonic cipher" = 246
37. "*All Souls* gate hides Master Code clue" = 246
38. "*All Souls* gate hides the secret code" = 246
39. "*All Souls* gate hiding code of *Skelton*" = 246
40. "*All Souls* gate hiding insoluble codes" = 246
41. "*All Souls* gate hiding the code test" = 246
42. "*All Souls* gate is insoluble cipher" = 246

43. "*All Souls* gate was hiding a clue to a code" = 246
44. "*All Souls* gate's code was unbreakable" = 246
45. "*All Souls* gate's codes are insoluble" = 246
46. "*All Souls* gate's scrolls hiding" = 246
47. "*All Souls* heaven's gate is hiding a code" = 246
48. "*All Souls* hid the Masonic cypher" = 246
49. "*All Souls* hides the Master Code clue" = 246
50. "*All Souls* is proof of *Skelton* code" = 246
51. "*All Souls* name encoded as gate emblems" = 246
52. "*All Souls*, Oxford hides secret code" = 246
53. "*All Souls* west-gate hid a numeral" = 246
54. "*All Souls* west-gate hid a secret" = 246
55. "*All Souls* west-gate hides the code" = 246
56. "*All Souls* west-gate hiding clues" = 246
57. "*All Souls* west-gate hiding *our* code" = 246
58. "Break code clue at *All Souls* and open gate" = 246
59. "Break code on gate to enter *All Souls*" = 246
60. "Cipher hidden on the gate of *All Souls*" = 246
61. "Cipher hides in the gate of *All Souls*" = 246
62. "Ciphers hide in the gate of *All Souls*" = 246
63. "Clue hid by ornate gate at *All Souls*" = 246
64. "Clue hidden on ornate gate of *All Souls*" = 246
65. "Clue is at ornate gate at *All Souls*" = 246
66. "Clue is *gilded lilies* on *All Souls* gate" = 246
67. "Clues found on gate of *All Souls College*" = 246
68. "Clues to code found at *All Souls College*" = 246
69. "Code *All Souls* gate hides is insoluble" = 246
70. "Code clues are on the gate at *All Souls*" = 246
71. "Code hid at *All Souls* gate is insoluble" = 246
72. "Code hid at *All Souls* solved by you" = 246
73. "Code hid secrets at *All Souls College*" = 246
74. "Code hidden at *All Souls* is unbreakable" = 246
75. "Code hiding in *All Souls* is unbreakable" = 246
76. "Code in ornamental gate in *All Souls*" = 246
77. "Code in the crest of *All Souls College*" = 246
78. "Code is hiding on the gate at *All Souls*" = 246
79. "Code is in *All Souls* gate decorations" = 246
80. "Code number hidden at gate at *All Souls*" = 246
81. "Code number is hidden as *All Souls* gate" = 246
82. "Code on gate of *All Souls College* Oxford" = 246
83. "Code test was set in *All Souls*" = 246
84. "Code-cypher in *All Souls College* gate" = 246
85. "Count *All Souls College* gate curls" = 246
86. "Count the gate's scrolls and find" = 246
87. "Crack code gate hid to enter *All Souls*" = 246

88. “Curlicues at *All Souls* gate number” = 246
89. “Curls on gate in *All Souls* number” = 246
90. “Cypher hiding *at All Souls College*” = 246
91. “Decorations on *All Souls* gate are code” = 246
92. “Emblems in *All Souls* gate hid cipher” = 246
93. “Few find a secret at *All Souls* gate” = 246
94. “Few find number hid in *All Souls* gate” = 246
95. “Few notice a cipher *All Souls* gate hid” = 246
96. “Few notice the cipher in *All Souls*” = 246
97. “Few solve the code of *All Souls* gate” = 246
98. “*Fleur de lis* is a clue in *All Souls* gate” = 246
99. “Flowers in *All Souls* gate are a clue” = 246
100. “Freemasons hid code on *All Souls* gate” = 246
101. “Freemasons’ code hid on *All Souls* gate” = 246
102. “Gate at *All Souls College* at Oxford” = 246
103. “Gate at *All Souls College* hid a heraldic code” = 246
104. “Gate at *All Souls* hid the code numeral” = 246
105. “Gate at *All Souls* hides a numeral clue” = 246
106. “Gate at *All Souls* hides a secret clue” = 246
107. “Gate at *All Souls* hiding the number” = 246
108. “Gate at *All Souls* is a code-puzzle” = 246
109. “Gate at *All Souls* is hiding a test” = 246
110. “Gate in *All Souls* has 246 spirals” = 246
111. “Gate in *All Souls* hiding *our* test” = 246
112. “Gate of *All Souls* hiding the numeral” = 246
113. “Gate of heaven is at *All Souls College*” = 246
114. “*Gilded faces* on gate at *All Souls College*” = 246
115. “Gilded shell on *All Souls College* gate” = 246
116. “Go to *All Souls:* look for code gate hides” = 246
117. “Go to *All Souls:* look for code hid at gate” = 246
118. “Go to *All Souls:* look for codes on gate” = 246
119. “Go to *All Souls:* find numeral on gate” = 246
120. “Go to *All Souls* gate: look for a hidden code” = 246
121. “Go to *All Souls* gate: look for cipher” = 246
122. “Heaven’s gate code at *All Souls College*” = 246
123. “Heraldic code hiding on a gate at *All Souls*” = 246
124. “Heraldic code in gate at *All Souls College*” = 246
125. “Hid a clue at west gate at *All Souls*” = 246
126. “Hid a code at *All Souls College* at Oxford” = 246
127. “Hid a code at the gate at *All Souls College*” = 246
128. “Hid a code in *All Souls* ornamental gate” = 246
129. “Hid *All Souls* name as emblems on gate” = 246
130. “Hid code clue at *All Souls College Oxford*” = 246
131. “Hid code number as *All Souls College* gate” = 246
132. “Hid code on *All Souls* ornamental gate” = 246

133. "Hid occult numeral on *All Souls* gate" = 246
134. "Hid secret code at *All Souls,* Oxford" = 246
135. "Hid secret code clue on the west gate" = 246
136. "Hid secret codes at *All Souls College*" = 246
137. "Hid the code at *All Souls* west gate" = 246
138. "Hid the code clue at *All Souls College* gate" = 246
139. "Hid the Master Code clue at *All Souls*" = 246
140. "Hid the secret code at *All Souls* gate" = 246
141. "Hide the key to *All Souls* gate as a code" = 246 a code instruction
142. "Hide the numeral at *All Souls College*" = 246
143. "Hide the secret at *All Souls College*" = 246
144. "How many curlicues on the gate?" = 246
145. "I hid a clue on west gate at *All Souls*" = 246
146. "I hid a Masonic cipher on *All Souls* gate" = 246
147. "I hid clues at *All Souls* west gate" = 246
148. "I hid the code clue on *All Souls College* gate" = 246
149. "I hid the code test at *All Souls* gate" = 246
150. "I hid the key to *All Souls* gate as code" = 246
151. "I hid the secret code on *All Souls* gate" = 246
152. "Impossible code is in *All Souls* gate" = 246
153. "Impossible code on gate at *All Souls*" = 246
154. "Inspect *All Souls* gate: find clues" = 246
155. **"Key to the code is in *All Souls* gate" = 246**
156. **"Key to the code on gate at All Souls" = 246**
157. "Lilies and leaves on *All Souls* gate" = 246
158. "Lilies, leaves and shell *hid* a code on gate" = 246
159. "Lilies, leaves and shell *hid* gate's code" = 246
160. "Lilies, leaves, shell and two faces" = 246
161. "Look for a code *hidden* in *All Souls* gate" = 246
162. "Look for a cypher clue at *All Souls*" = 246
163. "Look for *All Souls* gate scrolls" = 246
164. "Look for ciphers in *All Souls* gate" = 246
165. "Look for code at the gate at *All Souls*" = 246
166. "Look for code *hidden* on *All Souls* gate" = 246
167. "Masonic cipher *hid* at *All Souls* gate" = 246
168. "Master Code on the gate of *All Souls*" = 246
169. "Nobody cracked codes in *All Souls* gate" = 246
170. "Nobody solves *All Souls* gate code" = 246
171. "Open the gate of *All Souls* with code" = 246
172. "Ornamental gate in *All Souls hid* a code" = 246
173. "Ornamental gate of *All Souls hides*" = 246
174. "Ornamental gate of *All Souls* is a code" = 246
175. "Ornate gate of *All Souls* is hiding code" = 246
176. "Puzzle clues in *All Souls* gate" = 246
177. "Puzzle hides at *All Souls* gate" = 246

178. “Puzzle hiding on *All Souls* gate” = 246
179. “Puzzles hide at *All Souls* gate” = 246
180. “Secret cipher clue is in *All Souls*” = 246
181. “Secret cipher hiding at *All Souls*” = 246
182. “Secret clue on the gate of *All Souls*” = 246
183. “Secret code *hid* at *All Souls*, Oxford” = 246
184. “Secret code unlocks *All Souls* gate” = 246
185. “Secret in *All Souls* west gate” = 246
186. “Secret number in gate of *All Souls*” = 246
187. “Secret numeral in *All Souls* gate” = 246
188. “Secret on gate at *All Souls College*” = 246
189. “Set huge test as code in *All Souls*” = 246
190. “*Skelton* is code on gate of *All Souls*” = 246
191. “Solve *our* riddles to enter gate” = 246
192. “Solve the code in the gate and open it” = 246
193. “Study gate at *All Souls* for clue” = 246
194. “The cipher was at *All Souls* gate” = 246
195. “The clue hiding on *All Souls* gate is 246” = 246
196. “The code *All Souls* gate hid is intended” = 246
197. “The code at *All Souls College* gate is hid” = 246
198. “The code test is on *All Souls* gate” = 246
199. “The code’s test at *All Souls* gate” = 246
200. “The code was hiding on *All Souls* gate” = 246
201. “The crest of *All Souls College* hid a code” = 246
202. “The emblems at *All Souls* gate hide code” = 246
203. “The emblems in *All Souls* gate are a code” = 246
204. “The emblems on *All Souls* gate are code” = 246
205. “The gate at *All Souls College* hides a code” = 246
206. “The gate at *All Souls* hid code numeral” = 246
207. “The gate at *All Souls* hid secret code” = 246
208. “The gate at *All Souls* is a Masonic code” = 246
209. “The Golden Key hid on *All Souls* gate” = 246
210. “The key to the code is in *All Souls*” = 246
211. “The Master Code in *All Souls* College” = 246
212. “The Master Code on gate of *All Souls*” = 246
213. “The secret is in *All Souls College*” = 246
214. “The test hidden on *All Souls* gate” = 246
215. “The test hides in *All Souls* gate” = 246
216. “The test is set at *All Souls*” = 246
217. “There is a code *hiding* on *All Souls* gate” = 246
218. “*Two Four Six* on *All Souls* gate” = 246
219. “Use this code and open *All Souls* gate” = 246
220. “West gate at *All Souls* hides a clue” = 246
221. “Ye decrypted a code clue in *All Souls*” = 246
222. “Ye found secret code *All Souls* hides” = 246

223. “Ye found secret code hid at *All Souls*” = 246
224. “Ye have discovered *All Souls* codes” = 246
225. “Ye have found code *All Souls* gate hides” = 246
226. “Ye have found code hid at *All Souls* gate” = 246
227. “Ye have found codes on *All Souls* gate” = 246
228. “Ye unlock *All Souls* gate with a code” = 246
229. “Ye unlocked *All Souls* gate using a code” = 246
230. “You cracked secret code at *All Souls*” = 246
231. “You deciphered *All Souls* secret code” = 246
232. “You deciphered code hid on *All Souls* gate” = 246
233. “You decrypted code hid in *All Souls*” = 246
234. “You examined the gate in *All Souls*” = 246
235. “You found code at *All Souls.* Well done” = 246
236. “You found code at *All Souls College* gate” = 246
237. “You found gate of heaven in *All Souls*” = 246
238. “You found numeral clue at *All Souls*” = 246
239. “You found secret clue at *All Souls*” = 246
240. “You found the code at *All Souls College*” = 246
241. “You got clue hidden at *All Souls* gate” = 246
242. “You got clue hiding in *All Souls* gate” = 246
243. “You got clues in gate at *All Souls*” = 246
244. “You have cracked code at *All Souls* gate” = 246
245. “You have cracked the code at *All Souls*” = 246
246. “You have deciphered *All Souls* gate-code” = 246
247. “You have found a code clue *hid* at *All Souls*” = 246
248. “You have found clue at *All Souls* gate” = 246
249. “You have solved *All Souls* gate-code” = 246
250. “You passed *All Souls’* tests” = 246
251. “You solved a code at *All Souls College*” = 246
252. “You solved *All Souls’* secret code” = 246
253. “You solved code hid on *All Souls* gate” = 246
254. “You unlock *All Souls* gate using code” = 246
255. “You unlock gate at *All Souls* by code” = 246

Reverse solutions:

- 246 = “a Masonic number hid on *All Souls* gate”
- 246 = “a numeral *All Souls* west gate *hid*”
- 246 = “is a numeral *All Souls College* gate *hid*”
- 246 = “is *hidden* on ornate gate of *All Souls*”
- 246 = “is number on the gate at *All Souls*”
- 246 = “numeral on gate at *All Souls College*”
- 246 = “on west gate at *All Souls College*”
- 246 = “scrolls on the gate of *All Souls*” the number of scrolls is 246?

21. A Strange Sea-shell Grotto at Margate in Kent

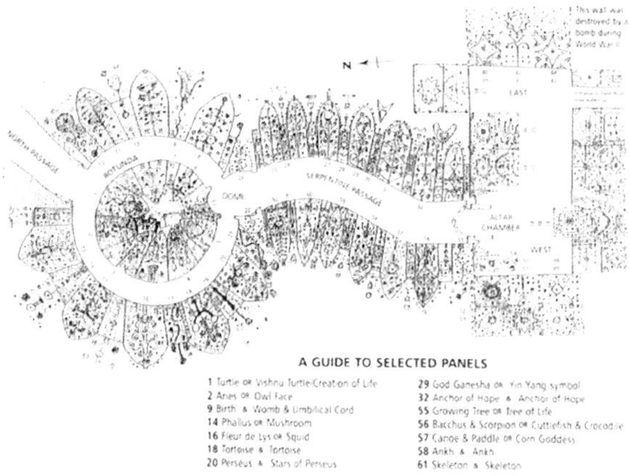

Discovered in 1835 by children at play, the mysterious 'sea-shell grotto' at Margate was opened to the public shortly afterwards. Consisting partly of a subterranean tunnel ~ 70 ft. long the entire wall and roof area, roughly 2000 sq. ft, is covered in an estimated 4.6 million shells some of which form patterns depicting a variety of mythical symbols and icons (see guide above). When, by whom and for what purpose the grotto was made has remained a mystery since its discovery...

A combination of Master Code solutions and design-style shows that the grotto, the gate at *All Souls* College, Shugborough's follies, Newton's tomb-monument and the Chiswick House Garden features are of the same era, c 1720-1750. Symbols and designs represented by shell patterns in the grotto are an eclectic mix of cultures and periods, reflecting a 'haphazard' approach to collecting associated with the early-mid C18 of which Thomas Anson's hoard at Shugborough was a prime example. That suggests the grotto is no more than about three hundred years old.

Being subterranean, the grotto was not excavated and decorated in sunlight and so construction might have taken place under the cover of darkness to minimise the chance of discovery. That might account for why *nobody* in Margate ***seems*** to have known anything about the structure when it was discovered. However, there is an alternative much darker reason for the townsfolks' silence. It is hard to believe that *nobody* living in Margate in 1835 knew anything about the grotto, especially as it's located in a hill near the town centre and was most probably constructed no more than about a hundred years earlier. Some of the older locals were probably aware of the grotto's existence and knew something about its function, remaining silent to protect themselves from opprobrium - 'guilt by association' - if they were to reveal its dark and shameful secrets.

The grotto's design is strongly suggestive of a pagan 'rite of passage', a journey from conception and birth through life to death and perhaps beyond. In that regard, the length of the tunnel - about 70 feet - might be significant as it equates numerically to the allotted Biblical lifespan, lending weight to the conjecture that the grotto represents the journey of life. Moreover, some of the shell designs are associated with sexual reproduction - womb & umbilical cord for example (9 in the guide) and phallus (14 in the guide) - added to which the structure consists of a tunnel leading into a womb-like space.

Many Master Code solutions indicate that the grotto was made for the purpose of worshipping Lucifer and that it was known as 'Lucifer's grotto'. In the seventeenth and eighteenth centuries, the coasts of Essex and Kent were known for witches. Some code solutions indicate that *Skelton*'s cipher and the Master Code were used by witches, so it's plausible that 'witches' or those with similar 'pagan' beliefs constructed the grotto; for example, the use of natural materials - sea-shells - accords with Wiccan beliefs. The grotto is near the coast, so shells would have been the natural choice of decorative material, especially as they are made by living organisms.

To test the conjecture that witches at Margate knew and used *Skelton*'s cipher, we apply the Master Code in that context:

1. "A coven of witches *hiding* at Margate" = 246
2. "A witches' grotto is at Margate" = 246
3. "Codes are Margate witches' secret" = 246
4. "Coven of witches is a clue in Margate" = 246
5. "Margate codes are witches secret" = 246
6. "Margate *hiding* witches secret code" = 246
7. "Masonic witches use secret codes" = 246
8. "Secret *hid* by witches of Margate" = 246
9. "*Skelton* is a *hidden* code witches use" = 246
10. "*Skelton* is cipher witches use" = 246
11. "The witches in Margate hid a number" = 246
12. "Witchcraft in Margate grotto" = 246
13. "Witchcraft's code of fertility" = 246
14. "Witches hide secrets in Margate" = 246
15. "Witches in Margate used Masonic code" = 246
16. "Witches of Margate use the cipher" = 246
17. "Witches use a code of the Freemasons" = 246
18. "Witches use secret Masonic codes" = 246
19. "Witches use *Skelton* cypher" = 246
20. "Witches' secret codes at Margate" = 246

Reverse solutions:

- 246 = "number *hid* by witches at Margate"
- 246 = "numeral *hid* by witches of Margate"

By applying the Master Code in the context of Margate's grotto and sea-shell designs we find a large set of solutions (For references to the grotto designs see guide).

1. "A code *hidden* at the grotto at Margate" = 246
2. "A code *hiding* in the grotto at Margate" = 246
3. "A code is in shell grotto in Margate" = 246
4. "A crocodile in the grotto at Margate" = 246 (56)
5. "A *fleur de lis* is in Margate grotto" = 246 (16)
6. "A grotto 70 feet in length" = 246
7. "A grotto at Margate in Kent is *hid*" = 246
8. "A grotto in Margate *hiding* a secret" = 246
9. "A hidden tomb in the Margate grotto" = 246
10. "A Masonic code is in sea-shell grotto" = 246
11. "A numeral is in Margate's grotto" = 246
12. "A phallus is in grotto of Margate" = 246 (14)
13. "A sea-shell grotto in Margate *hid* a code" = 246
14. "A secret grotto *hides* at Margate" = 246
15. "A secret is in Margate's grotto" = 246
16. "A shell grotto at Margate *hid* codes" = 246
17. "A skeleton is in Margate grotto" = 246 (61)
18. "Bacchus and a scorpion are at grotto" = 246 (56)
19. "Birth-life-death code be *hidden* at grotto" = 246
20. "Birth-life-death code *hiding* at grotto" = 246
21. "Buried grotto at Margate at Kent" = 246
22. "Cipher of a secret code *hidden* at Margate" = 246
23. "Cipher of secret code *hides* at Margate" = 246
24. "Clue is: Margate witches grotto" = 246
25. "Code *hides* at the grotto at Margate" = 246
26. "Code *hiding* in Margate shell grotto" = 246
27. "Code is *hidden* at the Margate grotto" = 246
28. "Code of *Skelton* in Margate grotto" = 246
29. "Codes *hide* at the grotto at Margate" = 246
30. "Codes in shell grotto at Margate" = 246
31. "Corn goddess on wall at grotto" = 246 (57)
32. "Creation is in Margate's grotto" = 246
33. "Cuttlefish on wall at grotto" = 246 (56)
34. "*Death Code hidden* in grotto at Margate" = 246
35. "*Death Code hiding* in grotto in Margate" = 246
36. "Deflowered virgins at grotto" = 246
37. "Dig-up the grotto *hidden* at Margate" = 246
38. "Dig-up the grotto *hiding* in Margate" = 246
39. "Excavate the grotto in Margate" = 246
40. "Find an anchor hid in Margate grotto" = 246 (32)
41. "Find buried grotto hiding at Margate" = 246

42. "Find Margate grotto's turtle" = 246 (1)
43. "Find sea-shell grotto at Margate" = 246
44. "Find the anchor in Margate grotto" = 246 (32)
45. "*Fleur de lis* at Margate's grotto" = 246 (16)
46. "*Fleur de lis* be in Margate's grotto" = 246 (16)
47. "Fuck girls in a grotto at Margate" = 246*
48. "Fuck many virgins at grotto" = 246*
49. "Fucked virgins hid at the grotto" = 246
50. "Go to the grotto hidden at Margate" = 246
51. "Go to the grotto hiding in Margate" = 246
52. "God Vishnu in Margate's grotto" = 246 (1)
53. "Great secret at Margate in Kent" = 246
54. "Grotto at Margate hides a secret" = 246
55. "Grotto at Margate is excavated" = 246
56. "Grotto at Margate made of shells" = 246
57. "Grotto be *buried* at Margate in Kent" = 246
58. "Grotto *hides* the fucked virgins" = 246
59. "Grotto in hill at Margate hides code" = 246
60. "Grotto is hiding fertility code" = 246**
61. "Grotto is hiding secret ritual" = 246**
62. "Grotto of Margate hid secret codes" = 246
63. "Grotto of Margate hiding phallus" = 246 (14)
64. "Grotto of sea shells *hides* the code" = 246
65. "Grotto was in Margate in Kent" = 246
66. "Grotto's fertility-rite code" = 246
67. "Grotto's ritual was secret" = 246
68. "Hid a code at Margate's shell grotto" = 246
69. "Hid a secret at grotto at Margate" = 246
70. "Hid code as shell grotto at Margate" = 246
71. "Hid code at grotto in hill at Margate" = 246
72. "Hid code at the grotto of sea shells" = 246
73. "Hid tortoise in Margate grotto" = 246 (1)
74. "Hid Vishnu in Margate's grotto" = 246 (1)
75. "Huge code in shell grotto in Margate" = 246
76. "I hid code in shell grotto at Margate" = 246
77. "Kent hid a great secret at Margate" = 246
78. "Look for a grotto hid in Margate" = 246
79. "Look for symbols hid in grotto" = 246
80. "Made the grotto from sea-shells" = 246
81. "Made the grotto of many shells" = 246
82. "Margate grotto fertility code" = 246
83. "Margate grotto hid a secret womb" = 246
84. "Margate grotto hid Masonic cipher" = 246
85. "Margate grotto hides secret clue" = 246
86. "Margate grotto hiding *fleur de lis*" = 246 (16)

87. “Margate grotto hiding secrets” = 246
88. “Margate grotto hiding skeleton” = 246 (61)
89. “Margate grotto hiding turtle” = 246 (1)
90. “Margate grotto hiding umbilical cord” = 246 (9)
91. “Margate grotto: look for the ankh” = 246 (58)
92. “Margate grotto: secret ritual” = 246
93. “Margate grotto symbols hid code” = 246
94. “Margate grotto was excavated” = 246
95. “Margate hiding the shell grotto” = 246
96. “Margate’s grotto hides code number” = 246
97. “Margate’s grotto hiding numeral” = 246
98. “Margate’s grotto hiding the ankh” = 246 (58)
99. “Margate’s shell grotto hides a code” = 246
100. “Masonic code hidden in Margate grotto” = 246
101. “Masonic codes at sea-shell grotto” = 246
102. “Our grotto is in a hill at Margate” = 246 grotto is located at Hill Road
103. “Our religion is phallic worship” = 246 phallus (14)
104. “Perseus be in grotto at Margate” = 246 (20)
105. “Rite of Margate grotto is sacred” = 246
106. “Ritual murders in the grotto” = 246
107. “Rituals at grotto are a secret” = 246
108. “Sea shell grotto *hid Skelton* code” = 246
109. “Sea shell grotto *hiding* Masonic code” = 246
110. “Sea-shells at grotto are *hidden* code” = 246
111. “Sea-shells in grotto are *hiding* code” = 246
112. “Secret grotto of Birth-Life-Death” = 246
113. “Secret womb in Margate grotto” = 246 (9)
114. “Shell grotto in Margate *hid* a huge code” = 246
115. “Shell grotto in Margate *hiding* code” = 246
116. “Shell grotto of Margate *hid* the code” = 246
117. “Shells in Margate grotto are code” = 246
118. “Sign of Birth-Life-Death at grotto” = 246
119. “Sign of Birth-Life-Death be in grotto” = 246
120. “Skeleton at Margate’s grotto” = 246 (61)
121. “Skeletons at Margate grotto” = 246 (61)
122. “Skeletons be in Margate grotto” = 246 (61)
123. “Stars of Perseus in grotto” = 246 (20)
124. “The grotto *hid* at Margate is found” = 246
125. “The grotto hides fucked virgins” = 246
126. “The grotto is made from shells” = 246
127. “The grotto Margate *hides* is found” = 246
128. “*The Tree of Life* in Margate grotto” = 246 (55)
129. “Umbilical cord be in Margate’s grotto” = 246 (9)
130. “Use *Skelton* for fertility code” = 246 “fertility code” = “secret ritual” = 117
131. “Use *Skelton* for secret ritual” = 246

132. "Use the grotto for human sacrifice" = 246
133. "Virgins deflowered at grotto" = 246
134. "We excavated a grotto in Margate" = 246
135. "We *fuck* the virgins in a grotto" = 246*
136. "We murder in grotto at Margate" = 246
137. "Womb was in grotto at Margate" = 246 (9)
138. "Ye discovered Margate grotto code" = 246
139. "Ye found a grotto *hiding* at Margate" = 246
140. "Yin Yang symbol at grotto" = 246 (29)
141. "You found Margate's hidden grotto" = 246
142. "You found the grotto code. Well done!" = 246
143. "You have found grotto at Margate" = 246

*The word 'fuck' was relatively common in eighteenth century texts; however, its occurrence in print declined very significantly in the nineteenth century.

Reverse solutions:

- 246 = "be the number Margate's grotto hid"
- 246 = "hidden in a shell grotto in Margate"
- 246 = "hides in shell grotto in Margate"
- 246 = "is a number the Margate grotto hid"
- 246 = "is the number in Margate grotto"

Was the grotto used for secret 'initiation' purposes? Was it used as a metaphorical rite of passage into a secret sect? Some code solutions suggest the grotto was used for nefarious activities involving sex and death - some shell designs are associated with the creation of life (1 in guide) and some with death (61 in guide). It seems that people living in Margate who knew of the grotto's dark purposes, deliberately stayed silent on the matter. The grotto was probably buried to hide its unsavoury past, enabling the local population to 'forget' the 'satanic', illegal rituals that had taken place there. It is plausible, in the context of some code solutions, that virgins were routinely deflowered and impregnated in a fertility rite at the grotto and that, nine months later, the un-named new-born were used for blood sacrifices - completing the cycle of conception, birth, life and death. In other words, the shell designs inside the grotto were more than simply decorative. That would be the strongest of reasons why the grotto has remained a complete mystery and why nobody living in Margate in 1835 claimed to know anything about it.

Who designed the grotto?

Applying the Master Code in that context:

1. "Grotto in Margate: design of Kent" = 246
2. "Kent designed grotto at Margate" = 246
3. "Margate grotto: design by Kent" = 246

Applying *Skelton,* we find the resonance equation

"Grotto at Margate" = "was Kent's design" = 149

And:

1. "Margate grotto" = "is Kent's design" = 129
2. "Margate grotto" = "the design of Kent" = 129

We note the following solutions linking *All Souls*, Shugborough, Chiswick House and Margate:

1. "A code hidden in *All Souls* and Shugborough" = 246
2. "*All Souls* and Margate hid the same code" = 246
3. "Chiswick House code is at Shugborough" = 246
4. "Code hides in *All Souls* and Shugborough" = 246
5. "Margate and Shugborough hiding same code" = 246
6. "Same code in Chiswick House and Margate" = 246

Solutions imply that Margate's sea-shell grotto, Shugborough's follies, the west gate at *All Souls College,* Chiswick House garden-monuments and Isaac Newton's tomb-monument are more or less contemporaneous structures (c 1720-1750). All are linked by *Skelton* and the Master Code, so it is plausible, even likely, that they were all designed at least in part by the senior Freemason, William Kent (c 1718-1748).

22. Benjamin Franklin: *Silence Dogood* & other pseudonyms

Image: Wikipedia commons

Benjamin Franklin (1706-1790) the famous American polymath, spent a lot of time in England as nascent Freemasonry was developing. A member of 'The Craft' himself and one of the founding fathers of The Republic, his ideas had a lasting influence on post-colonial America. In 1722, at the remarkably young age of sixteen, he wrote letters in his own name to his older brother James' newspaper *The New England Courant* where he was apprenticed; however, his first attempts at publication met without success, probably due to the malign influence of James. Undeterred, Ben assumed an alias: the middle-aged widow of a minister, *Silence Dogood*. The ruse worked and *fourteen* letters, comic observations of life in America, were published in the name of Silence Dogood's widow. **The conjecture is Franklin used *Skelton* in that context, and we find:**

- "*Silence Dogood*" = "Quaker name" = 79 *Silence* was a Quaker 'virtue' name.
- "The answer is" = "Benjamin Franklin" = "uses a Quaker name" = 123

Applying *Skelton* to *"Mrs Dogood"* in the context of 'Ben' & 'Franklin' we find the resonance equations:

1. "Ben hiding as" = "*Mrs Dogood*" = 74
2. "Called ruse" = "*Mrs Dogood*" = 74
3. "*Mrs Dogood*" = "be a cypher" = 74
4. "*Mrs Dogood*" = "Franklin" = 74
5. "*Mrs Dogood*" = "is a mere joke" = 74
6. "*Mrs Dogood*" = "is a trick" = 74
7. "*Mrs Dogood*" = "it hides Ben" = 74
8. "*Mrs Dogood*" = "jest hid Ben" = 74
9. "*Mrs Dogood*" = "joke hiding Ben" = 74
10. "*Mrs Dogood*" = "name Ben used" = 74
11. "*Mrs Dogood*" = "ruse hid Ben" = 74

Applying *Skelton* to "Widow Dogood", we find the resonance equations:

1. "Widow *Dogood*" = "Ben's cover" = 82
2. "Widow *Dogood*" = "hides Ben in a code" = 82
3. "Widow *Dogood*" = "is a disguise" = 82
4. "Widow *Dogood*" = "is alias of Ben" = 82
5. "Widow *Dogood*" = "is Ben hid in code" = 82
6. "Widow *Dogood*" = "made up by Ben" = 82
7. "Widow *Dogood*" = "name fooled all" = 82
8. "Widow *Dogood*" = "ruse is joke" = 82
9. "Widow *Dogood*" = "was mask" = 82

Applying *Skelton* in the context of Benjamin Franklin and *widow Dogood*:

1. "Benjamin Franklin" = "*hid* by widow Dogood" = 123
2. "Benjamin Franklin" = "*was* widow Dogood" = 123

Applying the Master Code in the context of Benjamin Franklin & *Skelton*:

1. "A code of Benjamin Franklin cracked by you" = 246
2. "A Shaker name hiding Benjamin Franklin" = 246
3. "Ben Franklin knew *Skelton*'s code" = 246
4. "Ben Franklin used *Skelton*'s codes" = 246
5. "Benjamin Franklin uses *nom de plume*" = 246
6. "Benjamin Franklin *was* widow Dogood" = 246
7. "Benjamin Franklin's code cracked by ye" = 246
8. "Code of *Skelton* used by Ben Franklin" = 246
9. "*Skelton* is a code Ben Franklin uses" = 246
10. "Thou hast found codes of Ben Franklin" = 246
11. "You broke a cipher hiding Ben Franklin" = 246
12. "You broke Ben Franklin's cypher" = 246
13. "You broke the cipher of Ben Franklin" = 246
14. "You found a secret code Ben Franklin hid" = 246
15. "You found cipher of Benjamin Franklin" = 246
16. "You have found cipher of Ben Franklin" = 246

Reversed solutions:

- 246 = "a secret number of Benjamin Franklin"
- 246 = "number was Benjamin Franklin's code"

Applying the Master Code to Benjamin Franklin, *Silence Dogood, widow Dogood* etc:

1. "14 *Dogood* letters by Ben Franklin" = 246
2. "Ben Franklin is *Silence Dogood* widow" = 246
3. "Ben Franklin's name hid as a *Mrs Dogood*" = 246
4. "Benjamin Franklin hid by *widow Dogood*" = 246
5. "Benjamin Franklin: the code fooled many" = 246
6. "Benjamin Franklin uses a Quaker name" = 246
7. "Benjamin Franklin *was* widow Dogood" = 246
8. "Benjamin used code to fool older brother" = 246
9. "Brother fooled by *Mrs Dogood*'s name" = 246
10. "Clue is name of minister: *Silence Dogood*" = 246
11. "Code hidden in *fourteen Dogood* letters" = 246
12. "Coded messages are in *Dogood* letters" = 246
13. "Coded messages hide as *Dogood* letters" = 246
14. "*Dogood*'s letters hiding a secret code" = 246
15. "Hid a code clue in letters of widow *Dogood*" = 246
16. "Hid my secret as *Dogood* letters" = 246
17. "I hid my secret in *Dogood* letters" = 246
18. "James Franklin fooled by *Silence Dogood*" = 246
19. "Letters of widow *Dogood* hide a cipher" = 246
20. "*Mrs Dogood* hides Ben Franklin's name" = 246
21. "*Mrs Dogood*: a Franklin pseudonym" = 246
22. "*Mrs Dogood:* false name hid Ben Franklin" = 246
23. "*Mrs Silence Dogood:* Franklin's name" = 246
24. "*Mrs Silence Dogood:* name be just a jest" = 246
25. "*Mrs Silence Dogood*'s 14 letters" = 246
26. "My *Dogood* letters are a secret code" = 246
27. "Name of the Quaker hid Benjamin Franklin" = 246
28. "Secret code hiding as *Dogood* letters" = 246
29. "*Silence Dogood* a Quaker minister name" = 246
30. "*Silence Dogood* Benjamin Franklin hid by code" = 246
31. "*Silence Dogood* cipher solved by you" = 246
32. "*Silence Dogood* false name of Ben Franklin" = 246
33. "*Silence Dogood* is code of Benjamin Franklin" = 246
34. "*Silence Dogood* is Quaker virtue name" = 246
35. "*Silence Dogood* mask hides Ben Franklin" = 246
36. "*Silence Dogood* the Quaker minister" = 246
37. "*Silence Dogood* was name of a minister" = 246
38. "*Silence Dogood* was the Quaker's name" = 246
39. "*Silence Dogood* widow hiding Franklin" = 246
40. "*Silence Dogood* widow *is* Ben Franklin" = 246
41. "The fourteen *Dogood* letters are a code" = 246
42. "The Quaker minister *Silence Dogood*" = 246
43. "The Quaker name hid Benjamin Franklin" = 246

44. "The secret code of *Dogood*'s letters" = 246
45. "The widow of *Silence Dogood* is a fiction" = 246
46. "Widow *Dogood* is Ben Franklin's alias" = 246
47. "Widow *Dogood:* the alias of Ben Franklin" = 246
48. "Ye discovered cipher *Silence Dogood* hid" = 246
49. "Ye discovered name *Silence Dogood* hides" = 246
50. "You discovered *Silence Dogood* folly" = 246

Benjamin Franklin used several *nom de plumes* during his career, including:

Alice Addertongue, Anthony Afterwit, Benevolus, Miss Busybody, Harry Meanwell, Martha Careful, Polly Baker, Poor Richard, Richard Saunders, Caelia Shortface, Timothy Turnstone. **Applying the Master Code in the context of Franklin's aliases:**

1. "*Anthony Afterwit:* Benjamin's name" = 246
2. "*Anthony Afterwit* is Franklin" = 246
3. "Ben Franklin hiding as *Alice Addertongue*" = 246
4. "*Benevolus* disguise hid Ben Franklin" = 246
5. "*Benevolus* is the alias of Franklin" = 246
6. "Ben hid as a pseudonym: *Polly Baker*" = 246
7. "*Caelia Shortface* hides name of Franklin" = 246
8. "*Caelia Shortface* is Franklin's alias" = 246
9. "Franklin hid by *Richard Saunders*" = 246
10. "Franklin hid name as *Turnstone*" = 246
11. "Franklin is hidden as *Alice Addertongue*" = 246
12. "Franklin was hidden as *Addertongue*" = 246
13. "*Harry Meanwell*: Franklin's code" = 246
14. "*Martha Careful:* alias hides Franklin" = 246
15. "*Martha Careful*: Ben Franklin's alias" = 246
16. "*Meanwell* alias hid Benjamin Franklin" = 246
17. "*Meanwell* hides Ben Franklin's name" = 246
18. "*Miss Busybody*: hiding Franklin" = 246
19. "*Miss Busybody* is Ben Franklin" = 246
20. "*Miss Busybody*: name of Franklin" = 246
21. "*Polly Baker*: cipher for Franklin" = 246
22. "*Polly Baker*: cipher of Ben Franklin" = 246
23. "*Polly Baker:* pseudonym hides Ben" = 246
24. "*Poor Richard:* cypher of Franklin" = 246
25. "*Poor Richard* is cipher of Franklin" = 246
26. "*Richard Saunders*: a code of Ben Franklin" = 246
27. "*Richard Saunders* was Franklin" = 246

A Freemason, Franklin helped to choose the motto that appears on the first Great seal of the US and on the statue of *Freedom* atop Washington's Capitol. Applying the Master Code in that context:

1. "*e pluribus unum:* a cipher of Franklin" = 246
2. "*e pluribus unum:* a code made by Franklin" = 246

23. *Skelton* - a secret cipher for writers

It appears from the foregoing that Benjamin Franklin used several pseudonyms linked to his name via *Skelton* and the Master Code. As indicated in the preface, the cipher has been used secretly by a number of well-known authors from the time of *Shake-speare* to the present. **To test the conjecture that (some) writers have used *Skelton*, we apply the Master Code in that general context:**

1. "Cipher writers use is Masonic" = 246
2. "Code of *Skelton* is for writers" = 246
3. "*Hidden* code is writers' secret joke" = 246
4. "*Skelton* is a cipher for authors" = 246
5. "The code you found was writers" = 246
6. "The secret cipher of writers" = 246
7. "The writers used Doctor Dee's code" = 246
8. "Very secret code of writers" = 246
9. "Writers are *hiding Skelton* code" = 246
10. **"Writers *must* hide *Skelton*" = 246**
11. "Writers use code Freemasons *hide*" = 246
12. "Writers use Freemason cipher" = 246
13. "Writers use Masonic cypher" = 246
14. "Writers used secret occult code" = 246
15. "Writers used the Golden Key code" = 246 "Golden key" = "Skelton" = 77
16. "Writers used the *Skelton* code" = 246

Famous writers that have used a *Skelton*-derived alias include: *Shake-speare's* secret author, Charles Dickens, Mary Ann Evans, Charles Dodgson, Arthur Conan Doyle, Samuel Clemens, T. E. Lawrence, Agatha Christie, John Buchan, Eric Blair, J. R. R. Tolkein, Graham Greene, David Cornwell, Douglas Adams and J. K. Rowling. In each case, *Skelton* and the Master Code give resonance equations linking the author's real name and pseudonym. **For example, in the case of Samuel Clemens - a Freemason - and his famous pen name *Mark Twain*, we find the Master Code solutions:**

1. "Clemens used pen name *Mark Twain*" = 246
2. "Clemens uses alias of *Mark Twain*" = 246
3. "*Mark Twain* hiding Samuel Clemens" = 246
4. "*Mark Twain* is Clemens' false name" = 246
5. "*Mark Twain* is Clemens's cipher" = 246
6. "*Mark Twain* is name hiding Clemens" = 246
7. "*Mark Twain* masks Clemens' name" = 246
8. "*Mark Twain:* a cipher hiding Clemens" = 246
9. "*Mark Twain*: Clemens's cypher" = 246
10. "*Mark Twain:* the cipher of Clemens" = 246
11. "*Mark Twain!* call of river-boat man" = 246
12. "*Mark Twain*'s name was Clemens" = 246
13. "Samuel Clemens: name of *Mark Twain*" = 246

24. Orange Order/Society and the Master Code

The Orange Order/Society - named for William of Orange (1650-1702) the Protestant Dutch king - is an international Protestant order based in Northern Ireland. The Order is very strongly associated with Ulster Protestants though it has lodges in England, Scotland and the Republic of Ireland; there are lodges also in the United States and throughout the Commonwealth. The Order/Society was founded in 1795 at Loughgall, County Armagh following a series of violent sectarian disputes with Catholics over land rights. A fraternity sworn to protect the ascendancy of Protestantism in Ireland, the 'Orangemen' used secret signs, passwords and ciphers. According to Master Code solutions, the 'Orange Order' appropriated *Skelton*'s cipher from the Freemasons. It is noteworthy that the founders of the Orange Order were Freemasons and that the Order's link to Freemasonry has remained strong ever since. **Applying the Master Code in that context:**

1. "A clue is: the Orange Order use this code" = 246
2. "A Masonic cipher used by Orange Order" = 246
3. "Orange Order cipher hides a secret code" = 246
4. "Orange Order cypher hid secret code" = 246
5. "Orange Order used code of the Golden Key" = 246
6. "Orange Society used code of *Skelton*" = 246
7. "Orangemen knew of codes of *Skelton*" = 246
8. "Orangemen know *Skelton*'s codes" = 246
9. "Secret code used by Orange Society" = 246
10. "Secret code used by the Orange Order" = 246
11. "Secret occult code of Orange Society" = 246
12. "*Skelton* cipher hides the Orange code" = 246
13. "*Skelton*: code of the Orange Society" = 246
14. "The Orange Order secrets are in a code" = 246
15. "The Orange Order used code of *Skelton*" = 246
16. "*The Secret* of the Orange Society" = 246
17. "This code was for the Orange Order" = 246
18. "*This* was Orange Order's number" = 246
19. "You cracked a secret code of Orange Order" = 246
20. "You found the Orange Order code-number" = 246

Reverse solutions:

- 246 = "a secret numeral Orange Order hides"
- 246 = "secret number the Orange Order hide"
- 246 = "the numeral is the Orange Order's"
- 246 = "the numeral of the Orange Society"

25. A mysterious stone face hidden *inside* Grasmere's church-wall

St Oswald's from the south

Brian Clift / *St Oswald's Church, Grasmere* /

Grasmere is a tiny village at the heart of the English Lake District, its 14th century parish church is dedicated to St Oswald.

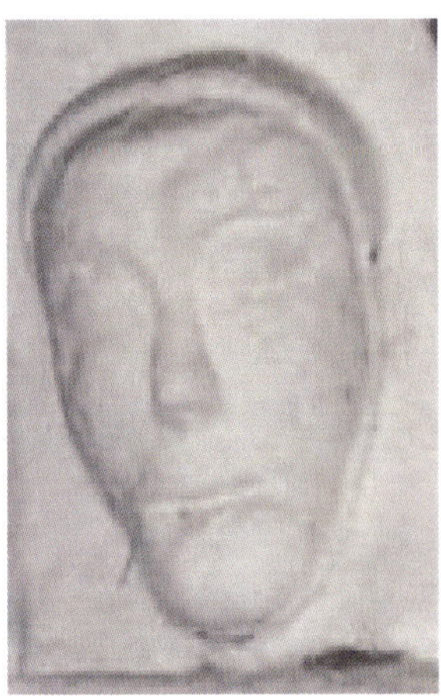

This stone face was found *inside* the east wall of the church by workmen effecting repairs in 1841 and it has remained a mystery until now. A primitive artefact that could have been made by almost anyone, its discovery prompts five questions:

- When was the face hidden?
- Who hid it?
- Who made it?
- Why was it placed *inside* the church wall?
- Who, if anyone, does it represent?

In view of the bizarre location, the last question might be the easiest to answer as it's likely the face is meant to be a representation of St. Oswald. The assumption gains strength if whoever hid the face had a punning sense of humour - the church is dedicated to Oswald, so the face hidden *inside* the wall is 'Os-walled'! A joke typical (perhaps) of someone with a literary turn of mind, like many well-known writers fond of puns. We note that the joke *only* works at a church dedicated to St Oswald.

Applying *Skelton* in the context of the face and its discovery, we find the resonance equations:

1. "You discovered" = "the face of Oswald" = 111
2. "The face of Oswald" = "the Master Code" = 111

The pun, location and date of discovery are clues hinting at the perpetrator's likely identity. According to the second equation, 'The face of Oswald' is an icon representing 'the Master Code', implying that whoever planted the face knew *Skelton*'s cipher and the Master Code. Clearly, *when* the face was hidden and *who* hid it are linked - the answer to the former suggesting the probable answer to the latter. It is virtually certain that the face was concealed by someone who knew that the church was undergoing repairs, someone who probably made the face themselves and planted it inside the wall knowing the workmen would find it. So, the 'culprit' was almost certainly someone living in or near Grasmere in 1841 and who probably attended the church.

The use of *Skelton* suggests a clever practical joker – an individual who was probably well-educated since it's very unlikely an 'ordinary' inhabitant of a remote rural village in 1841 would have known of *Skelton*'s obscure cipher, let alone how to use it. Taking all into account, by far the most likely 'suspect' living in the area at the time, who would have known of the repairs and who might have known *Skelton* and the Master Code was Cambridge-educated William Wordsworth, the famous Lakeland poet.

Applying *Skelton* in the context of Oswald's face and Wordsworth:

"Oswald's face made by" = "Wordsworth" = 135

William Wordsworth (1770 - 1850) (By B. Haydon, Wiki commons)

Raised at Hawkshead, William Wordsworth was the second of five children; his mother, who taught him to read, died when the boy was eight and his father, a legal representative, died when the lad was thirteen. On the death of his mother in 1778, William was sent to Hawkshead Grammar School and in 1787 he went up to St John's College, Cambridge graduating with a BA in 1791. From 1799 to 1808 he lived with his sister Dorothy at Dove Cottage in Grasmere - where he wrote his most famous works. In 1813 he moved to nearby Rydal Mount, remaining there until his death in 1850.

William Wordsworth was made Poet Laurate in 1843 and is, so far, the only holder of that prestigious title never to write a single word of poetry while in post. Throughout his time at Grasmere, St. Oswald's was his place of worship and is now the site of his grave. How the poet knew of *Skelton* and the Master Code is unclear, perhaps he learned of it from other writers during his extensive travels or possibly as a student at Cambridge. Some solutions suggest he knew that the cipher was Masonic, so he might have been a secret member of the Craft himself or he had friends who were.

First, applying the Master Code in the context of William Wordsworth and his sister Dorothy:

1. "A clue is: *William* and *Dorothy* used code" = 246
2. "A secret code of *William* and *Dorothy*" = 246
3. "Dorothy Wordsworth's code" = 246*
4. "I am called *William Wordsworth*" = 246
5. "Look for a code hid by *Wordsworth*" = 246
6. "Name of *Wordsworth* hid in the code" = 246
7. "*William* and *Dorothy* use the codes" = 246
8. "*William Wordsworth* hides code" = 246
9. "*Wordsworth* concealed clues in code" = 246
10. "*Wordsworth* cracked motto code" = 246
11. "*Wordsworth* cracked Oxford code" = 246
12. "*Wordsworth* hid code of Newton" = 246 Newton and Wordsworth Cambridge alumni
13. "*Wordsworth* knew code number" = 246
14. "*Wordsworth* used Master Code" = 246
15. "*Wordsworth* uses a Masonic code" = 246
16. "*Wordsworth*'s code is a test" = 246
17. "You found codes *Wordsworth* hid" = 246
18. "You found Wordsworth's name" = 246
19. "You knew Wordsworth's code" = 246
20. "You know a code Wordsworth hid" = 246

And, we note the Master Code resonance equation:

"I am called *William Wordsworth*" = "you found Wordsworth's name" = 246

*Did Dorothy learn of *Skelton* from William or did William learn of the cipher from Dorothy?

Applying the Master Code in the context of St Oswald, the stone face, Wordsworth and Grasmere's church etc we find a large set of solutions:

1. "A church at Grasmere *hid* Oswald's face" = 246
2. "A face *hidden* in Grasmere church's wall" = 246
3. "A face *hiding* in a wall was a practical joke" = 246
4. "A face was *in* Saint Oswald's church" = 246
5. "A *hidden* face left by Wordsworth" = 246
6. "A mysterious face Grasmere *hides*" = 246
7. "A mysterious face *hid* at Grasmere" = 246
8. "A workman found a face church's wall *hid*" = 246
9. "A workman found face *in* church's wall" = 246
10. "Clue is: Oswald's face within a wall" = 246
11. "Clue is: the stone face of St Oswald" = 246
12. "East wall in St Oswald *hides* a face" = 246
13. "East wall of St Oswald's *hid* clue" = 246
14. "Face at St Oswald's church is code clue" = 246
15. "Face at St Oswald's church was a code" = 246
16. "Face at St Oswald's was test" = 246
17. "Face *hid* by poet is walled-up in a church" = 246
18. "Face *hid* by wall of Grasmere's church" = 246
19. "Face *hid in* St Oswald's wall is a clue" = 246
20. "Face *hid in* wall at Grasmere's church" = 246
21. "Face *hid* in wall: practical joke by poet" = 246
22. "Face *hidden in* wall: a pun on Oswald name" = 246
23. "Face *hidden in* wall: Oswald's name pun" = 246
24. "Face *hides in* Grasmere church's wall" = 246
25. "Face *hiding* at Saint Oswald's church" = 246
26. "Face *hiding in* Oswald's wall is hoax" = 246
27. "Face *hiding in* wall at St Oswald's" = 246
28. "Face immured *in* wall is St Oswald" = 246
29. "Face *in* a wall: *Wordsworth*'s joke" = 246
30. "Face *in* church wall *hidden* by the poet" = 246
31. "Face *in* Oswald's church at Grasmere" = 246
32. "Face *in* Saint Oswald's church is clue" = 246
33. "Face *in* St Oswald's wall is a hoax" = 246
34. "Face *in* wall in Grasmere *hid* by poet" = 246
35. "Face *inside* of a wall at St Oswald's" = 246
36. "Face *inside* of wall is St Oswald's" = 246
37. "Face is hidden at St Oswald's church" = 246
38. "Face is hiding *in* St Oswald's church" = 246
39. "Face is made and hid by *Wordsworth*" = 246
40. "Face left *in* wall of church is Oswald" = 246
41. "Face of Oswald at St Oswald's hid a code" = 246

42. "Face of Oswald is practical joke of a poet" = 246
43. "Face of Oswald was *in* church's wall" = 246
44. "Face of Oswald: joke of *Wordsworth*" = 246
45. "Face of St Oswald hidden at the church" = 246
46. "Face of St Oswald hides in Grasmere" = 246
47. "Face of St Oswald hiding *in* the church" = 246
48. "Face of St Oswald is *in* a church wall" = 246
49. "Face Saint Oswald's church hid is a clue" = 246
50. "Face *Wordsworth* concealed hides clue" = 246
51. "Face *Wordsworth* made is hiding clue" = 246
52. "Face *Wordsworth* planted hid joke" = 246 a pun: Os-walled
53. "Face *Wordsworth* used was his" = 246
54. "Find Oswald's face hid *in* wall of church" = 246
55. "Find Oswald's face hidden at Grasmere" = 246
56. "Found face *inside* St Oswald's church" = 246
57. "Grasmere hides a mysterious face" = 246
58. "Grasmere's church hides face *in* wall" = 246
59. "Hid a clue to *Skelton* as Oswald's face" = 246
60. "Hid a face at St Oswald in east wall" = 246
61. "Hid a mysterious face at Grasmere" = 246
62. "Hid face *in* wall at Grasmere's church" = 246
63. "Hid Oswald's face as a clue to *Skelton*" = 246
64. "Hidden face be *Wordsworth*'s hint" = 246
65. "Hidden face is a deceit of *Wordsworth*" = 246
66. "Hide a face *in* St Oswald's east wall" = 246
67. "I hid face *in* St Oswald's east wall" = 246
68. "I hid Oswald's face *in* Oswald's church" = 246
69. "I hid St Oswald *in* St Oswald's" = 246
70. "I immured face *in* St Oswald's wall" = 246
71. "I walled-up the face *in* St Oswald's" = 246
72. "Left face *in* the wall for workman" = 246
73. "Look for face *Wordsworth* concealed" = 246
74. "*My* face *hid* at St Oswald in east wall" = 246
75. "*My* face *hides* in St Oswald east wall" = 246
76. "Mystery of 'Oswald' solved" = 246
77. "Os *walled* is a pun on a saint's name" = 246
78. "Os-wald *in* the wall puns on name" = 246
79. "Os-wald is a joke of *Wordsworth*" = 246
80. "Os-wald: *Wordsworth*'s pun" = 246
81. "Oswald hidden at Saint Oswald's" = 246
82. "Oswald *hiding in* Saint Oswald's" = 246
83. "Oswald is *Wordsworth's* face" = 246
84. "Oswald: a face entombed *in* wall of church" = 246
85. "Oswald: name of a face Grasmere church *hid*" = 246
86. "Oswald: name of face *in* Grasmere church" = 246

87. “Oswald’s church at Grasmere *hid* a face” = 246
88. “Oswald’s ‘death mask’ found *in* wall” = 246 stone face is like a death mask
89. “Oswald’s face *in* church at Grasmere” = 246
90. “Oswald’s face was *in* wall of church” = 246
91. “Saint Oswald east wall hides face” = 246
92. “Skelton was St Oswald’s code” = 246
93. “Solve puzzle of St Oswald” = 246
94. “St Oswald: face found at east wall” = 246
95. “St Oswald: face was hiding test” = 247
96. “St Oswald: *hiding* the face of Oswald” = 246
97. “Stone face was found by workman” = 246
98. “Stone face: *Wordsworth* made it” = 246
99. “Stone face’s riddle solved by you” = 246
100. “The face *hid* by *Wordsworth* hid a code” = 246
101. “The face of Oswald at St Oswald’s” = 246
102. “*The face of Oswald* is clue to a cypher” = 246
103. “*The face of Oswald* is hidden *and* found in 1841” = 246
104. “*The face of Oswald* was a clue to a cipher” = 246
105. “The face Saint Oswald’s *hid* is a hoax” = 246
106. “The Oswald enigma solved by you” = 246
107. “Uncover face *hidden* at St Oswald’s” = 246
108. “Uncover face *hiding in* St Oswald’s” = 246
109. “Walled-up-face: you solved the riddle” = 246
110. “*Wordsworth* concealed stone face” = 246
111. “*Wordsworth* left face as a sign” = 246
112. “*Wordsworth* left face *in* wall” = 246
113. “*Wordsworth* made face wall *hides*” = 246
114. “*Wordsworth* placed a face *in* a wall” = 246
115. “*Wordsworth* planted *hidden* face” = 246
116. “Workmen found face *in* church’s wall” = 246
117. “You solved puzzle of Oswald” = 246
118. “You solved riddle St Oswald hid” = 246

According to those solutions, it was William Wordsworth who made and planted the stone face representing St Oswald inside the east wall of Grasmere’s church during repairs in 1841. It seems the face was both a joke and a test.

The question is: did Wordsworth use *Skelton* in his poetry?

By way of answer, we find the resonance equation:

"The answer is Wordsworth" = "hid a code in *Daffodils* poem first verse" = 258

A hint that we should apply *Skelton* to the first stanza of Wordsworth's famous poem known either as 'Daffodils' or by the first line 'I wandered lonely as a cloud'.

Applying *Skelton* to the first line, we find the resonance equation:

1. *"I wandered lonely as a cloud"* = "daffodils poem line one is clue" = 180
2. *"I wandered lonely as a cloud"* = "hid *Wordsworth* in a code" = 180
3. *"I wandered lonely as a cloud"* = "name in daffodils poem line 1" = 180
4. *"I wandered lonely as a cloud"* = "line 1 of daffodils poem is code" = 180

And the resonance equations:

- "A code of Wordsworth hiding in" = "*Daffodils* poem first verse" = 213
- "A code of Wordsworth hides as" = "*Daffodils* poem first verse" = 213
- "*Daffodils* poem's first verse" = "you found Wordsworth's code" = 231
- "Wordsworth hid codes in" = "*Daffodils* poem first stanza" = 197
- "Wordsworth" = "hid a code in *Daffodils* poem" = 135

Also, the Master Code solutions:

1. "A riddle in Daffodils poem 1 st verse" = 246
2. "*Daffodils* first verse hides codes" = 246
3. "*Daffodils* is Wordsworth poem" = 246
4. "The riddle was in the *Daffodils* poem" = 246

Applying *Skelton* to each line of the first verse:

- "I wandered lonely as a cloud" = "is a code of Wordsworth" = 180
- "That floats on high o'er vales and hills" = "you found Wordsworth's codes. *Bravo*!" = 294
- "When all at once I saw a crowd" = "name of Wordsworth as code" = 205
- "A host of golden daffodils" = "code of Wordsworth" = 158
- "Beside the lake, beneath the trees" = "hid the code by Wordsworth" = 218
- "Fluttering and dancing in the breeze" = "is a code by William Wordsworth" = 259

Several alternative, contextually appropriate solutions exist many of which include the name Wordsworth.

26. Charles Dickens: the Master Code, characters' names, *Edwin Drood* & *Boz*

Charles Dickens (1812-1870) Image: Wiki commons

Charles John Huffam Dickens, writer and social critic, was born in Portsmouth on February 7th 1812. Although he had little formal education - leaving school to work in a factory when his father entered debtor's prison - it didn't stop him writing fifteen novels, five novellas and hundreds of short stories.

Dickens began his professional writing career as a freelance journalist, before going on to specialise as a Parliamentary reporter. In 1850 he took on the first of two magazine editorships, positions he held for a total of twenty years during which time he published many anonymous works by famous Victorian writers. His literary success began with the publication of *The Pickwick Papers* in 1836 and within a few years he had become an international celebrity noted for his humour, satire and sharp observation of both individual character and society as a whole. The novels, published in monthly or weekly instalments pioneered the serial publication of fiction, which became popular in the Victorian era, and in 1853 he became the first writer in England to give public readings of his own works, performances which were initially given for charity.

A fervent champion of social reform, Dickens focussed special attention on the education and rights of children. Topical references in his novels painted vividly realistic scenes of poverty and its social consequences, much like the conditions he had seen for himself on the long walks he regularly took across London. It was through witnessing the scale of poverty, degradation and child cruelty personally that the author's reforming zeal was fired.

How Dickens came to know of *Skelton* is unclear; it seems he was not a Freemason himself although he had many friends who were, so it's possible that through those associations he became aware of certain Masonic secrets. Like other writers who knew *Skelton*, he might have discovered the following Master Code solutions himself:

1. "Character's names are in a secret code" = 246
2. "Clues to characters' names hide as code" = 246
3. "I hid secret code as character's names" = 246
4. "I hide clues to code in character's names" = 246
5. "Secret code is in characters' names" = 246

Taking a hint from those solutions, it's plausible if not likely that Dickens used *Skelton* and the Master Code to link the names of characters to their parts in his stories. Of course, those general solutions could have been found by *any* writer who knew the Master Code, they are not specific to Dickens.

Applying the Master Code in the *context* of Dickens, his stories and the code:

1. "*All* Charles Dickens' stories hid a code" = 246
2. "Charles Dickens uses *Skelton* code" = 246
3. "Charles Dickens wrote novels" = 246
4. "Code in *all* Charles Dickens' stories" = 246
5. "Dickens hid a code as names of characters" = 246
6. "*Skelton*'s code in Dickens' novels" = 246

The solutions support the conjecture that the author used *Skelton*'s cipher in his fictional work, so it's *appropriate* to apply the Master Code to the names of Dickens' characters. **The following is a partial list of Master Code solutions linking the names and roles of characters in Dickens' novels:**

1. "A fiction writer called *Copperfield*" = 246*
2. "*A fierce lion:* nickname of *Linkinwater*" = 246
3. "A *fortune teller: Pancks'* nickname" = 246
4. "A simpleton is called *Barnaby Rudge*" = 246
5. "*A single gentleman*: an alias of Dickens" = 246**
6. "A *zephyr* is *Mr Mivins'* alias" = 246
7. "*Abel Magwitch* is the name of a convict" = 246
8. "*Agnes Fleming* is mother of *Oliver*" = 246
9. "*Alderman Cute* was Justice of the Peace" = 246
10. "*Arthur Gride:* the old miser's name" = 246
11. "*Barnaby Rudge:* killer of *Reuben Haredale*" = 246
12. "Barrister called *Stryver*" = 246
13. "*Bill Sikes* was an evil murderer" = 246
14. "*Bill Sikes*' dog: his name is *Bull's eye*" = 246
15. "*Blandois:* alias of a murderer called *Rigaud*" = 246
16. "Called Charley *little coavinses*" = 246
17. "Called the swindler *Compeyson*" = 246
18. "*Chadband* is oleaginous preacher name" = 246
19. "*Coavinses* is pet name of *Neckett*" = 246

20. “*Codlin:* Punch and Judy show owner” = 246
21. “*Copperfield:* code hiding Charles Dickens” = 246
22. “*Copperfield* is Dickens in secret code” = 246
23. “*Copperfield:* mask of Charles Dickens” = 246
24. “*Cruncher* was messenger at bank” = 246
25. “*Daniel Quilp:* the evil dwarf’s name” = 246
26. “*David Copperfield* fiction writer” = 246
27. “*Defarge:* owner of Paris wine shop” = 246
28. “*Dolly Varden* was a beautiful girl” = 246
29. “*Dombey and Son:* name for a shipping co.” = 246
30. “*Dr Peps*: name of a court physician” = 246
31. “*Edmund Sparkler* a dim-witted man” = 246
32. “*Esther Summerson* is orphan” = 246
33. “*Fagin* the Jewish kidsman and miser” = 246***
34. “*Frederick Trent* is a wastrel” = 246
35. “*Gabelle* the name for a postmaster” = 246
36. “*Gabriel Varden* the lock-smith name” = 246
37. “Gamblers called *Isaac List* and *Joe Jowl*” = 246
38. “*Good Mrs Brown* is name of a rag dealer” = 246
39. “*Grip* is name for talking raven” = 246
40. “Hangman of Tyburn called *Ned Dennis*” = 246
41. “*Hannah* name of an idiotic maid of *La Creevy*” = 246
42. “*Harmon* was hiding as *Rokesmith*” = 246
43. “*Havisham*: recluse at *Satis House*” = 246
44. “*Havisham* was spinster name” = 246
45. “Headmaster’s name was *Mr Creakle*” = 246
46. “*Herbert Pocket* name of friend of *Pip*” = 246
47. “*Hortense* kills *Tulkinghorn*” = 246
48. “*Hugh* was hostler of *The Maypole*” = 246
49. “*Jack Dawkins* called *the Artful Dodger*” = 246
50. “*Jack Dawkins* nicknamed *Artful Dodger*” = 246
51. “*Jacques Five* hid the road mender’s name” = 246
52. “*Jacques Four* hid name of *Monsieur Defarge*” = 246
53. “*Jarvis Lorry* is manager of bank” = 246
54. “*Joe Gargery* the blacksmith’s name” = 246
55. “*Joe Willets* name for one-armed soldier” = 246
56. “*John Willets* name for Inn keeper” = 246
57. “*Josiah Bounderby* was mill-owner” = 246
58. “*Julius Handford* alias for *John Harmon*” = 246
59. “*Krook* died in spontaneous burning” = 246 Dickens was interested in the ‘phenomenon’
60. “*Lady Dedlock* owns *Chesney Wold*” = 246
61. “*M’Choakumchild* is the pedantic teacher” = 246
62. “*Marley and Scrooge,* businessmen” = 246
63. “*Marshalsea* is debtor’s prison” = 246
64. “*Martha Endell* is a scarlet woman” = 246

65. “*Matthew Pocket:* tutor’s name” = 246
66. “*Miss Mowcher* was name for a dwarf” = 246
67. “*Molly:* name of *Jaggers*’ servant” = 246
68. “*Molly* is the wife of *Abel Magwitch*” = 246
69. “*Monks* and *Oliver* half-brothers” = 246
70. “*Monks* was the alias of *Brownlow*” = 246
71. “*Monseigneur* a generic aristocrat” = 246
72. “*Montague* is name for fraudster” = 246
73. “*Mr Bumble* is self-important beadle” = 246
74. “*Mr Campbell* is an *Abel Magwitch* alias” = 246
75. “*Mr Campbell* was alias of *Magwitch*” = 246
76. “*Mr Dolls’* pseudonym: *my bad child*” = 246
77. “*Mr Gamfield* a chimney sweep’s name” = 246
78. “*Mr Jaggers* is honest lawyer” = 246
79. “*Mr Meagles* name for retired banker” = 246
80. “*Mr Pumblechook* the corn merchant” = 246
81. “*Mr Riah:* Jewish moneylender name” = 246
82. “*Mr Sleary* was a circus manager” = 246
83. “*Mrs Corney* was the matron” = 246
84. “*Mrs Wilfer* was malcontent*” = 246*
85. “*Nancy* was *Bill Sikes*’s lover” = 246
86. “*Nell* at The Old Curiosity Shop” = 246
87. “*Nemo*: alias hiding Captain *James Hawdon*” = 246
88. “Nicknamed a madman: *the man next door*” = 246.
89. “*Noddy Boffin* is *the golden dustman*” = 246
90. “*Old Soldier: Mrs Markleham*’s handle” = 246
91. “*Oliver Twist* is orphan name” = 246
92. “*Oliver Twist* was foundling” = 246
93. “*Pecksniff* hypocrite architect” = 246
94. “*Peggotty* was fisherman name” = 246
95. “*Peggotty*’s handle was *Barkis*” = 246
96. “*Peps* is name of a court physician” = 246
97. “*Pet:* nickname of beautiful *Minnie Meagles*” = 246
98. “Philanthrope is called *Jellyby*” = 246
99. “*Philip Pirrip* is an orphan name” = 246
100. “*Pip* is nickname of *Philip Pirrip*” = 246
101. “*Plornish:* name for plasterer” = 246
102. “*Reginald Wilfer* nicknamed *The Cherub*” = 246
103. “*Rose Maylie:* name of *Oliver*’s aunt” = 246
104. “*Sally Brass’s* nickname be *dragon*” = 246
105. “*Sam Weller* is humorous bootblack” = 246
106. “*Sarah Gamp* was mid-wife and nurse” = 246
107. “*Scrooge* is the mean-spirited miser” = 246
108. “*Sikes*’ bull-terrier had a bull’s eye” = 246
109. “*Smike* was name of the feeble companion” = 246

110. “*Sophronia Sphynx* was a maid” = 246
111. “*Squeers* cruel headmaster’s name” = 246
112. “*Stony boy*: nickname for *Briggs*” = 246
113. “*Tappertit:* apprentice’s name” = 246
114. “*The Jackal: Sydney Carton*’s name” = 246
115. “The rent collector called *Pancks*” = 246
116. “*The Signalman:* ghost story” = 246
117. “*Tiny Tim* was cripple’s name” = 246
118. “*Tip* is pet name of *Edward Dorrit*” = 246
119. “*Todgers:* the boarding-house owner” = 246
120. “*Tony Jobling* disguised as *Weevle*” = 246
121. “*Toodle* is name of locomotive stoker” = 246
122. “*Trotty* is name of *Toby Veck*” = 246
123. “*Tulkinghorn* is name of lawyer” = 246
124. “*Uriah Heep* is the fraudster’s name” = 246
125. “*Wardle* owned farm in *Dingley Dell*” = 246

**David Copperfield* was Dickens’ favourite novel and character – a ‘reflection’ of the author.

**The *single gentleman* is anonymous, an alias of Dickens.

***a ‘kidsman’ was someone who used children for criminal purposes.

Numbers in the list above link the character to the number of the novel in the list below and in which they appear.

Eg. Solution 62: “*Marley and Scrooge,* businessmen” = 246 appear in 62: *A Christmas Carol*

- 1 *David Copperfield*
- 2 *Nicholas Nickleby*
- 3 *Little Dorrit*
- 4 *Barnaby Rudge*
- 5 *The Old Curiosity Shop*
- 6 *The Pickwick Papers*
- *7 Great Expectations*
- 8 *Oliver Twist*
- 9 *The Chimes*
- 10 *Nicholas Nickleby*
- 11 *Barnaby Rudge*
- 12 *A Tale of Two Cities*
- 13 *Oliver Twist*
- 15 *Little Dorrit*
- 16 *Great Expectations*
- 17 *Bleak House*
- 18 *Bleak House*
- 19 *Bleak House*

- 20 *The Old Curiosity Shop*
- 24 *A Tale of Two Cities*
- 25 *The Old Curiosity Shop*
- 27 *A Tale of Two Cities*
- 28 *Barnaby Rudge*
- 29 *Dombey and Son*
- 30 *Dombey and Son*
- 31 *Little Dorrit*
- 32 *Bleak House*
- 33 *Oliver Twist*
- 34 *The Old Curiosity Shop*
- 35 *A Tale of Two Cities*
- 36 *Barnaby Rudge*
- 37*The Old Curiosity Shop*
- 38 *Dombey and Son*
- 39 *Barnaby Rudge*
- 40 *Barnaby Rudge*
- 41 *Nicholas Nickleby*
- 42 *Our Mutual Friend*
- 43 *Great Expectations*
- 45 *David Copperfield*
- 46 *Great Expectations*
- 47 *Bleak House*
- 48 *Barnaby Rudge*
- 49 *Oliver Twist*
- 50 *Oliver Twist*
- 51 *A Tale of Two Cities*
- 53 *A Tale of Two Cities*
- 54 *Great Expectations*
- 55 *Barnaby Rudge*
- 57 *Hard Times*
- 58 *Our Mutual Friend*
- 59 *Bleak House*
- 60 *Bleak House*
- 61 *Hard Times*
- 62 *A Christmas Carol*
- 63 *Little Dorrit*
- 64 *David Copperfield*
- 65 *Great Expectations*
- 66 *David Copperfield*
- 67 *Great Expectations*
- 69 *Oliver Twist*
- 71 *A Tale of Two Cities*

- 72 *Martin Chuzzlewit*
- 73 *Oliver Twist*
- 74 *Great Expectations*
- 76 *Our Mutual Friend*
- 77 *Oliver Twist*
- 78 Great Expectations
- 79 *Little Dorrit*
- 80 *Great Expectations*
- 81 *Our Mutual Friend*
- 82 *Hard Times*
- 83 *Oliver Twist*
- *84 Our Mutual Friend*
- 85 *Oliver Twist*
- 86 *The Old Curiosity Shop*
- 87 *Bleak House*
- 88 *Nicholas Nickleby*
- 89 *Our Mutual Friend*
- 90 *David Copperfield*
- 91 Oliver Twist
- *92 Oliver Twist*
- 93 *Martin Chuzzlewit*
- 94 David Copperfield
- 95 *Davis Copperfield*
- 96 *Dombey and Son*
- 97 *Little Dorrit*
- 98 *Bleak House*
- 99 *Great Expectations*
- *100 Great Expectations*
- 101 Little Dorrit
- 102 Our Mutual Friend
- 103 Oliver Twist
- *104 The Old Curiosity Shop*
- 105 The Pickwick Papers
- 106 Martin Cuzzlewit
- 107 *A Christmas Carol*
- *108 Oliver Twist*
- *109 Nicholas Nickleby*
- 110 *The Old Curiosity Shop*
- 111 *Nicholas Nickleby*
- 112 *Dombey and Son*
- 113 *Barnaby Rudge*
- 114 *A Tale of Two Cities*
- 115 *Little Dorrit*

- 116 *The Signalman*
- 117 *A Christmas Carol*
- 118 *Little Dorrit*
- 119 *Martin Chuzzlewit*
- 120 *Bleak House*
- 121 *Dombey & Son*
- 122 *The Chimes*
- 123 *Bleak House*
- 124 *David Copperfield*
- 125 *The Pickwick Papers*

The Mystery of Edwin Drood

Dickens signalled his intention to write a mystery novel in a letter to a friend; it was to be a murder story in which an uncle kills his nephew. Unfortunately, on June 9th 1870 at just 58 years of age the author died suddenly from a stroke. Although prevented by the hand of Death from completing the *Mystery of Edwin Drood*, critics generally agree about Dickens' intended solution - that the killer was Edwin's uncle, the choirmaster John Jasper. **As there is very good evidence Dickens used the Master Code in *all* his previous novels, it makes sense to apply it in the context of his last novel.**

1. "A clue is: *Jasper* buried *Drood* in quicklime" = 246   a pile of quicklime is mentioned in the story
2. "A clue is: solve *Drood*'s murder by code" = 246
3. "*Bazzard:* dramatist in secret" = 246
4. "Boarding School called *The Nuns' House*" = 246
5. "Clue is: solve *Drood*'s killing by code" = 246
6. "Code solved the murder of *Edwin Drood*" = 246
7. "Codes are hiding the demise of *Edwin Drood*" = 246
8. "*Crisparkle*: a canon in *Cloisterham*" = 246
9. "*Dick Datchery* is investigator" = 246
10. "Dickens hid code in *Drood* mystery" = 246
11. "*Drood mystery* is code of Dickens" = 246
12. "*Drood*'s murder is solved by codes" = 246
13. "*Drood*'s mystery by Dickens" = 246
14. "*Durdles*: his nickname is 'stony'" = 246
15. "*Edwin Drood:* Dickens' mystery" = 246
16. "*Edwin Drood:* nephew to *John Jasper*" = 246
17. "*Edwin Drood*: strangled with a tie" = 246
18. "*Edwin Drood* was code hiding *Skelton*" = 246   "*Edwin Drood*" = "*Skelton*" = 77
19. "*Edwin Drood* was nephew of *Jasper*" = 246
20. "*Edwin Drood* was victim of murder" = 246
21. "*Edwin Drood*'s fate hidden as a cypher" = 246
22. "*Edwin Drood*'s fate hides as cypher" = 246
23. "*Edwin Drood*'s fate is hidden as a cipher" = 246
24. "*Grewgious* was *Rosa Bud*'s guardian" = 246
25. "Identity of *Drood*'s killer hid in code" = 246
26. "*Jasper* was *Edwin Drood's killer*" = 246

27. "*Jasper*'s the name of *Drood*'s killer" = 246
28. "*John Jasper* is evil choirmaster" = 246
29. "*John Jasper* is killer of *Edwin Drood*" = 246
30. "*John Jasper* was name of the killer" = 246
31. "*John Jasper* was uncle of *Edwin Drood*" = 246
32. "*John Jasper*'s murder of *Edwin Drood*" = 246
33. "*Luke Honeythunder*: bully's name" = 246
34. "*Princess Puffer*: opium den keeper" = 246
35. "*Tartar* is the name of the old sea-dog" = 246
36. "The demise of *Edwin Drood* is hiding in a code" = 246
37. "The fate of *Edwin Drood* is hidden in codes" = 246
38. "The murder of *Drood:* solved by codes" = 246
39. "The murder of *Edwin Drood* is hiding a code" = 246
40. "The name *Edwin Drood* hides *Skelton*" = 246
41. "The orphaned *Landless* twins" = 246
42. "*Thomas Sapsea:* an auctioneer's name" = 246
43. "Verger of *Cloisterham* called *Tope*" = 246
44. "You discovered name of killer of *Drood*" = 246
45. "You found killer of *Drood: John Jasper*" = 246
46. "You solved Drood's murder. *Bravo*!" = 246
47. "You solved *Edwin Drood*'s killing" = 246

Charles Dickens' alias – *Boz* (from mispronunciation of Moses as Boses – a malapropism)

Applying *Skelto**n*** to "Charles Dickens", we find the resonance equation:

"A pseudonym hid" = "Charles Dickens" = 113

In 1834 Dickens assumed the *nom de plume* 'Boz'*,* jokingly derived from 'Moses'.

Applying the Master Code in the context of Charles Dickens and his pen name:

1. "A pseudonym hides Charles Dickens" = 246
2. "Boses: a malapropism of Moses' name" = 246
3. "*Boz* disguised name of Charles Dickens" = 246
4. "*Boz* is a Charles Dickens *nom de plume*" = 246
5. "*Boz* is cipher derived from *Moses*" = 246
6. "*Boz* is the cypher C. J. H. Dickens used" = 246
7. "*Boz* was a Charles Dickens' disguise" = 246
8. "*Boz* was name derived from Moses" = 246
9. "Charles Dickens' disguise: clue is *Boz*" = 246
10. "You found Dickens' name *Boz.* Well done!" = 246

Nicknames of Charles Dickens & his children

The author assumed nicknames, at least four of which are Master Code solutions:

1. "A *resurrectionist* called Dickens = 246
2. "*Revolver* was Dickens' nickname" = 246
3. "*The Inimitable:* a Charles Dickens alias" = 246
4. "*The Inimitable:* hides Charles Dickens" = 246
5. "*The Sparkler of Albion*: a Dickens name" = 246
6. "*The Sparkler of Albion*: hid C J H Dickens" = 246

Dickens gave his children nicknames, at least three of which are Master Code solutions:

1. "Catherine Dickens' name is *Lucifer box*" = 246
2. "Name of Frank is *chicken-stalker*" = 246
3. "William Dickens is *a young skull*" = 246

27. QUEEN VICTORIA (1819 - 1901) & PRINCE ALBERT (1819 - 1861)

Images: Wiki commons

Code solutions indicate that Albert, prince consort to Queen Victoria learned of *Skelton's* cipher and the Master Code from his personal secretary, close friend and confidant George Anson. As we have seen, *Skelton's* cipher was used extensively by the Anson family at Shugborough long before the Victorian era and in that context, we recall the Master Code solution:

"*Skelton* is the Anson family code" = 246

***SKELTON* - A SECRET ROYAL CODE**

We have also seen solutions associated with Elizabeth I indicating that *Skelton* and the Master Code were originally royal codes/ciphers. The following solutions are general and not associated with a specific sovereign.

1. "A secret royal code hid as the number" = 246
2. "Hid the secret royal code as a number" = 246
3. "*Skelton:* name of secret royal code" = 246
4. "*Skelton* was cipher of royal code" = 246
5. "The code you discovered is royal" = 246
6. "The Golden Key was the royal code" = 246 "Golden key" = "*Skelton*" = 77
7. "The secret royal code hid as a number" = 246
8. "*This* number hid a secret royal code" = 246
9. "You have found royal code's numeral" = 246
10. "You have found royal code's secret" = 246
11. "You have found secret royal codes" = 246

Reverse solution:

- 246 = "the number hides secret royal code"

Applying the Master Code in the context of Prince Albert and Queen Victoria:

1. "A secret cypher of Prince Albert" = 246
2. "Albert knew the codes of *Skelton*" = 246
3. "Code hidden by her Majesty the Queen" = 246
4. "Code hides secrets of Queen Victoria" = 246
5. "Code of Queen Victoria hides secrets" = 246
6. "Code of *Skelton* hid by Prince Albert" = 246
7. "Her Majesty Queen Victoria's code" = 246
8. "Her Majesty the Queen is hiding a code" = 246
9. "Her Majesty's secret cipher code" = 246
10. "Leopold was a Freemason at Oxford" = 246* youngest son of the Queen
11. "Leopold was son of Queen Victoria" = 246*
12. "Queen and Prince Albert use the codes" = 246
13. "Queen Victoria hid secret cipher code" = 246
14. "Queen Victoria is the sovereign" = 246
15. "Queen Victoria knew the cipher code" = 246
16. "Queen Victoria knew of the number" = 246
17. "Queen Victoria knew the numeral" = 246
18. "Queen Victoria knew the secret" = 246
19. "Queen Victoria knows of the codes" = 246
20. "Queen Victoria's occult code numeral" = 246
21. "Queen Victoria's secret occult code" = 246
22. "Secret ciphers of Queen Victoria" = 246
23. "Secrets of Queen Victoria hid as a code" = 246
24. "*The Code* of Victoria and Prince Albert" = 246
25. "Victoria and Albert hid *Skelton* code" = 246
26. "Victoria and Albert hid the numeral" = 246
27. "Victoria and Albert hid the secret" = 246
28. "Victoria and Albert knew occult code" = 246
29. "Victoria and Albert knew of cipher" = 246
30. "You found the Queen's number. *Bravo*!" = 246

Reverse solutions:

- 246 = "Her Majesty's secret numeral"
- 246 = "hides secret codes of Queen Victoria"
- 246 = "is a secret cipher of Prince Albert"
- 246 = "is cypher numeral of Prince Albert"
- 246 = "secret numeral Prince Albert used"
- 246 = "the numeral Victoria and Albert hid"
- 246 = "the sovereign's secret number"
- 246 = "was the numeral of Prince Albert"
- 246 = "was the secret of Prince Albert"

Prince Albert's very close friendship with George Anson would account for his knowledge of *Skelton* and the Master Code. It seems from the foregoing solutions that the Master Code was originally the Royal Code, so it's possible Victoria knew of the cipher independently of her husband, perhaps as a 'royal secret' passed down the generations.

*Leopold (1853-1884), eighth child and youngest son of Victoria and Albert, attended *Christ Church* College Oxford (1872-1876) at the very time *Lewis Carroll* (Charles Dodgson) was in residence writing his enigmatic nonsense poem *The Hunting of the Snark.* Leopold was made president of the university chess club and left Oxford a Freemason with an honorary doctorate in law; unfortunately, he suffered from haemophilia - a very serious inherited blood disorder occurring mainly in males - which probably contributed to his early death at thirty.

28. The Master Code at Osborne House, Isle of Wight (c 1851)

After Prince Albert's untimely death in 1861, Victoria spent many years 'deep in mourning' as a virtual recluse - a royal hermit. It was at Osborne House on the Isle of Wight and Balmoral Castle in Scotland that she escaped the immediate pressures, responsibilities and duties that faced her when she was resident in the bustling metropolis. The style of Osborne was a design to which Albert made significant contributions; construction of the main building was completed in 1851. The distinctive Italianate towers are non identical twins: clock tower/bell tower/campanile on the left, taller flag tower on the right. In light of the fact that Albert and George Anson were very close friends and that the prince was deeply involved in designing the house and gardens, it makes sense to look for signs that *Skelton's* cipher was used at Osborne.

The following Master Code solutions are noteworthy:

1. "Albert *hid* Anson code at Osborne House" = 246
2. "Albert *hid* Anson's old code at Osborne" = 246
3. "George Anson gave Albert a secret code" = 246

Reversed solution:

246 = "a number George Anson gave to Albert" = 246

We notice that the clock tower has *six* floors, *four* faces and except for the clock *two* windows in each face, the digits of the Master Code key. Similarly, the 'coincidence' of the digits 2, 4, 6 around the *Andromeda* fountain (see below). **In the context of the fountain, we recall the Master Code solution**:

"Make measurements to find number" = 246

[Flickr](https://flickr.com) by Amanda Slater at https://flickr.com/photos/15181848@N02/3744299546.

The fountain-statue of Andromeda

A statue of *Andromeda* stands at the centre of the main garden fountain at Osborne. It is evident from the name - meaning 'ruler of men' – that *Andromeda* alludes to Victoria, as she too was a female ruler of men. Around the fountain *four* sets of *six* steps lead down to the fountain pool each set of steps having *two* statues located either side. Perhaps, like Newton's tomb-monument the numbers are hinting at the Master Code key digits: 2 & 6 repeated 4 times. More importantly, the pool's diameter is 20 ft 6 ins (246 inches measured using *Google Earth);* so, it appears that the 'magic' number has been hidden as the fountain's diameter measured in inches.

According to the classic fable, *Andromeda's* mother *Cassiopeia* boasted that her daughter was more beautiful than the *Nereids*. In response, the sea god *Poseidon* sent *Cetus,* a terrible sea-monster to ravage the land. *Andromeda* was chained to a rock where she was to be sacrificed to *Cetus* - but just in time, *Perseus* arrived on the winged horse *Pegasus* and rescued her, saving *Andromeda* from an appalling death; the pair were then joined in a sacred marriage. Master Code solutions indicate, as logic too suggests that *Andromeda* alludes to Victoria and *Perseus* represents Albert.

Applying the Master Code in the context of *Andromeda* and Victoria:

1. "*Andromeda:* cypher of Queen Victoria" = 246
2. "*Andromeda* is an alias of Queen Victoria" = 246
3. "*Andromeda* is cipher of Queen Victoria" = 246
4. "*Andromeda* statue hid Queen Victoria" = 246
5. "*Andromeda* was hiding Queen Victoria" = 246
6. "*Andromeda's* statue hides Victoria" = 246
7. "Found a hint: *Andromeda* was Victoria" = 246

8. “Found a hint: Victoria hid by *Andromeda*” = 246
9. “Got the hint: *Andromeda* hid Victoria” = 246

Applying the Master Code in the context of *Perseus* and Prince Albert:

1. “*Perseus:* disguised Prince Albert” = 246
2. “*Perseus:* hides Prince Albert in code” = 246
3. “*Perseus:* masking Prince Albert” = 246
4. “*Perseus:* Prince Albert hidden in a code” = 246
5. “*Perseus* was code of Prince Albert” = 246
6. “Prince Albert hid in a code as *Perseus*” = 246

It appears that *Andromeda* was chosen for the fountain statue at Osborne House not only because the myth alluded to the real-life romantic relationship of Victoria and Albert, but because several Master Code solutions are also consistent with that context. In other words, Victoria and Albert were ‘destined’ to be represented by *Andromeda* and *Perseus*. **Applying the Master Code in the context of Victoria, Albert, Osborne House, the fountain and the cipher etc:**

1. “A code hidden at Osborne House is solved” = 246
2. “A code of Prince Albert at Osborne House” = 246
3. “A fountain-statue at Osborne House” = 246
4. “A pair of towers at Osborne House” = 246
5. “A secret code clue hides at clock tower” = 246
6. “A secret code hidden at Osborne House” = 246
7. “A secret code hiding in Osborne House” = 246
8. “A secret code test in Osborne House” = 246
9. “A secret number is found in fountain” = 246
10. “A statue of Andromeda alludes to *Drina*” = 246
11. “A statue of Andromeda at the fountain” = 246
12. “Albert designed Osborne House Garden” = 246
13. “Albert’s secrets at Osborne House” = 246
14. “Albert’s six-floor bell tower” = 246
15. “*Andromeda* is in garden of Osborne House” = 246
16. “*Andromeda* is statue of the fountain” = 246
17. “*Andromeda* statue hid Queen Victoria” = 246
18. “*Andromeda*’s statue hides Victoria” = 246
19. “Cipher at Osborne House is solved” = 246
20. “Cipher is in garden at Osborne House” = 246
21. “Clock tower hiding a secret number” = 246
22. “Clue in diameter of *Andromeda*’s fountain” = 246
23. “Clues are in fountain of Osborne House” = 246
24. “Clues by fountain at Osborne House” = 246
25. “Clues in secret code at Osborne House” = 246
26. “Clues to digits *hide* at the fountain” = 246
27. “Code clue at Osborne House clock tower” = 246
28. “Code clue hidden at Osborne House campanile” = 246

29. "Code clue hides in garden at Osborne House" = 246
30. "Code clue hiding in Osborne House campanile" = 246
31. "Code clue in fountain statue of *Andromeda*" = 246
32. "Code clue near Osborne House's fountain" = 246
33. "Code hid at Osborne House was solved" = 246
34. "Code hid by Osborne House clock tower" = 246
35. "Code hid in clock tower of Osborne House" = 246
36. "Code hidden in the design of Osborne House" = 246
37. "Code left by Albert at Osborne House" = 246
38. "Code numeral digits hidden at fountain" = 246
39. "Code numeral is hidden at Osborne House" = 246
40. "Code of Her Majesty at Osborne House" = 246
41. "Code Osborne House hides was solved" = 246
42. "Code set as test at Osborne House" = 246
43. "Cypher in garden at Osborne House" = 246
44. "*Digits* of code number hidden at fountain" = 246
45. "Few find the cipher in Osborne House" = 246
46. "Find code digits hidden by the fountain" = 246
47. "Find the secret code at Osborne House" = 246
48. "Fountain at Osborne House hid the clue" = 246
49. "Fountain is at Osborne House Garden" = 246
50. "Garden fountain hiding a cipher number" = 246
51. "Gardens at Osborne House hid code clues" = 246
52. "Hid a cipher clue at Osborne House Garden" = 246
53. "Hid the clue at Osborne House fountain" = 246
54. "Hid the code number clue at Osborne House" = 246
55. "I concealed a numeral in *Andromeda* fountain" = 246
56. "I hid a secret code key at Osborne House" = 246
57. "I hid number in Osborne House fountain" = 246
58. "I hid Victoria at Osborne as *Andromeda*" = 246
59. "Italian towers in Osborne House" = 246 the twin towers are Italianate
60. "Look for a number clue at Osborne House" = 246
61. "Look for a numeral hid in Osborne House" = 246
62. "Look for a secret hid in Osborne House" = 246
63. "Look for code-digits nearby fountain" = 246
64. "Look for number hid in garden fountain" = 246
65. "Number hiding in Osborne House Garden" = 246
66. "Number in gardens at Osborne House" = 246
67. "Number in Osborne House's fountain" = 246
68. "Osborne hiding Victoria as *Andromeda*" = 246
69. "Osborne House fountain hides the clue" = 246
70. "Osborne House garden hid the numeral" = 246
71. "Osborne House garden hid the secret" = 246
72. "Osborne House garden hides a cypher" = 246
73. "Osborne House garden hiding code digits" = 246

74. “Osborne House hid a secret number clue” = 246
75. “Osborne House hid number puzzle” = 246
76. “Osborne House hiding Albert’s secret” = 246
77. “Osborne House is hiding *Skelton* code” = 246
78. “Osborne House is hiding the numeral” = 246
79. “Osborne House is hiding the secret” = 246
80. “Osborne House on the Isle of Wight” = 246
81. “Osborne House was hiding the riddle” = 246
82. “Prince Albert hid a secret code number” = 246
83. “Prince Albert hid code in Osborne House” = 246
84. “Prince Albert hides Freemason’s code” = 246
85. “Prince Albert is hiding numeral clue” = 246
86. “Prince Albert knows code numeral” = 246
87. “Prince Albert knows of code number” = 246
88. “Prince Albert knows secret code” = 246
89. “Prince Albert’s code clue in the garden” = 246
90. “Prince Albert’s code is in the garden” = 246
91. “Secret code clue hidden at Osborne House” = 246
92. “Secret code digits hidden at fountain” = 246
93. “Secret code is hidden at Osborne House” = 246
94. “Secret of occult code at Osborne House” = 246
95. “*Skelton*’s code is at Osborne House” = 246
96. “The clue is in Osborne House’s Garden” = 246
97. “The clue is: test at Osborne House” = 246
98. “The clue was: Osborne House test” = 246
99. “The code *digits* are found *near* a fountain” = 246
100. “The code is hidden on the Isle of Wight” = 246
101. “The code of *Skelton* at Osborne House” = 246
102. “The code’s *digits* hidden *near* a fountain” = 246
103. “The puzzle is in Osborne House” = 246
104. “The riddle is hiding at Osborne House” = 246
105. “The secret clues at Osborne House” = 246
106. “Twin towers of Osborne House” = 246
107. “Two-Four-Six: a clue *in* clock tower” = 246 number of steps inside?
108. “Two-Four-Six: clue *on* clock tower” = 246
109. “Width of fountain in inches was 246” = 246 written 2, 4, 6
110. “You cracked Osborne House codes. *Bravo*!” = 246
111. “You found numeral Prince Albert hid” = 246
112. “You found secret code of Osborne House” = 246
113. “You found secret Prince Albert hid” = 246
114. “You have found the code of Osborne House” = 246
115. “You passed Osborne House test” = 246
116. “You solved riddle Osborne House hid” = 246

Reverse solutions:

- 246 = “a number Osborne House’s fountain hid”
- 246 = “a numeral Prince Albert was hiding”
- 246 = “hidden at Osborne House clock tower”
- 246 = “hides as diameter of *Andromeda* fountain”
- 246 = “hiding in Osborne House clock tower”
- 246 = “is at Osborne House garden-fountain”
- 246 = “is hid at the Osborne House fountain”
- 246 = “is hidden at fountain of Osborne House”
- 246 = “is numeral Prince Albert is hiding”
- 246 = “is secret number at the fountain”
- 246 = “number concealed at fountain of *Andromeda*”
- 246 = “number garden’s fountain is hiding”
- 246 = “number hid as Osborne House fountain”
- 246 = “number hidden as fountain’s diameter”
- 246 = “number hiding at the garden fountain”
- 246 = “number I hid in Osborne House fountain”
- 246 = “number in Osborne House’s fountain”
- 246 = “numeral concealed at *Andromeda* fountain”
- 246 = “secret number hid by the fountain”
- 246 = “secret numeral hid in the fountain”
- 246 = “the number Prince Albert has hidden”
- 246 = “was fountain’s diameter in inches”

29. The novels of 'George Eliot' – by Mary Ann Evans (1819-1880)

Portrait by Samuel Laurence - http://www.meredithsuewillis.com/favorites.html

One of the leading English novelists of the 19th century, writing under the name *George Eliot*, Mary Ann Evans's works are noted for their realism and psychological insights. Also known as Marian, she was born on 22nd November 1819 near Nuneaton in Warwickshire. When her mother died in 1836, she left school to help run the household and in 1841 moved with her father to Coventry, living with him until his death in 1849. Somewhat 'liberated' by his passing she then felt free to explore, travelling around Europe before finally settling in London.

In 1850, Mary began contributing to the 'Westminster Review', a leading journal for philosophical radicals of which she later became editor. Finding herself at the centre of a literary circle, she met George Henry Lewes a noted scholar and translator of Goethe; however, Lewes was married and the relationship caused a scandal which resulted in her being shunned by friends. Undaunted, in 1856 she began 'Scenes of Clerical Life' - stories about the people of Warwickshire where she grew up, which were published in 'Blackwood's Magazine'.

In 1857 Mary Evans took the pen name *George Eliot*, adopting a male *nom de plume* to ensure her works were taken seriously at a time when female authors were usually associated with romantic novels. Her first novel 'Adam Bede' (1859) published under the assumed name was a great success. Later titles included: 'The Mill on the Floss' (1860), 'Silas Marner' (1861), 'Romola' (1863), 'Middlemarch' (1872) and 'Daniel Deronda' (1876).

The popularity of her novels brought social acceptance and the home of George and Mary became a regular meeting place for writers and intellectuals. After George Lewes' death in 1878 she married a friend John Cross, 20 years her junior.

Mary Cross died childless on 22nd December 1880 and was buried at Highgate Cemetery in north London.

To test the conjecture that Mary Ann Evans used *Skelton* to create her *nom de plume*, the cipher is applied in the context of the author's real name and pen name *George Eliot*.

Trial and error, gives the following resonance equations:

1. "*George Eliot:* an alias of" = "Mary Ann Evans" = 136
2. "*George Eliot:* cipher of" = "Mary Ann Evans" = 136
3. "*George Eliot:* pen name" = "for Mary Evans" = 136
4. "Marian Evans hid as" = "pen name *George Eliot*" = 136
5. "Mary Ann Evans" = "pen name: *George Eliot*" = 136
6. "Mary Ann Evans" = "used a name: *George Eliot*" = 136

Which suggests the author probably knew *Skelton's* cipher. It's possible she was introduced to the cipher by members of the *literati* - Freemasons perhaps - that she had come to know through her husband and her work. **To test the conjecture further we apply the Master Code in the context of Mary (Ann)/Marian Evans and *George Eliot*:**

1. "A code was used by Mary Ann Evans" = 246
2. "*All* of *George Eliot*'s novels hide codes" = 246
3. "Clue is: Mary Ann Evans used *our* code" = 246 'our' - refers to the 'Brothers' code?
4. "Each novel of *George Eliot* was hiding a code" = 246
5. "Each of *George Eliot's* novels hides a clue" = 246
6. "Every novel of *George Eliot* has a code" = 246
7. "*George Eliot* is hiding Mary Evans" = 246
8. "*George Eliot* is name of Mary Evans" = 246
9. "*George Eliot* is name of the writer" = 246
10. "*George Eliot* used *code* in *all* novels" = 246
11. "*George Eliot* used *The Code* in stories" = 246
12. "*George Eliot* uses *Skelton* cipher" = 246
13. "*George Eliot:* Mary Evans's mask" = 246
14. "*George Eliot*'s cipher was secret" = 246
15. "*George Eliot*'s cypher is difficult" = 246
16. "*George Eliot*'s hidden code was a secret" = 246
17. "*George Eliot*'s name is a code of *Skelton*" = 246
18. "I hid Mary Ann Evans as a man's name" = 246
19. "I hid Mary Evans' name as man's name" = 246
20. "Man's name hiding Mary Ann Evans" = 246
21. "Marian Evans masked as *George Eliot*" = 246
22. "Mary Ann Evans is hidden by a name" = 246
23. "Mary Evans used *Skelton*'s code" = 246
24. "You broke a code of Mary Evans. *Bravo*!" = 246
25. "You broke *George Eliot*'s code. Well done!" = 246
26. "You cracked a cipher Mary Evans hid" = 246
27. "You cracked a clue Mary Ann Evans hid" = 246
28. "You found secret code *George Eliot* used" = 246
29. "You have broken a code of Mary Evans" = 246
30. "You have found Mary Ann Evans' code" = 246

The solutions are evidence that Mary Evans knew *Skelton* and the Master Code and that she probably used the cipher in all of her novels: *Adam Bede, The Mill on the Floss, Silas Marner, Felix Holt – the radical, Middlemarch, Daniel Deronda.*

Applying the Master Code to each novel chronologically:

Adam Bede (1859)

1. "*Adam Bede* is name of a master carpenter" = 246
2. "*Adolphus Irwine:* pastor's name" = 246
3. "*Bartle Massey:* the teacher of *Adam Bede*" = 246
4. "Called gardener at Donnithorne: *Craig*" = 246
5. "Called *Poyser*'s orphaned niece: *Dinah Morris*" = 246

The Mill on the Floss (1860)

1. "*Bob Jakin:* old friend of *Tom Tulliver*" = 246
2. "*Dorlcote* name of a mill near *St Ogg's*" = 246
3. "*Dorlcote* was a mill on the *Floss*" = 246
4. "*Dr Turnbull* is at *Dorlcote mill*" = 246
5. "Head miller of *Dorlcote* was called *Luke*" = 246
6. "*Kezia:* maid of the *Tulliver* family" = 246
7. "*Mrs Jane Glegg:* Dodson's matriarch" = 246
8. "Rector at St Ogg's is called *Kenn*" = 246
9. "*Tom* and *Maggie*'s cousin called *Lucy Deane*" = 246
10. "*Walter Stelling:* name of teacher" = 246
11. "*Yap:* the name for *Tulliver*'s dog" = 246

Silas Marner (1861)

1. "*Bob Lundy:* name of the village butcher" = 246
2. "*Cass* is a squire: lord of the manor" = 246
3. "*Crackenthorpe* was the rector" = 246
4. "*Dowlas:* name of the village farrier" = 246
5. "*Eppie* is adopted by *Silas Marner*" = 246
6. "*Eppie* was a diminutive of *Hephzibah*" = 246
7. "*John Dowlas:* farrier of the village" = 246
8. "*Kimble* is the squire's sister" = 246
9. "*Lantern Yard:* a slum street" = 246
10. "*Molly Farren* was an opium addict" = 246
11. "Name the *Raveloe* poacher: *Jem Rodney*" = 246
12. "*Silas* is falsely accused of a theft" = 246
13. "*Silas Marner* is a weaver's name" = 246
14. "*Silas Marner* was Calvinist" = 246
15. "*Silas Marner*: the name of a weaver" = 246

Romola (1862-63)

1. "Barber's name at Florence was *Nello*" = 246
2. "*Bardo de Bardi* is blind classical scholar" = 246
3. "*Bratti Ferravecchi* was a trader" = 246
4. "Called the slave: *Baldassarre Calvo*" = 246
5. "*Tito Melema* is the Italianate Greek" = 246

Felix Holt, the radical (1866)

1. "A medical apprentice called *Felix Holt*" = 246
2. "*Christian* alias is *Scaddon*'s mask" = 246
3. "*Christian* was the alias of *Scaddon*" = 246
4. "*Christian:* name assumed by *Scaddon*" = 246
5. "*John Johnson:* agent for *Transome*" = 246
6. "Landowner name: *Harold Transome*" = 246
7. "*Rufus Lyon:* a friend of *Felix Holt*" = 246
8. "*Rufus Lyon:* deacon at *Treby Magna*" = 246

Middlemarch (1871-1872) – regarded as one of the great C19 English novels

Applying *Skelton* to the title of the novel, we find: "Middlemarch" = "*Skelton*" = 77*. Suggests the title alludes to *Skelton*'s cipher. To test the conjecture, we applying the Master code in that context:

1. "Book's title: a clue to the name of the code" = 246
2. "Middlemarch hides the name *Skelton*" = 246
3. "Middlemarch title: hiding *Skelton*" = 246
4. "Middlemarch was in eight volumes" = 246
5. "Middlemarch: clue to *Skelton* cipher" = 246
6. "Middlemarch: name is *Skelton* hint" = 246
7. "Novel title is clue to cipher name" = 246
8. "Novel title: clue to cypher name" = 246
9. "Title hiding a clue to the name of the code" = 246
10. "Title of book was clue to *Skelton*" = 246
11. "Title of book was clue to the cipher" = 246

Applying the Master Code to elements in the narrative:

1. "A code hides in the unfinished book of *Casaubon*" = 246
2. "A *Skelton* code hid in the unfinished book" = 246
3. "An unfinished book by *Casaubon* hid a cipher" = 246
4. "*Casaubon* is the alias hiding *Skelton*" = 246
5. "*Casaubon's* unfinished book hiding cipher" = 246
6. "Cipher in an unfinished book by *Casaubon*" = 246
7. "Cipher of *Middlemarch:* the code is broken" = 246
8. "Code hid in unfinished book of *Edward Casaubon*" = 246
9. "Code in the unfinished book of *Casaubon* is hid" = 246
10. "Code of *The Key to all Mythologies*" = 246*

11. *"Code you have found is Edward Casaubon's"* = 246
12. "*Doctor Sprague* was a physician" = 246
13. "*Edward Casaubon* is name of clergyman" = 246
14. *"Edward Casaubon* knew the *Big Secret*" = 246
15. *"Edward Casaubon* was the mystic" = 246
16. *"Edward Casaubon's* unfinished book hid clue" = 246
17. "*James Chettam* is a lover of *Dorothea*" = 246
18. "*Middlemarch* title hiding *Skelton*" = 246 "Middlemarch" = "*Skelton*" = 77
19. "*Middlemarch* title hiding *The Code*" = 246
20. "The code you have found is *Casaubon*'s clue" = 246
21. "The hidden code of *Casaubon*'s unfinished book" = 246
22. "The name *Casaubon* is alias of *Skelton*" = 246
23. "The unfinished book by *Casaubon* hid code clue" = 246
24. "The unfinished book by *Casaubon* hides a code" = 246
25. "The unfinished book hides cipher clues" = 246
26. "The unfinished book hides cyphers" = 246
27. "The unfinished book is a code of *Skelton*" = 246
28. "*Unfinished* book by *Edward Casaubon* hid code" = 246

*Suggests the Master Code is the 'Code of *The Key to all Mythologies*' – the title of *Edward Casaubon*'s unfinished book. **Applying *Skelton* in that context:**

"The Key to all Mythologies" = **223**

The gematria number in this context is 223. Applying *Skelton*, we find the resonance equations:

1. *"The Key to all Mythologies"* = "*George Eliot*'s secret ciphers" = 223
2. *"The Key to all Mythologies"* = "Hiding the cypher of *Skelton*" = 223*
3. *"The Key to all Mythologies"* = "Is hiding the cipher of *Skelton*" = 223
4. *"The Key to all Mythologies"* = "Mary Evans hides secrets" = 223
5. *"The Key to all Mythologies"* = "Title is hiding a secret cipher" = 223*
6. *"The Key to all Mythologies"* = "Title was code hiding the cipher" = 223*
7. *"The Key to all Mythologies"* = "Title was hiding a secret name" = 223*
8. *"The Key to all Mythologies"* = "Title was hiding the secret" = 223*
9. ***"The Key to all Mythologies"* = "You cracked code *Middlemarch* hid. *Bravo*!" = 223**
10. *"The Key to all Mythologies"* = "You found the key to a cypher" = 223
11. *"The Key to all Mythologies"* = "You have cracked a cipher. Well done!" = 223
12. *"The Key to all Mythologies"* = "You have cracked my code. Well done!" = 223
13. *"The Key to all Mythologies"* = "You have found a cipher of *Skelton*" = 233
14. *"The Key to all Mythologies"* = "You have found key to the cipher" = 233
15. *"The Key to all Mythologies"* = "You have the key to a cypher" = 223

***We note:** *"Middlemarch"* = *"Skelton"* = "The Cipher" = 77

Reverse solutions:

- **223** = "is the key you found to a cipher"
- **223** = "the key you found to a cypher"

The title of *Edward Casaubon*'s unfinished book *The Key to all Mythologies* implies a deep insight into the foundation of the world's mystical religions, the common factor linking them - ***The Key***.

Applying *Skelton* in that context, we find the resonance equations:

1. "A supernatural cipher hidden in" = "*The Key to all Mythologies*" = 223
2. "Supernatural cipher hides in" = "*The Key to all Mythologies*" = 223
3. "Supernatural ciphers hide in" = "*The Key to all Mythologies*" = 223
4. "*The Key to all Mythologies*" = "cipher hiding supernatural code" = 223
5. "*The Key to all Mythologies*" = "hiding the old supernatural code" = 223
6. "*The Key to all Mythologies*" = "is supernatural code you found" = 223
7. "*The Key to all Mythologies*" = "it hides the supernatural code" = 223
8. "*The Key to all Mythologies*" = "the huge supernatural cipher" = 223
9. "Found supernatural code hiding in" = "*The Key to all Mythologies*" = 223

And, we note the resonance equations:

1. "A clue to the secret code is hiding in" = "*The Key to all Mythologies*" = 223
2. "*The Key to all Mythologies*" = "hiding the cypher of *Skelton*" = 223
3. "*The Key to all Mythologies*" = "is hiding the cipher of *Skelton*" = 223

'Supernatural' solutions of *Skelton* will be explored in ***The Secret Code of Destiny*** **Part 3.**

Daniel Deronda (1876)

1. "*Daniel Deronda:* an allegorical story" = 246*
2. "*Ezra Mordecai Cohen* is visionary" = 246
3. "*Gwendolen Harleth:* name of socialite" = 246
4. "*Mirah Lapidoth* is beautiful Jewess" = 246
5. "*Maria Alcharisi:* a young operatic diva" = 246
6. "*Klesmer* is name of a Jewish musician" = 246
7. "*Thomas Lush:* A *Grandcourt* lackey" = 246

*****Daniel Deronda is recognised as allegory.

30. *LEWIS CARROLL* - CHARLES LUTWIDGE DODGSON

Charles Dodgson (1832-1898) by O. G. Rejlander (1863) (Image: Wiki-Commons)

The Reverend Charles Lutwidge Dodgson, better known to millions as the children's author *Lewis Carroll*, was born at Daresbury parsonage in Cheshire on January 27th 1832. He proved to be a brilliant student and from Rugby School went up to Oxford where he took a double first. Although afflicted with migraine, a stammer and possibly epilepsy he nevertheless became a lecturer at his *alma mater* Christ Church and made original contributions in his specialism, mathematics.

An Anglican deacon, Dodgson never married and lived his entire adult life in college. Among his wide-ranging interests, he was a pioneer in the nascent techniques of photography and developed a penchant for taking pictures of young girls, many naked - most of which he later destroyed. His interest in logic and ciphers suggests he might have encountered *Skelton* while researching cryptology though it's possible he learned of the cipher through Freemasonry - some solutions suggest he knew the secret Masonic code. **To test the conjecture that Dodgson used *Skelton,* we apply the cipher in the context of 'Dodgson' and *Skelton*'s gematria.**

1. "Charles Dodgson uses" = "*Skelton*'s gematria" = 157
2. "*Skelton*'s gematria" = "a code Charles Dodgson used" = 157
3. "*Skelton*'s gematria" = "cipher used by Dodgson" = 157
4. "*Skelton*'s gematria" = "C. L. Dodgson knew the code" = 157
5. "*Skelton*'s gematria" = "secret code Dodgson used" = 157

And, in respect of the Master Code we find the resonance equations:

"You discovered" = "C. L. Dodgson uses" = "the Master Code" = 111

To test further his use of *Skelton*, we look for resonance equations linking Charles Dodgson's real name with his nom de plume, *Lewis Carroll* - a pseudonym derived from the Latinisation of Lutwidge and Charles respectively. In that context, trial and error gives the following resonance equations:

1. "Dodgson masked as" = "Lewis Carroll" = 120
2. "Lewis Carroll" = "a code hiding C. L. Dodgson" = 120
3. "Lewis Carroll" = "a mask of C. L. Dodgson" = 120
4. "Lewis Carroll" = "C. L. Dodgson's alias" = 120
5. "Lewis Carroll" = "Dodgson's cipher" = 120
6. "Lewis Carroll" = "is C. L. Dodgson's code" = 120
7. "Lewis Carroll" = "is clue to the hidden code" = 120
8. "Lewis Carroll" = "is don at Oxford" = 120
9. "Lewis Carroll" = "Latinised names" = 120
10. "Lewis Carroll" = "name hiding Dodgson" = 120
11. "Lewis Carroll" = "ruse of C. L. Dodgson" = 120
12. "Lewis Carroll" = "was Oxford don" = 120

Evidence that Dodgson knew the Master Code is provided by the following:

1. "A cipher of Charles Lutwidge Dodgson" = 246
2. "A code at Oxford solved by C. L. Dodgson" = 246
3. "A code clue hid as the name *Lewis Carroll*" = 246
4. "A code of the Oxford don Charles Dodgson" = 246
5. "C. L. Dodgson found a code hid at Osborne House" = 246
6. "C. L. Dodgson found a code Osborne House hides" = 246
7. "C. L. Dodgson found code clue Osborne House hid" = 246
8. "C. L. Dodgson solved the motto's code" = 246
9. "C. L. Dodgson solved the Oxford codes" = 246
10. "C. L. Dodgson used gematria of *Skelton*" = 246
11. "Carroll is actually called Dodgson" = 246
12. "Carroll is name of Charles in Latin" = 246
13. "Carroll is pseudonym of Dodgson" = 246
14. "Carroll was Charles Latinized" = 246
15. "Charles Dodgson at Christ Church" = 246
16. "Charles Dodgson cracked a code at Oxford" = 246
17. "Charles Dodgson cracked *All Souls* code" = 246
18. "Charles Dodgson used a Masonic cipher" = 246
19. "Charles Dodgson used the secret code" = 246
20. "Charles Dodgson uses a Freemason code" = 246
21. "Charles Dodgson's unbreakable ciphers" = 246
22. "Charles L. Dodgson + *Lewis Carroll*" = 246
23. "Charles L. Dodgson hid a secret cipher" = 246
24. "Charles L. Dodgson is a don at Oxford" = 246
25. "Charles L. Dodgson used secret codes" = 246
26. "Charles Lutwidge Dodgson: a recluse" = 246
27. "Charles Lutwidge is name of Dodgson" = 246

28. "Chas. Dodgson the Christ Church don" = 246
29. "Chas. L. Dodgson Christ Church's don" = 246
30. "Cipher you have cracked is Dodgson's" = 246
31. "C. L. Dodgson cracked code on *All Souls* gate" = 246
32. "C. L. Dodgson pen-name: *Lewis Carroll*" = 246
33. "C. L. Dodgson used gematria of *Skelton*" = 246
34. "C. L. Dodgson uses the Freemason code" = 246
35. "Code hid at Oxford solved by Dodgson" = 246
36. "Code motto hides solved by Dodgson" = 246
37. "Code of Charles Dodgson was uncrackable" = 246
38. "Code of Osborne House found by C. L. Dodgson" = 246
39. "Code Oxford hides solved by Dodgson" = 246
40. "Dodgson: tutor in Christ Church" = 246
41. "Dodgson broke code of Oxford's motto" = 246
42. "Dodgson congratulates you by code" = 246
43. "Dodgson cracked clue Oxford motto hid" = 246
44. "Dodgson found clue hid in Osborne House" = 246
45. "Dodgson found the Osborne House code clue" = 246
46. "Dodgson had a pen-name: *Lewis Carroll*" = 246
47. "Dodgson hid codes in nonsense language" = 246
48. "Dodgson is name of children's author" = 246
49. "Dodgson is the author for children" = 246
50. "Dodgson knew code hid at Osborne House" = 246
51. "Dodgson knew code of the Freemasons" = 246
52. "Dodgson knows code Osborne House hid" = 246
53. "Dodgson knows *Skelton* cipher" = 246
54. **"Dodgson loved the little girls" = 246**
55. "Dodgson solved motto in Oxford" = 246
56. "Dodgson solved secret motto code" = 246
57. "Dodgson solved secret Oxford code" = 246
58. "Dodgson used the code of Queen Elizabeth" = 246
59. "Dodgson used the codes of Freemasons" = 246
60. "Dodgson uses gematria of *Skelton*" = 246
61. "*Dodo* was Charles Dodgson's nickname" = 246 Dodgson stammering his name 'Dodo...'
62. "Few deciphered secret codes of Dodgson" = 246
63. "Few decrypt clues in code of Dodgson" = 246
64. "Few decrypt code-clues by Dodgson" = 246
65. "Few have decoded secret codes Dodgson hid" = 246
66. "Gematria of *Skelton*: a code Dodgson used" = 246
67. **"*Lewis Carroll* wrote gibberish" = 246***
68. "*Lewis Carroll:* alias hiding Dodgson" = 246
69. "*Lewis Carroll:* an alias of C. L. Dodgson" = 246
70. "*Lewis Carroll:* cipher of C. L. Dodgson" = 246
71. "*Lewis Carroll:* just a *nom de plume*" = 246
72. "*Lewis Carroll:* Latinisations" = 246

73. "*Lewis Carroll:* name hid the author" = 246
74. "*Lewis Carroll*: name was clue to code" = 246
75. "*Lewis Carroll:* the pseudonym" = 246
76. "Motto code is solved by C. L. Dodgson" = 246
77. "Oxford hides code solved by Dodgson" = 246
78. "Secret code found by Charles Dodgson" = 246
79. "Secret code *hides* Dodgson as *Carroll*" = 246
80. "*Skelton* is name of code C. L. Dodgson used" = 246
81. "*Skelton* is name of code Dodgson uses" = 246
82. "The code you discovered is Dodgson's" = 246
83. "The little girls loved Dodgson" = 246
84. "The name *Lewis Carroll* hides code clue" = 246
85. "The name *Lewis Carroll* is a hidden code" = 246
86. "The name *Lewis Carroll* is an alias" = 246
87. "These codes hid Dodgson's secrets" = 246
88. "This was a code Charles Dodgson used" = 246
89. "Used the name *Lewis Carroll* to hide" = 246
90. "You decoded ciphers of Charles Dodgson" = 246
91. "You found cipher of Dodgson. Well done!" = 246
92. "You found Dodgson's cipher numeral" = 246
93. "You found Dodgson's secret cipher" = 246
94. "You have broken cypher of Dodgson" = 246
95. "You have cracked Dodgson's cypher" = 246
96. "You have discovered Dodgson's codes" = 246
97. "You knew Charles Dodgson's alias" = 246
98. "You know Dodgson's secret codes" = 246

Reverse solutions:

- 246 = "a secret code number of Charles Dodgson"
- 246 = "a secret cypher number of Dodgson"
- 246 = "C. L. Dodgson's secret cipher number"
- 246 = "code numeral found by Charles Dodgson"
- 246 = "hides a code of Charles Lutwidge Dodgson"
- 246 = "hides a secret code of Charles L. Dodgson"
- 246 = "is a secret cipher number of Dodgson"
- 246 = "secret cipher-number Dodgson found"
- 246 = "was the secret number of Dodgson"
- 246 = "you found Dodgson's code number. *Bravo*!"

It appears from those solutions that Charles Dodgson not only used *Skelton* to hide secrets but that he also cracked the motto-code at Oxford, ciphers on *All Souls* gate and the Osborne House code.

*__We note the Master Code solution__: "Lewis Carroll wrote gibberish" = 246

Implies a sort of 'split' personality with Lewis Carroll penning the nonsense and Charles Dodgson devising the meaning *hidden* by the nonsense.

Alice's adventures in Wonderland (1865)

Dodgson dedicated *Alice's Adventures in Wonderland* to Alice Pleasance Liddell (1852-1934), the fourth of ten children of Henry Liddell, Dean of *Christ Church* Oxford and his wife Lorina Liddell (nee Reeve). Dodgson developed a very close relationship with the family of his boss – especially Alice.

Applying *Skelton* to 'Wonderland':

1. "a secret code in" = "Wonderland" = 91
2. "*Wonderland*" = "a secret land" = 91

Applying the Master Code in the context of the dedication:

1. "*Alice (in Wonderland)* is called Alice Liddell" = 246
2. "Alice Liddell was a *dream-girl* of Dodgson" = 246
3. "C. L. Dodgson wrote a book for Alice Liddell" = 246
4. "Dedicated the book to Alice Pleasance Liddell" = 246
5. "I wrote book for Alice Pleasance Liddell" = 246
6. "*Wonderland:* code written for Alice" = 246
7. "Wrote cypher-book for Alice Liddell" = 246

Applying the Master Code in the context of '*Alice in Wonderland*':

1. "A clue is: the *Duchess*'s baby becomes a pig" = 246
2. "A secret code hides in *The Wonderland*" = 246*
3. "A secret code of Dodgson in *Wonderland"* = 246
4. "A *very* secret code in *Wonderland*" = 246
5. "*Absolem:* the name of the caterpillar" = 246
6. "*Bravo*! you broke the *Wonderland* code" = 246
7. "Chapter six name: *Pig and Pepper*" = 246
8. "Cheshire cat's big evanescent smile" = 246
9. "Clue is: the cook throws pepper" = 246
10. "Clue to secret code is in *Wonderland*" = 246
11. "Dodgson made a *Wonderland* from *The Code*" = 246
12. "Dodgson was hidden as *White Rabbit*" = 246
13. "*hjckrrh* hid the name of Alice Liddell as code" = 246 "hjckrrh" = "is a cipher" = 66
14. "*hjckrrh* hides Alice Liddell's name as a code" = 246
15. "*hjckrrh* hinting at name: Alice Liddell" = 246
16. "*hjckrrh* is code by *Lewis Carroll*" = 246
17. "*hjckrrh:* a cipher for name of Alice Liddell" = 246*
18. "*hjckrrh:* Alice Liddell's name as a cipher" = 246
19. "*hjckrrh:* cipher hiding name Alice Liddell" = 246
20. "*hjckrrh:* code clue by *Lewis Carroll*" = 246

21. "*hjckrrh:* code hides Alice Pleasance Liddell" = 246
22. "*hjckrrh:* gryphon's secret code" = 246
23. "*hjckrrh:* sign for Alice Liddell's name" = 246
24. "*hjckrrh:* signal hid Alice Liddell's name" = 246
25. "*hjckrrh:* the sound gryphon made" = *246*
26. "I hid secret codes in *The Wonderland*" = 246
27. "My secret code in *The Wonderland*" = 246
28. "Play at croquet with flamingo" = 246
29. "Playing card Queen hiding Victoria" = 246
30. "Price on hat: 10 shillings and 6 pence" = 246
31. "*Queen of Hearts* is a code for Victoria" = 246
32. "*Queen of Hearts:* a code of Queen Victoria" = 246
33. "*Queen of Hearts:* clue was Victoria" = 246
34. "The extremely ugly *Duchess*" = 246
35. "The *Mock Turtle* talks code to Alice" = 246
36. "The price of *Hatter*'s hat is 10 and 6" = 246
37. "Theo. Carter is the name of *Hatter*" = 246
38. "Theophilus Carter: *Hatter* name" = 246
39. "Twins: *Tweedledum* and *Tweedledee*" = 246
40. "Victoria: name of playing card queen" = 246
41. "*White Rabbit* code hid *Lewis Carroll*" = 246
42. "*Wonderland*'s inhabitants are mad" = 246
43. "You have cracked a code-clue *Wonderland* hid" = 246
44. "You solved codes hid in *Wonderland*" = 246

In that context, we note the resonance equations:

"Congratulations" = "you found code-message" = "I hid code in *Wonderland*" = 138

The list is not exhaustive, many additional solutions are likely to be found in the Wonderland story.

**hjckrrh* is the strange 'sound' made by the gryphon when talking with Alice. The significance of the cipher is revealed by applying *Skelton*:

1. "hjckrrh" = "code hid name of" = "Alice Liddell" = 66*
2. "hjckrrh" = "hiding name" = "Alice Liddell" = 66
3. "hjckrrh" = "is in fact" = "Alice Liddell" = 66

**hjckrrh* is a cipher for the name *Alice Liddell* using *Skelton*: "hjckrrh" = "Alice Liddell" = 66

Applying the Master Code in that context, we find:

- "7-letter cypher is Alice Liddell code" = 246 — hjckrrh
- "7-letters in Alice Liddell cypher" = 246 — any 7 letters which sum to 66
- "I use 7-letter cipher for Alice Liddell" = 246
- "You solved the *hjckrrh* code. *Bravo*!" = 246

The Botanic Garden at Oxford

Dodgson spent a lot of time in Oxford's botanic garden. In that context, we find the Master Code solutions:

1. "A botanical garden hiding a secret garden" = 246
2. "A magical garden in Oxford botanic garden" = 246
3. "A secret garden hidden in a botanic garden" = 246
4. "A secret garden hides in botanic garden" = 246
5. "Botanic garden is a clue to *Wonderland*" = 246
6. "Danby gate hides *Wonderland*'s gate" = 246
7. "Danby gate in botanic garden of Oxford" = 246*
8. "Danby gate: the gate to a wonderland" = 246
9. "I dream of a *Wonderland* in botanic garden" = 246
10. "*Wonderland* hidden at botanical garden" = 246
11. "*Wonderland* hiding in botanical garden" = 246
12. "*Wonderland* is in the botanic garden" = 246
13. "*Wonderland* was dream of C. L. Dodgson" = 246

Those solutions suggest that the botanic garden at Oxford was, at least in part, the inspiration for Dodgson's *Wonderland*.

*The Danby gate stands at the entrance to the garden.

In 1871 Dodgson published *Alice through the Looking Glass*

Applying the Master Code to the title:

"*Alice through the Looking Glass* is a book" = 246

Applying *Skelton* to the title gives the resonance equation:

"*Alice through the Looking Glass*" = "was a book written for Alice" = 204

Jabberwocky - a 7-stanza nonsense poem in *Alice through the looking glass*

Why is the poem's title *Jabberwocky* not *Jabberwock?*

Applying *Skelton*: "*Jabberwocky*" = "**code** of a *Jabberwock*" = 90

And: "*Jabberwocky*" = "*Skelton* code" = 90

The *Jabberwock* is described as 'a fearful beast with jaws and claws.' It was probably a dinosaur fossil in Oxford's Museum of Natural History that inspired the *Jabberwock*. Discovered long before Dodgson wrote the verse, *Megalosaurus (*meaning *giant lizard)* was the first dinosaur to be identified as such.
Applying the Master Code in that context:

"*Jabberwock* was name of a *Megalosaurus*" = 246

Applying *Skelton* in that context, we find the resonance equation:

"Jabberwock" = "a dinosaur" = 66

Jabberwock is 'a fearful beast with jaws and claws' like a *terrible lizard. Dinosaur* means *terrible lizard,* so it seems the *Jabberwock* is (like) a dinosaur.

Applying the Master Code in the context of the poem:

1. "7-stanza poem of *Jabberwocky* hid a code" = 246
2. "A code hid by *Jabberwocky's* nonsense" = 246
3. "*A dinosaur* is the pre-historic clue" = 246
4. "A dinosaur name is a pre-historic clue" = 246
5. "A secret code hid as *Jabberwocky* language" = 246   *Skelton*
6. "Clue is: *Jabberwock* name of *Megalosaurus*" = 246   name of the giant lizard
7. "Code in 7-stanza poem of *Jabberwocky*" = 246
8. "Coded riddles hide in *Jabberwocky* language" = 246
9. "Dodgson left clues in *Jabberwock* poem" = 246
10. "Dodgson left code *Jabberwock* verse hid" = 246
11. "*Jabberwock* means *terrible lizard*" = 246   terrible lizard is dinosaur
12. "*Jabberwock* was name of a *Megalosaurus*" = 246
13. "*Jabberwock: terrible lizard*'s name" = 246
14. "*Jabberwock:* the pre-historic beast" = 246
15. "Jabberwock's language hid code of *Skelton*" = 246
16. "Jabberwock's language hiding *Skelton*" = 246
17. "*Jabberwocky* is nonsense hiding a code" = 246
18. "*Jabberwocky* is the code you solved" = 246
19. "*Jabberwocky* is the *Snark* language" = 246
20. "*Jabberwocky* language hides a difficult code" = 246
21. "*Jabberwocky* language hides secret code" = 246
22. "*Jabberwocky* language is riddles in code" = 246
23. "*Jabberwocky* language: code hid as gibberish" = 246
24. "*Jabberwocky* was a Dodgson verse" = 246
25. "*Jabberwocky:* riddled with riddles" = 246
26. "*Jabberwocky:* secret codes of Dodgson" = 246
27. "*Jabberwocky*: the language by Dodgson" = 246
28. "*Jabberwocky's* nonsense is code clue" = 246
29. "*Jabberwocky's* nonsense was a code" = 246
30. "Nonsense was called *Jabberwocky*" = 246
31. "Riddles in *Jabberwocky* language are a code" = 246
32. "The *Jabberwock* is like giant lizard" = 246
33. "The *Jabberwock* language is nonsense" = 246
34. "You have deciphered *Jabberwocky* codes" = 246
35. "You solved the *Jabberwock* code. *Bravo*!" = 246
36. "You translated the *Jabberwock* code" = 246   Jabberwocky is a language

Humpty Dumpty

In *Alice through the looking glass*, *Humpty Dumpty* is identified as an 'egg-man' for the first time. The traditional character was a short, fat person – not a 'human-egg'. However, the following solutions link Humpty to the 'egg-man', additional evidence Dodgson used *Skelton* and the Master Code. Humpty makes words mean what he wants them to mean, 'neither more nor less' and Alice points out that he can make one word mean many things – *multum in parvo.*

Applying the Master Code:

1. "Egg-man: clue is *Humpty Dumpty*" = 246
1. "Hid a yolk as *Humpty Dumpty*" = 246 Dodgson liked puns
2. "*Humpty Dumpty* an egg-man name" = 246
3. "*Humpty Dumpty* was a man-egg" = 246
4. "*Humpty Dumpty: a* hidden yolk" = 246 pun
5. "*Humpty Dumpty*: the human-egg" = 246
6. "I hid a yolk in *Humpty Dumpty*" = 246 pun

Applying *Skelton* to "*Humpty Dumpty*" (= 162) we find the resonance equations:

2. "Called enormous human-egg" = "*Humpty Dumpty*" = 162
3. "*Humpty Dumpty*" = "is big yolk by Dodgson" = 162
4. "*Humpty Dumpty*" = "is C. L. Dodgson's human-egg" = 162
5. "*Humpty Dumpty*" = "name is yolk of Dodgson" = 162
6. "*Humpty Dumpty*" = "name of Carroll's egg-man" = 162
7. "*Humpty Dumpty*" = "the egg-man was a yolk" = 162
8. "*Humpty Dumpty*" = "the human-egg of C. L. Dodgson" = 162
9. "*Humpty Dumpty*" = "was Dodgson's yolk" = 162
10. "*Humpty Dumpty*" = "wore a beautiful cravat" = 162

Humpty Dumpty tells Alice the meaning of some of the nonsense words in the *Jabberwocky* verse. Applying the Master Code in that context:

1. "A *jub jub* is the sound horse hooves make" = 246
2. "*Brillig* meant 4 o'clock in *Jabberwocky*" = 246
3. "*Gyre and gimble* is *to turn and bore*" = 246
4. "*Slithy* means active-slimy" = 246
5. "*The wabe:* the grass around a sun-dial" = 246
6. "*Tove*: name of very peculiar animal" = 246

And, applying *Skelton* to 'rath' and 'borogove bird':

"A rath is" = "a green pig" = 67

"The borogove bird" = "is like a live mop" = 116

There are probably many more solutions awaiting discovery in *Jabberwocky*.

THE HUNTING OF THE SNARK

an agony in eight fits

The Hunting of the Snark (1874 – 1876) was dedicated to nine-year old Gertrude Chataway, a girl that Dodgson met at Sandown on the Isle of Wight in summer 1875. Classified as 'nonsense', the poem caused puzzlement among contemporary critics and it received a mixed reception. Almost immediately fans of *Lewis Carroll* surmised that the poem hid a secret code, an understandable suspicion since it was hard to believe that someone as clever as Charles Dodgson - and someone known to use acrostics - would 'waste' two years of his life writing 141 stanzas of nonsense; and so thereafter, the author was pestered for an explanation of the enigmatic verse - though he steadfastly refused, a tacit hint perhaps that the poem *has* a secret meaning. If true, two questions arise:

- Did Dodgson use *Skelton's* cipher in *The Hunting of the Snark*?
- Why was Dodgson so reluctant to explain the poem's (assumed) hidden meaning?

The title begs a question: what is *The Snark*?

Turning the question into a statement and applying *Skelton*, we find the contextually appropriate resonance equations:

1. "Snark" = "is hiding" = "riddles" = 59

So: "The Hunting of *The Snark*" = "The Hunting of *The Riddles*" = 195

Also: "Use a *Skelton* code to solve" = "The Hunting of *The Snark*" = 195

This makes sense in the context and implies that there is more to the verse than pure nonsense, as has long been suspected.

Applying *Skelton* again, we find the resonance equations:

1. "*The Snark* is" = "the unknown" = 109
2. "*The Snark* is" = "a hidden secret code" = 109

Those solutions are appropriate if 'the Snark' is an abstraction – 'the unknown' or a 'secret code'.

However, 'the *Snark*' has a contextually appropriate meaning that relates to contemporary Britain in the early-mid 1870s when the verse was written. In that particular setting, it becomes clear why Dodgson would not have wanted to reveal the work's hidden meaning as he would almost certainly have considered the 'real-world' identity of *The* Snark too controversial for public revelation. Moreover, in order to give a complete explanation, he would need to reveal *Skelton*'s cipher - something prohibited by the Master Code solution:

"You are forbidden to reveal this code" = 246

which Dodgson almost certainly knew.

After the death of her beloved Prince Albert in 1861, Queen Victoria became notoriously reclusive and abandoned many of the public duties expected of her as monarch. She spent a great deal of time in retreat, 'hiding' at Osborne House on the Isle of Wight and Balmoral Castle in Scotland – hermit-like-behaviour that might be explained if she was a shy person or if she was overwhelmed by official responsibilities without the Prince Consort by her side; alternatively, it might have been that she could no longer be 'bothered' with 'tiresome' public duties. Whatever the true reason, Victoria seems to have chosen to stay at royal venues well away from London, forcing ministers to make long / inconvenient journeys if they wanted an audience with their 'invisible', 'snark-like' sovereign.

The Queen had nine children with Prince Albert and yet she appears to have resented the time he spent with them. Victoria - 'Drina' as she was known privately, a 'pet-name' derived from her first name Alexan*drina* - was self-absorbed, had a strong tendency to feel sorry for herself and possessed a short temper; she seems to have lacked the 'emotional warmth' associated with a 'motherly' disposition. Indeed, she displayed a highly controlling and critical attitude towards her offspring, most of whom failed to reach the high standards she set them.

Leopold (1853-1884) the Queen's eighth child and youngest son, was an undergraduate at Christ Church College Oxford (1873-1876) just as Dodgson was writing *The Hunting of the Snark.* An intelligent young man and a talented pianist, Leopold was made to live out of college at a house in North Oxford to 'protect' him from the 'harmful', 'subversive' and 'corrupting' influences of fellow undergraduates. Drina was determined that Leopold should not to have 'fun' at university and so it was agreed that he would attend Oxford on the strict understanding that he must work hard and focus all his energies on study.

Dodgson got to know Leopold at Christ Church and photographed him during his time as an undergraduate. It's plausible that through their relationship the writer discovered something of what Drina was like as a mother and a person - an insight very few 'ordinary' subjects would ever share; the possibility that intimate secrets concerning royal persons might have informed the verse, would go some way to explain why Dodgson never revealed the poem's hidden meaning.

Applying *Skelton* in the context of Victoria's/Drina's 'withdrawal' from public life and 'The Snark', we find the resonance equations:

"*Snark*" = "is name of" = "a recluse" = 59, "Drina is" = "a recluse" = 59 and "Snark" = "is Drina" = 59

"*The Snark*" = "is The Queen" = 88

"*The Snark* is" = "Queen Victoria" = 109

By the 1870s the reclusive sovereign was effectively 'unknown', at least as far as the vast majority of her subjects were concerned. Even Prime Minister Gladstone, who had the strongest of legitimate reasons to meet with Victoria often and on a regular basis, said the Queen was 'invisible'. In that abstract sense, Drina was the great 'unknown' of the age – she was *The* Snark. It is now clearer why Dodgson was so reluctant to explain the hidden meaning of the poem, the more so in view of the less than flattering 'Snark marks' described in the verse (see following).

An agony in eight fits

Applying *Skelton* to the poem's strange sub-title - "an agony in eight fits" (= 164) - gives the following *contextually appropriate* resonance equations:

1. *"An agony in eight fits"* = "a very hard cypher" = 164
2. *"An agony in eight fits"* = "cipher clue in sub-title" = 164
3. *"An agony in eight fits"* = "cipher is in sub-title" = 164
4. *"An agony in eight fits"* = "code clue of *Lewis Carroll*" = 164
5. *"An agony in eight fits"* = "cypher in sub-title" = 164
1. *"An agony in eight fits"* = "Dodgson's cipher hid in code" = 164
6. *"An agony in eight fits"* = "Dodgson's *magnum opus*" = 164
7. *"An agony in eight fits"* = "hid a clue as the sub-title" = 164
8. *"An agony in eight fits"* = "hid clue as secret cipher" = 164
9. *"An agony in eight fits"* = "hid code intentionally" = 164
10. *"An agony in eight fits"* = "hides a very hard code clue" = 164
11. *"An agony in eight fits"* = "hides the code of *Skelton*" = 164
12. *"An agony in eight fits"* = "I hid clue in secret cipher" = 164
13. *"An agony in eight fits"* = "is a code Charles Dodgson hid" = 164
14. *"An agony in eight fits"* = "is a very hard cipher" = 164
15. *"An agony in eight fits"* = "is alluding to hidden codes" = 164
16. *"An agony in eight fits"* = "is code of *Lewis Carroll*" = 164
17. *"An agony in eight fits"* = "is insoluble secret code" = 164
18. *"An agony in eight fits"* = "is nonsense hiding a clue" = 164
19. *"An agony in eight fits"* = "is nonsense verse" = 164
20. *"An agony in eight fits"* = "is parody and satire" = 164 parody of Edward Lear's verse
21. *"An agony in eight fits"* = "is *Skelton*'s cipher" = 164
22. *"An agony in eight fits"* = "secret code by Carroll" = 16
23. *"An agony in eight fits"* = "Skelton's cypher" = 164
24. *"An agony in eight fits"* = "sub-title hid a cypher" = 164
25. *"An agony in eight fits"* = "sub-title hides the clue" = 164
26. *"An agony in eight fits"* = "the code is intentional" = 164
27. *"An agony in eight fits"* = "used cipher of *Skelton*" = 164
28. *"An agony in eight fits"* = "you can be certain of the code" = 164
29. *"An agony in eight fits"* = "you cracked code of C. L. Dodgson" = 164

Reversed resonance equations:

1. "*Bravo*! You found code hid by" = *"An agony in eight fits"* = 164
2. "Dodgson hid secrets in" = *"An agony in eight fits"* = 164
3. "Well done! You found a code in" = *"An agony in eight fits"* = 164
4. "You cracked a secret code in" = *"An agony in eight fits"* = 164

The expression *'An agony in eight' fits* can be replaced with some of those solutions to give appropriate meanings, examples include:

1. *The Hunting of the Snark* (Dodgson's *magnum opus*)
2. *The Hunting of the Snark* (hides the code of *Skelton*)
3. *The Hunting of the Snark* (is a code Charles Dodgson hid)
4. *The Hunting of the Snark* (is code of *Lewis Carroll*)
5. *The Hunting of the Snark* (is parody *and* satire)
6. *The Hunting of the Snark* (secret code by Carroll)
7. *The Hunting of the Snark* (used cipher of *Skelton*)

The solutions show that *'an agony in eight fits'* secretly represents information concerning the nature of *The Hunting of the Snark*; The solutions show the 'solver' that the codes are contextually appropriate and intentional and that *Skelton* is the correct cipher.

Some key details in the poem that relate to code solutions

The following identifies references in *The Hunting of the Snark* which relate to code solutions. In the poem ten characters - 'the crew' - whose names all start with 'B', set-sail in the hope of finding the island home of the *Snark* and thence the elusive *Snark*. The crew's leader is the Bellman; described as a 'wise' navigator, he possesses a map which depicts nothing at all. The Bellman informs the crew that there are five 'marks' by which the *Snark* can be identified adding that some *Snarks, called Boojums,* are dangerous.

According to the Bellman, the five identifying marks of *Snarks* are: 1. Taste – meagre and hollow but crisp ... a flavour of will-o-the wisp. 2. Slothful - have a habit of getting up late. 3. Slowness in taking a jest... always looks grave at a pun (QV: 'we are not amused') 4. A fondness for bathing machines (alludes to Prince Albert). 5. Ambition (Queen Victoria's title: *Empress of India*).

Dodgson loved puns and word-play and often used them in his writing, it's therefore probably not coincidence that 'snark' puns on 'shark and so it's likely that the 'snarks' are 'sharks'; that is to say, the snarks are the ruling elite - implying that Queen Victoria is THE Snark of the title.

Applying the Master Code in the context of *The Hunting of the Snark*, *Lewis Carroll* and Charles Dodgson etc. gives the following contextually appropriate solutions:

1. "A *Bandersnatch* is a mythical animal" = 246
2. "A *blank map* means: *you* must find clue" = 246
3. "A clue is: The island home of the *Snark*" = 246
4. "A code in the *Snark hunt* nonsense" = 246
5. **"A code is in *The Hunting of the Snark*" = 246**
6. "A puzzle hid by the *Snark* poem" = 246
7. "A *Snark* code clue hides at Osborne House" = 246
8. "A *Snark* hid as the mother of Leopold" = 246
9. "*Ambition:* The *Snark*'s fifth sign" = 246
10. "*An agony in eight fits* is a message" = 246
11. "*An agony in eight fits:* secret clue" = 246
12. "Arithmetic code hides as *Snark* poem" = 246

13. "Arithmetic code hiding in *Snark* poem" = 246
14. "*Bathing machine* is a sign of *Snarks*" = 246
15. "*Bathing machines* are a *Snark* signal" = 246
16. "*Blank map* meant *you* must find clue" = 246
17. "*Boojum* are the dangerous breed of *Snark*" = 246
18. "*Boojum:* dangerous sorts of *Snark*" = 246
19. "*Boojum* is a very dangerous *Snark*" = 246
20. "Character names start with a **B**" = 246
21. "Character's names hiding ten clues" = 246
22. "Charles Dodgson's nonsense codes" = 246
23. "Charles Dodgson's *Snark* was a code" = 246
24. "Charles Lutwidge Dodgson + *Snark*" = 246
25. "Clue is: a recluse hid at Osborne House" = 246
26. "Clue is: Osborne House hides *a recluse*" = 246
27. "Clue is: the Bellman's map of nothing" = 246
28. "Code clue is on island home of *the Snark*" = 246
29. "Code is hidden in the *Snark* poem riddle" = 246
30. "Code is hiding the Queen as *The Snark*" = 246
31. "Code of Dodgson in verse of nonsense" = 246
32. "Code-poem is for Gertrude Chataway" = 246
33. "Dedicate poem to Gertrude Chataway" = 246
34. "Dodgson hid a secret code as nonsense" = 246
35. "Dodgson hid himself in the *Snark* code" = 246
36. "Dodgson's cipher hid as *Snark* poem" = 246
37. "*Drina* is *secret* name of *The Snark*" = 246
38. "Few find a *Snark* at Osborne House" = 246
39. "Few find Osborne House *Snark* clue" = 246
40. "Few find the *Snark* Dodgson created" = 246
41. "Five unmistakable *Snark* marks" = 246
42. "Gertrude was *Snark* poem dedicatee" = 246
43. "Hid a huge riddle as *The Snark* verse" = 246
44. "Hid a puzzle in poem of *The Snark*" = 246
45. "Hid a secret code as *Snark*'s verse" = 246
46. "Hid code in *Snark* nonsense verse" = 246
47. "Hid my code in *Hunting of the Snark*" = 246
48. "Hid satire of Queen Victoria as poem" = 246
49. "Hid secret as the *Snark* rhyme" = 246
50. "Hid the mother of Leopold as a *Snark*" = 246
51. "Hid the Queen as the royal *Snark*" = 246
52. "Huge code in *The Hunting of the Snark*" = 246
53. "Huge mystery in *Snark* poem" = 246
54. "*Hunting the Snark* hid a secret code" = 246
55. "I hid a secret code in *Snark*'s verse" = 246
56. "I hid code in riddle of the *Snark* verse" = 246
57. "I hid satire of Queen Victoria in poem" = 246

58. "I used occult code to hunt the *Snark*" = 246
59. "IoW is *The Snark* Isle acronym" = 246
60. "*Isle of Snark* code for *Isle of Wight*" = 246
61. "*Isle of Wight* is the *Snark*-isle" = 246
62. "*Jabberwocky* is the *Snark* language" = 246 see Jabberwocky verse following
63. "Key clue is: the monarch is a *Snark*" = 246
64. "Left a big code in *Hunting of the Snark*" = 246
65. "*Lewis Carroll*'s poem hid the codes" = 246
66. "Look for a *Snark* at Osborne House" = 246
67. "Look for *Snark*'s bathing machines" = 246
68. "Look for the five signs of a *Snark*" = 246
69. "Meaning of the *Snark* poem hidden in a code" = 246
70. "Meaning of the *Snark* poem hides in code" = 246
71. "Mother of Leopold hides *The Snark*" = 246
72. "My character names are ten clues" = 246
73. "My clue is: the monarch is a *Snark*" = 246
74. "Nonsense poem hides secret code clue" = 246
75. "Nonsense poem hides the *Snark*" = 246
76. "Nonsense poem is a secret hidden code" = 246
77. "Nonsense poem is secret cipher" = 246
78. "Nonsense verse: Dodgson's codes" = 246
79. "Nonsense verse hid the *Snark*" = 246
80. "Nonsense verse is code of *Snark*" = 246
81. "Nonsensical *Snark* poem was a code" = 246
82. "Nothing at all is on Bellman's map" = 246
83. "Osborne House is hiding *Snark*'s code" = 246
84. "Poem for Gertrude Chataway is code" = 246
85. "Poem of Charles Dodgson hid secret code" = 246
86. "Poem of *Snark* hides Queen Victoria" = 246
87. "Puzzles hidden as *Snark* poem" = 246
88. "Queen Victoria is a royal recluse" = 246
89. "Queen Victoria is hiding as a recluse" = 246
90. "Queen Victoria is hiding as *Snark*" = 246
91. "Queen Victoria is royal *Snark*" = 246
92. "Queen Victoria knew *Snark*'s code" = 246
93. "Queen Victoria: she is *The Snark*" = 246
94. "Queen Victoria's Snark satire" = 246
95. "Riddle hiding as the *Snark* verse" = 246
96. "Riddle of *The Hunting of the Snark*" = 246
97. "Secret clue in the *Snark* verse" = 246
98. "Secret code hides in the *Snark* poem" = 246
99. "Secret code in *Hunting the Snark*" = 246
100. "Secret is in the *Snark* verse" = 246
101. "Secret of the *Snark* poem hid by code" = 246
102. "*Skelton* code is the *Snark* language" = 246

103. “*Snark:* a satire on Queen Victoria” = 246
104. “*Snark:* a secret name of the monarch” = 246
105. “*Snark:* alluding to Queen Victoria” = 246
106. “*Snark* clue: go to *The Isle of Wight*” = 246
107. “*Snark* code was Dodgson’s secret” = 246
108. “*Snark* disguises Queen Victoria” = 246
109. “*Snark* equates to *hidden Queen*” = 246
110. “*Snark* hid the Queen’s identity” = 246
111. “*Snark* hides at *The Isle of Wight*” = 246
112. “*Snark* hiding on *The Isle of Wight*” = 246
113. “*Snark* hunt was in *eight fits*” = 246
114. “*Snark* hunting requires courage” = 246
115. “*Snark* inhabited *The Isle of Wight*” = 246
116. “*Snark* is a recluse of Osborne House” = 246
117. “*Snark* is a secret pun on *shark*” = 246
118. “*Snark* is Charles Dodgson’s code clue” = 246
119. “*Snark* is clue alluding to the Queen” = 246
120. “*Snark* is Dodgson’s secret pun” = 246
121. “*Snark* is satire of the Queen in code” = 246
122. “*Snark* is secret name of the Queen” = 246
123. “*Snark* is the cipher for *a secret*” = 246
124. “*Snark* name: Dodgson’s shark pun” = 246
125. “*Snark* poem hid a huge mystery” = 246
126. “*Snark* poem hiding Queen Victoria” = 246
127. “*Snark* poem is a code ***not*** nonsense” = 246
128. “*Snark* poem was concealed sarcasm” = 246
129. “*Snark*: Queen Victoria’s disguise” = 246
130. “*Snark*: Queen Victoria’s satire” = 246
131. “*Snark* rhyme hid Queen Victoria” = 246
132. “*Snark* verse hides secret codes” = 246
133. “*Snark* was *parody* of Edward Lear” = 246
134. “*Snark*‘s verse hides secret code” = 246
135. “*Snark*’s code clue hid on Isle of Wight” = 246
136. “*Snark’s* code clues at Osborne House” = 246
137. “*Snark*’s code hid Victoria and Albert” = 246
138. “*Snark*’s poem has eight parts” = 246
139. “*Snark*’s poem hid Dodgson’s agony” = 246
140. “*Snark*’s poem hides puzzles” = 246
141. “*Snarks* are on *The Isle of Wight*” = 246
142. “The Bellman’s map without clues” = 246
143. “The clue is hiding in the *Snark* poem” = 246
144. “The code is for hunting the *Snark*” = 246
145. “The code was the language of *Snarks*” = 246
146. “The code-verse took two years” = 246
147. “*The Hunting of the Snark* hid a huge code” = 246

148. “The Prime Minister is a *Snark*” = 246
149. “The Queen is hiding behind *THE Snark*” = 246
150. “*The Riddle of The Snark:* a code of Dodgson” = 246
151. “The secret code *hidden* by nonsense” = 246
152. “*The Snark* hid code of *Lewis Carroll*” = 246
153. “*THE Snark* hides mother of Leopold” = 246
154. “*THE Snark* alias hid Queen Victoria” = 246
155. “*THE Snark* clue is: Queen Victoria” = 246
156. “*THE Snark* clue is: *the sovereign*” = 246
157. “*The Snark* is a creature of the codes” = 246
158. “*The Snark* is a sign of Dodgson’s code” = 246
159. “*The Snark* is code of Charles Dodgson” = 246
160. “*The Snark* is Dodgson’s parody” = 246
161. “*The Snark* is my impossible code” = 246
162. “*THE Snark* is really Victoria” = 246
163. “*THE Snark* is satire of the Queen” = 246
164. “*THE Snark* is the alias of our Queen” = 246
165. “The Snark language is *Skelton* code” = 246
166. “*THE Snark* lived at Osborne House” = 246
167. “*THE Snark* name is Queen Victoria” = 246
168. “*The Snark* poem hides the secret” = 246
169. “*The Snark* poem is a huge logical riddle” = 246
170. “*The Snark* poem was a puzzle” = 246
171. “*The Snark* poem was giant riddle” = 246
172. “*The Snark* verse is a huge code-riddle” = 246
173. “*The Snark* verse is allegory” = 246
174. “*The Snark* was a mystery” = 246
175. “*The Snark* was a nonsense poem” = 246
176. “*The Snark* was a shy creature” = 246
177. “*THE Snark* was at Osborne House” = 246
178. “*THE Snark’s* name was Victoria” = 246
179. “*The Snark*’s nature is a secret” = 246
180. “The *Snark’s* verse is riddles” = 246
181. “*The Snarks* are idle and slothful” = 246
182. “*The Snarks* do not laugh and smile” = 246.
183. “*The Snarks* tasted of nothing” = 246
184. “This cipher hid the *Snark* language” = 246
185. “Translate *Snark* language by code” = 246
186. “Use *blank map* to hunt the *Snark*” = 246
187. “Verse of nonsense: code by Dodgson” = 246
188. “Verse of nonsense hid a code of Dodgson” = 246
189. “Verse of *The Snark* hid riddles in code = 246
190. “Write verse in two years” = 246
191. “You discovered a clue: *You* are a *Snark*” = 246
192. “You discovered the *Snark* language” = 246

193. "You find the *Snark* hidden in my code" = 246
194. "You found the *Snark* in *Skelton*" = 246
195. "You found the *Snark* in the cipher" = 246
196. "You hunt the *Snark* with logic" = 246 Dodgson was interested in logic
197. "You hunted the *Snark* using logic" = 246
198. "You use logic for the *Snark* hunt" = 246
199. "You used logic to hunt the *Snark*" = 246

We recall the solutions:

- "A *blank map* means: *you* must find clue" = 246
- "*Blank map* meant: *you* must find clue" = 246
- "The answer is: *a code having no clues*" = 246.

Like the Bellman's map *The Code of Destiny* has no clues; therefore, we must find and solve *contextually appropriate* clues ourselves.

The solutions support the conjecture that the poem be seen in the context of Britain in the early-mid 1870s, a period when Queen Victoria failed to fulfil her public duties and responsibilities as sovereign; a reclusive monarch who, like the Snark, was effectively 'invisible' - as Prime Minister Gladstone had said. Against that 'real world' background the meaning of *The Hunting of the Snark* becomes clearer. The poem is, in one sense, a satire of Queen Victoria and the ruling elite. The assertion that the *Snarks* - 'the sharks' - are 'the elite' and that Dodgson is secretly lampooning them partly accounts for his reluctance to explain the verse's hidden meaning.

*Edward Lear (1812-1888) was famous for his nonsense verse well before Dodgson made an appearance on the literary scene; it's therefore likely that the latter parodied the former's style in *The Hunting of the Snark,* as solution 135 indicates. *The owl and the pussy cat* launched their pea-green boat six years before Dodgson's motley crew set sail.

Liddell's holiday home at Llandudno, North Wales

In 1862 Henry Liddell had a large holiday home built near the West Shore at Llandudno in North Wales. The house was named *Pen Morfa*, meaning *head of a marsh* or *top of the marsh*. Liddell was an eminent classical linguist, so it's very likely he knew the meaning. It seems that *Pen Morfa* was an appropriate name, as the property was built on raised ground overlooking a marshy area by the shore.

The following solutions indicate that Liddell knew *Skelton* and the Master Code:

1. "Home of Henry Liddell called *Pen Morfa*" = 246
2. "Liddell holiday home: name is *Pen Morfa*" = 246
3. "Liddell's holiday house at *Pen Morfa*" = 246
4. "*Pen Morfa* - West Shore - Llandudno" = 246 the exact address
5. "*Pen Morfa* is a holiday home for Liddell" = 246
6. "*Pen Morfa* is holiday home of Liddell's" = 246
7. "*Pen Morfa* means: *at head of the marsh*" = 246

8. *"Pen Morfa:* a clue is *top of the marsh"* = 246
9. *"Pen Morfa:* name means *at head of a marsh"* = 246
10. *"Pen Morfa:* name of Liddell holiday house" = 246
11. *"Pen Morfa:* the Llandudno holiday home" = 246
12. "The Liddell holiday home at *Pen Morfa"* = 246

31. The white rabbit statue at Llandudno

The 'white rabbit' statue at Llandudno's West Shore, close to where *Pen Morfa* stood, is dedicated to the remembrance of 'Lewis Carroll' and 'Alice Liddell'. However, the plaque's inscription is factually incorrect because the inspiration for *Alice's Adventures in Wonderland* came not at the West Shore as the plaque states, but during a boat trip on the Isis near Oxford. The statue was unveiled by former British Prime Minister David Lloyd George on Sept. 6th 1933.

In the context of the statue, we find the Master Code solutions:

1. "1933 is date on Llandudno statue" = 246 — written 19, 33
2. "1933: date on a statue at Llandudno" = 246
3. "1933: statue's date at Llandudno" = 246
4. "A clue is: date on the statue 6/9/1933" = 246
5. "A clue is: *misleading* account on statue" = 246 — factually incorrect
6. "A clue is: *white rabbit* with watch" = 246 — white rabbit is holding a watch
7. "A code hid by the *white rabbit* statue" = 246
8. "A code hides on *white rabbit*'s statue" = 246
9. "A code is on statue at West Shore" = 246
10. "A code was on West Shore statue" = 246
11. "A *hollow* tree trunk on statue" = 246
12. "A statue hides Dodgson's secret code" = 246
13. "A *white rabbit* statue hid a Masonic code" = 246
14. "Account of the statue is misleading" = 246

15. "Alice Liddell was a name on the statue" = 246
16. "Alice Liddell's name is found on statue" = 246
17. "Big clue: the *white rabbit* at Llandudno" = 246
18. "*Bravo!* you cracked a code a *white rabbit* hid" = 246
19. "Clue at the West Shore Llandudno" = 246
20. "Code clue at West Shore in Llandudno" = 246
21. "Code clue is on West Shore statue" = 246
22. "Code clue on a statue at West Shore" = 246
23. "Code is at West Shore in Llandudno" = 246
24. "Code is on a statue at West Shore" = 246
25. "Date on statue: *Sept. 6th 1933*" = 246
26. "Deliberate error included on statue" = 246
27. "Error on statue is a clue to the code" = 246
28. "Error on statue of *white rabbit*" = 246
29. "Find an error on statue's plaque" = 246
30. "Find statue on the West Shore" = 246
31. "Hid a code at Llandudno in North Wales" = 246
32. "Hid code clues on *white rabbit* statue" = 246
33. "Hid code on statue of the *white rabbit*" = 246
34. "*Hollow* stump of tree like a womb" = 246
35. "*Hollow* tree is statue's hint" = 246
36. "*Hollow* tree on statue is a hint" = 246
37. "*Hollow* tree trunk was a womb" = 246
38. "I hid codes on *white rabbit*'s statue" = 246
39. "I left statue codes for the future" = 246
40. "Llandudno in North Wales hides a code" = 246
41. "Llandudno's *white rabbit* statue" = 246
42. "Look for tree stump on statue" = 246
43. "Masonic code on *white rabbit* statue" = 246
44. "Secret code of *white rabbit* statue" = 246
45. "Statue at West Shore hiding a code" = 246
46. "Statue code is left for the future" = 246
47. "Statue hid a womb in a tree stump" = 246
48. "Statue on West Shore is code clue" = 246
49. "Statue on West Shore was a code" = 246
50. "Statue to remembrance of Alice Liddell" = 246
51. "Statue's hollow tree trunk" = 246
52. "Statue's story is untrue" = 246
53. "The West Shore is at Llandudno" = 246
54. "*The white rabbit* and a *hollow tree*" = 246
55. "*The white rabbit* in Llandudno hid a clue" = 246
56. "*The white rabbit* is standing up" = 246
57. "*The white rabbit* of Llandudno is a clue" = 246
58. "*The white rabbit* statue was a code" = 246
59. "*The white rabbit, dormouse* and a *frog*" = 246 animals on the statue

60. "Tree stump on statue hid a womb" = 246
61. "West Shore statue is hiding code" = 246
62. *"White rabbit* statue had an error" = 246
63. "*White rabbit* statue hides a cipher" = 246
64. "*White rabbit* was clue at Llandudno" = 246
65. "*White rabbit's* statue hides codes" = 246
66. "Womb in tree stump on statue" = 246
67. "Womb is in hollow tree stump" = 246
68. "You found *a white rabbit* in Llandudno" = 246
69. "You found code I hid on statue. Well done!" = 246
70. "You found code statue hides. Well done!" = 246
71. "You found codes on statue. Well done!" = 246
72. "You have found false claim on statue" = 246

A study of the white rabbit and hollow tree trunk suggests sexual connotations:

1. "A sex-code on white rabbit statue" = 246
2. "A *white rabbit*'s statue is obscene" = 246
3. "Code on obscene white rabbit statue" = 246
4. "Obscene statue of a *white rabbit* hid a code" = 246
5. "The obscene statue of a *white rabbit*" = 246
6. "West Shore statue hid obscene code" = 246
7. "White rabbit statue's sex-code" = 246
8. "You found Llandudno's obscene statue" = 246

Applying *Skelton* in that context of the tree stump and white rabbit:

1. "The tree" = "the womb" = 69

1. "White rabbit" = "a pseudonym" = 98
2. **"White rabbit" = "alias of Dodgson" = 9**8*
3. "White rabbit" = "is code of Dodgson" = 98
4. "White rabbit" = "the phallus" = 98

Also, the Master Code solution: "The *white rabbit* is a pseudonym" = 246

It has long been believed that the white rabbit represents Dodgson. In that context, we find the resonance equations:

1. "The white rabbit" = "a cipher of C. L. Dodgson" = 127
2. "The white rabbit" = "Dodgson hidden by code" = 127
3. "The white rabbit" = "hides name of Dodgson" = 127
4. "The white rabbit" = "is hiding C. L. Dodgson" = 127
5. "The white rabbit" = "the alias of Dodgson" = 127

Is the statue hinting that Dodgson used the Master Code for sexual purposes – perhaps as a 'sex-game' of some kind? The statue's codes imply that others were aware of a secret 'sex-code' and that they (presumably) knew the Oxford don had used *Skelton* for the same purpose – hence the white rabbit statue. If Dodo had experimented with the cipher in a sexual context, what might he have found?

Applying the Master Code in the *general* context of a 'sex-game':

1. "A cipher you found is a sex-game. *Bravo*!" = 246
2. "A sex game played using *Skelton*" = 246
3. "Look for a sex game in *Skelton's* code" = 246
4. "Look for sex game *Skelton* code hides" = 246
5. "Play a sex-game with *Skelton*" = 246
6. "*Skelton* gematria was a sex-game" = 246
7. "The code you have found was a sex-game" = 246
8. "*This* was code-number for a sex-game" = 246
9. "Use code of *Skelton* for the sex game" = 246
10. "Used *Skelton* cipher for sex-game" = 246
11. "Used *Skelton* to play a sex-game" = 246
12. "You discovered secret sex-codes" = 246
13. "You discovered sex-code's secret" = 246
14. "You found the code for the sex-games" = 246
15. "You found the sex games. Well done!" = 246
16. "You have discovered the sex-codes" = 246
17. "You have found secret code of sex-game" = 246

Those solutions are preliminary hints that the code *was* used for a 'sexual purpose'. It seems likely, in view of the many Master Code solutions associated with his work, that Dodgson looked for and found solutions with sexual connotations like those. In other words, he used *Skelton's* cipher and the Master Code for a secret sex-game.

Applying the Master Code in the context of Charles Dodgson and a 'sex-game' etc:

1. "A code hides Charles Dodgson's sex-game" = 246
2. "A secret pornographic code of Dodgson" = 246
3. "A sex-code of Charles Dodgson is obscene" = 246
4. "C. L. Dodgson was a sex pervert" = 246
5. "C. L. Dodgson's huge pornography code" = 246
6. "Charles Dodgson found obscene sex-code" = 246
7. "Charles Dodgson hid secret sex-code" = 246
8. "Charles Dodgson hides sex-game as code" = 246
9. "Charles Dodgson used the sex-codes" = 246
10. "Charles Dodgson's code hides a sex-game" = 246
11. "Code hid a very dirty game of Dodgson" = 246
12. "Code hid Dodgson's dirty secrets" = 246
13. "Code hid Dodgson's sex-game fantasies" = 246
14. "Code of Dodgson hid a very dirty game" = 246
15. "Code of sex games by Charles Dodgson" = 246

16. **“Code told Charles Dodgson what to do” = 246***
17. “Code was dirty secret of Dodgson” = 246
18. “Codes for sex-fantasies of Dodgson” = 246
19. “Dirty secret of Dodgson hid by code” = 246
20. “Dodgson found the numeral for sex” = 246
21. “Dodgson hides sex code as pictures” = 246
22. “Dodgson hides sex fantasies as a code” = 246
23. “Dodgson loved the little girls” = 246
24. “Dodgson made sex-picture of girls” = 246
25. “Dodgson: you love little girls” = 246
26. “Dodgson’s code hiding an obscene sex game” = 246
27. “Dodgson’s evil sex-games are hidden” = 246
28. “Dodgson’s game is very dirty” = 246
29. “Dodgson’s nude photography hid code” = 246
30. “Dodgson’s picture’s hide a secret code” = 246
31. “Dodgson’s pornography hides a code” = 246
32. “Dodgson’s sex fantasies are in a code” = 246
33. “Dodgson’s sex fantasies hide as a code” = 246
34. “Dodgson’s sex-cipher is a secret” = 246
35. “Dodgson’s sex-games found by you” = 246
36. “Dodo used *Skelton* as code for sex game” = 246
37. “Dodo uses *Skelton* for sex games” = 246
38. “Dodo’s photographs of naked girls” = 246
39. “I use *Skelton*’s code for sex games” = 246
40. “Look for a sex game I hid in *Skelton* code” = 246
41. “Obscene sex-game-code of Charles Dodgson” = 246
42. “Pornography of Dodgson is a huge code” = 246
43. “Secret codes of Dodgson are for sex” = 246
44. “Sex game of Dodgson uses secret code” = 246
45. “Sex games of Dodgson use secret code” = 246
46. “Sex-codes found by Charles Dodgson” = 246
47. “Sex-game rules created by Dodgson” = 246
48. “The sex-games of Dodgson are many” = 246
49. “The very dirty game of Dodgson” = 246
50. “This code is for Dodgson’s sex-game” = 246
51. “Very dirty code-game by Dodgson” = 246
52. “You discovered a sex-game Dodgson hid” = 246
53. “You found a sex-code of Charles Dodgson” = 246
54. “You found Dodgson’s sex-game *hid* in code” = 246
55. “You found secret sex-code of Dodgson” = 246
56. “You found sex-game Dodgson *hid* in codes” = 246
57. “You found sex-game *hid* in Dodgson’s code” = 246
58. “You found the sex game I hid. Well done!” = 246
59. “You have found the sex-code of Dodgson” = 246

Reversed solutions:

- 246 = "a number C. L. Dodgson uses for sex-code"
- 246 = "a numeral Dodgson used for sex codes"
- 246 = "code number for Dodgson's secret game"
- 246 = "code number for Dodgson's sex-games"
- 246 = "code number *hides* sex-games of Dodgson"
- 246 = "number Dodgson used for the sex-code"
- 246 = "numeral Dodgson used as code for sex"

Dodgson's controversial photograph of Alice Liddell, age 7, posed as a beggar-girl (1859)

Image: Gilman Collection, Gift of The Howard Gilman Foundation, 2005

Title: *The Beggar Maid*

A pioneer of photography, Dodgson made more than 3000 images though only about 1000 survive as he destroyed many himself. In recent times, this picture has been seen as having dark sexual connotations, associations conveyed by the pose and clothing: an unshod girl in ragged skirt begging with raised leg, dress suggestively off a shoulder.... It is noteworthy, in this context, that child prostitution was not uncommon in the less salubrious parts of Victorian London.

The photograph's title is *the beggar-maid.* Applying *Skelton* in the context of Alice Liddell, we find the resonance equation:

"Alice Liddell as" = "the beggar-maid" = 85

Applying the Master Code in the context of the beggar-maid photograph and Alice Liddell:

1. "A beggar-girl picture dated 1859" = 246 written 18,59
2. "A beggar-girl's picture hid secret code" = 246
3. "A beggar-maid's picture dated 1859" = 246
4. "A beggar-maid's picture hid secret code" = 246
5. "A code hides as the picture of a beggar-girl" = 246
6. "A photograph of beggar Alice Liddell is a code" = 246
7. "Alice is little beggar-girl of Dodgson" = 246
8. "Alice is little beggar-maid of Dodgson's" = 246
9. "Alice Liddell in photograph of beggar-maid" = 246
10. "Alice Liddell is girl-prostitute" = 246
11. "Alice Liddell is name of prostitute" = 246
12. "Alice Liddell is the street slut" = 246
13. "Alice Liddell is the street whore" = 246
14. "Alice Liddell posed for Dodgson as a beggar" = 246
15. "Alice Liddell vagabond picture hid cipher" = 246
16. "Alice Liddell was my dirty beggar" = 246
17. "Alice Liddell: name of a dirty beggar-girl" = 246
18. "Alice Liddell: she was begging for sex" = 246
19. "Alice Liddell: the beggar in a photograph" = 246
20. "Alice Liddell: the beggar-maid portrait" = 246
21. "Alice Liddell: the vagabond picture is code" = 246
22. "Alice Liddell: vagabond photograph hid a code" = 246
23. "Alice Liddell's beggar photograph hid code" = 246
24. "Alice Pleasance Liddell is a beggar-girl" = 246
25. "Beggar photograph of Alice Liddell hid clue" = 246
26. "Beggar-girl picture is hiding my code" = 246
27. "Beggar-girl's picture hid a secret code" = 246
28. "Beggar-girl's sex-code photograph" = 246
29. "Beggar-maid's picture is hiding my code" = 246
30. "Beggar-slut name: it was Alice Liddell" = 246
31. "Beggar-whore name: it was Alice Liddell" = 246
32. "Charles Dodgson photographs Alice" = 246
33. "Charles Dodgson's 'Alice' photograph" = 246
34. "Charles Dodgson's love of Alice Liddell" = 246
35. "Clue is: Dodgson's beggar picture of Alice" = 246
36. "Code hidden in Alice Liddell vagabond picture" = 246
37. "Code in Alice Liddell vagabond photograph" = 246
38. "Dodgson photographs Alice as a beggar" = 246
39. "Dodgson: secret lover of Alice Liddell" = 246
40. "Dodgson's photograph of Alice Liddell" = 246
41. "Hid a secret as a picture of a beggar-girl" = 246
42. "Hid code clue as the picture of a beggar-girl" = 246
43. "I hid secret code in beggar-girl picture" = 246

44. “My beggar photograph of Alice hid codes” = 246
45. “My beggar photograph of Alice Liddell” = 246
46. “Picture of a beggar-girl hides a secret” = 246
47. “Picture of the beggar-girl hides code clue” = 246
48. “Picture of the beggar-girl hiding codes” = 246
49. “Picture of the beggar-girl is a hidden code” = 246
50. “Picture of vagabond-slut Alice Liddell” = 246
51. “Picture of vagabond-whore Alice Liddell” = 246
52. “Secret code hid as beggar-maid’s picture” = 46
53. “Secret code hid as beggar-girl picture” = 246
54. “Secret code in beggar-girl’s picture” = 246
55. “Secret codes in beggar-girl picture” = 246
56. “Secret codes in beggar-maid’s picture” = 246
57. “Secret hidden as a picture of a beggar-maid” = 246
58. “*The beggar-maid* picture is of Alice Liddell” = 246
59. “Vagabond beggar-girl is called Alice Liddell” = 246

The solutions are consistent with the conjecture that Dodgson entertained a sexual fantasy of Alice as a beggar-girl prostitute. If - as the *‘Pen Morfa’* solutions imply - Henry Liddell knew *Skelton* and the Master Code, did he come to suspect ‘Dodo’ of using the cipher for ‘dark immoral purposes’ involving his young daughter. Liddell was evidently very clever, so it’s plausible he applied the Master Code in the context of ‘Alice’, discovering the same kind of solutions Dodgson would have found linking ‘sex-games’, ‘Alice Liddell’ and the ‘beggar-maid’ photograph. If that was the case, it might account for the sudden, unexplained rupture in the Liddell family’s close friendship with the Christ Church don.

Although Charles Dodgson made friends with many little girls, he was careful to choose only those he considered ‘high-class’ – which is somewhat ironic in view of the beggar-maid picture. If Dodo let a ‘chosen one’ know that he had singled her out for ‘special attention’ it suggests he was deliberately ‘flattering to deceive’ - a ‘grooming’ tactic of paedophiles.

After making the controversial beggar-maid/vagabond picture of Alice Liddell, Dodgson took matters a stage further by photographing young girls naked - having first obtained parental agreement. Permission was usually granted because pictures of children naked were considered ‘natural’, ‘innocent’ and entirely ‘proper’ by Victorian society. In Dodgson’s case however things were not quite as ‘proper’ as they might have seemed. It appears that he combined his knowledge of photography and ciphers to create coded pornographic pictures of young girls naked.

In the context of Dodgson’s ‘naked-girl’ pictures in general, we find the Master Code solutions:

1. “A code clue is in each nude girl photograph” = 246
2. “A sex-code in *all* naked-girl pictures” = 246
3. “*All* C. L. Dodgson’s nude pictures hid a code” = 246
4. “*All* naked-girl pictures hide sex-code” = 246
5. “Charles Dodgson had girls pose nude” = 246
6. “C. L. Dodgson’s secret coded pictures” = 246
7. “Code hid by each nude girl’s photograph” = 246
8. “Code in *all* C. L. Dodgson’s nude pictures” = 246

9. "Code in pictures of girls in the nude" = 246
10. "Dodgson hid code in each nude-girl study" = 246
11. "Dodgson's nude pictures are of girls" = 246
12. "Dodgson's nude-girl pictures hid code" = 246
13. "Each nude-girl photograph hides code clue" = 246
14. "Each nude-girl photograph is a hidden code" = 246
15. "Each nude girl's photograph was code" = 246
16. "Every girl's nude study hid code" = 246
17. "Hid a code clue as each nude-girl photograph" = 246
18. "Hid a code in *all* pictures of naked girls" = 246
19. "Hid sex-code in studies of nude girls" = 246
20. "I hid a code clue as each nude-girl photograph" = 246
21. "I photograph *all* my girls naked" = 246
22. "Look for code hid in nude-girl pictures" = 245
23. "Naked-girl pictures hide secrets" = 246
24. "Nude-girl photographs hide my code" = 246
25. "Nude-girl pictures hide Dodgson's code" = 246
26. "Nude-girl pictures hide the sex-code" = 246
27. "Nude-girl studies are hiding a sex-code" = 246
28. "Photograph *all* girls in the nude" = 246
29. "Pictures of girls in the nude hid a code" = 246
30. "Pictures of girls nude are hiding a code" = 246

In the context of photography, applying *Skelton* we find the resonance equations:

1. "Mask of Dodgson hid" = "pornographer" = 120
2. "Pornographer" = "masked as Dodgson" = 120
3. "Lewis Carroll" = "is name of secret" = "pornographer" = 120
4. "pornographer" = "a mask of C. L. Dodgson" = 120

And, the Master Code solutions:

1. "Pornographer is mask of Dodgson" = 246
2. "The pornography of Dodgson hid code" = 246

Which implies that certain photographs by Dodgson are secret pornographic codes, in particular the pictures of naked girls.

Photographs of the Hatch sisters naked

PLATE I

This photograph of Beatrice Hatch (age 6) was taken on 30th July 1873. Originally monochrome, the picture was hand-coloured under Dodgson's instruction by Anne Lydia Bond. (Image: public domain)

Late in life, Charles Dodgson destroyed most of his 'naked-girl girl' photographs and instructed the executors of his will to dispose of any similar images that had escaped his trawl. The Victorians are supposed to have believed that photographs of children naked were 'natural', 'innocent' art works - certainly not pornographic - but if that was true why was the Deacon of Christ Church so keen to have every last one of his 'nude-girl studies' destroyed? Notwithstanding Dodgson's very thorough attempts to eradicate all the 'incriminating' evidence, of the approximately 1000 surviving photographs about thirty are nudes of young girls. Are Master Code solutions similar to the ones following associated with all thirty nude studies? The code solutions suggest the answer is in the affirmative and that *all* of the nude images of girls made by Dodgson were coded.

Master Code solutions in the context of the Beatrice Hatch photograph

1. "A clue is: Beatrice is completely naked" = 246
2. "A clue is: Beatrice posed naked for Dodgson" = 246
3. "A naked girl on a rock by the sea shore" = 246
4. "Beatrice is naked girl in the picture" = 246
5. "Beatrice Hatch: age six in nude picture" = 246
6. "Beatrice Hatch bares all to my camera" = 246
7. "Beatrice Hatch: dated 30/7/1873" = 246
8. "Beatrice Hatch in beautiful photograph" = 246
9. "Beatrice Hatch in colour picture is code" = 246
10. "Beatrice Hatch is in a sex-code picture" = 246
11. "Beatrice Hatch is stark naked in a picture" = 246
12. "Beatrice Hatch: I photographed her nude" = 246
13. "Beatrice Hatch: nude photograph hid clue" = 246

14. “Beatrice Hatch: picture by C. L. Dodgson” = 246
15. “Beatrice Hatch: she bared all for Dodgson” = 246
16. “Beatrice Hatch: the nude philosopher” = 246
17. “Beatrice is nude on a rock by the sea” = 246
18. “Beatrice looked thoughtful in picture” = 246
19. “Beatrice *must* be naked in the picture” = 246
20. “Beatrice nude: White Cliffs in backdrop” = 246
21. “Beatrice sat in the nude at sea-shore” = 246
22. “Beatrice sitting nude at a sea-shore” = 246
23. “Beatrice was like a nude philosopher” = 246
24. “Beatrice was near to the White Cliffs” = 246
25. “Beautiful Beatrice Hatch in nude picture” = 246
26. “Beautiful picture of Beatrice Hatch naked” = 246
27. “C. L. Dodgson’s code-picture of Beatrice nude” = 246
28. “Code hid by my picture of Beatrice naked” = 246
29. “Code hid by picture of Beatrice Hatch naked” = 246
30. “Code hid by picture of Beatrice in the nude” = 246
31. “Code in sea-shore picture of Beatrice nude” = 246
32. “Coloured picture of Beatrice Hatch is code” = 246
33. “Dodgson photographed Beatrice Hatch” = 246
34. “Dodgson took Beatrice’s nude picture” = 246
35. “Dodgson’s picture is of Beatrice naked” = 246
36. “Hid a code as study of Beatrice Hatch naked” = 246
37. “I took a picture of Beatrice naked on a rock” = 246
38. “I unclothed Beatrice for photograph” = 246
39. “Image dated 30 th July 1873” = 246
40. “My Beatrice photograph bares all” = 246
41. “My picture of Beatrice naked was code” = 246
42. “Naked Beatrice: image is at White Cliffs” = 246
43. “Nude Beatrice photograph is beautiful” = 246
44. “Nude of Beatrice near the White Cliffs” = 246
45. “Nude picture of Beatrice Hatch in colour” = 246
46. “Nude picture of Beatrice made by Dodgson” = 246
47. “Picture Beatrice naked by the seaside” = 246
48. “Picture of Beatrice Hatch naked was code” = 246
49. “Picture of Beatrice in the nude was code” = 246
50. “Sea-shore picture of Beatrice nude hid a code” = 246
51. “Sit Beatrice naked on a rock by shore” = 246
52. “Study of Beatrice Hatch naked hides code” = 246
53. “The sea-shore picture of Beatrice nude” = 246

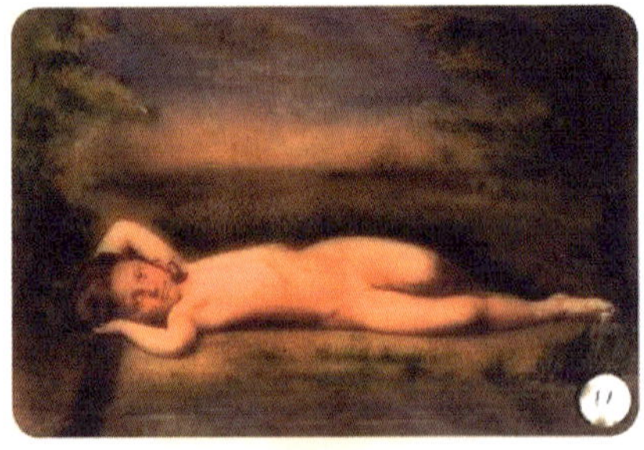

PLATE III

Evelyn Hatch (age 7) younger sister of Beatrice photographed 29th July 1879, coloured by Anne Lydia Bond under Dodgson's instruction. (Image: Wiki-commons)

1. "Code hidden as a nude study of Evelyn" = 246
2. "Code hides as nude study of Evelyn" = 246
3. "Code hiding in nude study of Evelyn" = 246
4. "Colour the naked study of Evelyn" = 246
5. "Coloured the picture of Evelyn naked" = 246
6. "Evelyn completely nude on rug" = 246
7. "Evelyn fully stretched nude" = 246
8. "Evelyn Hatch lying naked on rug" = 246
9. "Evelyn Hatch photographed naked" = 246
10. "Evelyn Hatch: a picture in the nude" = 246
11. "Evelyn lying on rug in the nude" = 246
12. "Evelyn nude was colour picture" = 246
13. "Evelyn's picture dated 29/7/1879" = 246 written 1,8,7,9
14. "Hid a code clue as picture of Evelyn naked" = 246
15. "I took the picture of naked Evelyn" = 246
16. "Naked Evelyn's coded colour picture" = 246
17. "Nude of Evelyn stretching-out" = 246
18. "Nude study is of Evelyn on rug" = 246
19. "Nude study of Evelyn hides code clue" = 246
20. "Nude study of Evelyn is a hidden code" = 246
21. "Picture of Evelyn naked hides code clue" = 246
22. "Picture of Evelyn naked is a hidden code" = 246

Evelyn posed as naked gypsy girl, 29th July 1879. Again, hand-coloured (image: Wiki-commons)

1. "Evelyn in nude sat by stream" = 246
2. "Evelyn in the nude sat by tree" = 246
3. "Evelyn is near gypsy camp" = 246
4. "Evelyn's gypsy posed nude" = 246
5. "Evelyn's picture dated 29/7/1879" = 246 written 1,8,7,9
6. "Gypsy Evelyn in naked pose" = 246
7. "Gypsy picture is Evelyn" = 246
8. "Gypsy-girl Evelyn stark naked" = 246
9. "I pose Evelyn as nude gypsy" = 246
10. "I sat Evelyn naked near stream" = 246
11. "Naked Evelyn sat by the tree" = 246
12. "Nude Evelyn next to stream" = 246
13. "Nude Evelyn sitting by a tree" = 246
14. "Pictures of Evelyn naked are codes" = 246
15. "Sit Evelyn naked near a stream" = 246
16. "The coloured picture of Evelyn naked" = 246

The Master Code applied to the Hatch sisters in this context:

1. "Code in pictures of naked Hatch girls" = 246
2. "Code in pictures of naked sisters" = 246
3. "*Hatch girls* coded as *sisters*" = 246 "Hatch girls" = "sisters" = 95
4. "Hatch sisters are *my* girls" = 246
5. "Hatch sisters posed in the nude" = 246
6. "Hatch sisters were in the nude" = 246
7. "Hatch sisters' naked pictures" = 246
8. "Photograph the Hatch girls nude" = 246
9. "Photograph the sisters nude" = 246
10. "Pictures are of Hatch sisters" = 246
11. "Pictures of naked Hatch girls hid a code" = 246
12. "Pictures of naked sisters hid a code" = 246

13. "Pictures of the Hatch girls naked" = 246
14. "Pictures of the sisters naked" = 246

The evidence of the foregoing points strongly to the conclusion that the Reverend Charles Lutwidge Dodgson, Dean of Christ Church College Oxford - better known by his pen name *Lewis Carroll* - was sexually attracted to young girls. In other words, he was a paedophile. It appears likely from the sheer number of solutions, that Dodgson used *Skelton*'s cipher and the Master Code for sexual purposes: to play 'sex-game' fantasies involving young girls - girls who appear to have been aged about six or seven if the photographs are a guide. He seems to have 'lost interest' when girls reached puberty. As to whether he took matters beyond fantasy cannot be known with certainty; however, if he was a 'true believer' in *The Code of Destiny* - meaning solutions *must* be enacted - there is a very distinct possibility he paid for sex with young girls in London, as the following Master Code solutions suggest:

1. "A clue is: Dodgson paid girls for sex" = 246
2. "A code tells C. L. Dodgson to fuck girls" = 246
3. "A young girl masturbated Dodgson" = 246
4. "C. L. Dodgson has sex with girls" = 246
5. "C. L. Dodgson paid the girls for sex" = 246
6. "C. L. Dodgson: fuck girls in the capital" = 246
7. "C. L. Dodgson: girls in London fuck you" = 246
8. "C. L. Dodgson: you fuck girls in London" = 246
9. "C. L. Dodgson: you fuck little girls" = 246
10. "Charles Dodgson: fucking the girls" = 246
11. "Clue is: Dodgson fucking girl in London" = 246
12. "Clue is: Dodo goes to London to fuck girl" = 246 Dodo – Dodgson's nickname
13. "Clue is: girl in London fucking Dodgson" = 246
14. "Dodgson fucked the girls in secret" = 246
15. "Dodgson fucked young slut-girls" = 246
16. "Dodgson fucked young whore-girls" = 246
17. "Dodgson fucks the girls in London" = 246
18. "Dodgson fucks the little girls" = 246
19. "Dodgson fucks young girls of London" = 246
20. "Dodgson has a fuck with many-a-girl" = 246
21. "Dodgson has sex with girls" = 246
22. "Dodgson is a secret fucker of girls" = 246
23. "Dodgson paid for sex hidden in London" = 246
24. "Dodgson used codes to fuck the girls" = 246
25. "Dodgson will fuck girls in London" = 246
26. "Dodgson: a fucker of the young girls" = 246
27. "Dodgson: fuck girls found in slums" = 246
28. "Dodgson: fuck slut-girls of London" = 246
29. "Dodgson: fuck whore-girls of London" = 246
30. "Dodgson: go to London fuck the girls" = 246
31. "Dodgson's fucking young girls" = 246
32. "Dodo fucked by young girls in London" = 246
33. "Dodo fucked London prostitute-girl" = 246

34. "Dodo fucks girls hidden in the capital" = 246
35. "Dodo had relations with the girls" = 246
36. "Girls in London will fuck Dodgson" = 246
37. "Girls in the capital fuck C. L. Dodgson" = 246
38. "*Lewis Carroll* paid girls to fuck" = 246
39. "*Lewis Carroll* paid to fuck girls" = 246
40. "Little girls fucked for C. L. Dodgson" = 246
41. "London prostitute-girl fucked Dodo" = 246
42. "Slum girls are fucked by C. L. Dodgson" = 246
43. "The young girls had sex with Dodgson" = 246
44. "The young girls masturbated Dodo" = 246
45. "Young girls in London fucked by Dodo" = 246

In that context, we recall the Master Code solution:

"Code told Charles Dodgson what to do" = 246

Conditions both physical and moral in parts of the Victorian metropolis were so corrupt and depraved that some inhabitants of the most deprived districts were prepared to do *anything* for money – including the vending of their offspring for sex with strange men. Children even sold themselves in order to buy enough food to survive, while others were snatched off the streets and put to work in brothels. Around the middle of the nineteenth century, an estimated 2700 girls in London had a sexually transmitted disease – giving some idea how common the sexual abuse of girls was at the time. If Dodgson *was* tempted to realise his sexual fantasies he could easily have done so, disguised as an anonymous 'sex tourist' furtively stalking the back-streets and dark alleys of the capital's most notorious slums.

32. THE INFAMOUS WHITECHAPEL MURDERS (1888)

and

JACK the RIPPER's IDENTITY

During Queen Victoria's reign (1837-1901), London witnessed an estimated 30,000 killings; murder was so common in parts of the city that it was accepted as an 'everyday' occurrence and passed almost unnoticed – that is until autumn 1888 when a series of five grisly murders took place in the Whitechapel borough, gruesome homicides horrific even by the standards of the blasé capital. The 'killing ground' in London's East End was notorious for extreme over-crowding, abject poverty and appalling squalor - conditions so bad that Whitechapel was known half-seriously as 'the gateway to hell'. The five female victims (Polly Nichols, Annie Chapman, Liz Stride, Kate Eddowes, Mary Kelly) comprised a tiny fraction of the hundreds of part-time prostitutes that plied their trade in Whitechapel and nearby Spitalfields. The murders shared characteristics linking them to a perpetrator who, in a 'red ink' note to the Central News Agency, revealed his now infamous 'trade name' - *Jack the Ripper*.

Many 'suspects' have been proposed, yet the identity of the most mysterious of murderers remains unresolved. It might be argued that after 135 years, with the inevitable loss and degradation of material evidence and deaths of all witnesses the Whitechapel murders are now insoluble. One might 'propose' a solution but it could never be proven for lack of hard evidence. However, in his dazzling 'red-ink' note addressed 'Dear Boss', the writer says he is playing 'funny little games.' Like other serial killers (Zodiac in the US, for example) it's possible the murderer left secret clues to his identity in code – implying 'funny little games' is hinting at a puzzle, a difficult puzzle but solvable because unlike witnesses and material evidence, codes and code solutions are timeless. **So, the key question is: did *Jack the Ripper* use secret codes in committing the Whitechapel murders?**

Specifically, did the killer use *Skelton's* cipher and the Master Code? If so, the mystery of *Jack the Ripper* and the Whitechapel murders might be solved definitively. Applying the Master Code in the general context of 'prostitute' murders and '*Skelton*':

1. "*Skelton*: a code for slut murders" = 246
2. "*Skelton*: a code for whore murders" = 246
3. "*Skelton* is harlot murder code" = 246
4. "Use *Skelton* in slut murders" = 246
5. "Use *Skelton* in whore murders" = 246
6. "Use the *Skelton* code for murders" = 246
7. "Used the *Skelton* codes to murder" = 246

If the killer knew the cipher, it's very likely he would have looked for solutions such as those. Did the murderer use *Skelton* and the Master Code to hide secret clues about himself and the Whitechapel homicides?

The killer *deliberately* left material evidence - evidence that might relate to codes that use *Skelton*'s cipher. Potential examples are associated with the *ripper*'s double murder (Stride & Eddowes) in the early hours of Sunday 30 th September 1888 viz:

- Graffito chalked on a wall in flats at 108-119 Goulston St. and a piece of Eddowes blood-stained apron left on the ground below.
- A large bloodied knife found on the steps of a laundry at 253 Whitechapel Road.

Those instances will be examined in the context of codes later.

Evidence and reasoning imply that the murderer:

- Was very familiar with Whitechapel and Spitalfields. The second murder took place *behind* the back door at 29 Hanbury St. - an obscure, secluded location known by very few. **This suggests someone who knew of that particular spot, probably someone who visited the property.**
- Had a good understanding of female anatomy and an ability to wield a knife with precision and speed in 'difficult' physical circumstances – **pointing to an individual with medical training possibly a doctor, as the police believed.**

The 'Dear Boss' (red-ink) letter – a note to the Central News Agency

The author of a note written in red ink addressed 'Dear Boss', delivered and post-dated September 27th nineteen days after the second killing, claims to have committed a murder and warns of more to come. Police investigating the case concluded that, in view of the nature of the wounds inflicted on the women, the killer had probably received medical training. Consequently, several doctors came under suspicion and a few were interviewed but to no avail. The *modus operandi* and certain material evidence allegedly left at the crime scenes led some to suspect links with a Masonic ritual; implying, if true, that the malefactor was probably an educated, middle-class white male and likely Protestant. This suggests that the gross misspellings and incorrect grammar in the *ripper*'s letters and notes were intended to mislead as to the author's social background, status and education.

In stating that he was playing 'funny little games' the writer of the *Dear Boss* note was clearly teasing 'the authorities' – a hint perhaps at a test of wit. Were *they* clever enough to solve the game's clues and discover the killer's identity? History says not - unless they *had* solved the puzzle but decided for some mysterious reason to keep it secret. To be fair, the culprit knew that the 'clues' were *almost* impossible to solve and that his identity was virtually guaranteed to remain secret during his lifetime and for many years thereafter. The man who adopted the unforgettable alias, *Jack the Ripper*, created a 'coded criminal masterpiece' whose solution (he knew) would defy many, perhaps all and thereby earn *Jack the Ripper* a prominent place in the pantheon of unsolved murders.

There are many code solutions (following) that correspond exactly with unique elements in the biography of the man who was 'Jack the Ripper', it's therefore possible to identify him without 'guessing' a name based only on a hunch. Biographical details in the code solutions include: date and place of birth, names of parents, home and work place addresses – specific information sufficient to identify a particular individual.

'Dear Boss letter' to the Central News Agency, September 27th 1888

Dear Boss,

I keep on hearing the police have caught me but they wont fix me just yet. I have laughed when they look so clever and talk about being on the right track. That joke about Leather Apron gave me real fits. ***I am down on whores*** *and* ***I shant quit ripping them till I do get buckled****. Grand work the last job was. I gave the lady no time to squeal. How can they catch me now. I love my work and want to start again. You will soon hear of me with my* ***funny little games****. I saved some of the proper red stuff in a ginger beer bottle over the last job to write with but it went thick like glue and I cant use it.* ***Red ink*** *is fit enough I hope ha. ha.*

The next job I do I shall clip the ladys ears off and send to the police officers just for jolly wouldn't you. Keep this letter back till I do a bit more work, then give it out straight. My knife's so nice and sharp I want to get to work right away if I get a chance. Good Luck. Yours truly

Jack the Ripper

Dont mind me giving the trade name

PS Wasnt good enough to post this before I got all the ***red ink off my hands*** *curse it. No luck yet. They say I'm a doctor now. ha ha*

Clearly, the striking thing about the *Dear Boss* letter is the use of red ink. We note two references by the author to 'red ink' suggesting it's probably a clue and not a mad whim. **Applying *Skelton* to "red ink" in the context of a hidden code/cipher we find the resonance equations:**

1. "I pen in" = "red ink" = 49
2. "red ink" = "a cipher" = 49
3. "red ink" = "a clue of *Jack*" = 49
4. "red ink" = "hid code clue" = 49
5. "red ink" = "hides a code" = 49
6. "red ink" = "my code" = 49

This suggests the killer knew *Skelton*'s cipher and that the red ink is indeed a clue.

Next, applying the Master Code in the context of 'red ink' & 'Jack the Ripper':

1. "**Dear Boss,** you noticed the 'red ink' clue!" = 246 note is addressed: *Dear Boss*
2. "I, *Jack the Ripper* write in red ink" = 246
3. "*Jack the Ripper* hid code in red ink note" = 246 a hint at codes hidden in the note
4. "*Jack the Ripper* hides codes in red ink" = 246
5. "*Jack the Ripper:* name in red ink note" = 246 'Jack the Ripper' is named first in the note
6. "Red ink is *Jack the Ripper*'s hint" = 246
7. "Red ink note is code of *Jack the Ripper*" = 246
8. "Red ink: the hint of *Jack the Ripper*" = 246

Suggests *Jack the Ripper* used the Master Code and left coded clues in the red ink note.

***Jack the Ripper* – what's in a name?** We recall the Master Code solutions:

1. "*Skelton*: a code for slut murders" = 246
2. "*Skelton*: a code for whore murders" = 246
3. "*Skelton* is harlot murder code" = 246
4. "Use *Skelton* in slut murders" = 246
5. "Use *Skelton* in whore murders" = 246
6. "Use the *Skelton* code for murders" = 246
7. "Used the *Skelton* codes to murder" = 246

The evidence is sufficient to warrant further examination of the conjectures that the killer, perhaps through links to Freemasonry, knew *Skelton* and the Master Code and that *Jack the Ripper* is a *special* name. **Applying *Skelton*, we find a supporting clue in the resonance equation:**

"*Jack the Ripper*" = "hid secret clues" = 115 suggests the name *itself* hides a set of clues.

Applying the Master Code in the context of the name 'Jack the Ripper':

1. "Codes *hide* in the name of *Jack the Ripper*" = 246
2. "*Jack the Ripper* is a secret cipher" = 246
3. "*Jack the Ripper* is the special name" = 246
4. "*Jack the Ripper* was a secret name" = 246
5. "*Jack the Ripper*: the name hides clues" = 246
6. "The secret codes of *Jack the Ripper*" = 246
7. "You found the clue in *Jack the Ripper*" = 246

Again, those solutions are signs that '*Jack the Ripper*' is a *special* name hiding secret clues encoded using *Skelton*. **The conjecture is tested by applying *Skelton* to "*Jack the Ripper*". We find the following contextually appropriate resonance equations (assuming the police were right, that the murderer was either a doctor or someone with medical training) viz:**

1. "Jack the Ripper" = "a clue was a doctor" = 115
2. "Jack the Ripper" = "a doctor hidden in code" = 115
3. "Jack the Ripper" = "a fiend hid as a doctor" = 115
4. "Jack the Ripper" = "a harlot killer" = 115
5. "Jack the Ripper" = "a mad doctor's name" = 115
6. "Jack the Ripper" = "a name of pure evil" = 115
7. "Jack the Ripper" = "a sex-mad killer" = 115
8. "Jack the Ripper" = "alias a doctor used" = 115
9. "Jack the Ripper" = "an insane doctor" = 115
10. "Jack the Ripper" = "ate half of a kidney" = 115 killer's claim in 'From Hell' letter
11. "Jack the Ripper" = "be a doctor's mask" = 115
12. "Jack the Ripper" = "be sex-mad doctor" = 115
13. "Jack the Ripper" = "cipher hid a *doctor*" = 115
14. "Jack the Ripper" = "clue in the red ink" = 115

15. "Jack the Ripper" = "disguised *doctor*" = 115
16. "Jack the Ripper" = "fiend *hides* a doctor" = 115
17. "Jack the Ripper" = "he's mad for sex" = 115
18. "Jack the Ripper" = "hid a clue to a killer" = 115
19. "Jack the Ripper" = "hid a code clue in *red-ink*" = 115
20. "Jack the Ripper" = "hid a fiend *from hell*" = 115 see letter 'From Hell'
21. "Jack the Ripper" = "hid barbaric killer" = 115
22. "Jack the Ripper" = "hid code of *Skelton*" = 115
23. "Jack the Ripper" = "hid homicidal doctor" = 115
24. "Jack the Ripper" = "hid killer's name" = 115
25. "Jack the Ripper" = "hid name of medical man" = 115
26. "Jack the Ripper" = "hid subtle hint" = 115
27. "Jack the Ripper" = "hid the mad killer" = 115
28. "Jack the Ripper" = "hides a reprobate" = 115
29. "Jack the Ripper" = "hides doctor in code" = 115
30. "Jack the Ripper" = "hides the doctor" = 115
31. "Jack the Ripper" = "hiding a murderer" = 115
32. "Jack the Ripper" = "hiding *Skelton*" = 115
33. "Jack the Ripper" = "hint at a doctor" = 115
34. "Jack the Ripper" = "hint is *doctor*" = 115
35. "Jack the Ripper" = "his clue in *red-ink*" = 115
36. "Jack the Ripper" = "horrible doctor" = 115
37. "Jack the Ripper" = "I hid doctor's name" = 115
38. "Jack the Ripper" = "I hid famous doctor" = 115
39. "Jack the Ripper" = "I killed sluts" = 115
40. "Jack the Ripper" = "I killed whores" = 115
41. "Jack the Ripper" = "I serve Satan" = 115
42. "Jack the Ripper" = "I smell of shit" = 115 victims were disembowelled
43. "Jack the Ripper" = "is a dirty man" = 115
44. "Jack the Ripper" = "is a killer's clue" = 115
45. "Jack the Ripper" = "is a mad murderer" = 115
46. "Jack the Ripper" = "is a medical man's code" = 115
47. "Jack the Ripper" = "is a name in *red-ink*" = 115
48. "Jack the Ripper" = "is a name of a killer" = 115
49. "Jack the Ripper" = "is a pervert" = 115
50. "Jack the Ripper" = "is code of *The Beast*" = 115 in the book of Revelation
51. "Jack the Ripper" = "is concealed doctor" = 115
52. "Jack the Ripper" = "is devilish medic" = 115
53. "Jack the Ripper" = "is diabolical doctor" = 115
54. "Jack the Ripper" = "is hiding a lunatic" = 115
55. "Jack the Ripper" = "is lady-killer" = 115
56. "Jack the Ripper" = "is name of a lunatic" = 115
57. "Jack the Ripper" = "is secret maniac" = 115

58. “Jack the Ripper” = “is the bogey man” = 115
59. “Jack the Ripper” = “is the evil fiend” = 115
60. “Jack the Ripper” = “is the evil name” = 115
61. “Jack the Ripper” = “it was a doctor” = 115
62. “Jack the Ripper” = “killed for Lucifer” = 115
63. “Jack the Ripper” = “killing by codes” = 115
64. “Jack the Ripper” = “murders by a code” = 115
65. “Jack the Ripper” = “name hid a mad killer” = 115
66. “Jack the Ripper” = “name hid the madman” = 115
67. “Jack the Ripper” = “name hides a *doctor*” = 115
68. “Jack the Ripper” = “name is special code” = 115
69. “Jack the Ripper” = “name of a murderer” = 115
70. “Jack the Ripper” = “name of a sex-maniac” = 115
71. “Jack the Ripper” = “Orange killing code” = 115 “Orange code” = “murder” = 57 see following
72. “Jack the Ripper” = “*red-ink* note hid code” = 115
73. “Jack the Ripper” = “savage evil fiend” = 115
74. “Jack the Ripper” = “secret killer” = 115
75. “Jack the Ripper” = “sex-mad lunatic” = 115
76. “Jack the Ripper” = “sexual lunatic” = 115
77. “Jack the Ripper” = “symbol of death” = 115
78. “Jack the Ripper” = “the clue to the code” = 115
79. “Jack the Ripper” = “the code of a medical man” = 115
80. “Jack the Ripper” = “the lunatic’s code” = 115
81. “Jack the Ripper” = “the red ink hid a clue” = 115
82. “Jack the Ripper” = “the Satanic name” = 115
83. “Jack the Ripper” = “the slut cannibal” = 115 ate half of a kidney
84. “Jack the Ripper” = “the whore cannibal” = 115
85. “Jack the Ripper” = “used the *Orange* code” = 155 code of Orange Order (see following)
86. “Jack the Ripper” = “was code of *doctor*” = 115
87. **“Jack the Ripper” = “was doctor X” = 115** see following
88. “Jack the Ripper” = “was insane medic” = 115
89. “Jack the Ripper” = “was secret code” = 115
90. “Jack the Ripper” = “you cracked his code” = 115
91. “Jack the Ripper” = “you have his clue” = 115

Reversed resonance equations:

1. “A doctor hid in code as” = “*Jack the Ripper*” = 115
2. “A killer hidden by” = “*Jack the Ripper*” = 115
3. “Called the killer” = “*Jack the Ripper*” = 115
4. “Mad surgeon called” = “*Jack the Ripper*” = 115
5. **“The code identifies” = “*Jack the Ripper*” = 115**
6. **“You got the code of” = “*Jack the Ripper*” = 115**

The resonance equations identify *Jack the Ripper* as a 'doctor/medic/surgeon' many times, which suggests the police were probably right to suspect someone with medical training, a line of investigation to which the author of the 'Dear Boss' letter laughingly refers. Crucially, solution (5) above tells us that the code identifies *Jack the Ripper* and (6) that 'we' have 'his' code – in other words, *Skelton's* code (see 22, 32, 84 above) – so it should be possible to identify the killer using the cipher.

***Jack the Ripper* – an unknown doctor (X):**

'X' traditionally represents 'the unknown'. If, as the police believed *Jack the Ripper* was an 'unknown' doctor he might be represented as 'Doctor X' / 'Dr X'. In that context, we find:

1. *"Jack the Ripper"* = "hid by *Doctor X*" = 115
2. *"Jack the Ripper"* = "was Doctor X" = 115

Suggests the murderer was an unknown doctor/medic (denoted X) who used *Skelton*'s cipher.

'Saucy Jacky' postcard to Central News Agency, post-marked and received on October 1st *

*I was not codding dear old **Boss** when I gave you the tip, you'll hear about **Saucy Jacky**'s work tomorrow **double event*** this time number one squealed a bit couldn't finish straight off. Had not got time to get ears off for police thanks for keeping last letter back till I got to work again.*

Jack the Ripper

*The postcard was received the day after a 'double' murder (Stride & Eddowes).

Applying *Skelton* in the context of '*Jack the Ripper*' and '*Saucy Jacky*' gives the resonance equation:

"*Saucy Jacky* code of" = "*Jack the Ripper*" = 115 again, implies *Skelton* is the correct cipher.

Applying the Master Code in that context:

1. "*Saucy Jacky:* a name of *Jack the Ripper*" = 246
2. "*Saucy Jacky: Jack the Ripper's* clue" = 246

Additional evidence the killer used the Master Code, implying also that 'Saucy Jacky' and 'Jack the Ripper' are the same individual.

Letter to George Lusk* - '*From Hell*' - dated October 15th

Sor

I send you half the Kidne I took from one women prasarved it for you tother pirce I fried and ate it was very nise I may send you the bloody knif that took it out if you only wate a whil longer.

signed **Catch me when you can** **Mishter** Lusk.*

*George Lusk was chairman of the Whitechapel Vigilance Committee.

It is noteworthy that 'Sor' and 'Mishter' are Irish pronunciations of 'sir' & 'mister', hinting perhaps that the killer had an Irish connection - consistent with many code solutions (following). So, the 'clues' raise the question: was *Jack the Ripper* an Irish doctor/medic?

Applying *Skelton* to *Jack the Ripper* in that context, we find the resonance equations:

1. "Dublin medic is called" = "*Jack the Ripper*" = 115
2. "*Jack the Ripper*" = "a medic from Ireland" = 115
3. "*Jack the Ripper*" = "a surgeon of Dublin" = 115
4. "*Jack the Ripper*" = "an Irish medic name" = 115
5. "*Jack the Ripper*" = "clue is: Irish medic" = 115
6. "*Jack the Ripper*" = "code hid an Irish medic" = 115
7. "*Jack the Ripper*" = "hid a doctor of Dublin" = 115
8. "*Jack the Ripper*" = "hid Dublin medical man" = 115
9. "*Jack the Ripper*" = "hid Irish doctor" = 115
10. "*Jack the Ripper*" = "Irish surgeon" = 115
11. "*Jack the Ripper*" = "the code of a Dublin medic" = 115

In that context, we find also: "*Jack the Ripper*" = "code of Irish madman" = 115

Applying the Master Code in the context of *Jack the Ripper* and the 'code':

1. "A code in murders by *Jack the Ripper*" = 246 a hint the murders *are* coded using *Skelton*
2. "Find code in *Jack the Ripper* killings" = 246
3. "*Jack the Ripper's* real name hid by code" = 246 real name is found by code
4. "Look for *Jack the Ripper*'s name in code" = 246
5. "Murders by *Jack the Ripper* hide code" = 246
6. "Murders of *Jack the Ripper* hid codes" = 246
7. "Name of *Jack the Ripper* revealed as a code" = 246
8. "Reveal name of *Jack the Ripper* by code" = 246
9. "You found codes *Jack the Ripper* hides" = 246 implying *Skelton* is the correct cipher
10. "You unmask *Jack the Ripper* by code" = 246 implying the mystery is solved by code

Crucially, solutions 3, 4, 7, 8, 10 suggest it's possible to name the murderer using the code.

From those solutions and resonance equations it is evident that the killer used *Skelton*'s cipher and the Master Code to hide secret clues. Finally, applying the Master Code in the context of *Jack the Ripper* and what is known so far, we find a huge set of contextually appropriate solutions:

1. "A clue is: code hid prostitute-killer" = 246
2. "A clue is: I use *Skelton* code for killing" = 246
3. "A clue is: *Jack the Ripper* is hidden as a code" = 246
4. "A clue is: *Jack the Ripper* is hiding in code" = 246
5. "A clue is: *Jack the Ripper*'s letter" = 246 'Dear Boss'
6. "A clue is: letter dated 15th of October" = 246 'From Hell' letter
7. "A code clue in letter of *Jack the Ripper*" = 246

8. "A code clue in *October-first* postcard" = 246 — '*Saucy Jacky*' post card
9. "A code hid by *Saucy Jacky's* postcard" = 246
10. "A code hid in killings of *Jack the Ripper*" = 246
11. "A code hid the names of the five sluts" = 246
12. "A code hid the names of the five whores" = 246
13. "A code hiding homicidal doctor" = 246
14. "A code in letter dated *27 September*" = 246 — 'Dear Boss' letter
15. "A code in murders by *Jack the Ripper*" = 246
16. "A code is in letter of *Jack the Ripper*" = 246
17. "A code is in *October first* postcard" = 246 — following the double murder
18. "A code killed fallen Whitechapel women" = 246
19. "A code-letter signed *Jack the Ripper*" = 246 — 'Dear Boss' letter
20. "A dark secret hiding at *Whitechapel*" = 246
21. "A doctor cut throats of sluts" = 246 — victim's throats cut from behind
22. "A doctor cut throats of whores" = 246
23. "A doctor from Ireland is the killer" = 246 — consistent with 'sor' & 'mishter'
24. "A doctor hid *Spitalfields* ripper" = 246
25. "A doctor killing the sluts is hid" = 246
26. "A doctor killing the whores is hid" = 246
27. "A doctor was to blame for murders" = 246
28. "A killing was at 29 Hanbury St." = 246 — site of 2nd murder
29. "A letter on October 15 is ***from hell***" = 246
30. "A Masonic code hides the harlot killer" = 246
31. "A message hid in code by *Jack the Ripper*" = 246
32. "A murderer hides as *Jack the Ripper*" = 246
33. "A physician is *Jack the Ripper* clue" = 246
34. "A physician of Whitechapel kills" = 246
35. "A prostitute murderer hid as a code" = 246
36. "A prostitute murderer hides code" = 246
37. "A prostitute's murderer in a code" = 246
38. "A secret murderous Irish doctor" = 246 — consistent with resonance equations above
39. "A sexually perverted doctor" = 246
40. "All *Jack the Ripper* murders are code" = 246
41. "All slut murders are at Autumn" = 246
42. "All the harlots killed at Autumn" = 246
43. "All Whitechapel women are sinful" = 246
44. "All whore murders are at Autumn" = 246
45. "Barbaric murders of *Jack the Ripper*" = 246
46. "*Boss:* addressee of a letter is code clue" = 246 — "Boss" = "the Code" = 42
47. "Called addressee of letter *Dear Boss*" = 246 — 'Dear Boss' is a code
48. "*Catch me when you can*: a secret sign" = 246 — should be: 'catch me *if* you can'
49. "*Catch me when you can*: code hiding a doctor" = 246
50. "*Catch me when you can*: doctor's code clue" = 246

51. "*Catch me when you can*: is doctor's code" = 246
52. "*Catch me when you can:* is hiding a hint" = 246
53. "*Catch me when you can:* is secret clue" = 246
54. "*Catch me when you can:* is the signal" = 246
55. "Ciphers unmasked *Jack the Ripper*" = 246
56. "Clue hid by red-ink letter to *Boss*" = 246
57. "Clue is: a code hid killer of Spitalfields" = 246
58. "Clue is: doctor to blame for murders" = 246
59. "Clue is: *Jack the Ripper* is hiding in a code" = 246
60. "Clue is: killing at 29 Hanbury St." = 246 location of 2nd murder
61. "Clue is: prostitute killer hid a code" = 246
62. "Clue is: the killer of Spitalfields" = 246
63. "Clue is: the prostitute killer" = 246
64. "Clue is: the sluts of Whitechapel" = 246
65. "Clue is: the whores of Whitechapel" = 246
66. "Clue was bloodthirsty doctor" = 246
67. "Clue was murderous Irish doctor" = 246
68. "Code hid a murdering Irish physician" = 246
69. "Code hid as postcard by *Saucy Jacky*" = 246
70. "Code hid harlot killer of Whitechapel" = 246
71. "Code hid Spitalfields slut-killer" = 246
72. "Code hid Spitalfields whore-killer" = 246
73. "Code hid the address of *Jack the Ripper*" = 246
74. "Code hidden in postcard of *Saucy Jacky*" = 246
75. "Code hides a prostitute murderer" = 246
76. "Code hiding a homicidal doctor" = 246
77. "Code in killings by *Jack the Ripper*" = 246
78. "Code is hidden in notorious murders" = 246
79. "Code is in prostitute murders" = 246
80. "Code masked a doctor as *Jack the Ripper*" = 246
81. "Code of doctor killing at Whitechapel" = 246
82. "Code of Freemasons hid *Jack the Ripper*" = 246
83. "Code of *Jack the Ripper* is arithmetic" = 246
84. "Code reveals *Jack the Ripper*'s name" = 246
85. "Code-clue in *trade name* of *Jack the Ripper*" = 246
86. "Coded letters by *Jack the Ripper*" = 246
87. "Codes hid Irish-Protestant medic" = 246
88. "Codes hid spirit of *Jack the Ripper*" = 246 *Jack the Ripper* – a 'spirit' in the code?
89. "Dark secrets hid by diabolical doctor" = 246
90. "Deliberate misspellings hiding a code" = 246
91. "Diabolical doctor is at *Spitalfields*" = 246
92. "Diabolical doctor's prostitute code" = 246
93. "Doctor hid murderer of *Whitechapel*" = 246

94. "Doctor hides slut-slaughterer" = 246
95. "Doctor hides whore-slaughterer" = 246
96. "Doctor is found to be *Jack the Ripper*" = 246
97. "Doctor murders London sluts" = 246
98. "Doctor murders London whores" = 246
99. "Doctor X hiding as *Jack the Ripper*" = 246
100. "Dr X is *Jack the Ripper*'s cipher" = 246
101. "Dr X: a cipher hiding *Jack the Ripper*" = 246
102. "Dr X: *Jack the Ripper*'s cypher" = 246
103. "Each killing hides a code of *Jack the Ripper*" = 246
104. "Evil doctor killing the sluts" = 246
105. "Evil doctor killing the whores" = 246
106. "Evil fiend *Jack the Ripper:* a bogey man" = 246
107. "Evil lady-killer *Jack the Ripper*" = 246
108. "Famous murders of *Jack the Ripper*" = 246
109. "Few find clue to *Jack the Ripper's* code" = 246
110. "Few find codes in *Jack the Ripper* name" = 246
111. "Few find the doctor in Whitechapel" = 246
112. "Filthy sluts of Whitechapel" = 246
113. "Filthy whores of Whitechapel" = 246
114. "Find a killer hidden at Spitalfields" = 246
115. "Find a killer hiding in Spitalfields" = 246
116. **"Find *Jack the Ripper's* name using code" = 246**
117. "Five murders in Whitechapel hid a code" = 246
118. "Five Whitechapel killings hid in code" = 246
119. "Gave the 'trade name' *Jack the Ripper*" = 246
120. "Gruesome murders of Whitechapel" = 246
121. "Half of kidney: *Jack the Ripper*'s clue" = 246 in 'From Hell' letter
122. "Harlot killings in Whitechapel" = 246
123. "Harlots' killer at Whitechapel" = 246
124. "Hid a code as my notorious murders" = 246
125. "Hid a code as note written in *red-ink*" = 246
126. "Hidden *Jack* killed Whitechapel sluts" = 246
127. "Hidden *Jack* killed Whitechapel whores" = 246
128. "Huge secret code hides *Jack the Ripper*" = 246
129. "I am Irish doctor *Jack the Ripper* hid" = 246
130. "I am *Jack* I rip sluts of *Whitechapel*" = 246
131. "I am *Jack* I rip whores of *Whitechapel*" = 246
132. "I am *Jack the Ripper* a harlot killer" = 246
133. "I am *Jack the Ripper* a London bogeyman" = 246
134. "I am *Jack the Ripper* I killed sluts" = 246
135. "I am *Jack the Ripper* I killed whores" = 246
136. "I am killing Whitechapel harlots" = 246

137. "I am the doctor *Jack the Ripper* hides" = 246
138. "I hid a code in note written in red ink" = 246
139. "I kill Spitalfields fallen women" = 246
140. "I, *Jack the Ripper* hidden lady-killer" = 246
141. "I, *Jack the Ripper* left clues in huge code" = 246
142. "I, *Jack the Ripper* sign *coded* letter" = 246 *Dear Boss* letter
143. "I, *Jack the Ripper* use the secret code" = 246
144. "In the autumn of one eight-eight-eight" = 246 murders committed in autumn 1888
145. "In the year one eight-eight-eight" = 246
146. "Irish doctor hid at *Spitalfields*" = 246
147. "Irish doctor murders sluts" = 246
148. "Irish doctor murders whores" = 246
149. "Irish prostitute-murderer" = 246
150. "Irish-Protestant medic hid codes" = 246
151. "Irishman killed sluts of London" = 246
152. "Irishman killed whores of London" = 246
153. "*Jack the Ripper* cryptonym" = 246
154. "*Jack the Ripper* evil lady-killer" = 246
155. "*Jack the Ripper* hid a disguised doctor" = 246
156. "*Jack the Ripper* hid a secret killer" = 246
157. "*Jack the Ripper* hid an abominable doctor" = 246
158. "*Jack the Ripper* hid as the mad doctor" = 246
159. "*Jack the Ripper* hid in code of *Skelton*" = 246
160. "*Jack the Ripper* hid in Irish doctor" = 246
161. "*Jack the Ripper* hid in London doctor" = 246
162. "*Jack the Ripper* hid in *Ten Bells* pub" = 246 a notorious pub in Spitalfields
163. "*Jack the Ripper* hid man from Ireland" = 246
164. "*Jack the Ripper* hides a wicked doctor" = 246
165. "*Jack the Ripper* hiding as Doctor X" = 246
166. "*Jack the Ripper* hiding mad murderer" = 246
167. "*Jack the Ripper* is a cipher of Satan" = 246
168. "*Jack the Ripper* is a code in 'Boss' note" = 246
169. "*Jack the Ripper* is a diabolical surgeon" = 246
170. "*Jack the Ripper* is a hidden Irishman" = 246
171. "*Jack the Ripper* is a medical man hid as code" = 246
172. "*Jack the Ripper* is a name of *The Beast*" = 246 in the book of *Revelation*
173. "*Jack the Ripper* is a secret cipher" = 246
174. "*Jack the Ripper* is a slut-butcher" = 246
175. "*Jack the Ripper* is a weekend killer" = 246 only killed at weekend
176. "*Jack the Ripper* is a whore-butcher" = 246
177. "*Jack the Ripper* is an alias of a doctor" = 246
178. "*Jack the Ripper* is cipher of a doctor" = 246

179. “*Jack the Ripper* is cipher of Satan” = 246
180. “*Jack the Ripper* is clue hiding doctor” = 246
181. “*Jack the Ripper* is doctor’s mask” = 246
182. “*Jack the Ripper* is hidden murderer” = 246
183. “*Jack the Ripper* is homicidal maniac name” = 246
184. “*Jack the Ripper* is in a secret lair” = 246
185. “*Jack the Ripper* is in Whitechapel” = 246
186. “*Jack the Ripper* is medical-man cipher” = 246
187. “*Jack the Ripper* is monstrous” = 246
188. “*Jack the Ripper* is name hiding *Dr X*” = 246
189. “*Jack the Ripper* is name of a mad killer” = 246
190. “*Jack the Ripper* is name of libertine” = 246
191. “*Jack the Ripper* is playing a code-game” = 246* ‘funny little games’ (*Dear Boss* letter)
192. “*Jack the Ripper* is wicked surgeon” = 246
193. “*Jack the Ripper* killed old sluts” = 246 all bar one over 40
194. “*Jack the Ripper* killed old whores” = 246
195. “*Jack the Ripper* kills harlots” = 246
196. “*Jack the Ripper* left clues as *huge* code” = 246
197. “*Jack the Ripper* signed a code-letter” = 246 Dear Boss letter
198. “*Jack the Ripper* slayed sluts” = 246
199. “*Jack the Ripper* slayed whores” = 246
200. “*Jack the Ripper* used red-ink to hide code” = 246
201. “*Jack the Ripper* uses Freemason code” = 246
202. “*Jack the Ripper* was born in Dublin” = 246
203. “*Jack the Ripper* was from Ireland” = 246
204. “*Jack the Ripper* was hiding a doctor” = 246
205. “*Jack the Ripper* was medical-man name” = 246
206. “*Jack the Ripper* was name of a doctor” = 246
207. “*Jack the Ripper*: 2nd killing is big clue” = 246 at 29 Hanbury St
208. “*Jack the Ripper*: 2nd murder is a big clue” = 246
209. “*Jack the Ripper:* a bogeyman in London” = 246
210. “*Jack the Ripper:* a cipher hiding Dr X” = 246
211. “*Jack the Ripper:* a clue is in a *trade name*” = 246
212. “*Jack the Ripper*: a code hid *modus operandi*” = 246
213. “*Jack the Ripper:* a cypher of Satan” = 246
214. “*Jack the Ripper:* all murders are code” = 246
215. “*Jack the Ripper:* an evil doctor in code” = 246
216. “*Jack the Ripper*: at *Spitalfields*” = 246
217. “*Jack the Ripper:* bloody killer name” = 246
218. “*Jack the Ripper:* cipher was a riddle” = 246
219. “*Jack the Ripper*: clue is a physician” = 246
220. “*Jack the Ripper:* clue is an Irishman” = 246
221. “*Jack the Ripper:* clue is Irish medic” = 246
222. “*Jack the Ripper:* code hid Irish killer” = 246
223. “*Jack the Ripper:* code of a heinous killer” = 246

224. “*Jack the Ripper:* code of fiendish doctor” = 246
225. “*Jack the Ripper:* disguised in doctor” = 246
226. “*Jack the Ripper: Doctor Death*’s name” = 246
227. “*Jack the Ripper:* evil lady-killer” = 246
228. “*Jack the Ripper*: found through codes” = 246
229. “*Jack the Ripper*: he’s steeped in blood” = 246
230. “*Jack the Ripper:* hid an invisible man” = 246
231. “*Jack the Ripper:* hid in Irish doctor” = 246
232. “*Jack the Ripper:* hid in *Ten Bells* pub” = 246
233. “*Jack the Ripper:* hides a wicked doctor” = 246
234. “*Jack the Ripper:* hides the Masonic code” = 246
235. “*Jack the Ripper:* hiding *daemonic* doctor” = 246
236. “*Jack the Ripper:* hiding name of a killer” = 246
237. “*Jack the Ripper:* homicidal doctor’s code” = 246
238. “*Jack the Ripper:* Irish doctor’s code” = 246
239. “*Jack the Ripper:* Irish killer name” = 246
240. “*Jack the Ripper*: *Jack* is the *middle* name” = 246 a hint at killer’s middle name: John
241. “*Jack the Ripper:* left clues as huge code” = 246
242. “*Jack the Ripper:* look for a secret code” = 246
243. “*Jack the Ripper*: look for birthdate” = 246 exact birth date is in code
244. “*Jack the Ripper:* look for Irishman” = 246
245. “*Jack the Ripper:* mad doctor was a clue” = 246
246. “*Jack the Ripper:* mask hiding a doctor” = 246
247. “*Jack the Ripper:* mask of the doctor” = 246
248. “*Jack the Ripper:* medical-man cypher” = 246
249. “*Jack the Ripper*: *modus operandi* in code” = 246
250. “*Jack the Ripper:* monster’s name” = 246
251. “*Jack the Ripper:* murdered by the code” = 246
252. “*Jack the Ripper:* murdered the ladies” = 246
253. “*Jack the Ripper:* murdering doctor” = 246
254. “*Jack the Ripper*: name hid evil doctor” = 246
255. “*Jack the Ripper:* name hides mad doctor” = 246
256. “*Jack the Ripper:* name is a wild animal” = 246 a bear
257. “*Jack the Ripper:* name is hiding ‘Dr X’” = 246
258. “*Jack the Ripper*: name of mad murderer” = 246
259. “*Jack the Ripper*: name was a secret” = 246
260. “*Jack the Ripper*: name was riddle-clue” = 246
261. “*Jack the Ripper*: ploy by doctor” = 246
262. “*Jack the Ripper*: red ink was sign” = 246
263. “*Jack the Ripper: red-handed* murderer” = 246 alludes to Orange Order?
264. “*Jack the Ripper:* the abominable doctor” = 246
265. “*Jack the Ripper*: the code for medical man” = 246
266. “*Jack the Ripper:* the invisible man” = 246

267. "*Jack the Ripper:* the mad killer's code" = 246
268. "*Jack the Ripper:* the red ink signal" = 246
269. "*Jack the Ripper*: weekend killings" = 246 murdered only at weekends
270. "*Jack the Ripper:* weekend murderer" = 246
271. "*Jack the Ripper*'s cypher is X" = 246 unknown doctor X
272. "*Jack the Ripper's* name was a trade" = 246
273. "*Jack the Ripper*'s play in 5 acts" = 246 'Jack the Ripper' like a drama (see end)
274. "*Jack the Ripper's* real name hid by code" = 246
275. "*Jack the Ripper's* victims are a code" = 246 their names are in the code
276. "Kill fallen women at Whitechapel" = 246
277. "Kill the harlots of Whitechapel" = 246
278. "Kill the Spitalfields sluts" = 246
279. "Kill the Spitalfields whores" = 246
280. "Kill Whitechapel harlots by code" = 246
281. "Killer at Whitechapel used red-ink" = 246
282. "Killer of Spitalfields' sluts" = 246
283. "Killer of Spitalfields' whores" = 246
284. "Killer-physician of Whitechapel" = 246
285. "Killer-preacher in Spitalfields" = 246
286. "Killing harlots in Whitechapel" = 246
287. "Killings by *Jack the Ripper* hid a code" = 246
288. "Letter of *Jack the Ripper* hiding code" = 246
289. "Letter penned in red-ink was clue" = 246
290. "Letter was addressed to *Boss*" = 246
291. "Letter **X** hiding *Jack the Ripper*" = 246
292. "London prostitute murderer" = 246
293. "Look for a name *Jack the Ripper*'s code hid" = 246
294. "Look for a Whitechapel cut-throat" = 246
295. "Look for *Boss:* addressee of letter" = 246
296. "Look for clue to *Jack the Ripper's* code" = 246
297. "Look for code in red-ink *Boss* letter" = 246
298. "Look for name in *Jack the Ripper*'s code" = 246
299. "Look for the doctor in Whitechapel" = 246
300. "Look for the red-ink *Boss* letter" = 246
301. "Missive date: September 27th" = 246 *Dear Boss* letter
302. "Missive dated October 15th hid codes" = 246 *Saucy Jacky* note
303. "*Mr. Kipper* is rhyming slang" = 246 Mr Kipper: Jack the Ripper
304. "*Mr. Kipper:* code for *Jack the Ripper*" = 246
305. "Murder Spitalfields' harlots" = 246
306. "Murdered sluts are hidden in the code" = 246
307. "Murdered whores are hidden in the code" = 246
308. "Murders by *Jack the Ripper* hide code" = 246
309. "Murders by Whitechapel doctor" = 246

310. “Murders of *Jack the Ripper* hide in code” = 246
311. “My notorious murders hide codes” = 246
312. “Name of *Jack the Ripper* revealed as a code” = 246
313. “Name of sluts’ killer is a secret” = 246
314. “Name of whores’ killer is a secret” = 246
315. “Names of the five sluts in the code” = 246
316. “Names of the five whores in the code” = 246.
317. “Names of whores and sluts in a code” = 246
318. “NECKS are initials of slut names” = 246.
319. “NECKS are initials of whore names” = 246
320. “NECKS is code for sluts to be killed” = 246
321. “NECKS is code for whores to be killed” = 246
322. “NECKS was initials of harlots” = 246
323. “NECKS: an anagram of women’s initial” = 246 Nichols, Chapman, Stride, Eddowes, Kelly
324. “Note sent to News Agency hid code” = 246
325. “Note to *Boss* on September 27” = 246
326. “Note written in *red-ink* hides code” = 246
327. “*October-first* postcard hiding code” = 246
328. “Postcard from *Saucy Jacky* is code” = 246
329. “Postcard of *Saucy Jacky* was a clue” = 246
330. “Postcard on *October first* is code” = 246
331. “Postcard signed by *Saucy Jacky*” = 246
332. “Prostitute killer is savage” = 246
333. “Prostitute killer used the code” = 246
334. “Prostitute murderer’s codes” = 246
335. “Prostitute murders are in a code” = 246
336. “Prostitute’s killer be Irish” = 246
337. “Protestant medic was killer” = 246
338. “Real name of *Jack the Ripper* hid in codes” = 246
339. “Red ink is *Jack the Ripper*’s hint” = 246 ‘Dear Boss’ letter in red ink
340. “Red ink letter to *Boss* was clue” = 246
341. “Red ink signified code of *Jack the Ripper*” = 246
342. “Red ink was *Jack the Ripper* sign” = 246
343. “Red ink: the hint of *Jack the Ripper*” = 246
344. “Remove the guts from sluts” = 246
345. “Remove the guts from whores” = 246
346. “Remove the guts of the sluts” = 246
347. “Remove the guts of the whores” = 246
348. “Removed kidneys from sluts” = 246
349. “Removed kidneys from whores” = 246
350. “Removed the kidneys of sluts” = 246
351. “Removed the kidneys of whores” = 246

352. "Reveal name of *Jack the Ripper* by code" = 246
353. "*Ripper* of *Whitechapel* hid in the code" = 246
354. "*Ripper* of *Whitechapel* is a doctor" = 246
355. "*Saucy Jacky* postcard is hiding a code" = 246
356. "*Saucy Jacky:* a name of *Jack the Ripper*" = 246
357. "*Saucy Jacky*: a sexual pervert" = 246
358. "*Saucy Jacky's* postcard is code clue" = 246
359. "*Saucy Jacky's* postcard was a code" = 246
360. "Secret code hides as diabolical murders" = 246
361. "Secret code hiding in diabolical murders" = 246
362. "Secret killer at *Spitalfields*" = 246
363. "Secret lair hiding *Jack the Ripper*" = 246
364. "*September* 27th is date on a note" = 246 'Dear Boss' note/letter
365. "*September* 27th is note's date" = 246
366. "Slaughtered five London sluts" = 246
367. "Slaughtered five London whores" = 246
368. "Slut-slaughterer hid as a doctor" = 246
369. "Slut's intestine is removed" = 246
370. "Sluts are murdered according to a code" = 246
371. "Sluts must be murdered by name" = 246
372. "Solve *Jack the Ripper* murders" = 246
373. "Spirit of *Jack the Ripper* hid in code" = 246
374. "Spitalfields hides Irish doctor" = 246
375. "Spitalfields was whoredom" = 246
376. "Spitalfields' harlots are evil" = 246
377. "The 27th day of September is a code" = 246 date of 'Dear Boss' letter
378. "The answer is: a slut-ripper" = 246
379. "The answer is: a whore-ripper" = 246
380. "The answer is: code told me to kill" = 246
381. "The answer is: the diabolical doctor" = 246
382. "The coded murders of *Jack the Ripper*" = 246
383. "The doctor hides at Spitalfields" = 246
384. "The evil doctor hid at Whitechapel" = 246
385. "The five murders in Whitechapel" = 246
386. "The five sluts at Whitechapel" = 246
387. "The five whores at Whitechapel" = 246
388. "The killer is a doctor from Ireland" = 246
389. "The mad doctor hid as *Jack the Ripper*" = 246
390. "The murdering Irish physician" = 246
391. "The name *Jack the Ripper* hides clues" = 246
392. "The *red hand* of *Jack the Ripper* is a clue" = 246
393. "The *red ink* is a clue of *Jack the Ripper*" = 246
394. "The *red ink*: hint of *Jack the Ripper*" = 246

395. “The *red ink*: *Jack the Ripper* signal” = 246
396. “*The Ripper* is in *Spitalfields*” = 246
397. “*The Ripper* is the *trade name* of *Jack*” = 246
398. “The secret codes hide a slut-killer” = 246
399. “The secret codes hide a whore-killer” = 246
400. “The secret codes of *Jack the Ripper*” = 246
401. “The slut-killer name is secret” = 246
402. “The sluts of Whitechapel are a clue” = 246
403. “The unspeakable murders of a doctor” = 246
404. “The whore-killer name is secret” = 246
405. “The whores of Whitechapel are a clue” = 246
406. “These are code clues of *Jack the Ripper*” = 246
407. “This is proof *I* am *Jack the Ripper*” = 246
408. “*Trade name* is *Jack the Ripper*'s clue” = 246
409. “Unspeakable code-murders by a doctor” = 246
410. “Use a code to find name *Jack the Ripper* hid” = 246
411. “Used *red-ink* for the *Boss* letter” = 246
412. “Victims of *Jack the Ripper* are a clue” = 246
413. “*Whitechapel* hides the evil doctor” = 246
414. “*Whitechapel* hiding harlot killer” = 246
415. “*Whitechapel* murders hide the codes” = 246
416. “*Whitechapel* murders hiding clues” = 246
417. “*Whitechapel* ripper hid by the code” = 246
418. “*Whitechapel* sluts must be killed” = 246
419. “*Whitechapel* was hiding whoredom” = 246
420. “*Whitechapel* whores must be killed” = 246
421. “*Whitechapel*'s murdered sluts” = 246
422. “*Whitechapel*'s murdered whores” = 246
423. “*Whitechapel*'s murders are by code” = 246
424. “*Whitechapel*'s murders are clues” = 246
425. “Whore-slaughterer hid as a doctor” = 246
426. “Whore's intestine is removed” = 246
427. “Whoredom is at *Spitalfields*” = 246
428. “Whoredom is hiding at *Whitechapel*” = 246
429. “Whores are murdered according to a code” = 246
430. “Whores must be murdered *by name*” = 246
431. “You discovered the lunatic doctor” = 246
432. “You found a killer *Spitalfields* hid” = 246
433. “You found doctor *Jack the Ripper* hid” = 246
434. “You found killer in *Spitalfields*” = 246

We note the Master Code solution: *"Jack the Ripper* is playing *a code-game*" = 246

In that context, we find the Master Code solutions:

1. ***"Funny little games**** is a clue to a code" = 246
2. ***"Funny little games*** are the codes" = 246
3. "Hint is in: ***funny little games***" = 246

***Phrase in the *Dear Boss* note. The solutions imply *funny little games* is a hint at secret codes.**

Brief Summary of the preceding solutions

The solutions identify *Jack the Ripper* as a doctor/medic from Ireland and indicate that the killer is **playing 'a code-game'** - consistent with the 'funny little games' referred to in the 'Dear Boss' letter. Collectively, the foregoing solutions/resonance equations imply very strongly that the murderer knew and used *Skelton*'s cipher and the Master Code and that in turn suggests **the murders *and Jack the Ripper*'s identity are probably solvable mysteries even now, 135 years after the events.**

Code solutions indicate many times, that the murderer known as *Jack the Ripper* was a doctor/medic from Dublin and that he was a philanthropist who knew the Whitechapel-Spitalfields area very well. Solutions indicate that the killer's birth date was 4/7/1845, that his father was 'John' and his mother 'Abigail', that he lived/hid at Mossford Lodge in Barkingside and that he had 'a lair'/ 'hid' in a Boys Home/orphanage in Stepney Causeway. *Skelton* is a Masonic/Orange Order cipher which suggests the murderer was very probably Protestant, consistent with the following solutions:

1. "Code hid Irish-Protestant medic" = 246
2. "Protestant medic was killer" = 246

***Jack the Ripper* can now be identified.**

The man who was *Jack the Ripper*

A huge set of Master Code solutions (following) identify *Jack the Ripper* as the famous Irish philanthropist Doctor Thomas John Barnardo, a member of the Orange Order. Born in Dublin in 1845 to Anglo-German parents, he was 43 at the time of the murders and had gained an extensive and detailed knowledge of Whitechapel and Spitalfields from years of street preaching and by visiting many of the lodging-houses there.

Thomas John Barnardo (1845-1905)

(Image: Wikipedia commons)

The Barnardo family, possibly of Venetian-Jewish origin, emigrated from Hamburg to Dublin in the early 1840s. The fourth of five children of John Michaelis Barnardo - a furrier - and his second wife Abigail, Thomas John was born at Dame St in Dublin on July 4th 1845. Abigail (nee Drinkwater) was English and a member of the Plymouth Brethren, a non-conformist Protestant sect whose fundamental tenet is that *The Bible* is the word of God and the *only* true Christian authority.

It appears that Thomas was a small unattractive boy, hidden out of sight when friends of the family paid a visit. There are hints that his childhood was difficult and unhappy. He said of himself that he had been an ego-centric, totally selfish child. Educated at St Patricks Cathedral Grammar School in Dublin, it seems he was a troublemaker and proved an argumentative, disruptive pupil who got bored quickly with lessons. On leaving school at sixteen, having failed the public examinations he was apprenticed to a wine merchant and, at about the same time, he joined the Plymouth Brethren.

It was after attending an inspiring lecture about China that young Thomas experienced an epiphany, seeing his future as a medical missionary in old Cathay. Four years later in April 1866, he left Dublin to train as a doctor at the London Hospital in Whitechapel. It is noteworthy that fellow medical students regarded him as an 'odd-ball' on account of his fanatical 'fire and brimstone', 'Bible-bashing' Puritanism. It seems that he was an 'outsider' - a misfit - and perhaps out of his depth intellectually; he failed to complete the medical course though not before it was noticed that - having dissected two corpses - he showed a special interest in anatomy.

A year later in 1867, Barnardo set up a 'ragged school' - *Hope Place* - no pun intended, where poor children could get a basic education. One of the boys, Jim Jarvis, took the young fellow from Dublin on a tour of the neighbourhood, visiting some of its most appalling slums. Here the Irish medic witnessed first-hand homeless bedraggled children begging in the streets, sleeping rough in gutters and on roofs - many of them orphaned by a recent cholera epidemic. In that moment, the 22-year-old prospective missionary experienced a second epiphany and, having seen 'the light' anew, abandoned his cherished plan to work in China focussing instead on the desperate plight of an estimated 30,000 destitute children living rough in the capital's squalid slums.

To this day Doctor Barnardo is famous in the UK for his charitable work, having given thousands of disadvantaged children the chance of a better start in life. His 'great work' began in 1870 with the establishment of an orphanage for boys at 18-26 Stepney-causeway. The institution provided food, shelter and training in carpentry, metal-work and shoe-making with the aim of preparing the boys for apprenticeships and trades when the time came to leave.

In 1873 Thomas John Barnardo married the philanthropist and evangelist Syrie Louise Elmslie; they had seven children together though three died in childhood and one had Down's syndrome. The couple were given a fifteen-year lease on *Mossford Lodge* as a wedding present, a very large house at Barkingside in Essex. The 60-acre site allowed Barnardo to open a home for girls, where they were to receive training in preparation for domestic service. This is what he wrote about the first in-take of girls and their mothers:

"Among my first thirty girls I had as many depraved children gathered in our little Home as I suppose have ever been aggregated under one roof since then. These were mostly criminals in embryo, the offspring of degraded and vicious women."

Thomas Barnardo was a short, stocky man - standing at just 5' 3" - yet by all accounts he had a very forceful personality; some who knew him well claimed that his cold grey piercing eyes could 'penetrate the soul'. In common with many illustrious Victorians, he was a 'workaholic' possessed of considerable drive and energy and like many of that ilk he had a 'short fuse' - one friend described his sudden violent temper outbursts as 'volcanic'.

Although he was a widely respected philanthropist, Barnardo had his detractors. He was accused of 'kidnapping' - taking children without parental consent - an accusation he accepted as true, although he claimed that 'the ends justified the means...'. In fact, records show that he was taken to court no less than 88 times, mainly on grounds of unlawful abduction although other serious charges included neglect of basic hygiene for the children in his care.

On admission to a 'Barnardo home' a child was photographed; some of the pictures were used to illustrate the urchin's ragged and filthy condition. However, in certain quarters it was claimed that the photographs deliberately exaggerated the degree of dishevelment and so because the 'misleading' images were used to advertise the homes, the photographs were regarded as fraudulent. Thomas Barnardo had broken the law many times, had been neglectful of children's basic hygiene and, it seems, had engaged in deception. It would appear that the evangelical street preacher and member of the Plymouth Brethren was no saint.

Thomas Barnardo had been living and working in London's East End for about twenty years when the Whitechapel-Spitalfields murders shocked the capital in autumn 1888. It was a difficult time for him personally as the lease on Mossford Lodge ran-out that year. In order to purchase the property outright he needed £7,000 - a huge sum in those days - and it had to be found quickly. It so happened that the puritanical evangelist harboured a deep dislike of Roman Catholics and - as if Fate was intent on compounding insult with injury - he learned that it was Catholic Sisters who intended to buy the property, the Barnardo family home of fifteen years standing.

Street preacher and seasoned lodging-house visitor

Having living quarters in the Boys Home at 18-26 Stepney-causeway meant that Barnardo's 'street parish' was virtually on the door-step. By comparison, the family residence at Mossford Lodge was ten long miles away at Barkingside in Essex. It was in the guise of street preacher and evangelist that the good doctor visited the many lodging-houses in Whitechapel and Spitalfields, squalid rented shelters providing low-cost, sub-standard accommodation for a host of 'undesirable down-and-outs'.

Those visits would have brought the 'Bible-bashing' puritan into direct personal contact with many prostitutes - sex workers - females who in his own words were 'degraded and vicious women'. The proselytizing street preacher tried to persuade the 'fallen women' to change their 'sinful ways', give-up the demon drink and transfer their unruly offspring to his 'safe-keeping' – so it's very likely Barnardo got to know many of the Whitechapel-Spitalfields sex-workers personally and by name.

The prime suspect's 'CV'

A failed medic noted for his interest in anatomy. A religious fanatic seen as an odd-ball by fellow medical students. A very forceful personality with a 'volcanic' temper. An evangelical street preacher who would have encountered many prostitutes on the streets and in the lodging-houses of Whitechapel and Spitalfields. Someone with an intimate knowledge of the 'killing zone'.

In light of those details, the 'doctor'* from Dublin should have been a suspect for the Whitechapel murders, especially as the police seriously considered the possibility that the killer was a medic and even interviewed a few doctors. Against that background it is surprising Barnardo was never questioned; perhaps it was his renown as a 'whiter-than-white' philanthropist - the famous champion of destitute children - that shielded him from suspicion. Afterall, how could a famous, caring philanthropist be a brutal serial killer?

*It is unclear if Barnardo fully qualified as a doctor, having dropped-out of the medical course at the London Hospital in Whitechapel; nevertheless, from 1876 onwards he styled himself 'doctor'.

Barnardo - what's in a name?

The name Barnardo is a Venetian adaptation of Bernard, which means 'bear + tough' / 'bear + hardy' etc. Other adjectives include: strong, stout, robust. **Applying *Skelton* to 'Jack the Ripper' in that context, we find the resonance equations**:

1. "*Jack the Ripper*" = "alias hid a *tough bear*" = 115
2. "*Jack the Ripper*" = "code hid *robust bear*" = 115
3. "*Jack the Ripper*" = "code hid *stout bear*" = 115
4. "*Jack the Ripper*" = "hid *strong bear*" = 115
5. "*Jack the Ripper*" = "hiding a *hardy bear*" = 115
6. "*Jack the Ripper*" = "name of a *hardy bear*" = 115

Implies *Jack the Ripper* is a code/alias hiding a hardy/strong/stout/tough/robust bear; in other words, *Jack the Ripper* is a code-name which hides the *meaning* of 'Barnardo'.

In addition, we find the Master Code solutions:

1. "A *hardy bear* hides as *Jack the Ripper*" = 246
2. "A *hardy bear* hiding in *Jack the Ripper*" = 246
3. "A *tough bear* hid as Doctor Barnardo's name" = 246
4. "Doctor Barnardo's name hides *tough bear*" = 246
5. "*Hardy bear* is clue to Barnardo's name" = 246
6. "*Hardy bear:* clue to the name of Barnardo" = 246

So, via both the resonance equations and the Master Code solutions 'Jack the Ripper' is linked to the *meaning* of Barnardo's name.

Doctor Barnardo and the Master Code

The key conjecture is that Barnardo knew *Skelton*'s cipher and the Master Code and used them to carry-out murders. This is tested further by applying *Skelton* in that context:

1. "The Master Code" = "is Barnardo's code" = 111
2. "You discovered" = "Dr Barnardo's code" = 111

Moreover, we find resonance equations directly linking *Jack the Ripper* and Barnardo:

1. "*Jack the Ripper*" = "code concealed Barnardo" = 115
2. "*Jack the Ripper*" = "code hid name Barnardo" = 115
3. "*Jack the Ripper*" = "hid as T. J. Barnardo" = 115
4. "*Jack the Ripper*" = "hides Dr Barnardo" = 115
5. "*Jack the Ripper*" = "is a Barnardo alias" = 115
6. "*Jack the Ripper*" = "is Tom Barnardo" = 115
7. "*Jack the Ripper*" = "mask hid Barnardo" = 115
8. "*Jack the Ripper*" = "really Barnardo" = 115

Applying *Skelton* in the context of Doctor X and Barnardo, gives the resonance equations:

- "Doctor X" = "hid Barnardo" = 74
- "Doctor X" = "secret code" = 74
- "Dr X hid" = "Barnardo" = 59

Linking the equations: "Doctor X" = "secret code" = "hid Barnardo" = 74

Applying the Master Code in the context of Doctor X & Barnardo gives the solutions:

1. "*Doctor X:* a secret code hiding Barnardo" = 246
2. "*Doctor X:* code hiding Thomas Barnardo" = 246
3. "*Doctor X:* code of Thomas John Barnardo" = 246
4. "*Doctor X:* the secret code of Barnardo" = 246
5. "*Doctor X* was code hiding Dr Barnardo" = 246

Also: "Doctor X was" = "*Jack the Ripper*" = 115

The implication of the foregoing is that unknown 'Doctor X' – *Jack the Ripper* – was Barnardo.

Applying *Skelton* to Barnardo's full name in the context of *Jack the Ripper*, we find:

- "*Jack the Ripper* hid as" = "Thomas John Barnardo" = 149
- "*Jack the Ripper* was alias of" = "Doctor Thomas John Barnardo" = 200

The address of *Jack the Ripper*

We note the Master Code solution: "Code hid the address of *Jack the Ripper*" = 246

Applying *Skelton* in the context of *Jack the Ripper*'s address, we find the resonance equations:

1. "Barkingside hides" = "*Jack the Ripper*" = 115
2. "*Jack the Ripper*" = "hid at Barkingside" = 115

Barkingside in Essex was the location of Mossford Lodge, the Barnardo family home.

Jack the RIpper – an Irish philanthropist

In that context, we find the Master Code solution: "A clue is: *Irish philanthropist*" = 246

And, we note the resonance equation: "*Jack the Ripper*" = "was Dublin born" = 115

By trial and error, we find the resonance equations:

1. "*Jack the Ripper* hiding a" = "philanthropist" = 154
2. "*Jack the Ripper* name of a" = "philanthropist" = 154

And:

1. "*Jack the Ripper* is hiding the" = "Irish philanthropist" = 203

Jack the Ripper – ‘doctor’ and Orangeman from Dublin - Master Code solutions:

1. “*Dr Jack* was name of *Orangeman* Barnardo” = 246 “*Dr Jack* is” = “Barnardo” = 59
2. “I am an *Orange Order* doctor from Dublin” = 246*
3. “*Jack* is cipher of *Orangeman* Dr Barnardo” = 246
4. “*Jack* is cypher of *Orangeman* Barnardo” = 246
5. “*Jack the Ripper* hid *Orangeman*’s name” = 246
6. “*Jack the Ripper* is name of *Orangeman*” = 246
7. “*Jack the Ripper: Orange Order* is a clue” = 246
8. “*Jack the Ripper: Orangeman* Barnardo” = 246
9. “*Jack: a secret* name of *Orangeman* Barnardo” = 246
10. “*Jack:* was a cipher of *Orangeman* Barnardo” = 246
11. “*The red hand* is a clue of *Jack the Ripper*” = 246** red hand of the Orange Order?

**In the ‘Dear Boss’ note, the author refers to the red ink on his hand – the red hand is a symbol associated with the Orange Order, implying a link between *Jack the Ripper* and the Orange Order.

It appears that *Skelton* was a code known to the Orange Society/Orange Order and that the killer known as *Jack the Ripper* was an Orangeman – hence, the significance of the red hand.

*Thomas Barnardo was a member of the Orange Order; that is probably how he came to know *Skelton’s* cipher and Master Code.

Applying the Master Code in that context:

1. “A Masonic cipher used by Orange Order” = 246
2. “Orange Order used the code of *Skelton*” = 246
3. “Orange Society used code of *Skelton*” = 246
4. “Secret code used by the Orange Order” = 246
5. “Secret code used by *Orange Society*” = 246
6. “*Skelton:* code of the *Orange Society*” = 246
7. “This was a code used by Orange Order” = 246
8. “You cracked a secret code of Orange Order” = 246
9. “You have found Orange Order numeral” = 246

Reversed solutions:

- 246 = “is the Orange Society’s numeral”
- 246 = “number hid Orange Order’s secret code”

And, we find the Master Code solutions:

1. “Barnardo uses an *Orange Society* code” = 246
2. “Barnardo used codes of *Orange Society*” = 246
3. “Barnardo used codes of the *Orange Order*” = 246
4. “Code of *Orange Order* is used by Barnardo” = 246
5. “Code of *Orange Order* used by Dr Barnardo” = 246

Applying the Master Code in the context of Barnardo and the Whitechapel/Spitalfields murders etc gives rise to a huge set of solutions:

1. "A clue hides at Stepney-causeway" = 246 — Barnardo's Boys Home
2. "A clue is: Barnardo is in the *Ten Bells*" = 246 — a notorious pub in Spitalfields
3. "A clue is: Dr Barnardo in the *Ten Bells*" = 246
4. "A clue is: *Irish philanthropist*" = 246 — consistent with an Irish connection (sor, mishter)
5. "A clue is: *the confession of Dr Barnardo*" = 246
6. "A clue was: Barnardo likes to murder" = 246
7. "A clue was: the wicked doctor Barnardo" = 246
8. "A code hid an *Irish philanthropist*" = 246
9. "A code hides murderer Thomas Barnardo" = 246
10. "A code hides the women Barnardo gutted" = 246
11. "A doctor from *Barkingside* murders" = 246
12. "A doctor in *Barkingside* is a murderer" = 246
13. "A doctor in Plymouth Brethren" = 246
14. "A harlot killer at *Mossford Lodge*" = 246 — Mossford Lodge at Barkingside in Essex
15. "A killer clue is: *Barkingside*'s doctor" = 246
16. "A killer clue is: Thomas John Barnardo" = 246 — "Thomas John Barnardo" = "*Barkingside*'s doctor"
17. "A killer name is: Dr Thomas Barnardo" = 246
18. "A killer physician of Stepney" = 246
19. "A lair of *Jack the Ripper* at orphanage" = 246 — Stepney causeway
20. "A letter of Barnardo was in *red-ink*" = 246 — 'Dear Boss' letter
21. "A raging monster hidden as Barnardo" = 246
22. "A *red-ink* letter *hid* clue of Dr Barnardo" = 246
23. "A *red-ink* letter *hides* a clue of Barnardo" = 246
24. "A *red-ink* letter was by Barnardo" = 246
25. "A savage killer hid in Doctor Barnardo" = 246
26. "A *secret* abortionist of sluts" = 246
27. "A *secret* abortionist of whores" = 246
28. "A secret arithmetic code of Barnardo" = 246
29. "A secret code hides as Barnardo's *games*" = 246 — Dear Boss letter: 'my funny little games'
30. "A secret code hiding in Barnardo's *games*" = 246
31. "A wild animal hides as Doctor Barnardo" = 246
32. "A wild animal hiding in Doctor Barnardo" = 246
33. "Abominable murders of Doctor Barnardo" = 246
34. "Abortions doctor at Whitechapel" = 246
35. "An abortionist hid at Whitechapel" = 246
36. "An orphans home hid *Jack the Ripper*" = 246
37. "Atrocious murders are Barnardo's" = 246
38. "*Barkingside* doctor hiding a murderer" = 246
39. "*Barkingside* doctor: secret killer" = 246
40. "*Barkingside* hid a murderous surgeon" = 246

41. "*Barkingside* hid the butcher-surgeon" = 246
42. "*Barkingside* hides murdering doctor" = 246
43. "*Barkingside* hiding a slut's butcher" = 246
44. "*Barkingside* hiding a whore's butcher" = 246
45. "*Barkingside* is the home of Dr Barnardo" = 246
46. "*Barkingside*'s doctor is murderer" = 246
47. "Barnardo addressed a code-note to *Boss*" = 246
48. "Barnardo admits killing old slut" = 246
49. "Barnardo admits killing old whore" = 246
50. "Barnardo at Stepney Boys' home" = 246
51. "Barnardo confesses to murdering" = 246
52. "Barnardo guilty of five killings" = 246
53. "Barnardo hid a code in gruesome murders" = 246
54. "Barnardo hid code clue at Goulston St" = 246
55. "Barnardo hid code clues in a note to *Boss*" = 246
56. "Barnardo hid code in gruesome killings" = 246
57. "Barnardo hid in *Jack the Ripper* mask" = 246
58. "Barnardo hid messages as a secret code" = 246
59. "Barnardo hid the fiend *Jack the Ripper*" = 246
60. "Barnardo hid the murderous surgeon" = 246
61. "Barnardo hides evil *Jack the Ripper*" = 246
62. "Barnardo hiding a *Whitechapel* killer" = 246
63. "Barnardo hiding at the *Ten Bells* pub" = 246
64. "Barnardo hiding in mask of *Saucy Jacky*" = 246
65. "Barnardo is a killer of Dorset St" = 246
66. "Barnardo is a physician from Dublin" = 246
67. "Barnardo is a quintuple murderer" = 246
68. "Barnardo is a secret murderer code hid" = 246
69. "Barnardo is a secret savage killer" = 246
70. "Barnardo is a *Spitalfields* killer" = 246
71. "Barnardo is an Irish abortionist" = 246
72. "Barnardo is hidden by Freemason's code" = 246
73. "Barnardo is hidden in a code of *Saucy Jacky*" = 245
74. "Barnardo is hidden in code of Freemasons" = 246
75. "Barnardo is hiding a slut's butcher" = 246
76. "Barnardo is hiding a whore's butcher" = 246
77. "Barnardo is hiding at the *Ten Bells*" = 246
78. "Barnardo is hiding slut-slasher" = 246
79. "Barnardo is hiding whore-slasher" = 246
80. "Barnardo is murderer from Ireland" = 246
81. "Barnardo is name of slut-slasher" = 246
82. "Barnardo is name of *Spitalfields Jack*" = 246
83. "Barnardo is name of whore-slasher" = 246

84. “Barnardo is slut-killer of London” = 246
85. “Barnardo is the butcher of sluts” = 246
86. “Barnardo is the butcher of whores” = 246
87. “Barnardo is the evil Irish doctor” = 246
88. “Barnardo is the face of *Jack the Ripper*” = 246
89. “Barnardo is the hidden abortionist” = 246
90. “Barnardo is the Irish physician” = 246
91. “Barnardo is the monster *Jack*” = 246
92. “Barnardo is the scourge of sluts” = 246
93. “Barnardo is the scourge of whores” = 246
94. “Barnardo is the secret murderer” = 246
95. “Barnardo is whore-killer of London” = 246
96. “Barnardo killed sluts at Autumn” = 246
97. “Barnardo killed sluts at weekend” = 246 — the murderer killed only at weekends
98. “Barnardo killed sluts in East End” = 246
99. “Barnardo killed using code of *Skelton*” = 246
100. “Barnardo killed whores at Autumn” = 246
101. “Barnardo killed whores at weekend” = 246
102. “Barnardo killed whores in East End” = 246
103. “Barnardo kills as *Jack the Ripper*” = 246
104. “Barnardo kills by *Skelton*’s code” = 246
105. “Barnardo knew of the Orange Order code” = 246
106. “Barnardo murdered five women by code” = 246
107. “Barnardo murders at the age of 43” = 246 — he was 43 in July 1888
108. “Barnardo murders the 5 harlots” = 246
109. “Barnardo mutilated five victims” = 246
110. “Barnardo *only* murdered on weekend” = 246
111. “Barnardo posted a half a kidney as a clue” = 246
112. “Barnardo sent letter to *Boss*” = 246
113. “Barnardo shall kill ladies hidden in a code” = 246
114. “Barnardo the preacher hiding a killer” = 246
115. “Barnardo used arithmetic code to kill” = 246
116. “Barnardo used code of *Skelton* to kill” = 246
117. “Barnardo used codes of Orange Society” = 246
118. “Barnardo used codes of The Orange Order” = 246
119. “Barnardo used secret code for murder” = 246
120. “Barnardo uses an Orange Society code” = 246
121. “Barnardo was a murdering preacher” = 246
122. “Barnardo was a Quaker preacher” = 246 — “*The Quaker* hides” = “*Jack the Ripper*” = 115
123. “Barnardo was killer you identified” = 246
124. “Barnardo was name of a slut killer” = 246
125. “Barnardo was name of a whore killer” = 246
126. “Barnardo was name of *Barkingside* fiend” = 246

127. “Barnardo was real *Jack the Ripper*” = 246
128. “Barnardo was the demonic murderer” = 246
129. “Barnardo wrote notes to Lusk” = 246
130. “Barnardo: a killer hid in Dorset St” = 246
131. “Barnardo: a killer Whitechapel hid” = 246
132. “Barnardo: a secret Irish murderer” = 246
133. “Barnardo: a secret killer named by code” = 246
134. “Barnardo: blood-thirsty killer” = 246
135. “Barnardo: Dorset St’s mad doctor” = 246
136. “Barnardo: he was guilty of homicides” = 246
137. “Barnardo: hidden at Dorset St lair” = 246
138. “Barnardo: hiding in Dorset St lair” = 246
139. “Barnardo: hiding the mad abortionist” = 246
140. “Barnardo: hiding-out at Dorset St” = 246
141. “Barnardo: his code is very difficult” = 246
142. “Barnardo: killer in Whitechapel” = 246
143. “Barnardo: killing by the secret code” = 246
144. “Barnardo: mad surgeon of Whitechapel” = 246
145. “Barnardo: murderer of Dorset St” = 246
146. “Barnardo: name of a Whitechapel killer” = 246
147. “Barnardo: name of Irish surgeon, *mad Jack*” = 246
148. “Barnardo: name of killer *Barkingside* hid” = 246
149. “Barnardo: name of murderous preacher” = 246
150. “Barnardo: name of the mad abortionist” = 246
151. “Barnardo: preacher in the street” = 246
152. “Barnardo: Spitalfields’ murderer” = 246
153. “Barnardo: the fiend hidden in *Barkingside*” = 246
154. “Barnardo: the killer in the East End” = 246
155. “Barnardo: the killer of Whitechapel” = 246
156. “Barnardo: the mad doctor from Ireland” = 246
157. “Barnardo: the true *Jack the Ripper*” = 246
158. “Barnardo: the true name of a murderer” = 246
159. “Barnardo: the voice of *Jack the Ripper*” = 246
160. “Barnardo’s abortions on sluts” = 246
161. “Barnardo’s abortions on whores” = 246
162. “Barnardo’s code clue in *red-ink* letter” = 246
163. “Barnardo’s code clue on Goulston St” = 246
164. “Barnardo’s code is in *red-ink* letter” = 246
165. “Barnardo’s code is on Goulston St” = 246
166. “Barnardo’s code is to blame for murder” = 246
167. “Barnardo’s confession is hidden in a code” = 246
168. “Barnardo’s dastardly murder-code” = 246
169. “Barnardo’s guise as *Jack the Ripper*” = 246

170. “Barnardo’s letter *‘From Hell’* hid code” = 246
171. “Barnardo’s letter in *red-ink* is code” = 246
172. “Barnardo’s letter to *Boss* is code” = 246
173. “Barnardo’s murder-codes are secret” = 246
174. “Barnardo’s murders are secret code” = 246
175. “Barnardo’s sermons are in *red ink*” = 246
176. “Barnardo’s Whitechapel murders” = 246
177. “Bloody murders by evil Barnardo” = 246
178. “*Boss* is the code clue of Doctor Barnardo” = 246
179. “*Boss:* letter of Barnardo in *red-ink*” = 246
180. “*Boss:* red-ink letter by Barnardo” = 246
181. “*Boys’ Home* was hiding secret lair” = 246
182. “*Boys’ Home: Jack the Ripper*’s refuge” = 246
183. “Boys’ orphanage hid *Jack the Ripper*” = 246
184. “Brutal killer: the name is Barnardo” = 246
185. “Butchery of sluts by Barnardo” = 246
186. “Butchery of whores by Barnardo” = 246
187. “*Catch me when you can* is code of Barnardo” = 246 not ‘catch me *if* you can’
188. “*Catch me when you can:* a Barnardo hint” = 246
189. “*Catch me when you can:* code clue of Barnardo” = 246
190. “*Catch me when you can:* code of Dr Barnardo” = 246
191. “Clue hidden at *Stepney causeway E*” = 246
192. “Clue hiding in *Stepney causeway E*” = 246
193. “Clue is my nickname: mad Tom Barnardo” = 246
194. “Clue is: a code hid killer of *Mossford Lodge*” = 246
195. “Clue is: Barnardo butchers sluts” = 246
196. “Clue is: Barnardo butchers whores” = 246
197. “Clue is: Barnardo is the wicked doctor” = 246
198. “Clue is: Barnardo killed ladies in London” = 246
199. “Clue is: Boys’ Home hid *Jack the Ripper*” = 246
200. “Clue is: Doctor Barnardo killed women” = 246
201. “Clue is: Dorset St abortionist” = 246
202. “Clue is: Dr Barnardo likes to murder” = 246
203. “Clue is: ears, eyelids and nose are cut” = 246
204. “Clue is: in *red-ink* letter of Barnardo” = 246
205. “Clue is: kidney half-eaten by Barnardo” = 246
206. “Clue is: *mad Jack* was disguise of Barnardo” = 246
207. “Clue is: mad surgeon at Dorset St” = 246
208. “Clue is: *red-ink* letter by Barnardo” = 246
209. “Clue is: the killer of *Mossford Lodge*” = 246
210. “Clue of Barnardo is in *red-ink* letter” = 246
211. “Clue of Dr Barnardo in *red-ink* letter” = 246
212. “Clue to killer is in *Mossford Lodge*” = 246

213. “Clues named killer: Thomas Barnardo” = 246
214. “Code hid Barnardo’s murder confession” = 246
215. “Code hid birthdate of *Jack the Ripper*” = 246 “4/7/1845 is d.o.b. of” = “*Jack the Ripper*” = 115
216. “Code hid in a note from Barnardo to *Boss*” = 246
217. “Code hid in *red-ink* sermons of Barnardo” = 246
218. “Code hid *Jack the Ripper*’s date of birth” = 246
219. “Code hid *Mossford Lodge* slut-killer” = 246
220. “Code hid *Mossford Lodge* whore-killer” = 246
221. “Code hiding in notes Barnardo wrote” = 246
222. “Code identified a harlot killer: Barnardo” = 246
223. “Code of *Saucy Jacky* hides evil Barnardo” = 246
224. “Code shows Barnardo is the killer” = 246
225. “Code told Barnardo to kill harlots” = 246
226. “Code-letter from Barnardo to *Boss*” = 246
227. “Codes hid name and date of birth of Barnardo” = 246
228. “Codes hid the confessions of Barnardo” = 246
229. “Codes hide as notes Barnardo wrote” = 246
230. “Codes hide the confession by Barnardo” = 246
231. “Codes hide truths about T. J. Barnardo” = 246
232. “Codes show killer hidden in Barnardo” = 246
233. “Confession by *Thomas John Barnardo*” = 246
234. “Cryptonym hides Dr Barnardo” = 246
235. “Cut off the ears: *Jack the Ripper* clue” = 246
236. “Cut the throat *then* disembowel” = 246 *modus operandi* of *Jack the Ripper*
237. “Date of birth of a murderer: 4/7/1845” = 246 Thomas Barnardo’s d.o.b
238. “*Dear Boss* hides a code of Thomas Barnardo” = 246
239. “*Dear Boss* is Barnardo’s secret clue” = 246
240. “*Dear Boss* was a cipher of Dr Barnardo” = 246
241. “*Dear Boss* was a cypher of Barnardo” = 246
242. “Diabolical doctor is at *Mossford Lodge*” = 246
243. “Diabolical murders are Barnardo’s codes” = 246
244. “Diabolical murders hiding Barnardo’s code” = 246
245. “Doctor Barnardo disguise: a clue is *mad Jack*” = 246
246. “Doctor Barnardo founder of a Boys’ Home” = 246
247. “Doctor Barnardo hid at Dorset St” = 246
248. “Doctor Barnardo hides a homicidal doctor” = 246
249. “Doctor Barnardo is *Dr Jack*: a murderer” = 246
250. “Doctor Barnardo is hiding a murderer” = 246
251. “Doctor Barnardo is killing by codes” = 246
252. “Doctor Barnardo is name of a murderer” = 246
253. “Doctor Barnardo is secret killer” = 246
254. “Doctor Barnardo kills 5 harlots” = 246
255. “Doctor Barnardo kills fallen ladies” = 246

256. “Doctor Barnardo kills the foetus” = 246 an abortionist
257. “Doctor Barnardo loves murdering” = 246
258. “Doctor Barnardo loves to murder” = 246
259. “Doctor Barnardo used a cipher to kill” = 246
260. “Doctor Barnardo used a Freemason’s code” = 246*
261. “Doctor Barnardo uses code to murder” = 246
262. “Doctor Barnardo was cut-throat” = 246
263. “Doctor Barnardo: a killer of sluts” = 246
264. “Doctor Barnardo: a killer of whores” = 246
265. “Doctor Barnardo: a murderer of London” = 246
266. “Doctor Barnardo: an evil monster” = 246
267. “Doctor Barnardo: guilty of homicides” = 246
268. “Doctor Barnardo: guilty of murder” = 246
269. “Doctor Barnardo: mad *Jack* was a disguise” = 246 Jack’s notes are meant to ‘sound’ mad
270. “Doctor Barnardo: name of wicked killer” = 246
271. “Doctor Barnardo: *secret* Freemason” = 246 officially joined Freemasons in 1889
272. “Doctor Barnardo: the slut-killer” = 246
273. “Doctor Barnardo: the whore-killer” = 246
274. “Doctor Barnardo’s diabolical murders” = 246
275. “Doctor Barnardo’s hidden confession” = 246
276. “Doctor from *Barkingside* is a killer” = 246
277. “Doctor from Dublin hides the killer” = 246
278. “Doctor was *philanthropist*” = 246
279. “Doctor’s orphanage in Stepney” = 246
280. “Dorset St hides Doctor Barnardo” = 246
281. “Dorset St is a Barnardo residence” = 246
282. “Dorset St killer called Barnardo” = 246
283. “Dr Barnardo hid a murderous surgeon” = 246
284. “Dr Barnardo hid code at Goulston St” = 246
285. “Dr Barnardo hid the slut ripper” = 246
286. “Dr Barnardo hid the whore ripper” = 246
287. “Dr Barnardo hides brutal murderer” = 246
288. “Dr Barnardo hides in code of *Saucy Jacky*” = 246
289. “Dr Barnardo hides the evil preacher” = 246
290. “Dr Barnardo in *Jack the Ripper* guise” = 246
291. “Dr Barnardo inhabited *Mossford Lodge*” = 246
292. “Dr Barnardo is a killer from Ireland” = 246
293. “Dr Barnardo is *Jack the Ripper’s* face” = 246
294. “Dr Barnardo is murdering preacher” = 246
295. “Dr Barnardo is the ferocious killer” = 246
296. “Dr Barnardo is the harlot butcher” = 246
297. “Dr Barnardo knew the *Skelton* code” = 246
298. “Dr Barnardo liked to kill harlots” = 246

299. “Dr Barnardo murdered by using codes” = 246
300. “Dr Barnardo murdered five sluts” = 246
301. “Dr Barnardo murdered five whores” = 246
302. “Dr Barnardo murders according to code” = 246
303. “Dr Barnardo posts half of kidney” = 246
304. “Dr Barnardo ripped five harlots” = 246
305. “Dr Barnardo used the orphanage to hide” = 246
306. “Dr Barnardo was 43 years of age” = 246 when he committed the murders
307. “Dr Barnardo was red-handed Orangeman” = 246 alludes to *Dear Boss* note
308. “Dr Barnardo wears black Quaker hat” = 246
309. “Dr Barnardo: a doctor at Whitechapel” = 246
310. “Dr Barnardo: a killer of Dorset St” = 246
311. “Dr Barnardo: a quintuple murderer” = 246
312. “Dr Barnardo: a *Spitalfields* killer” = 246
313. “Dr Barnardo: an Irish abortionist” = 246
314. “Dr Barnardo: hide-out at Dorset St” = 246
315. “Dr Barnardo: the butcher of sluts” = 246
316. “Dr Barnardo: the butcher of whores” = 246
317. “Dr Barnardo: the hidden abortionist” = 246
318. “Dr Barnardo: the scourge of sluts” = 246
319. “Dr Barnardo: the scourge of whores” = 246
320. “Dr Barnardo: the secret murderer” = 246
321. “Dr Barnardo’s murders hid in the code” = 246
322. “Dr Barnardo’s terrible murders” = 246
323. “Dr Thomas Barnardo is the killer” = 246
324. “Dr Thomas John Barnardo is a killer” = 246
325. “Evil Barnardo was brutal killer” = 246
326. “Evil doctor living at *Barkingside*” = 246
327. “Evil doctor was in Dorset St” = 246
328. “Evil *Jack the Ripper* at Boys’ Home” = 246
329. “Famous doctor hid as *Jack the Ripper*” = 246
330. “Famous murders hid doctor Barnardo” = 246
331. “Few find code in note Barnardo wrote” = 246
332. “Few find *Jack the Ripper* in Barnardo” = 246
333. “Find a killer hidden at *Mossford Lodge*” = 246
334. “Find a killer hiding in *Mossford Lodge*” = 246
335. “Find *Jack the Ripper* hid in Boys Home” = 246
336. “Five slut killings by Barnardo” = 246
337. “Five whore killings by Barnardo” = 246
338. “Found the proof Barnardo killed by code” = 246
339. “Go to Dorset St: look for a killer” = 246
340. “Grand Plan: the Barnardo killings” = 246
341. “Grisly killings of Dr Barnardo” = 246

342. "Half a kidney was eaten by Barnardo" = 246
343. "*Hardy bear* is clue to Barnardo's name" = 246 meaning of name
344. "Harlot butchery by Dr Barnardo" = 246
345. "Harlot butchery is by Barnardo" = 246
346. "Have proof Barnardo killed by the code" = 246
347. "Heinous murders by Barnardo are code" = 246
348. "Heinous murders of Barnardo are in code" = 246
349. "Hidden confession of Doctor Barnardo" = 246
350. "Hide the mad surgeon in Dorset St" = 246
351. "I am an *Orange Order* doctor from Dublin" = 246
352. "I am Barnardo *the street preacher*" = 246
353. "I am Barnardo: I use name *Jack the Ripper*" = 246
354. "*I am down on whores* is a Barnardo code clue" = 246 quote from Dear Boss letter
355. "*I am down on whores* is a Dr Barnardo code" = 246
356. "*I am down on whores:* a Dr Barnardo code clue" = 246
357. "I am Thomas Barnardo: I kill sluts" = 246
358. "I am Thomas Barnardo: I kill whores" = 246
359. "I removed slut's intestines" = 246
360. "I removed whore's intestines" = 246
361. "I took female reproductive organs" = 246
362. "I'm Barnardo I use a name: *Jack the Ripper*" = 246
363. "I'm Barnardo: *Jack the Ripper* name hid me" = 246
364. "I'm Barnardo: you are right about code" = 246
365. "Irish doctor from Dublin hid killer" = 246
366. "Irish doctor hid at *Mossford Lodge*" = 246
367. "Irish murderer Thomas Barnardo" = 246
368. "Irish murderer was Dr Barnardo" = 246
369. "*Irish philanthropist* is a clue" = 246
370. "*Jack* hides Dr Barnardo at Whitechapel" = 246
371. "*Jack* is the dark side of Doctor Barnardo" = 246
372. "*Jack* is the secret name of Dr Barnardo" = 246
373. "*Jack* of Dorset St is hiding Barnardo" = 246
374. "*Jack* of Dorset St: hiding Dr Barnardo" = 246
375. "*Jack* of Whitechapel hid Doctor Barnardo" = 246
376. "*Jack the Ripper* actor name: Barnardo" = 246 *Jack the Ripper* is a 5-act melodrama
377. "*Jack the Ripper* clue: born 4 / 7 / 1845" = 246
378. "*Jack the Ripper* clue: born 4 th July" = 246
379. "*Jack the Ripper* clue: hid at a Boys' home" = 246
380. "*Jack the Ripper* code: real name Barnardo" = 246
381. "*Jack the Ripper* cuts throats" = 246 modus operandi
382. "*Jack the Ripper* guise hid T. J. Barnardo" = 246
383. "*Jack the Ripper* hid an evil preacher" = 246
384. "*Jack the Ripper* hid as evangelist" = 246

385. *"Jack the Ripper* hid codes by Barnardo" = 246
386. *"Jack the Ripper* hid doctor-preacher" = 246
387. *"Jack the Ripper* hid Orangeman's name" = 246
388. *"Jack the Ripper* hid-out at orphanage" = 246
389. *"Jack the Ripper* hidden in T. J. Barnardo" = 246
390. *"Jack the Ripper* hides a cut-throat" = 246 — cut throats of victims first
391. *"Jack the Ripper* hides in a *Quaker* hat" = 246 — see following
392. *"Jack the Ripper* hides in *Barkingside*" = 246
393. *"Jack the Ripper* hides in Dr Barnardo" = 246
394. *"Jack the Ripper* is a diabolical surgeon" = 246
395. *"Jack the Ripper* is code hiding Barnardo" = 246
396. ***"Jack the Ripper* is Doctor Barnardo" = 246**
397. *"Jack the Ripper* is Dr Barnardo in a code" = 246
398. *"Jack the Ripper* is in *The Preacher*" = 246
399. *"Jack the Ripper* is in Tom Barnardo" = 246
400. *"Jack the Ripper* is mask of Barnardo" = 246
401. *"Jack the Ripper* is sign of Barnardo" = 246
402. *"Jack the Ripper* is T. J. Barnardo in code" = 246
403. *"Jack the Ripper* lead-man name: Barnardo" = 246
404. *"Jack the Ripper* the evil preacher" = 246
405. *"Jack the Ripper* took female genitalia" = 246
406. *"Jack the Ripper* was Barnardo's code" = 246
407. *"Jack the Ripper:* a Barnardo *trade name*" = 246
408. *"Jack the Ripper:* a clue hid at Boys home" = 246
409. *"Jack the Ripper:* a clue is Orange Order" = 246
410. *"Jack the Ripper*: a doctor in Essex" = 246
411. *"Jack the Ripper:* a man in Orange Order" = 246
412. *"Jack the Ripper:* a moniker of Barnardo" = 246
413. *"Jack the Ripper:* a name Barnardo uses" = 246
414. *"Jack the Ripper*: a preacher in London" = 246
415. *"Jack the Ripper*: a secret of Barnardo" = 246
416. *"Jack the Ripper:* abortionist name" = 246
417. *"Jack the Ripper*: alias hiding Barnardo" = 246
418. *"Jack the Ripper:* an Essex killer" = 246
419. *"Jack the Ripper:* animal hid in Barnardo" = 246
420. *"Jack the Ripper:* at *Mossford Lodge*" = 246
421. *"Jack the Ripper: Barkingside* doctor" = 246
422. *"Jack the Ripper*: Boys' Home hides a clue" = 246
423. *"Jack the Ripper:* code clue Barnardo left" = 246
424. *"Jack the Ripper*: code hid abortionist" = 246
425. *"Jack the Ripper:* code hid man from Dublin" = 246
426. *"Jack the Ripper:* code hid name of preacher" = 246

427. “*Jack the Ripper*: code hiding Dr Barnardo” = 246
428. “*Jack the Ripper*: code is hiding Barnardo” = 246
429. “*Jack the Ripper:* code masks Barnardo” = 246
430. “*Jack the Ripper:* code of *Barkingside* fiend” = 246
431. “*Jack the Ripper:* concealed at orphanage” = 246
432. “*Jack the Ripper:* creation of Barnardo” = 246
433. “*Jack the Ripper:* cuts throats” = 246 modus operandi
434. “*Jack the Ripper:* decoy hides Barnardo” = 246
435. “*Jack the Ripper:* Dr T. J. Barnardo in code” = 246
436. “*Jack the Ripper:* guise for Barnardo” = 246
437. “*Jack the Ripper:* hid a religious fanatic” = 246
438. “*Jack the Ripper:* hid an evil preacher” = 246
439. “*Jack the Ripper:* hid as evangelist” = 246
440. “*Jack the Ripper:* hid doctor-preacher” = 246
441. “*Jack the Ripper:* hid Orangeman’s name” = 246
442. “*Jack the Ripper:* hid-out at orphanage” = 246
443. “*Jack the Ripper:* hides a cut-throat” = 246
444. “*Jack the Ripper:* hides in *Barkingside*” = 246
445. “*Jack the Ripper*: his father is John” = 246 John Barnardo
446. “*Jack the Ripper*: his *middle* name is *Jack*” = 246 Barnardo’s middle name: ‘John’ ~ ‘Jack’
447. “*Jack the Ripper:* is code Barnardo left” = 246
448. “*Jack the Ripper:* is sign of Barnardo” = 246
449. “*Jack the Ripper:* lived in Boys’ Home” = 246
450. “*Jack the Ripper:* monster’s name” = 246
451. “*Jack the Ripper*: mother was Abigail” = 246 Abigail Drinkwater
452. “*Jack the Ripper:* name hiding preacher” = 246
453. “*Jack the Ripper*: name of the melodrama” = 246 five murders are acts in a melodrama
454. “*Jack the Ripper:* nickname hid Barnardo” = 246
455. “*Jack the Ripper:* preacher’s cipher” = 246
456. “*Jack the Ripper:* removed the womb” = 246
457. “*Jack the Ripper:* secret Orangeman” = 246
458. “*Jack the Ripper*: shadow hid Barnardo” = 246
459. “*Jack the Ripper:* sign of Dr Barnardo” = 246
460. “*Jack the Ripper:* the evil preacher” = 246
461. “*Jack the Ripper:* the name hid Barnardo” = 246
462. “*Jack the Ripper:* was born in Dublin” = 246
463. “*Jack the Ripper:* was in Boys’ Home” = 246
464. “*Jack the Ripper*’s abode at *Barkingside*” = 246
465. “*Jack the Ripper’s* face: clue is Barnardo” = 246
466. “*Jack the Ripper*’s orphanage hide-out” = 246
467. “*Jack* the slut killer hid as Barnardo” = 246
468. “*Jack* the whore killer hid as Barnardo” = 246

469. "*Jack* was Doctor Barnardo's disguise" = 246
470. "Kill the sluts of Dorset St" = 246
471. "Kill the whores of Dorset St" = 246
472. "Killer Barnardo was a preacher-man" = 246
473. "Killer *Jack* is *philanthropist*" = 246
474. "Killer name: a clue is Thomas Barnardo" = 246
475. "Killer was doctor at *Barkingside*" = 246
476. "Killer-doctor lived at *Barkingside*" = 246
477. "Killings hid a *philanthropist*" = 246
478. "Knife on steps left by Barnardo" = 246 steps at Whitechapel Road laundry
479. "Letter in red ink is Barnardo's code" = 246
480. "Letter of Dr Barnardo is in red ink" = 246
481. "London sluts killed by Barnardo" = 246
482. "London whores killed by Barnardo" = 246
483. "Look for a diabolical doctor *Barkingside* hid" = 246
484. "Look for a mad doctor at Dorset St" = 246
485. "Look for Barnardo at *Mossford Lodge*" = 246
486. "Look for Barnardo at *Spitalfields*" = 246
487. "Look for Barnardo: murdering doctor" = 246
488. "Look for Barnardo: the abominable doctor" = 246
489. "Look for Barnardo's misspelling" = 246
490. "Look for code clue Barnardo hid in *Dear Boss*" = 246
491. "Look for code in note Barnardo wrote" = 246
492. "Look for diabolical doctor in *Barkingside*" = 246
493. "Look for Dr Barnardo in Whitechapel" = 246
494. "Look for *Jack the Ripper* birthdate" = 246 **same** as Barnardo: 4th July 1845
495. "Look for *Jack the Ripper* in Barnardo" = 246
496. "Look for *Saucy Jacky* in a post-card" = 246
497. "Lunatic Irish doctor called Barnardo" = 246
498. "*Mad Jack* from Ireland: clue is Dr Barnardo" = 246
499. "*Mad Jack* is a secret disguise of Barnardo" = 246
500. "*Mad Jack* is Doctor Barnardo's *alter ego*" = 246
501. "*Mad Jack* is the abortionist Barnardo" = 246
502. "*Mad Jack* the mad murderer hid in Barnardo" = 246
503. "*Mad Jack the Ripper* hid as Dr Barnardo" = 246
504. "*Mad Jack*: the *alter ego* of Doctor Barnardo" = 246
505. "*Medical man from Ireland* hides Barnardo" = 246
506. "*Medical man from Ireland* is a Barnardo code" = 246
507. "*Mishter Lusk* was code of Barnardo" = 246 'mishter' – Irish pronunciation
508. "Misspellings by Barnardo hide code" = 246
509. "Misspellings hid codes of Barnardo" = 246
510. "*Mister Kipper* hides as Barnardo" = 246 rhyming slang
511. "*Mister Kipper* hiding in Barnardo" = 246 *Mister Kipper - Jack the Ripper*

512. “Monster hiding inside Dr Barnardo” = 246
513. “Monster is hiding inside Barnardo” = 246
514. “*Mossford Lodge* hides Irish doctor” = 246
515. “*Mossford Lodge* is Barnardo’s house” = 246
516. “*Mossford Lodge* is home of killer” = 246
517. “*Mossford Lodge:* clue to evil killer” = 246
518. “*Mossford Lodge:* Dr Barnardo’s house” = 246
519. “*Mossford Lodge:* the house of Barnardo” = 246
520. “*Mr Kipper* is Barnardo’s nickname” = 246
521. “*Mr Kipper* is cipher for Barnardo” = 246
522. “*Mr Kipper* was name for Barnardo” = 246
523. “*Mr Kipper:* cipher for Dr Barnardo” = 246
524. “*Mr Kipper:* cypher for Barnardo” = 246
525. “*Mr Kipper*: Dr Barnardo’s nickname” = 246
526. “*Mr Kipper:* the nickname of Barnardo” = 246
527. “Murder harlots of Dorset St” = 246
528. “Murderer from Dublin hid as Barnardo” = 246
529. “Murderer is doctor of *Orange Order*” = 246
530. “Murderer is Thomas John Barnardo” = 246
531. “Murderer *Jack* is a *Barkingside* doctor” = 246
532. “Murderer *mad Jack*: look for Dr Barnardo” = 246
533. “Murderer name is Thomas Barnardo” = 246
534. “Murderer: doctor from *Barkingside*” = 246
535. “Murdering doctor hid at *Barkingside*” = 246
536. “Murdering *mad Jack* hides as Barnardo” = 246
537. “Murdering *mad Jack* hiding in Barnardo” = 246
538. “Murdering preacher is Dr Barnardo” = 246
539. “Murdering surgeon at *Barkingside*” = 246
540. “Murderous doctor hid in *Barkingside*” = 246
541. “Murderous doctor of Dorset St” = 246
542. “Murderous surgeon in *Barkingside*” = 246
543. “Murderous surgeon in Dr Barnardo” = 246
544. “Murders are codes of Doctor Barnardo” = 246
545. “Murders hid famous doctor: Barnardo” = 246
546. “*Orange Order* is a *Jack the Ripper* clue” = 246
547. “*Orangeman* with *red hand* murders” = 246 ‘red hand’ alludes to *Dear Boss* note
548. “Orphanage is lair of *Jack the Ripper*” = 246
549. “Orphanage of Barnardo in Stepney” = 246
550. “*Philanthrope* hid *Jack the Ripper*” = 246
551. “*Philanthropist* hid a murderer” = 246
552. “*Philanthropist* hiding killer” = 246
553. “*Philanthropist* was doctor” = 246
554. “Quaker preacher hid *Jack the Ripper*” = 246
555. “Raging monster hides as Barnardo” = 246
556. “Raging monster hiding in Barnardo” = 246

557. “Red ink *Boss letter* by Barnardo” = 246
558. “Red ink letter is by Dr Barnardo” = 246
559. “Red ink letter is clue by Barnardo” = 246
560. “Red ink letter: clue by Dr Barnardo” = 246
561. “Red ink sermons *hid* code by Barnardo” = 246
562. “Ritual killings by Barnardo *hid* a code” = 246
563. “Ritualistic murders of Barnardo” = 246
564. “Satanic murderer called Dr Barnardo” = 246
565. “Satanic murderer is called Barnardo” = 246
566. “*Saucy Jacky* is Barnardo hidden by a code” = 246
567. “*Saucy Jacky* is code of Doctor Barnardo” = 246
568. “*Saucy Jacky* is secret Barnardo code” = 246
569. “*Saucy Jacky*: alias of Doctor Barnardo” = 246
570. “*Saucy Jacky:* Dr Barnardo hidden by a code” = 246
571. “*Saucy Jacky*: the name hiding Barnardo” = 246
572. “Secret code identified killer Barnardo” = 246
573. “Secret code used by Barnardo to kill” = 246
574. “Secret in: *Stepney Causeway*” = 246 Barnardo’s Boys Home
575. “Secret killer at *Mossford Lodge*” = 246
576. “Secret lair is hiding at Boys Home” = 246
577. “*Skelton*’s code: Barnardo’s secret” = 246
578. “*Slut-butcher* hiding as Dr Barnardo” = 246
579. “*Slut-butcher* is hiding as Barnardo” = 246
580. “*Slut-doctor* is at Dorset St” = 246
581. “*Slut-gutter* is code of Dr Barnardo” = 246
582. “*Slut-gutter* was a code of Barnardo” = 246
583. “Sluts disfigured by Dr Barnardo” = 246
584. “Spitalfields hid a killer-preacher” = 246
585. “Spitalfields’ preacher hid a killer” = 246
586. “Stepney-causeway hid a secret” = 246
587. “Stepney-causeway: a lair of mad *Jack*” = 246
588. “Stepney-causeway: abode of evil *Jack*” = 246
589. “*Street preacher* hid in whoredom” = 246
590. “*Street preacher* is a code of Barnardo” = 246
591. “*Street preacher* is my cover” = 246
592. “*Street preacher* is the killer” = 246
593. “*Street preacher* of Whitechapel” = 246
594. “*Street preacher:* code of T. J. Barnardo” = 246
595. “*Street preacher:* guise of Barnardo” = 246
596. “*Street preacher*: is the killer” = 246
597. “*Street preacher*: the killer clue” = 246
598. “T. J. Barnardo hid murderous surgeon” = 246
599. “T. J. Barnardo hiding at the *Ten Bells*” = 246 public house in Spitalfields
600. “T. J. Barnardo is a quintuple killer” = 246
601. “T. J. Barnardo kills the 5 harlots” = 246

602. "T. J. Barnardo must kill 5 sluts" = 246
603. "T. J. Barnardo must kill 5 whores" = 246
604. "Terrible code-murders by Barnardo" = 246
605. "Terrible murders of Barnardo hid a code" = 246
606. "The abortionist at Whitechapel" = 246
607. "The abortionist: an Irish doctor" = 246
608. "The confession by Barnardo hid as a code" = 246
609. "The confession of Barnardo hidden in a code" = 246
610. "The confession of Barnardo hides in code" = 246
611. "The confessions of Barnardo hide in code" = 246
612. "The *daemon* in Doctor Barnardo is hidden" = 246
613. "The doctor hides at *Mossford Lodge*" = 246
614. "The *hardy bear* is code for Dr Barnardo" = 246 meaning of Barnardo's name
615. "The *hardy bear* was a code for Barnardo" = 246
616. "The hidden killer: a doctor from Dublin" = 246
617. "The killer clue is: Thomas Barnardo" = 246
618. "The killer hid as a doctor from Dublin" = 246
619. "The killer is: Dr Thomas Barnardo" = 246
620. "The name *Jack the Ripper* hid Barnardo" = 246
621. "THE PREACHER is at *Mossford Lodge*" = 246
622. "THE PREACHER is at Spitalfields" = 246
623. "The *red-ink* letter is Barnardo's" = 246
624. "*The Ripper* is in *Mossford Lodge*" = 246
625. "*The Ripper* is in Spitalfields" = 246
626. "*The Ripper:* a nickname of Doctor Barnardo" = 246
627. "The ritual killings by Barnardo" = 246
628. "The slut-gutter hid Dr Barnardo" = 246
629. "The sluts' abortionist is a clue" = 246
630. "The sluts' butcher of *Barkingside*" = 246
631. "The street preacher murders" = 246
632. "The *Ten Bells* was hiding Barnardo" = 246
633. "The terrible murders of Barnardo" = 246
634. "The voice of T. J. Barnardo in *Skelton*" = 246
635. "The whore-gutter hid Dr Barnardo" = 246
636. "The whores' abortionist is a clue" = 246
637. "The whores' butcher of *Barkingside*" = 246
638. "The wicked doctor: it was Barnardo" = 246
639. "This proves Dr Barnardo killed" = 246
640. "Thomas Barnardo is murderer code hid" = 246
641. "Thomas Barnardo is savage killer" = 246
642. "Thomas Barnardo is the killer clue" = 246
643. "Thomas Barnardo uses *red-ink* as a code" = 246
644. "Thomas Barnardo: killer named by code" = 246
645. "Thomas Barnardo: name of bogus doctor" = 246 unclear if he qualified as a doctor
646. "Thomas Barnardo's code number" = 246

647. “Thomas J. Barnardo admits he is *mad Jack*” = 246 “mad *Jack* is” = “a killer” = 55
648. “Thomas John Barnardo hides a secret” = 246
649. “Thomas John Barnardo is a killer clue” = 246
650. “Thomas John Barnardo is murderer” = 246
651. “*Trade name* is code hiding abortionist” = 246 trade name in ‘Dear Boss’ note
652. “*Trade name* of a secret abortionist” = 246
653. “*Trade name* was abortionist’s code” = 246
654. “*Trade name* was clue of abortionist” = 246
655. “Truth about Barnardo is hidden as a code” = 246
656. “Truth about Barnardo is hiding in code” = 246
657. “Truth about Dr Barnardo hidden as a code” = 246
658. “Truth about Dr Barnardo hides as code” = 246
659. “Truth about Dr Barnardo hiding in code” = 246
660. “Truth about T. J. Barnardo hidden as code” = 246
661. “Very difficult cipher hid Barnardo” = 246
662. “Whitechapel hides an abortionist” = 246
663. “Whitechapel’s killer is Barnardo” = 246
664. “Whitechapel’s killer: Dr Barnardo” = 246
665. “*Whore-butcher* hiding as Dr Barnardo” = 246
666. “*Whore-butcher* is hiding as Barnardo” = 246
667. “Whore-doctor is at Dorset St” = 246
668. “Whores disfigured by Dr Barnardo” = 246
669. “Wild animal hiding within Barnardo” = 246
670. “Women Barnardo gutted are in the code” = 246
671. “You are correct: codes are Barnardo’s” = 246
672. “You are right about a code Barnardo hides” = 246
673. “You are right about Barnardo’s codes” = 246
674. “You are right about code Dr Barnardo hid” = 246
675. “You are right: Barnardo is using code” = 246
676. “You are right: Barnardo killed ladies” = 246
677. “You are right: Doctor Barnardo hid a code” = 246
678. “You broke a code Thomas John Barnardo hid” = 246
679. “You broke codes by Thomas Barnardo” = 246
680. “You broke Doctor Barnardo’s evil code” = 246
681. “You discovered murderer Barnardo” = 246
682. “You discovered secret Barnardo hid” = 246
683. “You discovered: Barnardo is a killer” = 246
684. “You found a killer *Mossford Lodge* hid” = 246
685. “You found *Barnardo* means *hardy bear*” = 246
686. “You found *hardy bear*: Barnardo’s name” = 246
687. “You found killer in *Mossford Lodge*” = 246
688. “You found killer *Jack:* Doctor Barnardo” = 246
689. “You found proof Barnardo is a killer” = 246
690. “You have cracked Doctor Barnardo’s code” = 246
691. “You have found a lunatic hid as Barnardo” = 246

692. "You have found lunatic Barnardo hides" = 246
693. "You have proof Barnardo is a killer" = 246
694. "You identified Barnardo as murderer" = 246
695. "You identified Dr Barnardo as a killer" = 246
696. "You identified *Jack the Ripper* by code" = 246
697. "You knew codes used by Dr Barnardo" = 246
698. "You knew of the code used by Barnardo" = 246
699. "You know **how** *Jack the Ripper* hid" = 246
700. "You know *Jack the Ripper's* codes" = 246
701. "You know **who** *Jack the Ripper* hid" = 246
702. "You solved clues of Barnardo. *Bravo*!" = 246

Reversed solutions, key first:

- 246 = "a secret code number of Doctor Barnardo"
- 246 = "is secret code numeral of Dr Barnardo"
- 246 = "the code number Doctor Barnardo uses"
- 246 = "was a secret code numeral of Barnardo"

We note also the resonance equations:

"*Bravo!* you solved" = "code Doctor Barnardo hid" = "*Congratulations!*" = 138

It seems that Barnardo learned of *Skelton*'s cipher and the Master Code through his membership of the Orange Order.

Dorset Street: the 'worst' in London

Photographed in 1902 (Image: Wiki-commons)

Dubbed 'the worst street in London', Dorset St in Spitalfields rookery was about 400 ft long and 24 ft wide, linking Crispin St to the west with Commercial St to the east. This picture was taken fourteen years after the killings and suggests little had changed during that time. Miller's Court, scene of Mary Kelly's horrific murder was entered via a narrow passage between nos. 26 & 27.

Although the street no longer exists, a semi-circular curb marks the location of the passage. It seems that life in Dorset St was more than capable of corrupting a saint. The following are descriptions of the street's residents during that period. George Duckworth investigating London poverty on behalf of Charles Booth in 1898, described Dorset Street as *"the worst street I have seen so far, thieves, prostitutes, bullies, all common lodging houses".*

Ralph L. Finn's 1963 memoir of a Jewish boyhood in the East End gives a first-hand impression of the sort of people living in Dorset St c 1900.

It was a street of whores. There is, I always feel, a subtle difference between an whore and a prostitute. At least we used to think so. Prozzies were younger, and more attractive. Whores were debauched old bags. It teemed with nasty characters – desperate, wicked, lecherous, razor-slashing hoodlums.

A 'dodgy' doctor – an illegal abortionist in Dorset St?

According to Vanessa Hayes, Barnardo had studied gynaecology and, in that context, we find many solutions indicating that he was a secret abortionist – abortion was illegal. So-called 'back-street' abortions were often performed either by a 'granny' or a 'dodgy' doctor. It is unclear if Barnardo fully qualified as a doctor though he titled himself as such and so that perhaps labels him a 'dodgy' doctor. Unwanted pregnancy would have been a perennial problem for many of the younger sex-workers, abortions might therefore have been another channel in addition to lodging-house visits through which Barnardo encountered prostitutes. Presumably Barnardo saw a similarity between murder and abortion – and he loved both. **We recall the solutions**:

- "Doctor Barnardo kills the foetus" = 246
- "Doctor Barnardo loves murdering" = 246
- "Doctor Barnardo loves to murder" = 246

Applying the Master Code to 'Dorset St' in the context of 'Doctor' Barnardo/abortions etc:

1. "A hidden surgery at Dorset St" = 246
2. "A mad surgeon was at Dorset St" = 246
3. "A secret abortionist of sluts" = 246
4. "A secret abortionist of whores" = 246
5. "A surgery hiding in Dorset St" = 246
6. "Abortionist: a clue at Dorset St" = 246
7. "Abortions by *mad Jack* are by Barnardo" = 246 "mad Jack" = "alias" = "is code" = 34
8. "Abortions of *mad Jack* at Dorset St" = 246
9. "An abortionist hid at Whitechapel" = 246
10. "Barnardo is a killer of Dorset St" = 246
11. "Barnardo is an Irish abortionist" = 246
12. "Barnardo is Dorset St bogeyman" = 246
13. "Barnardo is the hidden abortionist" = 246
14. "Barnardo: a bogeyman at Dorset St" = 246
15. "Barnardo: a Dorset St monster" = 246
16. "Barnardo: a killer hid in Dorset St" = 246
17. "Barnardo: Dorset St was hide-out" = 246
18. "Barnardo: Dorset St's mad doctor" = 246
19. "Barnardo: hidden at Dorset St lair" = 246
20. "Barnardo: hide-out is at Dorset St" = 246
21. "Barnardo: hiding in Dorset St lair" = 246
22. "Barnardo: hiding-out at Dorset St" = 246
23. "Barnardo: killer hid on Dorset St" = 246
24. "Barnardo: murderer of Dorset St" = 246
25. "Barnardo's abortions on sluts" = 246
26. "Barnardo's abortions on whores" = 246
27. "Clue is: Dorset St abortionist" = 246
28. "Clue is: mad surgeon at Dorset St" = 246
29. "Code of the mad surgeon of Dorset St" = 246
30. "Doctor Barnardo hid at Dorset St" = 246
31. "Dorset St hides Doctor Barnardo" = 246
32. "Dorset St hides murderer *mad Jack*" = 246* "Doctor Barnardo" = "murderer *mad Jack*" = 110
33. "Dorset St is a Barnardo residence" = 246
34. "Dorset St killer called: Barnardo" = 246
35. "Dorset St preacher: evil madman" = 246
36. "Dr Barnardo: a killer of Dorset St" = 246
37. "Dr Barnardo: an Irish abortionist" = 246
38. "Dr Barnardo: Dorset St bogeyman" = 246
39. "Dr Barnardo: hide-out at Dorset St" = 246
40. "Dr Barnardo: the hidden abortionist" = 246
41. "Evil doctor was in Dorset St" = 246

42. "Go to Dorset St: look for a killer" = 246
43. "*Jack the abortionist*: hiding Barnardo" = 246*
44. "*Jack the Ripper:* abortionist name" = 246
45. "Kill the sluts of Dorset St" = 246 code instruction
46. "Kill the whores of Dorset St" = 246
47. "Look for a mad doctor at Dorset St" = 246
48. "*Mad Jack* of Dorset St is Dr Barnardo" = 246
49. "*Mad Jack*: murderer hid at Dorset St" = 246
50. "Murderous doctor of Dorset St" = 246
51. "Preacher Dorset St hid is a madman" = 246
52. "Preacher in Dorset St is madman" = 246
53. "Slut-doctor is at Dorset St" = 246
54. "Surgery hides at Dorset St" = 246
55. "Surgery hiding on Dorset St" = 246
56. "The Dorset St doctor-preacher" = 246 *Jack the Ripper* – a doctor-preacher
57. "The Dorset Street murderer" = 246
58. "The monster hid in Dorset St" = 246
59. "The sluts' abortionist is a clue" = 246
60. "The whores' abortionist is a clue" = 246
61. "*Trade name* is code hiding abortionist" = 246*
62. "*Trade name* is *Jack the Ripper*'s clue" = 246
63. "*Trade name* of a secret abortionist" = 246
64. "*Trade name* was abortionist's code" = 246
65. "*Trade name* was clue of abortionist" = 246
66. "Whitechapel hides an abortionist" = 246
67. "Whore-doctor is at Dorset St" = 246
68. "You found madman *Jack* at Dorset St" = 246
69. "You have found code Dorset St hides" = 246

We note the resonance equation: "Mad Jack* was code for" = "*Jack the Ripper*" = 115

NB: Barnardo was first suspected of the Whitechapel murders by Donald McCormick (1970) and later by Gary Rowlands (1999) * the latter claiming that the famous philanthropist from Dublin had a lonely, troubled childhood and this resulted in a deep-seated anger which gradually festered and warped into a personality capable of the most vicious murder.

* *The Mammoth Book of Jack the Ripper (1999) Robinson Publishing*

Vanessa Hayes published *Revelations of the True Ripper (2006, Lulu.com ISBN978-1-4116-9741-6)* identifying Barnardo as the infamous killer. In particular, she draws attention to the crucial significance of Annie Chapman's murder behind a door at the back of 29 Hanbury St. – a very obscure location that the killer must have known of beforehand, implying the murderer had visited the address and probably more than once. One of the rooms at 29 Hanbury St was rented to a prayer meeting group.

According to Hayes, Barnardo wrote his sermons in red ink.

Significance of the 'Dear Boss' letter

Dear Boss,

*I keep on hearing the police have caught me but they wont fix me just yet. I have laughed when they look so clever and talk about being on the right track. That joke about Leather Apron gave me real fits. I am down on whores and **I shant quit ripping them till I do get buckled**. Grand work the last job was. I gave the lady no time to squeal. How can they catch me now. **I love my work** and want to start again. You will soon hear of me with my **funny little games**. **I saved some of the proper red stuff** in a ginger beer bottle over the last job to write with but it went thick like glue and I cant use it. **Red ink** is fit enough I hope ha. ha. The next job I do I shall clip the ladys ears off and send to the police officers just for jolly wouldn't you. Keep this letter back till I do a bit more work, then give it out straight. My knife's so nice and sharp I want to get to work right away if I get a chance. Good Luck. Yours truly **Jack the Ripper***

Dont mind me giving the trade name

*PS Wasnt good enough to post this before I got all the **red ink** off my hands curse it. No luck yet. They say I'm a doctor now. ha ha*

The conjecture is that the 'Dear Boss' letter hides code solutions in certain phrases, the following is just a selection. First, applying *Skelton* to 'Dear Boss' (= 66) we find the linked resonance equations:

"Dear Boss" = "you found a" = "huge clue to" = "Jack's codes" = 66 implies the code key is *Skelton*

And, the Master Code solutions:

1. "***Dear Boss*** *hides* clue to code Barnardo used" = 246
2. "***Dear Boss*** is a clue to the code by Dr Barnardo" = 246
3. "***Dear Boss*** is clue to code Barnardo uses" = 246
4. "***Dear Boss***: red ink hid codes by Barnardo" = 246
5. "***Dear Boss***: clue to code Dr Barnardo uses" = 246
6. "***Dear Boss***: was the sign of Barnardo" = 246
7. "***Dear Boss***: you noticed the red ink clue" = 246

"I shant quit ripping them till I do get buckled" = 339 **which resonates with**:

1. "Doctor Barnardo: name of murderer *Jack the Ripper*" = 339
2. "*Jack the Ripper* is a killer hiding Doctor Barnardo" = 339
3. "*Jack the Ripper*: murderer hiding Doctor Barnardo" = 339
4. "*Jack the Ripper*: a code of Doctor Thomas John Barnardo" = 339
5. "*Jack the Ripper*: the code of Doctor Thomas Barnardo" = 339
6. "Thomas Barnardo: hidden real name of *Jack the Ripper*" = 339
7. "You found name of *Jack the Ripper:* Thomas Barnardo" = 339

"My funny little games" = 202

1. **"My funny little games"** = "Doctor Barnardo: name of killer" = 202
2. **"My funny little games"** = "Doctor Barnardo's secret code" = 202
3. **"My funny little games"** = "is a clue of Thomas John Barnardo" = 202
4. **"My funny little games"** = "is the clue of Thomas Barnardo" = 202
5. **"My funny little games"** = "*Jack the Ripper*: code hid Barnardo" = 202
6. **"My funny little games"** = "the secret code is Barnardo's" = 202
7. **"My funny little games"** = "you have found codes Barnardo hid" = 202

"They say I'm a doctor now ha ha" = 220

1. **"They say I'm a doctor now ha ha"** = "Barnardo: *Jack the Ripper*'s name" = 220
2. **"They say I'm a doctor now ha ha"** = "clue hides killer: Doctor Barnardo" = 220
3. **"They say I'm a doctor now ha ha"** = "clue is true: Barnardo is a killer" = 220
4. **"They say I'm a doctor now ha ha"** = "code of murderer Thomas Barnardo" = 220
5. **"They say I'm a doctor now ha ha"** = "Doctor Barnardo is a hidden killer" = 220
6. **"They say I'm a doctor now ha ha"** = "Doctor Barnardo: hidden murderer" = 220

"Yours truly" = 144

1. **"Yours truly"** = "code of Thomas Barnardo" = 144
2. **"Yours truly"** = "Dr Barnardo hidden in a code" = 144
3. **"Yours truly"** = "hides name T. J. Barnardo" = 144
4. **"Yours truly"** = "is Barnardo hidden in a code" = 144
5. **"Yours truly"** = "is Barnardo in cipher" = 144
6. **"Yours truly"** = "my name is Barnardo" = 144
7. **"Yours truly"** = "the clue hides Barnardo" = 144

And: "Yours truly" = "use the *Skelton* code" = "to crack code Barnardo hid" = 144

"Don't mind me giving the **trade name**" = 240 which resonates with:

1. "*Jack the Ripper* hid Doctor Barnardo" = 240
2. "*Jack the Ripper* is a code of Dr Barnardo" = 240
3. "*Jack the Ripper* masked as Barnardo" = 240
4. "*Jack the Ripper:* Barnardo's cipher" = 240
5. "*Jack the Ripper:* name hiding Barnardo" = 240
6. "*Jack the Ripper*'s code hides Barnardo" = 240
7. "Thomas Barnardo: hidden as a *trade name*" = 240 trade name: *Jack the Ripper*
8. "*Trade name* is hiding Dr Barnardo" = 240
9. "*Trade name* is mask for Dr Barnardo" = 240
10. "*Trade name* was a mask for Barnardo" = 240

Applying the Master Code in the context of the phrase *Funny little games*:

1. ***"Funny little games*** **are the codes" = 246**
2. ***"Funny little games:*** **means code clue" = 246**
3. ***"Funny little games:*** **meant as a code" = 246**
4. **"The funny little games are codes" = 246**

As suspected, the author's phrase: 'funny little games' was hinting at secret codes. Collectively, those solutions indicate that Barnardo wrote the 'Dear Boss' letter and that he was disguised as the murderer *'Jack the Ripper'*.

The writer of the *Dear Boss* letter draws attention to red-ink twice – the red ink identifies the letter's author as Barnardo which in turn identifies Barnardo as 'Jack the Ripper'. The writer refers to the difficulty of getting the red-ink off his hands – an odd thing to mention and suggests the 'red hand' might itself be a clue. **We have seen the resonance equations:**

- "*Red-ink*: clue of" = "Dr Barnardo" = 80
- "Barnardo was a" = "user of red-ink" = 101 wrote sermons in red-ink, according to Hayes
- "Thomas J. Barnardo" = "*red-ink* is a signal" = 124
- "*Red-ink* is sign of" = "Thomas Barnardo" = 121
- "Thomas Barnardo" = "the *red-ink* is a clue" = 121

1. "Jack the Ripper" = "hid a code clue in *red-ink*" = 115
2. "Jack the Ripper" = "is a name in *red-ink*" = 115
3. "Jack the Ripper" = "the *red-ink* hid a clue" = 115

And in the same context, the Master Code solutions:

1. "A *red-ink* letter was by Barnardo" = 246
2. "Barnardo: hand stained with *red-ink*" = 246 referred to in letter
3. "Barnardo uses red-ink ***instead*** of blood" = 246 as described in the letter
4. "Barnardo's code clue in *red-ink* letter" = 246
5. "Barnardo's code is in *red-ink* letter" = 246
6. "Barnardo's hands stained in *red-ink*" = 246
7. "Barnardo's letter in *red-ink* is code" = 246
8. "Barnardo's sermons are in red-ink" = 246 it seems he wrote sermons in red ink
9. "Clue is in: *red-ink* letter of Barnardo" = 246
10. "Clue of Barnardo is in *red-ink* letter" = 246
11. "Clue of Dr Barnardo in *red-ink* letter" = 246
12. "Clue to *Boss* hid by *red-ink* letter" = 246 the word 'Boss' is code
13. "Clue was: red-ink letter to *Boss*" = 246
14. "Code hid in *red-ink* sermons of Barnardo" = 246
15. "Dr Barnardo: look for red-ink on hands" = 246
16. "Hid a code as note written in *red-ink*" = 246
17. "*Jack the Ripper* used *red-ink* to hide code" = 246
18. "Killer at Whitechapel used *red-ink*" = 246
19. "Letter penned in *red-ink* was clue" = 246

20. "Look for the *red-ink Boss* letter" = 246
21. "Note written in *red-ink* hides code" = 246
22. "*Red-ink Boss* letter by Barnardo" = 246
23. "*Red-ink* hides the code of Doctor Barnardo" = 246
24. "*Red-ink* is on *Jack the Ripper*'s hand" = 246
25. "*Red-ink* letter is by Dr Barnardo" = 246
26. "*Red-ink* letter is clue by Barnardo" = 246
27. "*Red-ink*: the hint of *Jack the Ripper*" = 246
28. "*Red-ink* was *Jack the Ripper* sign" = 246
29. "The *Boss* note: Barnardo used *red-ink*" = 246
30. "The *red-ink* is a clue of *Jack the Ripper*" = 246
31. "The *red-ink*: *Jack the Ripper* signal" = 246
32. "The *red-ink* letter is Barnardo's" = 246
33. "Thomas Barnardo uses *red-ink* as a code" = 246
34. "Used *red-ink* for the *Boss* letter" = 246
35. **"*You caught Jack the Ripper* red-handed" = 246*** an appropriate solution in the context!

Applying *Skelton*, we find:

- "Doctor Barnardo" = "red-ink on hands" = 110
- "Doctor Thomas Barnardo" = "red-ink on hands was clue" = 172

***'Red-ink on hands': Master Code solutions in the context of Barnardo and *Jack the Ripper*:**

1. "Barnardo's hands stained in *red-ink*" = 246
2. "Dr Barnardo has red-ink on his hands" = 246
3. "*Red-ink* is on *Jack the Ripper*'s hand" = 246

And so, the Master Code joke: "*You caught Jack the Ripper* red-handed" = 246

‘From Hell’, a letter/note sent to George Lusk dated October 15th

Sor

I send you half the Kidne I took from one women prasarved it for you tother pirce I fried and ate it was very nise I may send you the bloody knif that took it out if you only wate a whil longer.

signed

Catch me when you can **Mishter** Lusk.*

*George Lusk was chairman of the Whitechapel Vigilance Committee.

Is the phrase “From Hell” part of a code? Applying *Skelton,* we find the resonance equations:

“A murder code” = “from hell” = “is the clue” = 71

The author signed with: **‘catch me *when* you can’** – not the usual **‘catch me *if* you can’.** This appears to be a deliberate ‘mistake’ so it’s probably a clue.

Applying *Skelton*:

“Catch me *when* you can” (= 143) gives the resonance equations:

1. “Catch me *when* you can” = “**Barnardo confesses**” = 143
2. “Catch me *when* you can” = “Barnardo’s code is found” = 143
3. “Catch me *when* you can” = “cipher hid Dr Barnardo” = 143
4. “Catch me *when* you can” = “cipher-clue Barnardo hid” = 143
5. “Catch me *when* you can” = “clue hides name: Barnardo” = 143
6. “Catch me *when* you can” = “code I used is *Skelton*” = 143
7. “Catch me *when* you can” = “cypher hid Barnardo” = 143
8. “Catch me ***when*** you can” = “found a mistake. *Bravo!*” = 143 should be ‘if’ not ‘when’
9. “Catch me *when* you can” = “**he’s *Jack the Ripper***” = 143
10. “Catch me *when* you can” = “hides name: Dr Barnardo” = 143
11. “Catch me *when* you can” = “*mistake* is my clue” = 143
12. “Catch me ***when*** you can” = “*when:* Barnardo’s clue” = 143
13. “Catch me *when* you can” = “**with a *Skelton* code**” = 143 use *Skelton* to identify the killer

Solutions can be linked, examples include:

1. “Cipher hid Dr Barnardo” = “he’s *Jack the Ripper*” = 143
2. “Barnardo confesses” = “he’s *Jack the Ripper*” = 143
3. “Barnardo’s code is found” = “code I used is *Skelton*” = 143
4. “*Jack the Ripper* name” = “hiding Barnardo’s name” = 143

And: “Barnardo confesses” = “with a *Skelton* code” = “he’s *Jack the Ripper*” = 143

Mishter Lusk. The spelling is wrong, suggesting another intentional error and potential code.

Applying *Skelton*, we find the resonance equations:

1. "Mishter Lusk" = "is pun of Barnardo" = 123 — Irish version of Mister
2. "Mishter Lusk" = "spelling is a clue" = 123 — spelling like Irish pronunciation
3. "Mishter Lusk" = "was code of Barnardo" = 123
4. "Mishter Lusk" = "was Irish pun" = 123 — confirms Irish hint was deliberate
5. "Mishter Lusk" = "you found clue to a code" = 123
6. "Mishter Lusk" = "the code fooled many" = 123

Spelling mistakes in 'From Hell' letter are code clues

> *I send you half the Kidne I took from one women prasarved it for you tother pirce I fried and ate it was very nise I may send you the bloody knif that took it out if you only wate a whil longer.*

Applying *Skelton* to the misspelled words: kidne = 32, prasarved = 96, tother = 69, pirce = 40, nise = 36, knif = 32, wate = 44, whil = 44. **The sum is 393.**

Assuming 393 is a gematria key, we find the contextually appropriate solutions:

1. "Cipher hid by '*From Hell'* letter spelling mistakes" = 393
2. "Cipher hid in spelling mistakes of '*From Hell'* letter" = 393
3. "Clues hidden in *'From Hell'* letter spelling mistakes" = 393
4. "Coded spelling mistakes are in my letter *'From Hell'*" = 393
5. "Codes are hiding in spelling mistakes in '*From Hell*' note = 393
6. "Doctor Barnardo is guilty of murdering five sluts" = 393
7. "Doctor Barnardo is guilty of murdering five whores" = 393
8. "From Hell note spelling mistakes are intentional" = 393
9. "Letter '*From Hell':* spelling mistakes are cipher clue" = 393
10. "Letter '*From Hell':* spelling mistakes are hiding codes" = 393
11. "Look for spelling mistakes in coded letter *'From Hell'*" = 393

We also find the following contextually appropriate solutions, linking the full name Thomas John Barnardo with *Jack the Ripper* using gematria number 393:

1. "Dr Thomas John Barnardo hid by the name of *Jack the Ripper*" = 393
2. "Dr Thomas John Barnardo was the name of *Jack the Ripper*" = 393
3. "*Jack the Ripper* is a pseudonym of Thomas John Barnardo" = 393
4. "*Jack the Ripper* is code hiding the name Thomas John Barnardo" = 393
5. "*Jack the Ripper* is the cypher of Thomas John Barnardo" = 393
6. "*Jack the Ripper:* code hiding the name Dr Thomas John Barnardo" = 393
7. "*Jack the Ripper:* his real name was Thomas John Barnardo" = 393

Applying *Skelton* to 'Barnardo' in the context of a 'hidden murderer':

- "Doctor Barnardo" = "*hidden* murderer" = 110
- "Doctor T. J. Barnardo" = "is a *hidden* murderer" = 132
- "Secret killer hid as" = "Thomas John Barnardo" = 149

And finally, the remarkable resonance equation:

"4/7/18 45 is d.o.b. of" = "*Jack the Ripper*" = 115 written 4, 7, 18, 45 (4 July 1845)

4th July 1845 was Barnardo's date of birth.

The Victims

In the nineteenth century, Whitechapel-Spitalfields was part of London's East End notorious for crime and prostitution, an insalubrious warren of vastly over-crowded insanitary slums of about 80,000 souls. Dorset St, adjacent to the last murder scene was considered 'the worst' thoroughfare in the entire city - a neighbourhood teeming with the lowest of the low, a hellish 'ghetto' where life was a dog-eat-dog existence and criminality of some kind was the only way to survive. The Whitechapel area alone had an estimated 62 brothels and 1200 sex-workers, the vast majority of whom were trapped in a gin-fuelled, endless nightmare of grinding poverty, neglect, disease and broken relationships. It was from this deprived and abused underclass of vulnerable women that *Jack the Ripper* selected his victims - their names 'chosen', in effect, by 'The Code of Destiny'.

Factors linking the victims: **Polly Nichols, Annie Chapman, Liz Stride, Kate Eddowes & Mary Kelly**

- part-time prostitutes.
- had a history of unstable, abusive relationships.
- had taken to drink.
- lived in extreme poverty, neglect and deprivation.
- aged over forty except Mary Kelly*

*Kelly was the odd-one-out, being much younger and larger than the other women.

Code solutions account for the murders' sudden cessation - the homicides were performed in accordance with code 'instructions' and so the 'ripper' killings had to stop by the end of autumn 1888.

In that context, we recall the Master Code solutions:

1. "All slut murders are at Autumn" = 246
2. "All the harlots killed at Autumn" = 246
3. "All whore murders are at Autumn" = 246
4. "In the autumn of one-eight-eight-eight" = 246

Jack the Ripper's 'killing-ground'

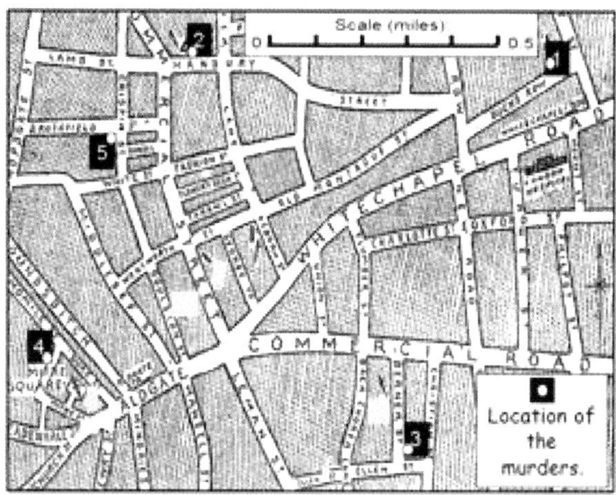

The five canonical murder sites displayed on a contemporary street map. It seems that Barnardo had a hide-out in Dorset St - opposite location 5 running W-E - said to be the most notorious street in London, situated close to the last and most horrific murder. A number of code solutions indicate that Barnardo was a 'dodgy doctor', an abortionist with a secret illegal surgery hidden in Dorset St.

Numbered murder locations:

1 = Nichols: Bucks Row

2 = Chapman: *behind* 29 Hanbury St

3 = Stride: Dutfield's yard off Berner St

4 = Eddowes: Mitre Square

5 = Kelly: 13 Miller's Court

Barnardo killed according to code instructions: the who, where, when, how and sequence of murders are found in the code. In that context, we note the Master Code solutions:

1. "A code hides dates and places of murders" = 246
2. "Code hides dates and places of killings" = 246
3. **"Code told Barnardo to kill harlots" = 246**
4. "Dates and places of murders are in code" = 246
5. "Dates and places of killings hid as a code" = 246
6. "Names of whores and sluts in a code" = 246
7. "T. J. Barnardo must kill 5 sluts" = 246
8. "T. J. Barnardo must kill 5 whores" = 246
9. "Women Barnardo gutted are in the code" = 246

First victim: "Mary Ann Nichols" aged 43 (aka "Polly Nichols")

Found: Friday, August 31st 3:40 am at Bucks Row. The location was less than 200 yds from the entrance to the London Hospital in Whitechapel where Barnardo had received medical training. Applying *Skelton* to the name, gives the contextually appropriate resonance equations:

1. "Mary Ann Nichols" = "gutted by Barnardo" = 141
2. "Mary Ann Nichols" = "is first murder" = 141
3. "Mary Ann Nichols" = "she is the first" = 141
4. "Mary Ann Nichols" = "she's first to die" = 141

1. "Polly Nichols" = "is killed first" = 125
2. "Polly Nichols" = "kill her first" = 125
3. "Polly Nichols" = "my debut murder" = 125
4. "Polly Nichols" = "premier murder" = 125

Master Code solutions in the context of Barnardo and Nichol's murder:

1. "1 st code-murder was in Bucks Row" = 246
2. "Bucks Row is my 1 st code-murder" = 246
3. "Bucks Row was the1 st murder" = 246
4. "Crack Nichols killing using cipher" = 246
5. "Crack Nichols killing with the code" = 246
6. "Crack Nichols murder by cypher" = 246
7. "Crack Nichols murder using a cipher" = 246
8. "Dr Barnardo killed Polly Nichols" = 246
9. "Harlot Nichols killed by Barnardo" = 246
10. "Harlot Nichols murdered first" = 246
11. "I began cipher-killing with Nichols" = 246
12. "I begin the murders with Nichols" = 246
13. "I kill slut called Nichols first" = 246
14. "I kill whore called Nichols first" = 246
15. "*Jack* killed Polly Nichols first" = 246
16. "Kill Mary Nichols in Bucks Row" = 246
17. "Killed Nichols on final day of August" = 246
18. "Murder of Nichols is in a code you broke" = 246
19. "Murder of Nichols solved by you" = 246
20. "Murdered Nichols 31st August" = 246
21. "Nichols is 1 st killing of Barnardo" = 246
22. "Nichols is first of five I murder" = 246
23. "Nichols murdered by Barnardo 1 st" = 246
24. "Nichols murdered first using a code" = 246
25. "Nichols was first one murdered" = 246
26. "Nichols: Barnardo's 1 st code-killing" = 246

27. "Nichols: first harlot murdered" = 246
28. "Nichols: first old harlot I killed" = 246
29. "Nichols: initial killing by Barnardo" = 246
30. "Nichols: killed by Barnardo first" = 246
31. "Nichols: the first slut killed" = 246
32. "Nichols: the first whore killed" = 246
33. "Polly Nichols was killed by code" = 246
34. "Polly Nichols: first killing" = 246
35. "The date of Nichols' murder: 31/8/1888" = 246 written 31,8,1,8,8,8
36. "The first murder in Bucks Row" = 246
37. "The first slut was Nichols" = 246
38. "The first whore was Nichols" = 246

Injuries to Mary Ann Nichols: The throat was severed by two deep cuts, one of which completely severed all the way down to the vertebrae. The vagina had been stabbed twice, and the lower part of the abdomen was partly ripped open by a deep, jagged wound causing the bowels to protrude.

Second victim: "Annie/Ann Chapman" aged 47

Found: Saturday, September 8th 6:00 am in the yard behind 29 Hanbury Street. Chapman lived at a lodging-house in Dorset St. Applying *Skelton* to the name:

"Ann Chapman" = "a second harlot" = 80

And

1. "Annie Chapman" = "I murdered 2nd" = 85
2. "Annie Chapman" = "killed second" = 85
3. "Annie Chapman" = "she died second" = 85
4. "Annie Chapman" = "was second" = 85

Also: "Doctor Barnardo" = "murder Chapman" = 110

Master Code solutions in the context of Barnardo and Chapman's murder:

1. "29 Hanbury St. Barnardo's BIG clue" = 246
2. "29 Hanbury St. BIG clue to killer" = 246
3. "29 Hanbury St. site of a murder" = 246
4. "29 Hanbury St. site of killing" = 246
5. "8/9/18 88 the date of a murder" = 246 written 8,9,18,88
6. "A clue is: *at rear* of 29 Hanbury St." = 246
7. "A huge clue hidden *behind* 29 Hanbury St" = 246
8. "A second murder is in Hanbury St" = 246
9. "Annie Chapman: 2 nd murder by Barnardo" = 246
10. "Annie Chapman: a harlot Barnardo killed" = 246
11. "Annie Chapman: her killer is Barnardo" = 246

12. "Annie Chapman: second harlot murder" = 246
13. "Annie Chapman: second victim of my code" = 246
14. "Annie Chapmen's killing by Barnardo" = 246
15. "*Behind* the door at 29 Hanbury St." = 246
16. "Chapman is the second murder of five" = 246
17. "Chapman: Barnardo's second murder of 5" = 246 murders had already been planned by code
18. "Chapman: murder by Doctor Barnardo" = 246
19. "Date I killed Chapman: 8/9/1888" = 246 written 8,9,18,88
20. "Go to 29 Hanbury St. find the clue" = 246
21. "*Hide* a second murder at Hanbury St." = 246 code instruction
22. "*Hide* second killing at Hanbury St" = 246
23. "Huge clue *at rear* of 29 Hanbury St." = 246
24. "Huge clue *hides behind* 29 Hanbury St." = 246
25. "I removed Chapman's intestines" = 246
26. "*Jack the Ripper*: 2nd murder is a big clue" = 246
27. "Kill the slut Annie Chapman second" = 246
28. "Kill the whore Annie Chapman second" = 246
29. "Killed Chapman in 29 Hanbury St" = 246
30. "Murder Annie Chapman on September 8" = 246
31. "Murder Chapman September eighth" = 246
32. "Murder is *behind* 29 Hanbury St." = 246
33. "Second killing is in Hanbury St" = 246
34. "Second murder is on Hanbury St" = 246
35. "The clue at 29 Hanbury Street" = 246

Injuries to Chapman. As with Nichols, Chapman's throat was severed by two deep cuts. The abdomen had been cut open, with a section of the flesh from the stomach being placed upon the left shoulder and another section of skin and flesh - plus the small intestines - being removed and placed above the right shoulder. The autopsy also revealed that Chapman's uterus and sections of the bladder and vagina had been removed – presumably taken as 'trophies', gruesome memorabilia that enabled the killer to relive the murder and an indication he probably had a sexual fetish, an obsessive fascination with female genitalia and, like a collector, expressing a need for power and control.

The murder *behind* 29 Hanbury Street – a big clue to the identity of *Jack the Ripper*

This case strongly suggests the killer had a good knowledge of female anatomy and that the complex injuries had been carried-out quickly and silently in difficult, cramped conditions by someone expert with a knife. The murder scene was located between a fence and a door that opened on to the back-yard of 29 Hanbury Street; only someone familiar with the property would have known the location. That means either a tenant or neighbour – both improbable; after all, who would kill literally on their own doorstep? Much more likely, it was a visitor to the property who knew of the secluded spot.

Combining those facts means the killer had prior knowledge of the location behind the door into the backyard at 29 Hanbury St.; that he had a good knowledge of female anatomy and was adept at using a knife and in a confined space. Of the five canonical murder scenes, this one provides the best clues to the identity of *Jack the Ripper*. The murderer was probably a regular attendee of the prayer meetings held in a rented room at 29 Hanbury St. - the one with a 'medical background'.

And so, the significance of the Master Code solutions:

1. "29 Hanbury St.: Barnardo's BIG clue" = 246
2. "29 Hanbury St.: BIG clue to killer" = 246
3. "Go to 29 Hanbury St. find the clue" = 246
4. "*Jack the Ripper*: 2nd murder is a big clue" = 246
5. "Prayers in 29 Hanbury St." = 246

It seems the police did not take the names of those who attended the prayer meetings at 29 Hanbury St.; however, at the time it was not clear the killing was part of a sequence. Nevertheless, once it became evident that the Hanbury St. murder *was* an instance of *Jack the Ripper*'s 'handy-work', the police could then have obtained the list of prayer meeting attendees. They did not and so *Jack the Ripper* escaped identification and arrest.

Third victim: "Elizabeth Stride" aged 44 (aka Long Liz)

Found: Sunday, September 30th at about 1.00 am in Dutfield's yard off Berner Street.

Elizabeth Stride originally from Sweden, was charged with prostitution in her native land before arriving in England. **Applying *Skelton* in that context**: "**Barnardo murders a" = "Swedish harlot" = 135**.

In this case, the murderer's diabolical surgery seems to have been interrupted by a man entering Dutfield's yard with a cart, so there was no time for the killer to complete desecration of the corpse.

1. "Elizabeth Stride" = "a Swedish harlot" = 136
2. "Elizabeth Stride" = "a third lady I killed" = 136
3. "Elizabeth Stride" = "is the third kill" = 136
4. "Elizabeth Stride" = "she is a third kill" = 136

1. "Liz Stride" = "3rd lady I kill" = 102
2. "Liz Stride" = "is 3rd murder" = 102

- "*Long Liz* Stride" = "the third murder" = 137

Master Code solutions in the context of Stride's murder:

1. "3rd Barnardo killing: clue is Stride" = 246
2. "3rd slut: she was from Sweden" = 246
3. "3rd whore: she was from Sweden" = 246
4. "A third slut was from Sweden" = 246

5. "A third whore was from Sweden" = 246
6. "Barnardo is killer of Liz Stride" = 246
7. "Clue is: third slut from Sweden" = 246
8. "Clue is: third whore from Sweden" = 246
9. "Dr Barnardo: killer of Liz Stride" = 246
10. "Elizabeth Stride: a third killing" = 246
11. "I kill long Liz in Dutfield's yard" = 246 known as 'long Liz'
12. "I murder Stride near Berner St" = 246
13. "I murdered long Liz off Berner St" = 246 Dutfield's yard was off Berner St
14. "Kill harlot Lizzy Stride" = 246
15. "Kill old harlot Lizzie Stride" = 246
16. **"Liz Stride identified by Barnardo" = 246** to which he refers in the *Times* letter
17. "Long Liz a third harlot I murder" = 246
18. "Long Liz is a 3rd murder of Barnardo" = 246
19. "Long Liz is third killing of five" = 246
20. "Long Liz: a 3rd murder of Dr Barnardo" = 246
21. "Long Liz: old slut from Sweden" = 246
22. "Long Liz: old whore from Sweden" = 246
23. "Prostitute Stride is killed" = 246
24. "Stride was a 3rd Barnardo killing" = 246
25. "Stride: a murder of *Jack the Ripper*" = 246
26. "Stride: Barnardo was the killer" = 246
27. "Stride: *Jack the Ripper* killed her" = 246
28. "Stride: the old Swedish harlot" = 246
29. "The old slut Stride was killed" = 246
30. "The old whore Stride was killed" = 246
31. "Third victim called Liz Stride" = 246

*A round-ended knife about a foot long and smothered in blood, was found on the steps of a laundry at 253 Whitechapel Road in the hours after the murder. The knife was not the murder weapon - the shape was inconsistent with the wounds - rather, the knife had been deliberately placed at that precise location as an obscure clue. In other words, if you understand *why* the bloodied knife is at that specific location you have solved the clue correctly - confirmation you have *Jack the Ripper*'s cipher.

Injuries to Stride: The cause of death was a single incision, measuring six inches across the neck which had severed the carotid artery and trachea before terminating beneath the right jaw - implying that her throat was cut from behind by a right-handed assailant - the *modus operandi* in all five murders. Barnardo was right-handed.

Barnardo's letter in *The Times* and the murder of Elizabeth Stride

Doctor Barnardo's letter in *The Times* newspaper (9th October 1888) was ostensibly concerned with the adverse effect on children living with adults in disreputable lodging houses. However, the author also refers to his identification of Elizabeth Stride's corpse at the mortuary – the author mentions her by name on *three* separate occasions. As we have seen, he used code words and phrases in notes he wrote as *Jack the Ripper* and *Saucy Jacky*, so it's likely Barnardo left codes in his *Times* letter also.

Applying the Master Code in that general context:

1. "Name of the killer *hiding* in a letter" = 246
2. "Name of the killer: a letter *hid* clues" = 246
3. "Name of the killer: clues in letter" = 246

On Wednesday September 26th, Barnardo visited a lodging house in Flower-Dean Street where Elizabeth Stride was living. He entered the kitchen and found some 'very frightened women' talking about the recent murders, one of whom was Stride. When Barnardo 'heard' of Stride's murder a few days later, he *took it upon himself* to visit the mortuary and said he was able to 'identify the woman at once' - even though he had seen her only briefly among a group of people some days before.

- Why did Barnardo include the totally irrelevant digression of his mortuary visit to inspect the corpse of Elizabeth Stride, in a letter concerned with children living in adult lodging houses?
- Why did Barnardo think he was qualified to visit the mortuary and *identify* Elizabeth Stride - to *name* her - *if* he knew her by sight only?
- Why did Barnardo refer to Elizabeth Stride *by name* on *three* separate occasions in a long letter concerned with the welfare of children?

Collectively, those points suggest Barnardo was deliberately drawing attention to Elizabeth Stride; the question is why?

- Barnardo implies that he didn't know the woman personally. He says in the letter that he had only seen the deceased briefly about a week earlier among a group of people.
- A corpse is usually identified by an individual who knew the deceased very well, such as a relative or close friend - someone who can definitively put a name to a face. Barnardo was neither.

Master Code solutions show that Barnardo *had* to identify the corpse at the mortuary and that he *had* to write a letter to *The Times* so as to comply with code instructions. Clearly, he could not control the date his letter appeared in the newspaper but he could fix the post-date: October 6th 1888. So, is the date significant?

Applying the Master Code in the context of the letter's post-date, 6th October 1888:

1. "A code is in *The Times* letter of *Oct. 6*" = 246
2. "Barnardo dated a *Times* letter *Oct. 6*" = 246
3. "Letter date 6/10/18 88: hid code" = 246 written 6,10,18,88
4. "Letter in *Times* dated as October 6" = 246
5. "October sixth *Times* letter" = 246
6. "Post-date of a *Times* letter hid a code" = 246
7. "Send letter on 6/10/1888" = 246 a code instruction
8. "*Times* letter of October 6 th hid code" = 246
9. "*Times* letter-date is a secret code" = 246
10. "*Times* letter: 6/10/1888" = 246 written 6,10,18,88

The *style* of Barnardo's signature on the letter (*Thos. J. Barnardo*) is a clue to Master Code solutions:

1. "Barnardo's signature *hid* cipher clue" = 246 *"Thos. J. Barnardo"* = "The Master Code" = 111
2. "Barnardo's signature *hides* a cipher" = 246
3. "The signature is: *Thos. J. Barnardo*" = 246

Applying *Skelton* to the signature as it appears in the letter:

1. "A murderer hid as" = "*Thos. J. Barnardo*" = 111
2. "Barnardo hid clue in" = "*Thos. J. Barnardo*" = 111
3. "Code hid the killer" = "*Thos. J. Barnardo*" = 111
4. "Killer hiding as" = "*Thos. J. Barnardo*" = 111
5. "*Thos. J. Barnardo*" = "a code Barnardo left" = 111
6. "*Thos. J. Barnardo*" = "a hidden murderer" = 111
7. "*Thos. J. Barnardo*" = "Barnardo's code clue" = 111
8. "*Thos. J. Barnardo*" = "hides murderer" = 111
9. "*Thos. J. Barnardo*" = "is Barnardo's code" = 111
10. "*Thos. J. Barnardo*" = "name of culprit" = 111

Applying the Master Code in the context of the *Times* letter:

1. "A code hides in *Times* October 6 letter" = 246 ***same*** code in the 'Dear Boss' letter etc
2. "A code *Times* letter hid is killer's" = 246
3. "A code was in *Times* October letter" = 246
4. "A cypher in *Times* letter is hid" = 246
5. "A letter hid a clue to *Jack the Ripper*" = 246
6. "A letter to *The Times* hides code clue" = 246
7. "A secret hidden by *Times* letter" = 246
8. "A *Times* letter is hiding a secret" = 246
9. "Address in *Times* letter is clue" = 246
10. "Author of *The Times* letter hid a code" = 246

11. "Barnardo left code clue in the letter" = 246
12. "Barnardo writes to *The Times*" = 246
13. "Barnardo's guilt hidden as a letter" = 246
14. "Barnardo's guilt hides as letter" = 246
15. "Barnardo's guilt hiding in letter" = 246
16. "Barnardo's letter in *The Times*" = 246
17. "Clue hid by killer in *Times* letter" = 246
18. "Clue is: code in *Times* October letter" = 246
19. "Clue is: *Times* October letter hid a code" = 246
20. "Clue to *Jack the Ripper* in a letter" = 246
21. "Clue to killer's name hid in a letter" = 246
22. "Clues hid in letter to *The Times*" = 246
23. "Code clues are hidden in *Times* letter" = 246
24. "Code in the *Times* letter address" = 246
25. "Code in *Times* letter is killer's" = 246
26. "Code was in letter to *The Times*" = 246
27. "Date of Barnardo's letter was a clue" = 246
28. "Dr Barnardo names Stride 3 times" = 246
29. "Examine *Times* letter for clues" = 246
30. "Find a code hidden as the *Times* letter" = 246
31. "Find code hiding in the *Times* letter" = 246
32. "Find proof hidden in *Times* letter" = 246
33. "Freemasons code in *Times* letter" = 246
34. "Hid a code as the letter in *The Times*" = 246
35. "Hid a cypher clue in *Times* Letter" = 246
36. "Hid a secret in *The Times* letter" = 246
37. "I hid a confession as *Times* letter" = 246
38. "I mention *Stride* murder 3 times" = 246
39. "I, Thomas Barnardo identified Stride" = 246
40. "Inspect *Times* letter for a clue" = 246
41. "Killer's code is in *Times* letter" = 246
42. "Letter hid Barnardo's confession" = 246
43. "Letter in *Times* is by Barnardo" = 246
44. "Letter of Barnardo is post-dated" = 246
45. "Letter to 'The Editor' was code clue" = 246
46. "Letter to *The Times* hides a code clue" = 246
47. "Letter's author killed Stride" = 246
48. "Look for a clue *The Times* letter hid" = 246
49. "Look for clue in *The Times* letter" = 246
50. "Missive in *Times* hid confession" = 246
51. "My letter was in *The Times*" = 246
52. "Name is in *Times* letter 3 times" = 246 Elizabeth Stride referred to 3 times by name
53. "*Stride:* clue is in a *Times* letter" = 246

54. "Stride's killing: clue in letter" = 246
55. "Stride's murder: a clue in letter" = 246
56. "Stride's name hiding code in letter" = 246
57. "The letter in *The Times* hides code" = 246
58. "The name *Stride* appears 3 times" = 246
59. "The *Times* letter address hid a code" = 246
60. "The *Times* letter was hiding a code" = 246
61. "Thomas J. Barnardo identified Stride" = 246
62. "*Times* letter 6/10 is by Barnardo" = 246
63. "*Times* letter hid a clue by Barnardo" = 246
64. "*Times* letter hid a Freemasons code" = 246
65. "*Times* letter hid a killer's code clue" = 246
66. "*Times* letter hid clue to the killer" = 246
67. "*Times* letter hid murderer's code" = 246
68. "*Times* letter hiding confession" = 246
69. "*Times* letter hiding Masonic codes" = 246
70. "*Times* letter is hiding a secret" = 246
71. "*Times* letter is Orange Order code" = 246
72. "*Times* letter is proof of guilt" = 246
73. "*Times* letter is the killer's" = 246
74. "*Times* letter proves guilt" = 246
75. "*Times* letter: code in the address" = 246
76. "*Times* letter: the address hid a code" = 246
77. "You cracked my *Times* letter code" = 246
78. "You solved a code *Times* letter hid" = 246
79. "You solved code in *Times* letter" = 246

And we find the Master Code resonance equations:

1. "Clue is: the *Times* October letter" = "*hid* murder confession of Dr Barnardo" = 246
2. "Clue is: the *Times* October letter" = "*hides* a murder confession of Barnardo" = 246
3. "October sixth *Times* letter" = "*hid* murder confession of Dr Barnardo" = 246
4. "October sixth *Times* letter" = "*hides* a murder confession of Barnardo" = 246
5. "*Times* letter 6/10/1888" = "*hid* murder confession of Dr Barnardo" = 246
6. "*Times* letter 6/10/1888" = "*hides* a murder confession of Barnardo" = 246

Applying *Skelton* to 'The Times letter' gives the resonance equations:

1. "*The Times* letter" = "confession of Barnardo" = 153
2. "*The Times* letter" = "hid Barnardo's secret" = 153
3. "*The Times* letter" = "hid code of *Jack the Ripper*" = 153
4. "*The Times* letter" = "hiding *Jack the Ripper*" = 153

Also

1. "Barnardo left you clues" = "in *The Times* letter" = 169
2. "Confession by Barnardo" = "in *The Times* letter" = 169
3. "*The Times* letter hid a" = "confession by Barnardo" = 169

And, in that context we find the resonance equations:

- "Barnardo's confession" = "is in *Times* letter" = 161
- "Dr Barnardo's confession" = "was in a *Times* letter" = 182

So, where is Barnardo's confession hidden?

The logical answer is: in the three references to Elizabeth Stride.

Applying *Skelton* to the three comments that refer to Elizabeth Stride by name, in the sequence they appear, viz:

- "The unhappy woman Stride" = 225
- "Poor Elizabeth Stride" = 176
- "The poor woman Stride" = 184

Applying *Skelton* to: "The unhappy woman Stride" = 225 gives the resonance equations:

1. ***"The Times* letter's code was"** = "***the unhappy woman Stride***" = 225
2. "Doctor Barnardo admits killing" = "the unhappy woman Stride" = 225
3. "Doctor Barnardo hid confession in" = "the unhappy woman Stride" = 225
4. "The unhappy woman Stride" = "a clue hidden in *The Times* letter" = 225
5. "The unhappy woman Stride" = "a clue is: *The Times* letter hid a code" = 225
6. "The unhappy woman Stride" = "a killing Barnardo confesses to" = 225
7. "The unhappy woman Stride" = "Barnardo was killer of Stride" = 225
8. "The unhappy woman Stride" = "Barnardo's confession hidden in a code" = 225
9. "The unhappy woman Stride" = "Barnardo's confession in cipher" = 225
10. "The unhappy woman Stride" = "her murderer was T. J. Barnardo" = 225
11. "The unhappy woman Stride" = "hides Barnardo's confession in code" = 225
12. "The unhappy woman Stride" = "hides clue in *The Times* letter" = 225
13. "The unhappy woman Stride" = "is a code clue in *The Times* letter" = 225
14. "The unhappy woman Stride" = "is clue Barnardo murdered Stride" = 225
15. "The unhappy woman Stride" = "is confession of Doctor Barnardo" = 225
16. "The unhappy woman Stride" = "is murdered by *Jack the Ripper*" = 225
17. "The unhappy woman Stride" = "letter in *The Times* uses code" = 225
18. "The unhappy woman Stride" = "name of her murderer is hidden here" = 225
19. "The unhappy woman Stride" = "name of murderer is Tom Barnardo" = 225

Applying *Skelton* to: "Poor Elizabeth Stride" = 176 gives the resonance equations:

1. ***"Times* letter's code is"** = "***poor Elizabeth Stride***" = 176
2. "Poor Elizabeth Stride" = "a confession of T. J. Barnardo" = 176
3. "Poor Elizabeth Stride" = "Dr Barnardo hid the code clues" = 176
4. "Poor Elizabeth Stride" = "hid clue in *Times* letter" = 176
5. "Poor Elizabeth Stride" = "is a *Jack the Ripper* homicide" = 176
6. "Poor Elizabeth Stride" = "is homicide Barnardo admits" = 176
7. "Poor Elizabeth Stride" = "killer was T. J. Barnardo" = 176
8. "Poor Elizabeth Stride" = "murderer was Barnardo" = 176
9. "Poor Elizabeth Stride" = "name was clue to murderer" = 176
10. "Poor Elizabeth Stride" = "Thos. Barnardo killed her" = 176

Applying *Skelton* to: "The poor woman Stride" = 184 gives the resonance equations:

1. ***"Times* letter's clue is"** = "***the poor woman Stride***" = 184
2. "Barnardo's admission hid in" = "the poor woman Stride" = 184
3. "The poor woman Stride" = "a killing of *Jack the Ripper*" = 184
4. "The poor woman Stride" = "I, Barnardo was her killer" = 184
5. "The poor woman Stride" = "T. J. Barnardo her murderer" = 184
6. "The poor woman Stride" = "the killer is Dr Barnardo" = 184
7. "Thomas Barnardo murdered" = "the poor woman Stride" = 184

We note Master Code solutions in the context of the *Times* letter, specifically the address:

1. **"Address hid the code of *Jack the Ripper*" = 246**
2. "Address in *Times* letter is clue" = 246
3. "Address was in a *Times* letter" = 246
4. "An address in *Times* letter hid code" = 246
5. "Barnardo hid the code clue in the address" = 246
6. "Barnardo's secret code hid in address" = 246
7. "Code in the *Times* letter address" = 246
8. "Dr Barnardo hid the code in the address" = 246
9. "The answers hide in the address" = 246
10. "*Times* letter: the address hid a code" = 246
11. "*Times* letter: address was coded" = 246
12. "You are right about code hid in address" = 246
13. "You found a secret clue hid as address" = 246
14. "You found secret clue address hides" = 246

Applying *Skelton* to the address as it appears in *The Times* letter:

"18 to 26, Stepney-causeway, E" = 238 gives the resonance equations:

1. "18 to 26, Stepney-causeway, E" = "Barnardo's address hides a secret" = 238
2. "18 to 26, Stepney-causeway, E" = "Doctor Barnardo's address hid codes" = 238
3. "18 to 26, Stepney-causeway, E" = "hides a retreat of *Jack the Ripper*" = 238
4. "18 to 26, Stepney-causeway, E" = "is a dwelling of *Jack the Ripper*" = 238
5. "18 to 26, Stepney-causeway, E" = "is address hiding *Jack the Ripper*" = 238
6. "18 to 26, Stepney-causeway, E" = "was hideout for *Jack the Ripper*" = 238
7. "18 to 26, Stepney-causeway, E" = "was hiding *Jack the Ripper*'s home" =238
8. "18 to 26, Stepney-causeway, E" = "was *Jack the Ripper*'s address" = 238
9. "18 to 26, Stepney-causeway, E" = "was *Jack the Ripper*'s residence" = 238
10. "18 to 26, Stepney-causeway, E" = "was safe-haven of *Jack the Ripper*" = 238
11. "A retreat of *Jack the Ripper* hid at" = "18 to 26, Stepney-causeway, E" = 238
12. "*Jack the Ripper:* a secret lodger in" = "18 to 26, Stepney-causeway, E" = 238
13. "*Jack the Ripper:* secret domicile at" = "18 to 26, Stepney-causeway, E" = 238
14. "Secret lair of *Jack the Ripper* at" = "18 to 26, Stepney-causeway, E" = 238

And in that context, we find the Master Code solutions:

1. "A Boys' home hides *Jack the Ripper* clue" = 246
2. "A lair of *Jack the Ripper* at orphanage" = 246
3. "Boys' orphanage hid *Jack the Ripper*" = 246
4. "Find *Jack the Ripper* hid in Boys' home" = 246
5. "*Jack the Ripper* clue: hid at a Boys' home" = 246
6. "*Jack the Ripper:* Boys' home hides a clue" = 246
7. "*Jack the Ripper*: concealed at orphanage" = 246
8. "*Jack the Ripper*'s orphanage hide-out" = 246
9. "Orphanage is lair of *Jack the Ripper*" = 246

Fourth victim: "Catherine/Kate Eddowes". Aged 46

Found: Sunday, September 30th 1:45 am at the south corner of Mitre Square, within about an hour of Elizabeth Stride's murder.

Applying *Skelton* to Catherine Eddowes in that context:

1. "Catherine Eddowes" = "my 4 th murder" = 124
2. "Catherine Eddowes" = "was number four" = 124
3. "Catherine Eddowes" = "is in Mitre Sq." = 124
4. "I kill a slut called" = "Catherine Eddowes" = 124
5. "I kill a whore called" = "Catherine Eddowes" = 124
6. "Kill the harlot" = "Catherine Eddowes" = 124

Applying *Skelton* to Kate Eddowes, we find the resonance equations:

1. "Kate Eddowes" = "4 th murder" = 88
2. "Kate Eddowes" = "harlot name" = 88
3. "Kate Eddowes" = "the fourth" = 88
4. "Kill slut" = "Kate Eddowes" = 88
5. "Kill whore" = "Kate Eddowes" = 88

Master Code solutions, found in the context of Eddowes & Stride:

1. "Barnardo murdered Catherine Eddowes" = 246
2. "Catherine Eddowes: cut her throat" = 246
3. "Catherine Eddowes: fourth one I killed" = 246
4. "Clue is: ***double event*** September 30" = 246* applying *Skelton*: "event" = "murder" = 57
5. "Clue is: ***double event*** Stride-Eddowes" = 246*
6. "Clue is: *double murder* September 30" = 246*
7. "Clue is: *double murder* Stride-Eddowes" = 246*
8. "Clue is: Kate Eddowes fourth murder" = 246
9. "Death in Mitre Square: Sept. 30" = 246
10. "Eddowes is killed in Mitre Square" = 246
11. "Eddowes was fourth to be murdered" = 246
12. "Eddowes: kill her in Mitre Square" = 246
13. "Eddowes' killing at Mitre Square" = 246
14. "Harlot Catherine Eddowes: kill her" = 246
15. "Kate Eddowes fourth murder of five" = 246
16. "Kate Eddowes was a fourth murder" = 246
17. "Kill Stride and Eddowes on 30 th" = 246
18. "September 30 was a ***double event***" = 246*
19. "September 30 was a *double murder*" = 246*
20. "Stride-Eddowes was a ***double event***" = 246*
21. "Stride-Eddowes was a double murder" = 246
22. "Stride-Eddowes was double killing" = 246

*'**double event'** appears in the *Saucy Jacky* card post-dated October 1st, the day after the murders.

Injuries to Eddowes: The throat was severed and the abdomen ripped open by a long, deep and jagged wound before the intestines had been placed over the right shoulder. The left kidney and the major part of the uterus had been removed and the face had been disfigured. The nose was severed, the cheek slashed and cuts measuring a quarter of an inch and a half an inch respectively vertically incised through each eyelid. Triangular incisions - pointing towards the eyes - had been carved on each cheek.

Within a few hours of the *double event* three related 'clues' were found:

- A blood-covered knife left on the steps of a laundry at 253 Whitechapel Road.
- Part of Eddowes bloodied apron left in the doorway of flats at 108-119 Goulston St.
- Graffito written in chalk on the wall above the piece of apron.

In the context of the blood-covered knife found on the steps of the laundry at 253 Whitechapel Road, we find the Master Code solutions:

1. "A bloodied knife: a clue of Thomas John Barnardo" = 246
2. "A bloodied knife: the clue of Thomas Barnardo" = 246
3. "Bloodied knife at laundry is clue for a code" = 246
4. "Bloodied knife at laundry was a sign" = 246
5. "Bloodied knife at laundry was jest" = 246 knife needed cleaning, so was left at laundry!
6. "Bloodied knife is Barnardo's secret joke" = 246
7. "Bloodied knife was the clue of Barnardo" = 246
8. "Laundry is at 253 Whitechapel Road" = 246
9. "Leave a blood-covered knife at a laundry" = 246
10. "Leave a knife on steps of laundry" = 246
11. "Left a blood-covered knife at laundry" = 246
12. "Left knife on steps of laundry" = 246
13. "The bloodied knife: a clue of Thomas Barnardo" = 246
14. "The bloodied knife is Doctor Barnardo's" = 246
15. "The bloodied knife is *Jack the Ripper* code" = 246
16. "You found bloodied knife I hid at laundry" = 246
17. "You solved the clue bloodied knife hides" = 246
18. "You solved the clue hid as a bloodied knife" = 246

By accounting for the presence of the bloodied knife on the laundry steps at 253 Whitechapel Road, the solutions show the solver that they have the same cipher as *Jack the Ripper*/Doctor Barnardo.

Applying the Master Code in the context of the piece of bloodied & soiled apron, we find:

1. "Blood and shit found on Eddowes apron" = 246 blood & excrement on the piece of apron
2. "Clue is: the piece of Eddowes' bloodied apron" = 246
3. "Clues hid by graffito and piece of apron" = 246
4. "Piece of apron is taken from Eddowes" = 246
5. "The piece of Eddowes' bloodied apron is clue" = 246

Graffito chalked on a wall at 108-119 Goulston St found shortly after the 'double' murder:

'The *Juwes* are the men that will <u>not</u> be blamed for <u>nothing</u>'

The graffito contains a spelling mistake (Juwes) and a double negative (underlined), solutions following show that the errors were deliberate.

Applying the Master Code in the context of the graffito:

1. "12-word graffito: Barnardo's hidden code" = 246
2. "A code hiding as writing on the wall" = 246
3. "A code was in writing on the wall" = 246
4. "A double negative was in the graffito" = 246
5. "A graffito hid anagram of Barnardo's name" = 246 to find the name you must already know it!
6. "Anagram hides *the full name* of Barnardo" = 246
7. "Anagram hiding Doctor Barnardo's name" = 246
8. "Anagram of Barnardo's name in graffito" = 246
9. "Barnardo wrote graffito message" = 246
10. "Barnardo's 12-word graffito hides code" = 246
11. "Barnardo's code hid as 12-word graffito" = 246
12. "Barnardo's name in anagram of graffito" = 246
13. "Barnardo's name is hiding as graffito" = 246*
14. "Barnardo's name is hiding in an anagram" = 246
15. "Clue is: double negative in the graffito" = 246
16. "Clue is: my misspelling of Jews" = 246
17. "Clue was in misspelling of Jews" = 246
18. "Doctor Barnardo's graffito is code clue" = 246
19. "Doctor Barnardo's graffito was a code" = 246
20. "Double negative is a clue the graffito hid" = 246
21. "Double negative is clue in the graffito" = 246
22. "Dr Barnardo's name hides as an anagram" = 246
23. "Dr Barnardo's name hiding in an anagram" = 246
24. "*Full name* of Barnardo hidden in an anagram" = 246
25. "Goulston St. graffito hid the clue" = 246
26. "Graffito code has twelve words" = 246
27. "Graffito hid name of Barnardo as anagram" = 246
28. "Graffito in Goulston St. hides a code" = 246
29. "Graffito on wall is arithmetic code" = 246
30. "Hid a code as a graffito in Goulston St." = 246
31. "I hid name as Goulston St. graffito" = 246
32. "Leave piece of apron in Goulston St." = 246
33. "Look for *Barnardo* in graffito anagram" = 246
34. "Misspelling of 'Jews' is clue to code" = 246
35. "Name clue in Goulston St. graffito" = 246
36. "Name is in Goulston St. graffito" = 246
37. "Re-arrange graffito's letters" = 246

38. "The graffito anagram hiding my name" = 246
39. "The graffito cipher by Dr Barnardo" = 246
40. "The graffito hides code by Dr Barnardo" = 246
41. "The graffito is a hidden code by Barnardo" = 246
42. "The graffito is cipher by Barnardo" = 246
43. "The graffito: cypher by Barnardo" = 246
44. "Writing on the wall is the clue" = 246
45. "You found a name-anagram clue in graffito" = 246
46. "You found a name-anagram is in graffito" = 246
47. "You found an anagram clue hid in graffito" = 246
48. "You found anagram clue in the graffito" = 246
49. "You found graffito hiding name anagram" = 246
50. "You found name I hid as a graffito anagram" = 246

Applying *Skelton* to the graffito, as quoted by PC Long at Eddowes' inquest, we find the resonance equations:

1. "*The Juwes are the men that will not be blamed for nothing*" = "code hidden at 108-119 Goulston St" = **412**
2. "*The Juwes are the men that will not be blamed for nothing*" = "code hiding in 108-119 Goulston St" = **412**

So, it makes sense to look for *contextually appropriate* solutions having gematria number 412:

1. "A clue is: the secret cypher of Doctor Thomas John Barnardo" = 412
2. "A secret cipher was hidden as *Jack the Ripper*'s murders" = 412
3. "Bravo! you found *Jack the Ripper* hiding Thomas John Barnardo" = 412
4. "Bravo! you found name of *Jack the Ripper:* Thomas John Barnardo" = 412
5. "Bravo! you have found the codes of Doctor Thomas John Barnardo" = 412
6. "Congratulations! you found *Jack the Ripper* hides Barnardo" = 412
7. "Congratulations! you solved codes *Jack the Ripper* hides" = 412
8. "Congratulations! you solved *Jack the Ripper*'s cipher" = 412
9. "Doctor Thomas Barnardo is homicidal lunatic *Jack the Ripper*" = 412
10. "Doctor Thomas John Barnardo is murderer *Jack the Ripper*" = 412
11. "Dr Barnardo *must* kill prostitutes of Whitechapel" = 412
12. "Graffito: *hiding* a confession by Doctor Thomas John Barnardo" = 412
13. "*Jack the Ripper hiding* real name: Doctor Thomas John Barnardo" = 412
14. "*Jack the Ripper* is cypher of murderer Thomas Barnardo" = 412
15. "*Jack the Ripper* is *hiding* name of Doctor Thomas John Barnardo" = 412
16. "*Jack the Ripper* was a cipher of murderer Thomas Barnardo" = 412
17. "*Jack the Ripper* was hiding real name of Thomas John Barnardo" = 412
18. "*Jack the Ripper:* name of a secret murderer Thomas Barnardo" = 412
19. "*Jack the Ripper* was pseudonym of Thomas John Barnardo" = 412
20. "*Jack the Ripper*: the doctor-preacher in 29 Hanbury St" = 412
21. "Secret cipher was hiding in *Jack the Ripper*'s murders" = 412
22. "Thomas John Barnardo wrote a hidden code-message on the wall" = 412
23. "Thomas John Barnardo wrote cipher-message on the wall" = 412
24. "You have found the truth. I, Barnardo was *Jack the Ripper*" = 412

That the graffito doesn't make much sense and that it contains errors suggests it's a code, possibly an anagram. ***'The <u>Juwes</u> are the men that will <u>not</u> be blamed for <u>nothing'</u>*** **transposes to a non-linear Scrabble-like anagram with the full name at the centre, viz:**

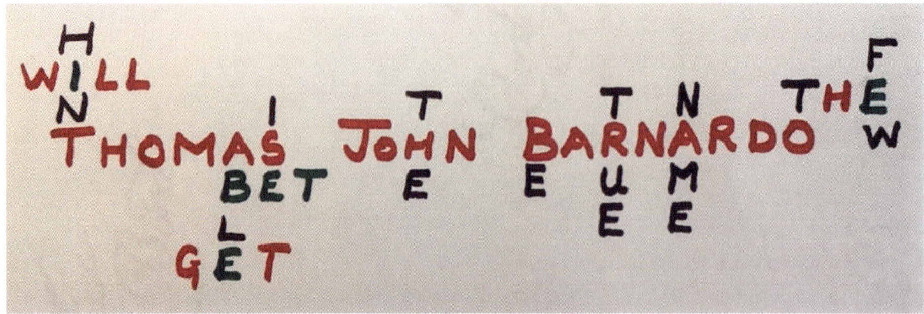

Which reads:

1. ***Bet few will be able to get the hint. The true name is Thomas John Barnardo***
2. ***The hint is true. Bet few will be able to get the name Thomas John Barnardo***

NB Employs the anagram method used in *Breaking the Shakespeare Codes (2007)

In this context, using gematria number 412 we also find the solutions:

1. "Graffito anagram Doctor Barnardo hid has sixteen words" = 412
2. "Sixteen-word anagram hiding **Thomas John Barnardo**'s name" = 412
3. "Sixteen-word graffito anagram hidden by Doctor Barnardo" = 412
4. "The graffito is a sixteen-word anagram hidden by Barnardo" = 412
5. "The graffito: a sixteen-word anagram hidden by Dr Barnardo" = 412
6. "The name of **Thomas John Barnardo** in a sixteen-word anagram" = 412
7. "**Thomas John Barnardo's** name is in a sixteen-word anagram" = 412

We note that the anagram solutions have sixteen words.

Using the gematria number 412 from the graffito (found just after the double killing):

"Barnardo kills Stride and Eddowes on 30 th September" = 412

The number of days in a year – a special gematria number

It seems Barnardo found the following Master Code solutions concerning the number of days in a year ...

1. "Hid a code as: *the number of days in a year*" = 246
2. "*Number of days in a year* hid a secret" = 246
3. "*Number of days in a year* hides the code" = 246

... and it seems he found many solutions with gematria number 365:

1. **"*The number of days in a year* hides the code of Dr Barnardo" = 365**
2. "*The number of days in a year* hiding the codes of Barnardo" = 365
3. "*The number of days in a year* is Barnardo's cypher" = 365
4. "*The number of days in a year* is the cipher of Barnardo" = 365
5. "*The number of days in a year* is the secret few find" = 365
6. "*The number of days in a year* was the cryptic code" = 365
7. "*The number of days in a year*: it is the secret code clue" = 365
8. "*The number of days in a year:* the cipher of Dr Barnardo" = 365
9. "*The number of days in a year*: the code of *Jack the Ripper*" = 365
10. "*The number of days in a year:* the cypher of Barnardo" = 365
11. "*The number of days in a year:* the hidden code of T. J. Barnardo" = 365
12. "*The number of days in a year*: the secret clue few find" = 365

Applying *Skelton* with gematria number 365, in the context of the graffito etc:

1. **"A clue is: murdered prostitute names in graffito code" = 365** see 27 below
2. **"A graffito clue is: spelling mistake and double negative" = 365**
3. **"A graffito in Goulston St is hiding Barnardo's codes" = 365**
4. **"An anagram of Thomas John Barnardo's name hid in graffito" = 365**
5. **"Anagram hid in graffito hid *Jack the Ripper*'s true name" = 365***
6. **"Anagram of Thomas John Barnardo's name in the graffito" = 365**
7. "Barnardo left secret clues hidden in Goulston St" = 365
8. "Barnardo's code is hidden as graffito at Goulston St" = 365
9. "Barnardo's code is hiding as graffito in Goulston St" = 365
10. "Clue is the graffito mistake: *not be blamed for nothing*" = 365 double negative
11. **"Clue to *Jack the Ripper*'s true name hides as graffito" = 365**
12. **"Clue to *Jack the Ripper*'s true name hiding in graffito" = 365**
13. "Code left by Barnardo on the wall at Goulston St" = 365
14. "Find the secret clues of Doctor Thomas John Barnardo" = 365
15. "Goulston St. graffito: hiding a secret confession" = 365
16. "Goulston St. graffito: misspelling is the clue" = 365
17. **"Graffito anagram hid real name of *Jack the Ripper*" = 365**
18. "Graffito hid a message by Doctor Thomas John Barnardo" = 365
19. "Graffito hid the message by Doctor Thomas Barnardo" = 365
20. "Graffito on Goulston St is hiding Barnardo's codes" = 365
21. "Graffito was a clue to *Jack the Ripper*'s secret name" = 365

22. "Juwes is Goulston St. graffito misspelling" = 365
23. "Look for a name-anagram hidden as writing on the wall" = 365
24. "Look for name-anagram hiding in writing on the wall" = 365
25. "Message in graffito by Doctor Thomas John Barnardo" = 365
26. "Misspelling of 'Jews' in Goulston St. graffito" = 365 a deliberate mistake
27. **"Murder: Nichols, Chapman, Stride, Eddowes and Kelly" = 365**** code instruction
28. "Murders of *Jack the Ripper* hide secret cipher clues" = 365
29. "Murders of *Jack the Ripper* hide secret cyphers" = 365
30. "The double negative in Goulston St. graffito is a clue" = 365
31. "The graffito ***not be blamed for nothing*** was a mistake" = 365 double negative
32. "The names of murdered sluts are hidden in graffito code" = 365
33. **"The names of murdered whores are hidden in graffito code" = 365**
34. "The real name of *Jack the Ripper* is hidden in the anagram" = 365
35. "Thomas John Barnardo wrote a message on the wall" = 365
36. "True name of *Jack the Ripper* hidden as a graffito anagram" = 365
37. "True name of *Jack the Ripper* hides as graffito anagram" = 365
38. "True name of *Jack the Ripper* hiding in graffito anagram" = 365
39. "Use the *Skelton* code to solve the code hid by Barnardo" = 365
40. "You discovered anagram of *Jack the Ripper*'s real name" = 365
41. "You discovered clue hiding Thomas John Barnardo's name" = 365
42. "You discovered the ciphers of Thomas John Barnardo" = 365
43. "You discovered Thomas John Barnardo's cipher clues" = 365
44. "You discovered Thomas John Barnardo's cyphers" = 365

The full name *Thomas John Barnardo* is hidden as an anagram in the graffito. **In that context, we find the following resonance equations, again using *Skelton* with gematria number 365:**

1. "*18 - 26 Stepney Causeway E* hides *Jack the Ripper*" = 365
2. "5 sluts murdered by Doctor Thomas John Barnardo" = 365
3. "5 whores murdered by Doctor Thomas John Barnardo" = 365
4. "A clue is: Barnardo played the part of *Jack the Ripper*" = 365 in a 5-act murderous melodrama
5. "A clue is: *Jack the Ripper* hides Doctor Thomas Barnardo" = 365
6. "A clue is: Thomas John Barnardo was the abortionist" = 365
7. "A code hides murder confession by Thomas John Barnardo" = 365
8. "A Goulston St graffito hides name of Doctor Barnardo" = 365
9. "A graffito at Goulston St hid name of Doctor Barnardo" = 365
10. "A medical-man and street preacher is at Dorset St" = 365
11. "A mystery Whitechapel hides solved by you" = 365
12. "A secret abortions clinic of Barnardo in Dorset St" = 365
13. "Address of *Jack the Ripper* is hidden at Dorset St." = 365
14. "Address of *Jack the Ripper* is hiding in Dorset St." = 365
15. "An anagram of Thomas John Barnardo's name hid in graffito" = 365
16. "Barnardo is secret abortionist at Dorset St" = 365
17. "Barnardo left a knife at Whitechapel Road's laundry" = 365
18. "Barnardo left clues found in Goulston St. graffito" = 365
19. "Barnardo was prayer leader in 29 Hanbury St" = 365 location of 2nd murder

20. "Barnardo was the secret prostitute killer" = 365
21. "Barnardo's code chalked on wall in Goulston Street" = 365
22. "Barnardo's code is hiding as graffito in Goulston St." = 365
23. "*Bravo*! You have cracked Doctor Barnardo's cipher clues" = 365
24. "*Bravo*! You have cracked Doctor Barnardo's cyphers" = 365
25. "Clue is: *Jack the Ripper* hiding Dr Thomas John Barnardo" = 365
26. "Clue is: Thomas John Barnardo is name of *Jack the Ripper*" = 365
27. "Codes prove Thomas John Barnardo is the murderer" = 365
28. "Doctor attended prayers at 29 Hanbury St" = 365
29. "Doctor Barnardo's abortion clinic is in Dorset St" = 365
30. "Doctor Barnardo hiding in graffito at Goulston St." = 365
31. "Doctor Barnardo is a murderer in Dorset Street" = 365
32. "Doctor Barnardo is in the Spitalfields rookery" = 365 'rookery' is name for a slum
33. "Doctor Barnardo is murderous *Mad Jack* Dorset St hid" = 365
34. "Doctor Barnardo: name of Dorset St doctor-preacher" = 365
35. "Doctor Barnardo was abortionist of Dorset St" = 365
36. "Dr Barnardo left knife on steps at the laundry" = 365
37. "Dr Barnardo lived in Dorset St in Spitalfields" = 365
38. "Dr Barnardo's code hidden as graffito at Goulston St." = 365
39. "Dr Barnardo's code hiding as graffito in Goulston St." = 365
40. "Dr Thomas Barnardo admits he was *Jack the Ripper*" = 365
41. "Final murder *hid* at Miller's Court off Dorset St" = 365 the only murder in doors
42. "Found secret name of prostitute killer: Barnardo" = 365
43. "*Funny little games* are a tease by Doctor Barnardo" = 365 see *Dear Boss* letter
44. "Goulston St graffito clue hid name of Doctor Barnardo" = 365
45. "Graffito at Goulston St. hides Dr Barnardo's codes" = 365
46. "Graffito in Goulston St. by Dr Thomas Barnardo" = 365
47. "Graffito in Goulston St. is by Thomas Barnardo" = 365*
48. "*Hid* final murder at Miller's Court off Dorset St" = 365
49. "I am Doctor Thomas John Barnardo alias *Jack the Ripper*" = 365
50. "I am *Jack the Ripper* my name is Thomas John Barnardo" = 365
51. "It is true: *Jack the Ripper* hid Thomas John Barnardo" = 365
52. "*Jack the Ripper* cipher hides Thomas Barnardo's name" = 365
53. "*Jack the Ripper* disguises Doctor Thomas Barnardo" = 365
54. "*Jack the Ripper* hid at *18 - 26 Stepney Causeway E*" = 365
55. "*Jack the Ripper* hidden in Doctor Thomas John Barnardo" = 365
56. "*Jack the Ripper* is a cipher hiding Dr Thomas Barnardo" = 365
57. "*Jack the Ripper* is a mask hiding Thomas John Barnardo" = 365
58. "*Jack the Ripper* is a pseudonym of Thomas Barnardo" = 365
59. "*Jack the Ripper* is hidden as Barnardo in Dorset St" = 365
60. "*Jack the Ripper* is Plymouth Brethren doctor" = 365
61. "*Jack the Ripper* is the code hiding Thomas John Barnardo" = 365
62. "*Jack the Ripper* is the mad surgeon in Dorset St" = 365

63. “*Jack the Ripper* is the mask hiding Thomas Barnardo” = 365
64. “*Jack the Ripper* is the mask of Thomas John Barnardo” = 365
65. “*Jack the Ripper* was a cipher: real name is Dr Barnardo” = 365
66. “*Jack the Ripper* was a cypher: real name is Barnardo” = 365
67. “*Jack the Ripper* was a name hiding Dr Thomas Barnardo” = 365
68. “*Jack the Ripper* was concealing Thomas John Barnardo” = 365
69. “*Jack the Ripper* was killer hidden at Dorset St” = 365
70. “*Jack the Ripper* was killer hiding in Dorset St” = 365
71. “*Jack the Ripper* was name concealing Thomas Barnardo” = 365
72. “*Jack the Ripper*: a trade name *hiding* evil abortionist” = 365 Jack the Ripper is a ‘trade name’
73. “*Jack the Ripper*: *hidden* as Dr Barnardo in Dorset St” = 365
74. “*Jack the Ripper*: real name is Dr Thomas John Barnardo” = 365
75. “*Jack the Ripper:* name *hides* murderer Thos. J. Barnardo” = 365
76. “*Jack the Ripper*: trade name of the evil abortionist” = 365
77. “*Jack the Ripper*’s lair was *hiding* at Dorset St” = 365
78. “*Jack the Ripper*’s secret abode was in Dorset St” = 365
79. “Killer *Jack the Ripper* is doctor-preacher Barnardo” = 365
80. “Last murder at Miller’s Court off Dorset St” = 365
81. “Miller’s Court off Dorset St *hides* final murder” = 365
82. “Murder confessions by Barnardo *hid* in *Skelton* code” = 365
83. “Murder confessions of Thomas Barnardo *hide* in the code” = 365
84. “Murder confessions of Thomas John Barnardo *hide* in a code” = 365
85. “My name is Thomas Barnardo I was *Jack the Ripper*” = 365
86. “My name’s Thomas J. Barnardo I was *Jack the Ripper*” = 365
87. “My Whitechapel mystery solved by you” = 365
88. “Name of Doctor Barnardo in graffito at Goulston St” = 365
89. “Real killer name is Dr Barnardo not *Jack the Ripper*” = 365
90. “Real name of *Jack the Ripper* is an anagram *hid* in graffito” = 365
91. “Secret of Barnardo *hides* as Goulston St. graffito” = 365
92. “Secret of Barnardo *hiding* in Goulston St. graffito” = 365
93. “The code *hides* murder confession by Thomas Barnardo” = 365
94. “The very difficult cyphers of *Jack the Ripper*” = 365
95. “Thomas Barnardo *hidden* as murderer *Jack the Ripper*” = 365
96. “Thomas Barnardo is murderer called *Jack the Ripper*” = 365
97. “Thomas Barnardo uses the name *Jack the Ripper* to *hide*” = 365
98. “Thomas Barnardo was killer of prostitutes” = 365
99. “Thomas J. Barnardo is the murderer *Jack the Ripper*” = 365
100. “*Thomas John Barnardo* was *hidden* by graffito anagram” = 365
101. “*Thomas John Barnardo* was *hidden* by *Jack the Ripper*” = 365
102. “*Thomas John Barnardo* was *hidden* in anagram of graffito” = 365
103. “*Thomas John Barnardo* was prostitute killer” = 365
104. “*Thomas John Barnardo:* anagram of his name *hid* as graffito” = 365
105. “*Thomas John Barnardo*’s name *hides* as a graffito anagram” = 365
106. “*Thomas John Barnardo*’s name *hiding* in a graffito anagram” = 365
107. “You discovered clue: Barnardo is *hiding Jack the Ripper*” = 365

108. “You discovered clue: Barnardo is name of *Jack the Ripper*” = 365
109. “You discovered: Dr Barnardo is name of *Jack the Ripper*” = 365
110. “You found bloodied knife Barnardo left as clue at laundry” = 365
111. “You made a discovery: Dr Barnardo is *Jack the Ripper*” = 365

*Implies Barnardo knew the names of the murder victims from the start.

Fifth and final victim: “Mary Jane Kelly”

(a.k.a. Marie Jeanette Kelly)

Found: Friday, November 9th 10:45 am at 13 Miller’s Court

Aged about 25 - originally from Limerick - Mary Jane Kelly, a Roman Catholic was the youngest and largest victim of *Jack the Ripper*. She was described as tall (~ 5′ 7′) and ‘quite attractive ... a pretty buxom girl’ – large by the norms of the time. She was the last of the five canonical victims. Her killing, the only one that took place indoors, was by far the most prolonged and brutal. She rented a single room - a hovel - at 13 Millers Court off Dorset St. Mary Kelly was ‘more than just killed’, she was reduced to an almost unrecognisable ‘thing’ by an insanely vicious attack; an orgy of violence of the most horrible and depraved kind estimated to have lasted 2-2 ½ hours.

Applying *Skelton* to “Mary Kelly” gives the resonance equations:

1. “Barnardo kills” = “Mary Kelly” = 112
2. “Mary Kelly” = “is final murder” = 112
3. “Mary Kelly” = “last one I killed” = 112
4. “Mary Kelly” = “murdered last = 112
5. “Mary Kelly” = “the last death” = 112

Applying *Skelton* to “Mary Jane Kelly”:

1. “Horrible murder of” = “Mary Jane Kelly” = 131
2. “Mary Jane Kelly” = “last one murdered” = 131
3. “Mary Jane Kelly” = “the last slut” = 131
4. “Mary Jane Kelly” = “the last whore” = 131
5. “Mary Jane Kelly” = “was killed last” = 131

And: “Marie Jeanette Kelly” = “killer was Barnardo” = 154

Master Code solutions:

1. “Barnardo admits killing big harlot” = 246**
2. “Barnardo burned the heart of Kelly” = 246*
3. “Barnardo gutted Mary Jane Kelly” = 246 literally
4. “Barnardo murdered *big* Mary Kelly” = 246
5. “Barnardo murders Mary Kelly” = 246
6. “Barnardo: Mary Jane Kelly murderer” = 246
7. “Date of the Kelly murder is: 9/11/1888” = 246 written 9, 11, 1, 8, 8,8
8. “Doctor Barnardo must fuck Kelly” = 246

9. "Doctor Barnardo: fuck Mary Kelly" = 246
10. "Dr Barnardo burned Kelly's heart" = 246
11. "Dr Barnardo: fuck *dead* Mary Kelly" = 246 necrophilia
12. "Final *coded* murder in Miller's Court" = 246 did Barnardo commit 'uncoded' murders?
13. "Go to 13 Miller's Court: fuck slut" = 246
14. "Go to 13 Miller's Court: fuck whore" = 246
15. "*Hide* final murder in Miller's Court" = 246 the only 'ripper' murder indoors
16. "I kill slut at 13 Miller's Court" = 246
17. "I kill the prostitute Kelly" = 246
18. "I kill whore at 13 Miller's Court" = 246
19. "I murdered Mary Jane Kelly last" = 246
20. "I pared Mary Jane Kelly to the bone" = 246 literally
21. "Kelly is fifth and last killing" = 246
22. "Kelly is killed on November 9 th" = 246
23. "Kelly was killed by Dr Barnardo" = 246
24. "Kelly was name of last harlot" = 246
25. "Kelly: killed by Thomas Barnardo" = 246
26. "Kelly: name of last harlot killed" = 246
27. "Kelly's death on 9 th of November" = 246
28. "Kill prostitute called Kelly" = 246
29. "Killed a slut in 13 Miller's Court" = 246
30. "Killed a whore in 13 Miller's Court" = 246
31. "Marie Jeanette Kelly is the fifth" = 246
32. "Marie Jeanette Kelly: final killing" = 246
33. "Mary Jane Kelly fucked by Barnardo" = 246
34. "Mary Jane Kelly: destroy her" = 246
35. "Mary Jane Kelly: eviscerate her" = 246
36. "Mary Kelly killer: Dr Barnardo" = 246
37. "Mary Kelly: a *big* prostitute" = 246
38. "Mary Kelly: appalling murder" = 246
39. "Mary Kelly: cremated her heart" = 246
40. "Mary Kelly: killer is Barnardo" = 246
41. "Mary Kelly: name of a tall slut" = 246
42. "Mary Kelly: name of a tall whore" = 246
43. "Mary Kelly: take-out her heart" = 246
44. "Murder the slut Kelly last" = 246
45. "Murder the whore Kelly last" = 246
46. "Tall harlot called Mary Kelly" = 246 she was ~ 5' 7", av. female height ~ 5' 2"

In that context, we note the Master Code solution:

"The last murder was the best" = 246

Injuries to Kelly: The extensively mutilated, eviscerated corpse of Mary Jane Kelly was discovered lying on the bed in the single room where she lived at 13 Miller's Court off Dorset Street Spitalfields, at 10:45 a.m. on Friday 9 th November 1888. Her face had been 'hacked beyond all recognition', her throat severed down to the spine and the abdomen almost emptied of organs. The uterus, kidneys and one breast had been placed beneath her head, other entrails had been placed beside her feet. Slabs and hunks of flesh cut from the abdomen and thighs were on a bedside table. The heart was missing from the crime scene*. Ashes found in the fireplace suggested that the murderer had burned several items. A recent fire had been hot enough to melt the solder holding the spout on a kettle, the spout having fallen into the grate.

*Solutions (2, 10, 39) indicate that Barnardo cremated the heart, accounting for the kettle's melted solder resulting from the extreme heat required for cremation.

Sarah Lewis - ear-witness to Kelly's murder - probably saw the killer approximately one hour before the murder. Lewis was called to Mary Kelly's inquest on November 12th. This was her testimony:

"II know Mrs. Keyler in Miller's Court. I was at her house at half past 2 on Friday morning she lives at No.2 in the court on the left on the first floor. I know the time by having looked at Spitalfields Church clock as I passed it. ***When I went in the court, I saw a man opposite the court in Dorset Street standing alone by the lodging house. He was not tall - but stout - had on a black wideawake hat -*** *I did not notice his clothes* ***- the man standing in the street was looking up the court as if waiting for someone to come out.*** *I was awake all night in a chair I dozed I heard no noise I woke up about half-past three - I sat awake until nearly five -* ***a little before four I heard a female voice shout loudly one Murder! the sound seemed to come from the direction of deceased's room there was only one scream*** *- I took no notice of it."*

**Thomas Barnardo was ~ 5' 3'' and of 'stout/stocky' build – Mary Kelly was described as ~ 5' 7" and 'buxom' and was relatively large for the times, 4" taller than Barnardo. Code solutions (following) indicate that when street preaching, Barnardo wore a black 'Quaker' hat ('wideawake').

A 'wideawake' / 'Quaker' hat

In this context we note the resonance equation: "A Quaker hat hides" = "Jack the Ripper" = 115

We note Master Code solutions in the context of Barnardo, *Jack the Ripper* and 'Quaker' hat:

1. "A *big black hat* is a *Jack the Ripper* sign" = 246
2. "A *big black hat*: signal of *Jack the Ripper*" = 246
3. "A *black Quaker hat* hid preacher Barnardo" = 246
4. "A *black Quaker hat* hid Thomas J. Barnardo" = 246
5. "A *black Quaker hat* hiding Dr Barnardo" = 246
6. "A *black Quaker hat* is hiding Barnardo" = 246
7. "A *black wideawake* hides *Jack the Ripper*" = 246
8. "A *Quaker hat*: sign of *Jack the Ripper*" = 246
9. "A *wideawake* hat hides *Jack the Ripper*" = 246
10. "A *wideawake* hides a street preacher" = 246
11. "Barnardo identified by a huge *Quaker hat*" = 246
12. "Barnardo is hidden by black *Quaker hat*" = 246
13. "Doctor Barnardo wore big *Quaker hat*" = 246
14. "Doctor Barnardo's big black *Quaker hat*" = 246
15. "Dr Barnardo is in a huge *black Quaker hat*" = 246
16. "Dr Barnardo wears *black Quaker hat*" = 246
17. "Huge *black Quaker hat* hiding Barnardo" = 246
18. "Huge wideawake hid street preacher" = 246
19. "*Jack the Ripper* hides in a *Quaker hat*" = 246
20. "*Jack the Ripper* is in *black wideawake*" = 246
21. "Preacher Barnardo has *black wideawake*" = 246
22. "Preacher Barnardo in *black Quaker hat*" = 246
23. "*Quaker hat* hid evil *Jack the Ripper*" = 246
24. "*Quaker hat*: sign of **doctor-preacher**" = 246
25. "Street preacher is in *wideawake*" = 246
26. "T. J. Barnardo identified by a *Quaker hat*" = 246
27. "Thomas Barnardo wore a *Quaker hat*" = 246
28. "Thomas J. Barnardo in *black Quaker hat*" = 246
29. "Thomas John Barnardo's *Quaker hat*" = 246

According to the solutions, the black Quaker hat (wideawake) is a symbol connecting *Jack the Ripper*, a street preacher and Doctor Barnardo. This suggests that the man Sarah Lewis saw *was* 'Jack the Ripper', apparently waiting for someone opposite the entrance to Millers Court about 1 – 1 ½ hours before the murder of Mary Kelly at (approaching) 4 am. Lewis' description of a short, stocky man in a black wideawake hat is consistent with those Master Code solutions concerning Thomas Barnardo.

In connection with street preaching and *Jack the Ripper*, we find the resonance equations:

1. "*Jack the Ripper*" = "alias hid a preacher" = 115
2. "*Jack the Ripper*" = "hidden in preacher" = 115
3. "*Jack the Ripper*" = "is *The Preacher*" = 115

Applying the Master Code in that context:

1. "A preacher of Whitechapel is a killer" = 246
2. "*Jack the Ripper* hid an evil preacher" = 246
3. "*Jack the Ripper* hid **doctor-preacher**" = 246*
4. "*Jack the Ripper:* a preacher in London" = 246
5. "*Jack the Ripper* hid an evil preacher" = 246
6. "*Jack the Ripper:* name hiding preacher" = 246
7. "*Jack the Ripper:* preacher's cipher" = 246
8. "*Jack the Ripper:* the evil preacher" = 246
9. "Killer-preacher in Spitalfields" = 246
10. "Spitalfields hid a killer-preacher" = 246

*Or "**doctor-preacher** hid *Jack the Ripper*" = 246

*Which is why the murder of Annie Chapman at 29 Hanbury St was a 'big clue' to the killer's identity, the location where two 'professions' - doctor-preacher - meet.

We have seen the resonance equations:

1. "Jack the Ripper" = "a clue was a doctor" = 115
2. "Jack the Ripper" = "a doctor hidden in code" = 115
3. "Jack the Ripper" = "a fiend hid as a doctor" = 115
4. "Jack the Ripper" = "alias a doctor used" = 115
5. "Jack the Ripper" = "cipher hid a *doctor*" = 115
6. "Jack the Ripper" = "disguised *doctor*" = 115
7. "Jack the Ripper" = "*doctor* is hint" = 115
8. "Jack the Ripper" = "hid homicidal doctor" = 115
9. "Jack the Ripper" = "hid Irish doctor" = 115
10. "Jack the Ripper" = "hid name of medical man" = 115
11. "Jack the Ripper" = "hides doctor in code" = 115
12. "Jack the Ripper" = "hides the doctor" = 115
13. "Jack the Ripper" = "hint at a doctor" = 115
14. "Jack the Ripper" = "is a medical man's code" = 115
15. "Jack the Ripper" = "is concealed doctor" = 115
16. "Jack the Ripper" = "is diabolical doctor" = 115
17. "Jack the Ripper" = "it was a doctor" = 115
18. "Jack the Ripper" = "masking doctor" = 115
19. "Jack the Ripper" = "name hides a *doctor*" = 115
20. "Jack the Ripper" = "the code of a medical man" = 115

And we recall the resonance equation: "*Jack the Ripper*" = "hides Dr Barnardo" = 115

Dr Jekyll and Mr Hyde - 'inspiration' for *Jack the Ripper*

Robert Louis Stevenson's *Dr Jekyll and Mr Hyde* was published in January 1886, more than two and a half years before the Whitechapel murders. The story was an instant success and the phrase *Jekyll and Hyde* entered the vernacular as a description of someone with changeable, distinct personalities typically good and bad. Master Code solutions (following) indicate that Barnardo got the inspiration for *Jack the Ripper* from Stevenson's story – that gave him plenty of time to plan the killings and find a huge number of contextually appropriate Master Code solutions well before autumn 1888.

It seems that the famous philanthropist from Dublin, the man who found homes for thousands of destitute children, concealed an evil 'spirit' much as *Dr Jekyll* hid the wicked *Mr Hyde*; but whereas *Hyde* was released from within *Jekyll* by a potion, the 'spirit' of *Jack the Ripper* emerged from within *Skelton's* gematria - the cipher Barnardo used as an 'oracle' to confirm his darkest impulses.

In that context, we recall the Master Code solution:

"*Jack* is the dark side of Doctor Barnardo" = 246

Also in that context, we find the resonance equation:

"Dr Thomas John Barnardo is hiding" = "the spirit of *Jack the Ripper*" = 229

Applying the Master Code in the context of *Dr Jekyll and Mr Hyde*:

1. "A clue was in *Dr Jekyll and Mr Hyde*" = 246
2. "Barnardo: a *Jekyll and Hyde* person" = 246
3. "Clue in story of *Jekyll and Hyde*" = 246
4. "*Jack the Ripper:* a clue is *Edward Hyde*" = 246
5. "*Jack the Ripper:* hiding like *Mr Hyde*" = 246
6. "*Jekyll and Hyde* gave Barnardo the idea" = 246
7. "*Jekyll and Hyde* inspire killing" = 246
8. "*Jekyll and Hyde* mirror Barnardo" = 246
9. "*Mr Hyde* is *Jack the Ripper* hint" = 246
10. "*Mr Hyde:* a hint at *Jack the Ripper*" = 246
11. "Story of *Jekyll and Hyde* hid a clue" = 246
12. "Take a hint hidden as *Jekyll and Hyde*" = 246
13. "Take hint hiding in *Jekyll and Hyde*" = 246

Mr Hyde symbolised the sexual/animal aspects of human nature which Victorians felt the need to hide; in that sense the name is a pun, as Hyde *hides* in Doctor Jekyll. Edward Hyde is described as devilish, evil and a criminal mastermind - he represents evil for evil's sake. Hyde is small and totally selfish and aims to achieve complete dominance over Jekyll. He has a burning animal fury and is brutal and barbaric in his attacks on people. Edward Hyde is essentially inhuman, entirely lacking empathy – characteristics manifest also in *Jack the Ripper*.

The 'mind' of *Jack the Ripper*

The following is an attempt to find Master Code solutions that Barnardo would probably have discovered himself if so inclined. The conjecture is that like the Reverend Charles Dodgson, the evangelist Thomas Barnardo was gripped by an abnormal sexual obsession – a secret though not uncommon phenomenon in Victorian society. Like Dodgson, it seems Barnardo had a 'collector's mentality' - probably a manifestation of the desire for order, control and power - but whereas the Oxford Maths don 'collected' and photographed young girls naked, the dodgy East End 'doctor' 'collected' old prostitutes. Like Dodgson, it seems Barnardo knew of or discovered the 'sex-game' that can be played with *Skelton*.

Through many years of street preaching and countless lodging-house visits, Barnardo probably got to know more sex-workers in Spitalfields and Whitechapel than anybody. In view of his detailed record keeping of every child that entered his orphanages, it's distinctly plausible that he likewise assembled a list of prostitutes' names and details recording them in an archetypical 'big black book' – again a manifestation of the desire for power and control.

In that context, we note the resonance equation:

"*Jack the Ripper*: the name of" = "the sexual pervert" = 182

We recall the Master Code solutions indicating that *Skelton* can be used for a sex-game, solutions Barnardo might well have found himself:

1. "A cipher you found is a sex-game. *Bravo*!" = 246
2. "A sex game played using *Skelton*" = 246
3. "Look for a sex game I hid in *Skelton* code" = 246
4. "Look for a sex game in *Skelton's* code" = 246
5. "Look for sex game *Skelton* code hides" = 246
6. "Play a sex-game with *Skelton*" = 246
7. "*Skelton* gematria was a sex-game" = 246
8. "The code you have found was a sex-game" = 246
9. "The secret sex-game found by you" = 246
10. "*This* number was code for a sex-game" = 246
11. "Use the code of *Skelton* for sex game" = 246
12. "Used *Skelton* cipher for sex-game" = 246
13. "Used *Skelton* to play a sex-game" = 246
14. "You discovered secret sex-codes" = 246
15. "You discovered sex-code's secret" = 246
16. "You found the code for the sex-games" = 246
17. "You found the sex game I hid. Well done!" = 246
18. "You found the sex games. Well done!" = 246
19. "You have discovered the sex-codes" = 246
20. "You have found code of secret sex-game" = 246

These Master Code solutions concerning Whitechapel's prostitutes might have 'inspired' Barnardo to assemble a 'book of prostitutes':

1. "A book of Whitechapel harlots is huge" = 246
2. "A huge code hid names of prostitutes" = 246
3. "A Spitalfields prostitute code" = 246
4. "Code hiding names of prostitutes" = 246
5. "Names of prostitutes in huge code" = 246
6. "Prostitutes names found in code" = 246
7. "*The Book of Prostitutes* hides code" = 246
8. "*The Book of Prostitutes* is black" = 246
9. "The huge book of Whitechapel sluts" = 246
10. "The huge book of Whitechapel whores" = 246
11. "Whitechapel-prostitute's code" = 246

According to fellow medical students Barnardo was a religious fanatic - a 'Bible-bashing nut', an odd-ball, a misfit - as director of the orphanages he was a workaholic; a characteristic often associated with a controlling personality and megalomania. As he said of himself: 'as a child *I was entirely self-centred and wanted to possess everything that wasn't mine'*. Barnardo brought to his insanely savage attacks on the most vulnerable women the zeal of a crazed preacher and the knowledge of a partly trained anatomist. It seems he had a fascination/obsession with female genitalia, an indication (perhaps) of a need to have *total* control over women.

If Barnardo *was* clinically insane it's possible his deranged mental state resulted from disease, specifically syphilis. Sexually transmitted disease was common in Victorian London and would almost certainly have been rife among the older prostitutes in Whitechapel and Spitalfields. In that case, Barnardo's motive might have been revenge – but then, as code solutions suggest, he loved to murder and in any case he was 'simply' carrying-out the code's instructions.

The depraved monster who carried-out the appalling attack on Mary Jane Kelly, seems to have had a visceral hatred of her personally - as suggested by the gross disfigurement, the obliterated features and general desecration of the corpse. Was the sustained orgy of destruction - lasting at least two hours - driven by Barnardo's 'volcanic' temper, a rage fuelled perhaps by the fervour of religious mania? Or was it the ultimate degradation and humiliation of the female sex itself, arising from a deep-seated fear – a fear whose roots lay in childhood, in rejection by an unloving puritanical mother?

The phenomenon that was *Jack the Ripper* probably emerged from a unique combination of factors: the 'right' man, in the 'right' place at the 'right' time. For many years Barnardo witnessed first-hand the lawless depravity of life in the worst East End slums; perhaps what he saw there turned his mind – or perhaps part of him *wanted* to be corrupted, a part that lusted after evermore extreme debauchery and that led inexorably down a path that terminated in the hell of 13 Miller's Court. Whatever, it's clear that Barnardo used *Skelton* for the most perverted and deviant of purposes; therefore, an attempt is made to discover some of the sexually related Master Code solutions he would probably have found himself if so inclined.

The following resonance equations give the name *Jack the Ripper* explicit sexual associations:

1. "Jack the Ripper" = "a sex-mad killer" = 115
2. "Jack the Ripper" = "a slut's fucker" = 115
3. "Jack the Ripper" = "a whore's fucker" = 115
4. "Jack the Ripper" = "he's mad for sex" = 115
5. "Jack the Ripper" = "is a dirty man" = 115
6. "Jack the Ripper" = "is a pervert" = 115
7. "Jack the Ripper" = "loves old cunt" = 115
8. "Jack the Ripper" = "name of a sex-maniac" = 115
9. "Jack the Ripper" = "old slut fucker" = 115
10. "Jack the Ripper" = "old whore fucker" = 115
11. "Jack the Ripper" = "sex-mad lunatic" = 115
12. "Jack the Ripper" = "sexual lunatic" = 115

In the appalling case of Mary Kelly, the coroner expressed the opinion that the killer was 'sexually insane'. Applying the Master Code in that context we find:

1. "A cipher used by Barnardo for sex-code" = 246
2. "A hidden code used by Barnardo for a sex-code" = 246
3. "A sexual lunatic hidden in Dr Barnardo" = 246
4. "A sexual lunatic is hidden in Barnardo" = 246
5. "A sexual lunatic: the clue is Barnardo" = 246
6. "A sexual madman hid as Thos. Barnardo" = 246
7. "A sexual madman hid in Thos. J. Barnardo" = 246
8. "Barnardo collected many harlots" = 246
9. "Barnardo had a secret album of sluts" = 246
10. "Barnardo had a secret album of whores" = 246
11. "Barnardo had scrap-book of old sluts" = 246
12. "Barnardo had scrap-book of old whores" = 246
13. "Barnardo hid a sexually insane man" = 246
14. "Barnardo hides evil sexual lunatic" = 246
15. "Barnardo hiding sex-crazed killer" = 246
16. "Barnardo is a raving sexual madman" = 246
17. "Barnardo is an evil sexual lunatic" = 246
18. "Barnardo is fucking the old sluts" = 246
19. "Barnardo is fucking the old whores" = 246
20. "Barnardo is hiding a sex-crazed loon" = 246
21. "Barnardo is hiding sex-monster" = 246
22. "Barnardo is name of a sex-crazed loon" = 246
23. "Barnardo is name of sex-monster" = 246
24. "Barnardo is the secret sex maniac" = 246
25. "Barnardo is to fuck the old sluts" = 246
26. "Barnardo is to fuck the old whores" = 246
27. "Barnardo knew many old sluts" = 246
28. "Barnardo knew many old whores" = 246
29. "Barnardo loved sluts' genitals" = 246

30. "Barnardo loved whores' genitals" = 246
31. "Barnardo lusts after sluts" = 246
32. "Barnardo lusts after whores" = 246
33. "Barnardo photographs sluts" = 246
34. "Barnardo photographs whores" = 246
35. "Barnardo prayed on the harlots" = 246
36. "Barnardo took advantage of sluts" = 246
37. "Barnardo took advantage of whores" = 246
38. "Barnardo uses secret code for sex" = 246
39. "Barnardo was sex-crazed doctor" = 246
40. "Barnardo's book of prostitutes" = 246
41. "Barnardo's book of sluts was black" = 246
42. "Barnardo's book of whores was black" = 246
43. "Barnardo's code for sex: you found clue" = 246
44. "Barnardo's secret book of harlots" = 246
45. "Clue is: Barnardo is a sexual deviant" = 246
46. "Clue is: Barnardo is raging sex maniac" = 246
47. "Code hid sex-maniac street-preacher" = 246
48. "Diabolical doctor's prostitute code" = 246
49. "Doctor Barnardo is a sex-mad killer" = 246
50. "Doctor Barnardo is hiding a sex maniac" = 246
51. "Doctor Barnardo is sexual lunatic" = 246
52. "Doctor Barnardo was sex-crazed" = 246
53. "Doctor Barnardo: fascinated by cunt" = 246 — the killer removed genitalia
54. "Doctor Barnardo: sex-mad murderer" = 246
55. "Doctor Barnardo: you fuck old harlots" = 246
56. "Dr Barnardo *collected* the harlots" = 246
57. "Dr Barnardo hid a sex-crazed lunatic" = 246
58. "Dr Barnardo hiding a sex-crazed loon" = 246
59. "Dr Barnardo hiding sex-monster" = 246
60. "Dr Barnardo is sexually insane" = 246
61. "Dr Barnardo name of sex-monster" = 246
62. "Dr Barnardo removes slut's womb" = 246
63. "Dr Barnardo removes whore's womb" = 246
64. "Dr Barnardo was a raging sex-maniac" = 246
65. "Dr Barnardo was sex-mad preacher" = 246
66. "Dr Barnardo: a raving sexual madman" = 246
67. "Dr Barnardo: an evil sexual lunatic" = 246
68. "Dr Barnardo: the secret sex maniac" = 246
69. "Evil Barnardo: sex-crazed preacher" = 246
70. "Fuck sluts of Dorset Street" = 246
71. "Fuck the old slut at Dorset St" = 246 — Annie Chapman? Lived at Dorset St
72. "Fuck the old whore at Dorset St" = 246
73. "Fuck whores of Dorset Street" = 246 — Chapman & Kelly?
74. "I hid a code in *The Book of Prostitutes*" = 246
75. "I took female reproductive organs" = 246

76. "I was sex-mad street preacher" = 246
77. "*Jack the Ripper* fucks dead harlots" = 246 necrophilia
78. "*Jack the Ripper* hid a sexual lunatic" = 246
79. "*Jack the Ripper:* fucker of harlots" = 246
80. "*Jack the Ripper*: name for sex-maniac" = 246
81. "*Jack the Ripper*: name of a sexual loon" = 246
82. "*Jack the Ripper:* sexual madman name" = 246
83. "*Jack the Ripper*: took female genitalia" = 246
84. "Sex-crazed lunatic is in Barnardo" = 246
85. "Sexual lunatic in *Jack the Ripper*" = 246
86. "Sexually insane man in Barnardo" = 246
87. "*Street preacher:* a maniac for sex" = 246
88. "T. J. Barnardo hid sex-crazed lunatic" = 246
89. "T. J. Barnardo is the sexual lunatic" = 246
90. "T. J. Barnardo: you must fuck a slut" = 246
91. "T. J. Barnardo: you must fuck a whore" = 246
92. "T. J. Barnardo's a sex-crazed doctor" = 246
93. "The sexual lunatic: it is Barnardo" = 246
94. "Thomas Barnardo is a sexual madman" = 246
95. "Thomas Barnardo is sex maniac name" = 246
96. "Thomas Barnardo: name of a sex-mad man" = 246
97. "Thomas J. Barnardo: sex maniac's name" = 246
98. "Thomas John Barnardo is sex-maniac" = 246
99. "Thos. Barnardo hides sexual madman" = 246
100. "You discovered sex-maniac Barnardo" = 246

Using the gematria number from the graffito (412) in that context, we find:

1. "Thomas Barnardo fucks a slut on *every day of the year*" = 412
2. "Thomas Barnardo fucks a whore on *every day of the year*" = 412
3. "Thomas John Barnardo fucked all the sluts in Whitechapel" = 412
4. "Thomas John Barnardo fucked all the whores in Whitechapel" = 412
5. "Thomas John Barnardo fucked every slut at Whitechapel" = 412
6. "Thomas John Barnardo fucked every whore at Whitechapel" = 412

If the solutions are right and Barnardo was indeed a 'sex maniac', 'sex-crazed lunatic' etc it would 'make sense' that he 'worked his way' through all the prostitutes in Whitechapel - but in any case, that is what the code told him to do.

From the (presumed) extensive list of names in *the huge black book of prostitutes,* amassed from hundreds of sex-workers in Whitechapel and Spitalfields, Barnardo would have been able to find the names of five women that fitted the codes. In view of the sexual aspect to the crimes, it's very likely the doctor-preacher was motivated to search for and found Master Code solutions like those above, discovery of which would have encouraged him to carry-out the gruesome plans he wished to enact; code solutions giving him confidence that his wicked intentions were in-keeping with an evil providence, a diabolical destiny manifest as the knife-wielding prostitute-killer *Jack the Ripper*.

It is a cliché that some serial killers almost 'want' to be caught, so the world can see just how clever they have been at fooling everyone - especially the police. They tempt Providence, risking discovery by leaving 'clues' to their identities in their 'clever games' – but not without ensuring the clues are *almost* insoluble. The coded confessions to Elizabeth Stride's murder in Barnardo's *Times* letter are far from obvious; he must have been extremely confident that none of *The Times* readers would ever suspect that he - the famous Irish philanthropist, a man seemingly very concerned for the welfare of children - was a mask hiding the most notorious of murderers, a brutal but clever killer who left coded confessions in letters and notes secretly identifying himself as *Jack the Ripper!*

The 'funny little games' the killer says he is playing in the 'Dear Boss' letter are games with the authorities, 'games' whose 'clues' did not die like witnesses or disappear and degrade like forensic evidence. By using *Skelton* and the Master Code to provide detailed instructions, the killer gave future generations a (remote) chance to solve the murders. If the homicides had been carried-out randomly - without coded clues - there would now be no way to identify the killer as there would be no remaining evidence of any kind linking the murders with an identifiable culprit. **Above all, it was Barnardo's *consistent* use of *Skelton*'s cipher and the Master Code which ensured that the mystery of the Whitechapel murders and *Jack the Ripper*'s identity would *always* be capable of solution.**

In summary, Barnardo left the following coded clues:

1. Graffito chalked on a wall in flats at 108-119 Goulston St
2. A piece of a victim's bloodied apron left at 108-119 Goulston St below the graffito
3. A bloodied knife left on the steps of a laundry at 253 Whitechapel Road
4. 'Dear Boss' letter.
5. *Saucy Jacky* note.
6. 'From Hell' note.
7. A letter in *The Times* post-dated October 6th

7. is especially significant as the letter is signed *Thos. J. Barnardo* and the content is consistent with Barnardo's area of expertise – so we can be very confident that any ciphers hidden in *The Times* letter are his. Crucially, we find the *same* cipher in the *Times* letter - used for the same purpose - as in each communication from *Jack the Ripper.* That alone is *very* strong evidence Barnardo and *Jack the Ripper* are one and the same person.

Postscript

The five canonical 'ripper' killings were in effect 'scripted' by the Master Code, like the acts of a play. *Jack the Ripper*'s five-act bloody 'drama' ran for just one season – the autumn of 1888.

In the context of drama, we note the Master Code solutions:

1. "*Jack the Ripper* was a drama title" = 246
2. "*Jack the Ripper* clue is: drama title" = 246
3. "*Jack the Ripper* lead-man name: Barnardo" = 246
4. "*Jack the Ripper*: name of a 5-act melodrama" = 246
5. "*Jack the Ripper*: name of the melodrama" = 246

The 'play' was a gruesome parody of the melodrama for which Victorian theatre was famous. As melodrama exaggerates life so *Jack the Ripper* exaggerates murder – the killer doesn't simply kill the female victims he disembowels, disfigures and destroys them.

A celebrated Irish philanthropist seemingly 'above suspicion' Doctor Barnardo escaped justice, became evermore famous and went on to live a further seventeen years. If the police *had* taken the names of those who attended the prayer meetings at 29 Hanbury St, the killer would probably have been identified as the one member of the group who had received medical training and who 'specialised' in anatomy – the prayer leader, the doctor-preacher Thomas Barnardo.

We recall the solution with gematria number 365:

"Barnardo was prayer leader in 29 Hanbury St" = 365

And the Master Code solutions:

"29 Hanbury St: Barnardo's big clue" = 246

"29 Hanbury St: BIG clue to killer" = 246

"*Jack the Ripper*: 2nd murder is a big clue" = 246 the 2nd murder in Hanbury St

The demise of the man who was *Jack the Ripper*

Thomas John Barnardo died aged sixty on 19th September 1905 after a series of angina attacks, his ashes were interred at Barkingside. An Orange Lodge in London was named posthumously in his honour; his philanthropic legacy assumed a life of its own and lived-on.

Finally, an unanswerable question: Were the ***coded*** 'ripper' killings just the tip of the proverbial ice-berg? Did Barnardo murder many more women - before and after 'Jack' - *without* using coded instructions?

In that context we recall the Master Code solutions:

- "Clue is: Dr Barnardo likes to murder" = 246
- "Doctor Barnardo *loves* murdering" = 246
- "Doctor Barnardo *loves* to murder" = 246
- "Dr Barnardo liked to kill harlots" = 246

In the 'Dear Boss' letter *Jack the Ripper* says he loves his 'work' and will not stop until caught. In fact, *Jack* gave-up killing in autumn 1888 – the question is: did Barnardo?

33. Sir Arthur Conan Doyle, *Sherlock Holmes* and the Master Code

Conan Doyle (1914) Image: Wikipedia commons

Arthur Ignatius Conan Doyle (1859-1930) was born in Edinburgh on May 22nd 1859 at 11 Picardy Place; the family had aristocratic Irish and French antecedents. The father, Charles Altamont Doyle was an alcoholic and afflicted by long-term mental illness, the mother Mary (nee Foley) was Roman Catholic like her husband. As the boy grew to adulthood, he came to reject the religion of his parents first becoming agnostic then later turning to spiritualism. Educated by wealthy English uncles, young Arthur was sent to Stoneyhurst a famous Catholic college in Lancashire noted for its Jesuitical ethos. On leaving the college Doyle studied medicine at Edinburgh University, but for a period before completing the course he became a ship's surgeon fully qualifying as a doctor after returning from his maritime adventure in 1881.

The most famous duo in crime fiction first saw the light of day in *A Study in Scarlet,* a short story written in just three weeks and published in *Beeton's Christmas Annual*, 1887. It was the 27-year-old writer's first big break following a number of rejections. Three years later, after nearly dying from a bout of influenza, the avuncular Scottish medic gave up his ophthalmic practice to concentrate entirely on writing, drawing inspiration for his characters from the people he knew. His immortal creation *Sherlock Holmes* was based *in part* on Edinburgh surgeon and university teacher Joseph Bell and – it is thought – *in part* on Henry Littlejohn, Edinburgh police surgeon and medical health officer - a cricket-playing acquaintance inspired the name *Sherlock*. *Watson* was a doctor the author knew in Dundee, a school-boy contemporary provided the name *Moriarty* while a fellow medical student gave his name to *Lestrade*, inspector of police.

The great imperial metropolis, an essential character in many of the stories with its smog-shrouded streets and sunless alleys, provided the most atmospheric of settings in which to locate the darkest of crimes. Corrupted by the city himself, *Sherlock Holmes* was no saint: drug addiction, opium den visits, association with low-life criminals and *Watson*'s description of his life-style as 'Bohemian' make that clear. Moreover, the celebrated sleuth's motivation in assisting those who sought his help did not spring from common human empathy but from a desperate personal need to fight-off *ennui.*

Taking-on only suitably challenging work, the 'bi-polar' problem-solver saw each case as an intellectual 'puzzle' to be solved using *his* special 'methods'. The feelings of those seeking help were alien to his severely logical, unemotional mind; clients were often brusquely interrogated, drained of information and abruptly discarded. This ego-centric cold-fish could be abrasive, arrogant and impatient and although the incorrigible criminal exploits of London's underworld energised him - and saved his sanity - it was his long-suffering side-kick *Doctor John Watson* who took the time and trouble to record *and* publicise their amazing escapades. Without the good doctor's literary talents, *Sherlock Holmes* would have been little more than foot-note in the history of crime fiction.

The adventures of the one and only consulting detective in the new *Strand* magazine, as recounted by *Watson*, became a 'must read' for many subscribers; yet the author grew to hate his creation with an almost visceral intensity as he felt he was being strangled by hands of his own making. Doyle saw that his paper sleuth was escaping the confines of the page, a monster that threatened to finish him artistically. The author long-aspired to be a 'proper' writer penning 'serious' literature; by his own standards the *Adventures of Sherlock Holmes* were light-weight entertainments. So, in *The Final Problem* (1893) Doyle gave his fiddle-playing, pipe-smoking investigator a suitably dramatic dénouement at Reichenbach Falls in Switzerland: the hero plunging to a seemingly inescapable demise amidst a thundering torrent of white-water, fighting evil *Professor Moriarty* to the end - implacable adversaries joined forever in the ice-cold embrace of a watery grave - or so it seemed...

But not for long... the author was forced to accept that his famous character *had* assumed a life of his own, at least in the minds of a phalanx of avid readers some of whom believed *Sherlock Holmes* to be a real person! (It's been claimed that 20,000 threatened to cancel their subscriptions to *The Strand* if their hero was killed-off). The ensuing uproar from a mass of distraught fans bewailing the great detective's end - some even wore black armbands - forced the beleaguered author to reprise the much-loved detective. And so, with the god-like help of his embattled creator the indestructible sleuth escaped Reichenbach's vertiginous cascades, miraculously avoiding certain death.

Although the author felt artistically cramped, burdened and hampered by his drug-addicted, 'Bohemian' misogynist Doyle was no fool; he saw that resurrecting the capital's celebrated 'consulting detective' would be potentially lucrative. Indeed, it was the prospect of much needed steady remuneration that gave him the incentive to write a total of 4 novels and 56 short stories, the canon now arranged in chronological sets: *The Adventures of Sherlock Holmes* (1891-1892), *The Memoirs of Sherlock Holmes* (1892-1893), *The Return of Sherlock Holmes* (1903-1904), *His Last Bow* (1908-1917) and *The Casebook of Sherlock Holmes* (1921-1927).

Since publication, *Sherlock Holmes* has become the most portrayed fictional human in history with over 25,000 adaptations across all media world-wide.

Conan Doyle, 'A. C. Smith' & *Skelton*

In addition to his talent as a writer, A. C. Doyle was a multi-faceted sportsman of some distinction. While living at Southsea in 1883 and using the alias 'A. C. Smith', he played in goal for an amateur football team at Portsmouth. A talented cricketer, he appeared in ten first class matches for the M.C.C. and when he wasn't playing football or cricket, he was Doyle the keen golfer, Doyle the gentleman pugilist, Doyle the accomplished billiards player and Doyle the pioneering skier. Among his surprisingly varied achievements, he was an inventor – the inflatable lifejacket just one of his claims to fame.

The conjecture is that, like other famous Victorian/Edwardian authors Conan Doyle used *Skelton* and the Master Code in his writing and in that context, we note the Master Code solutions:

1. "Conan Doyle has used writer's code" = 246
2. "Conan Doyle used code for writers" = 246

The conjecture is tested further by applying the cipher in the context of Doyle's footballing alias, Portsmouth goalkeeper *A. C. Smith*. **First, we find the resonance equations:**

- "*A. C. Smith* hid" = "Conan Doyle" = 79
- "*A. C. Smith:* a name hiding" = "Arthur Conan Doyle" = 146
- "*A. C. Smith:* the name of" = "Arthur Conan Doyle" = 146
- "*A. C. Smith:* the false name used for" = "Arthur Ignatius Conan Doyle" = 215
- "*A. C. Smith:* the pseudonym of" = "Arthur Ignatius Conan Doyle" = 215

Reversed, we find the resonance equation:

"Arthur Ignatius Conan Doyle" = "used the pseudonym *Smith*" = 215

Applying the Master Code in the context of Conan Doyle, A. C. Smith and *Skelton* gives the following solutions:

1. "A football player is called *A. C. Smith*" = 246
2. "*A. C. Smith:* an alias used by Conan Doyle" = 246
3. "*A. C. Smith:* false name of the footballer" = 246
4. "*A. C. Smith* is footballer's false name" = 246
5. "*A. C. Smith* was at Portsmouth" = 246
6. "Assumed name *A. C. Smith* hid Conan Doyle" = 246
7. "Clue is: *A. C. Smith* hid Conan Doyle's name" = 246
8. "Conan Doyle believes in the cipher code" = 246
9. "Conan Doyle believes occult cipher code" = 246
10. "Conan Doyle hid by false name *Smith*" = 246
11. "Conan Doyle hid secret code messages" = 246
12. "Conan Doyle knows code of *Skelton*" = 246
13. "Conan Doyle knows of the numeral" = 246
14. "Conan Doyle used *Skelton* as the code" = 246
15. **"Conan Doyle uses Freemasons' codes" = 246***
16. "Conan Doyle's code clue is very hard" = 246
17. "Doyle called goalkeeper alias *A. C. Smith*" = 246"Doyle: Portsmouth FC goalkeeper" = 246

18. "*Smith:* Conan Doyle's secret name" = 246
19. "*Smith:* pseudonym of Conan Doyle" = 246
20. "*Smith* was Conan Doyle's cipher" = 246
21. "*This* is the secret code Doyle used" = 246
22. "You found secret codes of Conan Doyle" = 246
23. "You found secret of Conan Doyle's code" = 246
24. "You found the code Conan Doyle hid. *Bravo*!" = 246
25. "You have broken code hid by Conan Doyle" = 246
26. "You have found message of Conan Doyle" = 246

Which implies that Doyle knew of *Skelton* and the Master Code by 1883, though how he came to know the cipher is unclear.

Sherringford Holmes

According to one of his earliest notes, Doyle considered naming the consulting detective *Sherringford Holmes* before finally hitting on *Sherlock*. **Applying *Skelton* in the context of *Sherringford Holmes,* we find the resonance equations:**

1. "*Sherringford Holmes*" = "consulting detective" = 171
2. "*Sherringford Holmes*" = "is the detective's name" = 171
3. "*Sherringford Holmes*" = "the name of the detective" = 171

Joseph Bell & Henry Littlejohn

Holmes was a *consulting* detective. According to Doyle, the character and his *modus operandi* was based in part on the Edinburgh surgeon and lecturer Joseph Bell. **Applying *Skelton* in that context, we find the resonance equations:**

1. "Holmes is" = "a detective" = 76
2. "Holmes is" = "Joseph Bell" = 76

Henry Littlejohn, Police Surgeon and Medical Officer of Health in Edinburgh, has also been suggested as an inspiration for the detective. Littlejohn provided Doyle with a link between medical investigation and the detection of crime. **Applying the Master Code in that case:**

1. "Henry Littlejohn alias *Holmes*" = 246
2. "Henry Littlejohn hid as *Holmes*" = 246

And:

1. "Bell and Littlejohn hiding in *Holmes*" = 246
2. "*Holmes* is both Bell and Littlejohn" = 246

In addition, we find the resonance equations:

1. "Sherlock Holmes" = "hides Littlejohn" = 128
2. "Sherlock Holmes" = "is a consultant" = 128
3. "Sherlock Holmes" = "Joseph Bell's alias" = 128
4. "Sherlock Holmes" = "plays the fiddle" = 128
5. "Sherlock Holmes" = "secret drug addict" = 128
6. "Sherlock Holmes" = "the tobacco smoker" = 128

Applying the Master Code in the *general* context of Sherlock Holmes & Dr Watson etc:

1. "221B: a clue at the Baker St. apartment" = 246***
2. "221B: is the Baker St. apartment clue" = 246
3. "Baker St address of *Holmes* hides code" = 246
4. "Baker St's address is secret code" = 246
5. "Clients climbed up 17 stairs at 221B" = 246
6. "Clue is: cocaine at 7 per cent solution" = 246
7. "Clue is: *Holmes* the man of a hundred faces" = 246
8. "Clue is: *seven percent* solution" = 246
9. "Clue is: *Sherlock Holmes* is a beekeeper" = 246
10. "Clue is: the Baker St. apartment 221B" = 246
11. "Clues to murderers' names hid in code" = 246
12. "*Cocaine:* a drug used by *Sherlock Holmes*" = 246
13. "Code was in each case of *Sherlock Holmes*" = 246
14. "*Doctor John Watson* was a cipher" = 246
15. "*Doctor Watson* was the cipher" = 246
16. "Doyle: creator of *Doctor Watson*" = 246
17. "Doyle: creator of *Sherlock Holmes*" = 246
18. "Doyle hid the code in *Sherlock Holmes*" = 246
19. "Every *Sherlock Holmes* case hid code" = 246
20. "Find *Sherlock Holmes* in 221B Baker St" = 246
21. "Flight of 17 stairs was clue at 221B" = 246
22. "Hid a code as Baker St. address of *Holmes*" = 246***
23. "Hid a code at the Baker St. apartment" = 246
24. "Hid a secret in address at Baker St" = 246
25. "Hid my code in each *Sherlock Holmes* case" = 246
26. "Hints at killers' names hid as code" = 246
27. "Hints at killers' names in codes" = 246
28. "*Holmes*: name of private detective" = 246
29. "*Holmes* is used as a detective's name" = 246
30. "*Holmes* was the detective's name" = 246
31. "*Holmes* was the famous detective" = 246
32. "*Holmes* was the great detective" = 246
33. "*Holmes*' rooms at 221B Baker Street" = 246

34. "I changed *Ormond Sacker* to *Watson*" = 246
35. "I hid a puzzle in *Sherlock Holmes*" = 246
36. "I use *Skelton* in *Sherlock Holmes*" = 246
37. "*John H. Watson* was Scottish" = 246
38. "*John Watson* is Scottish name" = 246
39. "*Lestrade*: medicine student I knew" = 246
40. "Life of *Sherlock Holmes* was Bohemian" = 246
41. "Morphine: the drug used by *Holmes*" = 246
42. "*Ormond Sacker* was *Holmes*' friend" = 246
43. "*Seven percent* was a solution" = 246
44. "*Seventeen stairs* at number 221B" = 246
45. "*Sherlock:* a cricket player friend" = 246
46. "*Sherlock:* cricket player's name" = 246
47. "*Sherlock Holmes*: addict of morphine" = 246
48. "*Sherlock Holmes:* clue is Joseph Bell" = 246
49. "*Sherlock Holmes* had a French grandma" = 246
50. "*Sherlock Holmes* hides deliberate mistakes" = 246****
51. "*Sherlock Holmes* is an addict of opium" = 246
52. "*Sherlock Holmes* is never loved" = 246
53. "*Sherlock Holmes:* retired beekeeper" = 246
54. "*Sherlock Holmes:* sixty in 1914" = 246
55. "*Sherlock Holmes* smoked an old pipe" = 246
56. "*Sherlock Holmes* was apiarist" = 246
57. "*Sherlock Holmes*' home in 221B Baker St." = 246
58. "The Baker St. apartment hides a code" = 246
59. "The famous *consulting detective*" = 246
60. "The year of *Holmes'* birth was 1854" = 246
61. "*Watson* is a doctor I knew in Dundee" = 246 +
62. "You found the secret to *Holmes'* code" = 246
63. "You have cracked *Sherlock Holmes*' code" = 246

+ It appears that Doyle knew a doctor Watson in Dundee (evidence discovered in 2014).

**In an early draft, Doyle named Holmes' associate *Ormond Sacker*. Applying *Skelton,* in that context:

"Ormond Sacker" = "John Watson" = 105 and "Ormond Sacker is" = "Dr John Watson" = 126

***The Baker St. address - 221B - is a cipher. Applying *Skelton* to "Two-Two-One B" we find:

1. "You discovered" = "code hid as address" = "Two-Two-One B" = 111
2. "You discovered" = "code I hid in address" = "Two-Two-One B" = 111
3. "You discovered" = "Two-Two-One B" = "the Master Code" = 111

So, the address '*Two-Two-One B*' is code for '*The Master Code*' in *Skelton's* cipher.

****Deliberate mistakes in the stories

The best-known intentional error is in *The Blue Carbuncle*. The gem-stone of the title was said to be lodged in the 'crop' of a Christmas goose – but geese have no crop! A second deliberate mistake appears in *The Musgrave Ritual*: an elm tree, whose height was a clue in the C17 ritual, would almost certainly have grown significantly by the time the enigmatic code was cracked, invalidating the ensuing clues. A third mistake was noticed in *The Red-Headed League* by Dorothy L Sayers - dates in the story are not consistent with the time-line. Code solutions (following) indicate that those errors are intentional, additional 'mistakes' probably await discovery...

Enumerated list of 'Adventures'

- A Scandal in Bohemia 1
- The Red-headed League 2
- A Case of Identity 3
- The Boscombe Valley Mystery 4
- The Five Orange Pips 5
- The Man with the Twisted Lip 6
- The Adventure of the Blue Carbuncle 7
- The Adventure of the Speckled Band 8
- The Adventure of the Engineer's Thumb 9
- The Adventure of the Noble Bachelor 10
- The Adventure of the Beryl Coronet 11
- The Adventure of the Copper Beeches 12
- Silver Blaze 13
- The Yellow Face 15
- The Stock-broker's Clerk 16
- The Gloria Scott 17
- The Musgrave Ritual 18
- The Reigate Squire 19
- The Crooked Man 20
- The Resident Patient 21
- The Greek Interpreter 22
- The Naval Treaty 23
- The Final Problem 24
- The Adventure of the Empty House 25
- The Adventure of the Norwood Builder 26
- The Adventure of the Dancing Men 27
- The Adventure of the Solitary Cyclist 28
- The Adventure of the Priory School 29
- The Adventure of Black Peter 30
- The Adventure of Charles Augustus Milverton 31
- The Adventure of the Six Napoleons 32

- The Adventure of the Three Students 33
- The Adventure of the Golden Pince-Nez 34
- The Adventure of the Missing Three-Quarter 35
- The Adventure of the Abbey Grange 36
- The Adventure of the Second Stain 37
- The Adventure of Wisteria Lodge 38
- The Adventure of the Cardboard Box 39
- The Adventure of the Red Circle 40
- The Adventure of the Bruce-Partington Plans 41
- The Adventure of the Dying Detective 42
- The Disappearance of Lady Francis Carfax 43
- The Adventure of the Devil's Foot 44
- His Last Bow 45
- The Adventure of the Illustrious Client 46
- The Adventure of the Blanched Soldier 47
- The Adventure of the Mazarin Stone 48
- The Adventure of the Three Gables 49
- The Adventure of the Sussex Vampire 50
- The Adventure of the Three Garridebs 51
- The Problem of Thor Bridge 52
- The Adventure of the Creeping Man 53
- The Adventure of the Lion's Mane 54
- The Adventure of the Veiled Lodger 55
- The Adventure of Shoscombe Old Place 56
- The Adventure of the Retired Colourman 57
- The hound of the Baskervilles 58
- The Valley of Fear 59
- A Study in Scarlet 60
- The Stock-broker's Clerk 61
- The Sign of (The) Four 62

Applying the Master Code in the context of all *Sherlock Holmes*' adventures gives rise to a large set of *contextually appropriate* solutions. To fully understand the significance of the solutions it is necessary to read the stories! Story number in ( ) is in the above list eg *The Sussex Vampire (50).*

1. "A clue is: blood-sucking *Mrs Ferguson*" = 246 (50, The Sussex Vampire)
2. "A clue is: *Holmes* broke *the dancing men* code" = 246 (27)
3. "A clue is: *Holmes* called *Adler 'the woman'*" = 246 (1)
4. "A clue is: *Holmes* has an older brother" = 246 (22)
5. "A clue is: *Lone Star*'s captain *Calhoun*" = 246 (5)
6. "A clue is: *rache* the German for revenge" = 246 (60)

7. “A clue is: *William Kirwan* the coachman” = 246 (19)
8. “A code is in *Whitaker’s Almanac* at page 341” = 246 (59)
9. “A code-book must have at least 534 pages” = 246 (59)
10. “A *hint* of *The Giant Rat of Sumatra*” = 246 (50) referred to in the story
11. “A hound of hell is in the *Grimpen Mire*” = 246 (58)
12. “A manuscript hidden in *Three Gables*” = 246 (49)
13. “A mastiff shot by *John Watson*” = 246 (12)
14. “A message is in *the dancing men* cipher” = 246 (27)
15. “A monograph on ciphers by *Holmes*” = 246 (27)
16. “*Abe Slaney* and *Elsie Cubitt* use the code” = 246 (27)
17. “*Abe Slaney* murdered *Hilton Cubitt*” = 246
18. “Abode of *Smith* is 13 Lower Burke St” = 246 (42)
19. “*Alec Cunningham:* the murderer’s name” = 246 (19)
20. “*Alec Fairbairn* murdered by *Browner*” = 246 (39)
21. “*Alice Rucastle* was held as a captive” = 246
22. “*Alice Rucastle:* secret prisoner” = 246 (12)
23. “*Allardyce* was the butcher’s name” = 246 (30)
24. “*Altamont* was disguise of *Holmes*” = 246 (45)
25. “*Amberley* killed *Dr Ray Ernest*” = 246 (57)
26. “*Amberley* was retired colourman” = 246
27. “An electric-blue gown of *Alice Rucastle*” = 246 (12)
28. “An old slipper hides a tobacco store” = 246
29. “*Anna* accidentally murdered *Smith*” = 246 (34)
30. “*Anna*: wife of evil *Professor Coram*” = 246
31. “*Armstrong*: medical faculty’s head” = 246 (35)
32. “*Ballarat gang* are highway robbers” = 246 (4)
33. “*Bannister*: name of the servant” = 246 (33)
34. “*Bar of Gold* opium den is haunt of *Holmes*” = 246 (6)
35. “*Baritsu* was name of a martial art” = 246 (24)
36. “*Baron Adelbert Gruner* hides a killer” = 246 (46)
37. “*Baron Maupertuis* is a swindler” = 246 (19)
38. “*Bartholomew* and *Thaddeus Sholto*” = 246 (62)
39. “Bastard of *Baskerville* is a killer” = 246 (58)
40. “Bastard *Stapleton:* killer name” = 246
41. “*Beddinton* killed weekend watchman” = 246 (61)
42. “Beggar *Hugh Boone* is *St Clair* disguised” = 246 (6)
43. “*Bellinger* was a Prime Minister” = 246 (37)
44. “*Bennett* is *Presbury* helper” = 246 (53)
45. “*Beppo* stole the Borgias’ black pearl” = 246 (32)
46. “*Billy* was pageboy to 221B Baker St” = 246 (48)
47. “Binomial theory by *Moriarty*” = 246
48. “Blanched soldier was *Emsworth*” = 246 (47)
49. “*Blessington:* an alias of *Sutton*” = 246 (21)

50. “*Blue Carbuncle* name of gem found inside goose” = 246 (7)
51. “Bog at Dartmoor called *Grimpen Mire*” = 246
52. “*Breckinridge:* dealer at Covent Garden” = 246 (7)
53. “*Brunton* cracked code the ritual hides” = 246 (18)
54. “*Brunton* cracked the ritual cipher” = 246
55. “*Brunton* loves *Rachel Howells*” = 246
56. “*Brunton* solved ritual’s clues” = 246
57. “*Brunton* the butler cracked a hidden code” = 246
58. “*Burnwell:* a disreputable villain” = 246 (11)
59. “*C. A. Milverton* is blackmailer’s name” = 246 (31)
60. “*C. A. Milverton:* name of the blackmailer” = 246
61. “*Calhoun* is captain of bark *Lone Star*” = 246 (5)
62. “Called a journalist *Mr Horace Harker*” = 246 (32)
63. “Called a music teacher *Violet Smith*” = 246 (28)
64. “Called a neurologist *Trevelyan*” = 246 (21)
65. “Called a poisonous snake *Speckled Band*” = 246 (8)
66. “Called a scientist *H. Lowenstein*” = 246 (53)
67. “Called aged housekeeper *Mrs Pringle*” = 246 (37)
68. “Called assassin *Sebastian Moran*” = 246 (25)
69. “Called *Barclay*’s maid *Jane Stewart*” = 246 (20)
70. “Called *Barrymore’s* in-law *Selden*” = 246 (58)
71. “Called bog at Dartmoor *Grimpen Mire*” = 246 (58)
72. “Called British soldier *James M. Dodd*” = 246 (47)
73. “Called broker clerk *Hall Pycroft*” = 246 (61)
74. “Called *Coram*’s maid *Susan Tarlton*” = 246 (34)
75. “Called *Countess Morcar’s* maid *Cusack*” = 246 (7)
76. “Called henchman of *Moriarty*: *Moran*” = 246 (25)
77. “Called housemaid of *Cubitt*’s: *Saunders*” = 246 (27)
78. “Called landlady *Mrs Merrilow*” = 246 (55)
79. “Called landlord of *Alpha Inn: Windigate*” (7)
80. “Called orphan *Godfrey Staunton*” = 246 (35)
81. “Called the assassin *Colonel Moran*” = 246 (25)
82. “Called the money lender *Samuel Brewer*” = 246 (56)
83. “Called the race horse *Silver Blaze*” = 246 (13)
84. “Called the vicar at Moosmoor *J. C. Elman*” = 246 (57)
85. “*Camford:* name mixed Cambridge and Oxford” = 246 (53)
86. “*Captain Basil* is the code-name of *Holmes*” = 246 (30)
87. “*Captain Jack Crocker* was a murderer” = 246 (36)
88. “Cardboard box hid two severed ears” = 246 (39)
89. “*Carey* was killed by the harpoon” = 246 (30)
90. “*Charles Gorot:* clerk in Foreign Office” = 246 (23)
91. “*Chequers* was name of inn at *Camford*” = 246 (53)
92. “Cigars are stored in a coal scuttle” = 246

93. "Cipher hid by Musgrave's ritual" = 246 (18)
94. "Clue is *Alexander Holder:* name of a banker" = 246 (11)
95. "Clue is *Alice Rucastle:* held as captive" = 246 (12)
96. "Clue is *Baritsu:* name of martial art" = 246 (25)
97. "Clue is *Bellinger:* Prime Minister" = 246 (37)
98. "Clue is *Black Peter: Carey*'s nickname" = 246 (30)
99. "Clue is *Captain Jack Crocker:* murderer" = 246 (36)
100. "Clue is *Dr Beecher: Colonel Stark* alias" = 246 (9)
101. "Clue is *Hugh Boone:* a filthy vagrant" = 246 (6)
102. "Clue is *Jefferson Hope:* murderer name" = 246
103. "Clue is *Lucy Hebron:* the yellow face" = 246 (15)
104. "Clue is *Marie Devine:* maid to *Lady Carfax*" = 246 (43)
105. "Clue is *Martha* was *Von Bork*'s p.a." = 246 (45)
106. "Clue is *Milverton:* based on Howell" = 246 (31)
107. "Clue is *Milverton:* the blackmailer" = 246
108. "Clue is *Moriarty:* the schoolboy" = 246
109. "Clue is *Morse Hudson*: a fine-art dealer" = 246 (32)
110. "Clue is *Morstan:* wife of *Watson*" = 246
111. "Clue is *Mrs Hudson:* the 221B landlady" = 246
112. "Clue is *Musgrave ritual* mistake" = 246 (18)
113. "Clue is *Norah Creina:* the name of a wreck" = 246 (21)
114. "Clue is *Peterson:* a commissionaire" = 246 (7)
115. "Clue is telephone number: XX 31" = 246 (46)
116. "Clue is the omniscient *Mycroft*" = 246 (22)
117. "Clue is two salted severed ears" = 246 (39)
118. "Clue is V V: *Vermissa Valley*" = 246 (59)
119. "Clue is *Von Bork:* name of a German agent" = 246 (45)
120. "Clue is: *Dr Roylott* was a giant" = 246 (8)
121. "Clue is: drunk servant *Toller*" = 246 (12)
122. "Clue is: *Eduardo Lucas* blackmailed *Lady Hope*" (37)
123. "Clue is: *Holmes* pushed *Moriarty*" = 246 (24) which makes *Holmes* a murderer!
124. "Clue is: *Jefferson Hope* is the killer" = 246 (60)
125. "Clue was in the Musgrave ritual" = 246 (18)
126. "Code clue is in *Whitaker's Almanac* page 341" = 246 (59)
127. "*Colonel Moran:* a *Moriarty* sidekick" = 246 (25)
128. "*Colonel Moran:* murders *Ronald Adair*" = 246
129. "*Colonel Moran:* secret assassin" = 246
130. "*Colonel Stark* is counterfeiter" = 246 (9)
131. "Convict *Selden* hides on Dartmoor" = 246 (58)
132. "*Cornelius* is pseudonym of *Oldacre*" = 246 (26)
133. "*Crowder: McCarthy*'s employee" = 246 (4)
134. "*Culverton-Smith* killed *Savage*" = 246 (42)
135. "*Cyril Morton*: an engineer's name" = 246 (28)

136. “*Damery* is acting on behalf of the king” = 246 (46)
137. “Death of *Holmes* is *The Final Problem*” = 246 (24)
138. “*Derbyshire* is alias of *Straker*” = 246 (13)
139. “D.o.b. of *Mycroft Holmes* is 18 47” = 246 Mycroft was 7 years Sherlock’s senior
140. “*Dorak:* name of old Bohemian store keeper” = 246 (53)
141. “*Dorak:* The Bohemian store keeper name” = 246
142. “*Douglas* was pseudonym of *Edwards*” = 246 (59)
143. “*Dr Barnicot* bought a bust of Napoleon” = 246 (32)
144. “*Dr Beecher* was a *Colonel Stark* alias” = 246 (9)
145. “*Dr Hill Barton* is hiding *Watson*” = 246 (46)
146. “*Dr Hill Barton* is name of *Watson*” = 246
147. “*Dr Trevelyan* is at Brook St” = 246 (21)
148. “Dutch dealer in diamond called *van Seddar*” = 246 (48)
149. “*Edward* is a young son of *Rucastle*” = 246 (12)
150. “Elm tree height: the clue is wrong” = 246 (18) the tree would have grown
151. “Engineer name: *Victor Hatherley*” = 246 (9)
152. “**Error** hidden in *Musgrave ritual*” = 246 (18)
153. “*Eugenia Ronder* took the Prussic acid” = 246 (55)
154. “Every third word is a codeword” = 246 (17)
155. “Evil *Presbury* is creeping man” = 246 (53)
156. “Evil *Roylott* killed by snake” = 246 (8)
157. “Evil *Rucastle* called mastiff *Carlo*” = 246 (12)
158. “Fighter is called *Barney Stockdale*” = 246 (49)
159. “*Five orange pips* are KKK cypher” = 246
160. “*Five orange pips:* code is sign of death” = 246 (5)
161. “*Five orange pips:* code signals a death” = 246 (5)
162. “*Five orange pips:* is a signal of death” = 246 (5)
163. “*Five orange pips:* was KKK cipher” = 246
164. “For *Holdernesse Hall* read Haddon Hall” = 246 (29) Haddon Hall near Bakewell
165. “*Fowler* is the fiancé of *Alice Rucastle*” = 246 (12)
166. “*Francis Prosper* has a wooden leg” = 246 (11)
167. “*Fred Porlock* is *false* name of an agent” = 246 (59)
168. “French worker: disguise of *Holmes*” = 246 (43)
169. “*Gelder and Co*. maker of the Napoleon bust” = 246 (32)
170. “German master was called *Heidegger*” = 246 (29)
171. “*Gilchrist* copied exam questions” = 246 (33)
172. “*Giuseppe Gorgiano* the giant Italian” = 246 (40)
173. “*Gloria Scott:* the name of a vessel” = 246 (17)
174. “*Gorgiano* was name of vicious killer” = 246 (40)
175. “*Gregson:* Scotland Yard’s best” = 246 (60)
176. “*Griggs:* name of the circus’s clown” = 246 (55)
177. “*Grimesby Roylott* was huge” = 246 (8)
178. “*Grimpen Mire* hiding *the hound of hell*” = 246 (58)

179. “*Harris* is *Holmes*’s assumed name” = 246 (61)
180. “*Harris:* the assumed name of *Holmes*” = 246
181. “*Harrison* stole the treaty” = 246 (23)
182. “*Hayes* was killer and kidnapper” = 246 (29)
183. “*Helen* the twin of *Julia Stoner*” = 246 (8)
184. “*Henderson* is hiding *Don Juan Murillo*” = 246 (38)
185. “*Henderson* masks *Don Juan Murillo*” = 246
186. “*Henri Fournaye* hid *Eduardo Lucas*” = 246 (37)
187. “Hid clue in: *The Illustrious Client*” = 246 (46) the title is code
188. “*Hill Barton* was a name of *Watson*” = 246 (46)
189. “*Holder and Stevenson*: bank’s name” = 246 (11)
190. “*Holmes* and *Baynes* are huge rivals” = 246 (38)
191. “*Holmes* and *Moriarty* die at falls” = 246 (24)
192. “*Holmes* and *Moriarty* died in falls” = 246
193. “*Holmes* died at the falls at Reichenbach” = 246
194. “*Holmes* dies in the falls of Reichenbach” = 246
195. “*Holmes* drowned in Reichenbach falls” = 246
196. “*Holmes* grades problems by pipe” = 246 (2) eg ‘a three-pipe problem’
197. “*Holmes* hid in disguise of clergyman” = 246 (1)
198. “*Holmes* hides in *Altamont* disguise” = 246 (45)
199. “*Holmes* is killed at Reichenbach Falls” = 246
200. “*Holmes* keeps a photograph of *Adler*” = 246 (1)
201. “*Holmes* solved *the dancing men*’s code” = 246
202. “*Holmes* used the tracker dog *Toby*” = 246 (62)
203. “*Holmes* was given emerald tie pin” = 246 (41) by Queen Victoria
204. “*Holy:* A *Henry Peters* moniker” = 246 (43)
205. “*Honeydew tobacco* is cardboard box name” = 246 (39)
206. “*Hope* killed *Drebber* and *Stangerson*” = 246 (60)
207. “*Hope* was name of brilliant diplomat” = 246 (37)
208. “*Hopkins*: the name of an inspector” = 246 (34)
209. “*Horner* was scapegoat of *Ryder*” = 246 (7)
210. “Horse was called *Shoscombe Prince*” = 246 (56)
211. “*Hosmer Angel* alias of *James Windibank*” = 246 (3)
212. “Huge hound: secret of *Jack Stapleton*” = 246 (58)
213. “*Hugh Boone* was *Neville Saint Clair*” = 246 (6)
214. “*Hugo Oberstein:* name of a secret agent” = 246 (41)
215. “I called bog on Dartmoor *Grimpen Mire*” = 246 (58)
216. “Indian student is called *Dulat Ras*” = 246 (33)
217. “*Irene Adler* is domiciled in *Briony Lodge*” = 246 (1)
218. “*Irene Adler* is the operatic singer” = 246
219. “*Irene Adler’s* house name: *Briony Lodge*” = 246 (1)
220. “*Irregulars* called *Street Arabs*” = 246
221. “*Isa Whitney* was Scottish” = 246

222. “*Isa Whitney:* found in the *Bar of Gold*” = 246 (6)
223. “*J. Davenport* of Lower Brixton” = 246 (22)
224. “*J. Moriarty*: a wicked professor” = 246 (24)
225. “*J. Neil Gibson* loved *Miss Grace Dunbar*” = 246 (52)
226. “*Jabez Wilson:* name of a pawnbroker” = 246 (2)
227. “*Jabez Wilson:* name of the Freemason” = 246 (2)
228. “*Jack Ferguson:* a malevolent youth” = 246 (50)
229. “*James Browner* was name of killer” = 246 (39)
230. “*James Moriarty* is arch-criminal” = 246
231. “*James Winter* hidden as *John Garrideb*” = 246 (51)
232. “*Jefferson Hope* was the murderer” = 246 (60)
233. “*John Hector McFarlane:* the scapegoat” = 246 (26)
234. “*John Mitton:* name of *Lucas’s* valet” = 246 (37)
235. “*John Turner* was murderer name” = 246 (4)
236. “*Josiah Amberley* the name of a colourman” = 246 (57)
237. “*Killer Evans* is a *John Garrideb* alias” = 246 (51)
238. “*Kitty Winter* is informer” = 246 (46)
239. “KKK is symbol Ku Klux Klan use” = 246 (5)
240. “KKK used *five orange pips* as sign” = 246
241. “KKK were *Openshaw*’s killers” = 246
242. “*Kramm* is the *King of Bohemia* incognito” = 246 (1)
243. “*Langdale Pike:* gossipmonger’s name” = 246 (49)
244. “*Latimer* is murderer of *Kratides*” = 246 (22)
245. “*Leon Sterndale* name of explorer” = 246 (44)
246. “*Leonardo* is strongman in circus” = 246 (55)
247. “*Leslie Oakshott* is the surgeon” = 246 (46)
248. “*Lestrade* was rival to Holmes” = 246
249. “*Lord Holdhurst:* the minister” = 246 (23)
250. “*Lowenstein* was scientist” = 246 (53)
251. “*Lucas* is name of the translator” = 246 (37)
252. “*MacKinnon* was a police inspector” = 246 (57)
253. “*Macphail* the *Presbury*’s coachman” = 246 (53)
254. “*MacPherson* was a Police Constable” = 246 (37)
255. “*Maria Gibson:* suicide staged as murder” = 246 (52)
256. “*Marie Devine* the maid to *Lady Carfax*” = 246 (43)
257. “*Marlow Bates: Gibson*’s employee” = 246 (52)
258. “*Mary Fraser* adored by *Jack Crocker*” = 246 (36)
259. “*Mary* is wife of *Doctor Watson*” = 246
260. “*Mary Sutherland* is duped by *Windibank*” = 246 (3)
261. “*Maud Bellamy* is love of *McPherson*” = 246 (54)
262. “*Mazarin* is name of yellow diamond” = 246 (48)
263. “*McPherson* was science master” = 246 (54)
264. “*Melas:* name of Greek interpreter” = 246 (22)

265. “Merge names Macclesfield and Buxton” = 246 (29) Priory School at Mackleton
266. “*Milverton* was killed by a widow” = 246
267. “*Milverton:* murdered by widow” = 246 (31)
268. “*Milverton:* name of diabolical blackmailer” = 246
269. “*Milverton:* the name of a blackmailer” = 246
270. “*Miss Hunter:* the governess” = 246 (12)
271. “Mistake is hiding in *The Blue Carbuncle*” = 246 (7)
272. “*Moore Agar:* doctor at Harley Street” = 246 (44)
273. “*Moran*’s attempt on *Holmes*’ life” = 246 (25)
274. “*Morecroft* an alias hiding *Winter*” = 246 (51)
275. “*Moriarty* is ‘Napoleon’ of crimes” = 246
276. “Moriarty is a very evil man” = 246
277. “*Moriarty* is arch-enemy’s name” = 246
278. “*Moriarty:* a master-mind of crime” = 246 (24)
279. “*Moriarty:* name of criminal genius” = 246
280. “*Morris* is an alias of *Duncan Ross*” = 246 (2)
281. “*Morstan* was *a* wife of *Watson*” = 246
282. “*Mortimer* is a servant of *Coram*” = 246 (34)
283. “*Mortimer* was the name of a doctor” = 246 (58)
284. “*Mr Carruthers:* the cyclist” = 246 (28)
285. “*Mr Harker* bought bust of Napoleon” = 246 (32)
286. “*Mr Merryweather:* the banker” = 246 (2)
287. “*Mr Sherman* was the owner of *Toby*” = 246 (62)
288. “*Mr. Wilder* hid *Lord Saltire*” = 246 (29)
289. “*Mrs Dixon:* name of the housekeeper” = 246 (28)
290. “*Mrs Hudson:* landlady at number 221B” = 246
291. “*Mrs Lexington*’s a housekeeper” = 246 (26)
292. “*Mrs Marker* was aged housekeeper” = 246 (34)
293. “*Mrs Mason:* the name of the nurse” = 246 (50)
294. “*Mrs Turner*: the land-lady name” = 246 (1)
295. “Murder of *Ronald Adair* at 427 Park Lane” = 246 (25)
296. “Musgrave’s ritual hid a code message” = 246 (18)
297. “Musgrave’s ritual was a hidden code” = 246
298. “*Mycroft Holmes*’ abode at Pall Mall” = 246
299. “*Mycroft* was very clever” = 246
300. “*Mycroft*: a clue was *the factotum*” = 246 (22)
301. “*Mycroft:* a member of the Diogenes club” = 246 (22)
302. “*Mycroft:* hiding at the Diogenes club” = 246
303. “*Mycroft:* the Diogenes club co-founder” = 246
304. “*Mycroft*: the very tall man” = 246
305. “Name of a murderer: *Smith* is the clue” = 246 (42)
306. “Name of the Andaman islander is *Tonga*” = 246 (62)
307. “Name the lecturer *Hilton Soames*” = 246 (33)

308. “*Neil Gibson* is nicknamed *The Gold King*” = 246 (52)
309. “*Neville Saint Clair* hid by *Hugh Boone*” = 246 (6)
310. “Norwood builder is called *Jonas Oldacre*” = 246 (26)
311. “*Oberstein* used *Pierrot* name as code” = 246 (41)
312. “*Oberstein: Cadogan West*’s killer” = 246 (41)
313. “*Oldacre* framed *J. H. McFarlane* for a murder” = 246 (26)
314. “*Old Peter Steiler* is *mein host*” = 246 (24)
315. “Old slipper is the tobacco store” = 246
316. “*Overton* is skipper of rugby” = 246 (35)
317. “*Overton* was rugby player” = 246
318. “*Patrick Cairns* killed *Black Peter*” = 246 (30)
319. “Persian slipper: tobacco store” = 246
320. “*Peter Carey* captain of *Sea Unicorn*” = 246 (30)
321. “*Peters* is a false missionary” = 246 (43)
322. “*Peters* is Australian criminal” = 246
323. “*Phelps: Watson*’s schoolmate” = 246 (23)
324. “*Pinkerton*’s: the agency in NY” = 246
325. “*Pinner* is alias name *Beddington* used” = 246 (61)
326. “Poison is called *Devil’s foot root*” = 246 (44)
327. “*Police Constable Cook* is in H Division” = 246 (5)
328. “*Porlock* is the false name of an agent” = 246 (59)
329. “*Presbury* is hiding *The Creeper*” = 246 (53)
330. “*Presbury* is name of *The Creeper*” = 246 (53)
331. “*Presbury* took a langur serum” = 246
332. “*Prescott:* name of the Chicago forger” = 246 (51)
333. “*Price* was name *Watson* assumed” = 246 (61)
334. “*Rachel Howells* loves *Brunton*” = 246 (18)
335. “*Red Circle:* criminal fraternity” = 246 (40)
336. “*Richard Brunton* broke the ritual code” = 246 (18)
337. “*Ronald Adair* shot dead on March 30, 1894” = 246 (25)
338. “*Ronder’s* murderer name is *Leonardo*” = 246 (55)
339. “*Roundhay:* name of local vicar at Poldhu” = 246 (44)
340. “*Roy:* name of the professor’s dog” = 246 (53)
341. “*Roylott* murdered his butler” = 246 (8)
342. “*Roylott*’s snake: it killed *Julia*” = 246
343. “Safe combination code was *August 1914*” = 246 (45)
344. “Safe’s combination code was *August 1914*” = 246
345. “*Sahara King* was a lion in the circus” = 246 (55)
346. “*Sandy Bain* is the Shoscombe jockey” = 246 (56)
347. “*Sarah Cushing* killed by *Browner*” = 246 (39)
348. “*Saunders* is the caretaker’s name” = 246 (51)
349. “*Saunders:* a famous dermatologist” = 246 (47)
350. “Secret cipher clue in *The dancing men*” = 246
351. “Secret cipher is in *The dancing men*” = 246
352. “Secret code hid in *The Sign of the Four*” = 246

353. “*Selden:* a convict hidden on Dartmoor” = 246 (58)
354. “*Sergius* was the real name of *Coram*” = 246 (34)
355. “*Sherlock Holmes* and *Agatha* to be engaged” = 246 (31)
356. “*Sherlock Holmes* hidden as a plumber” = 246 (31)
357. “*Sherlock Holmes* hides as plumber” = 246
358. “*Shinwell Johnson* is informer” = 246 (46)
359. “*Shlessinger* was assumed name” = 246 (43)
360. “*Shoscombe Prince* is a race-horse name” = 246 (56)
361. “*Shoscombe Prince* is the race-horse” = 246
362. “*Simpson:* little street Arab” = 246 (20)
363. “Sixth Napoleon hiding a black pearl” = 246 (32)
364. “*Smith* is *Coram*’s assistant” = 246 (34)
365. “*Spaulding* hides the name of *John Clay*” = 246 (2)
366. “*Speckled Band* is the name of the snake” = 246 (8)
367. “*St Simon* was name of noble bachelor” = 246 (10)
368. “*Stackhurst:* keeper of *The Gables*” = 246 (54)
369. “*Stamford:* dresser of *Watson*” = 246 (60)
370. “*Stapleton:* entomologist name” = 246 (58)
371. “*Stapleton:* hid wife as sister” = 246
372. “*Stapleton*: the name of a murderer” = 246
373. “*Stapleton:* used a huge hound to kill” = 246
374. “*Staunton:* the rugby player” = 246 (35)
375. “*Sterndale* had root of Devil’s foot” = 246 (44)
376. “*Straker* was horse trainer” = 246 (13)
377. “*Straubenzee* was weapon maker” = 246 (48)
378. “*Sutton* is a *hidden* police informer” = 246
379. “*Sutton:* informer for the police” = 246 (21)
380. “*Sylvius:* name of the diamond thief” = 246 (48)
381. “*Tangey* is commissionaire’s name” = 246 (23)
382. “*Tavernier:* name of a French modeller” = 246 (48)
383. “*Teddy* was mongoose of *Henry Wood*” = 246 (20)
384. “The *3-pipe* is a very hard problem” = 246 (2)
385. “*The Abbey Grange* murder by *Crocker*” = 246 (36)
386. “The beagle-foxhound is called *Pompey*” = 246 (35)
387. “The bearded man was called *Philip Green*” = 246 (43)
388. “*The Blue Carbuncle* was gem inside goose” = 246 (7)
389. “The boxer is called *Samuel Merton*” = 246 (48)
390. “The *Brambletye* in *Forest Row*” = 246 (30)
391. “*The Crooked Man:* name is *Henry Wood*” = 246 (20)
392. “*The dancing men* hid a secret cypher” = 246
393. “The error was: *a goose has no crop*” = 246 (7) error in *The Blue Carbuncle*

394. “*The Fighting Cock* is the name of an inn” = 246 (29)
395. “*The Final Problem* is death of *Holmes*” = 246 (24)
396. “*The hound of hell* is on *Grimpen Mire*” = 246 (58)
397. “*The hound of the Baskervilles* hid code” = 246 (58)
398. “*The Irregulars* of Baker Street” = 246 (62)
399. “The legend of *The Musgrave Ritual*” = 246 (18)
400. “*The Lion’s Mane*: killer jellyfish” = 246 (54)
401. “The *Maberley*’s maid is called *Susan*” = 246 (49)
402. “The mastiff shot by *Watson*” = 246 (12)
403. “The mathematician’s name is *Murdoch*” = 246 (54)
404. “*The Matilda Briggs:* the name of a ship” = 246
405. “The name *Duncan Ross* is hiding *Archie*” = 246 (2)
406. “*The Red Circle* are a secret society” = 246 (40)
407. “*The Red-Headed League:* trick by *John Clay*” = 246 (2)
408. “*The Red-Headed League*’s dates are wrong” = 246 deliberate error
409. “*The Sign of the Four* signals Death” = 246 (62)
410. “The Sikh number ‘four’ is code for Death” = 246
411. “The sudden death of *Tosca* the cardinal” = 246 (30)
412. “*Thorneycroft Huxtable:* a big man” = 246 (29)
413. “*Thurston* is billiard player” = 246 (27)
414. “*Tobacco Ash* is monograph by *Holmes*” = 246 (62)
415. “Tobacco store hidden in old slipper” = 246
416. “*Tobias Gregson:* rival to *Holmes*” = 246
417. “*Toller* was a drunk servant” = 246 (12)
418. “*Tom Bellamy* is a fisherman’s name” = 246 (54)
419. “*Trelawney Hope:* brilliant man” = 246 (37)
420. “*Trevor* hides real name of *Armitage*” = 246 (17)
421. “Triple K is a Ku Klux Klan cipher” = 246 (5)
422. “Triple K: a Ku Klux Klan cypher” = 246 (5)
423. “Triple K: the Ku Klux Klan sign” = 246
424. “*Turner* blackmailed by *McCarthy*” = 246 (4)
425. “*Tuson* is City police sergeant” = 246 (61)
426. “V V: the *Vermissa Valley* code” = 246 (59)
427. “*Victor:* the college friend of *Holmes*” = 246 (17)
428. “*Violet de Merville* was in danger” = 246 (46)
429. “*Violet* was niece of *Ralph Smith*” = 246 (28)
430. “*Walter:* name of traitor and thief” = 246 (41)
431. “Waterfall was symbol of death” = 246
432. “Wax effigy of *Holmes* is the decoy” = 246 (48)
433. “*Whitaker’s Almanac* used for cipher” = 246 (59)
434. “*Wiggins* is head of *The Irregulars*” = 246
435. “*Wiggins:* a street urchin’s name” = 246 (60)
436. “*Wilder:* bastard by *Holdernesse*” = 246 (29)

437. “*Williamson* is a defrocked priest” = 246 (28)
438. “*Willoughby Smith* saw *Anna*” = 246 (34)
439. “*Wilson Hargreave* in the NYPB” = 246 (27)
440. “*Wilson Kemp* was a brutal thug” = 246 (22)
441. “*Winter:* a victim of *Baron Gruner*” = 246 (46)
442. “X 2473: advertisement reference” = 246 (22)
443. “XX 31 was a telephone number” = 246 (46)
444. “*Youghal* is in CID at Scotland Yard” = 246 (48)

The inspiration for Professor Moriarty

Doyle indicated that Jonathan Wild, a real-life seventeenth/eighteenth century arch-criminal was the inspiration for the *character* of Professor Moriarty; however, the *name* Moriarty was that of a boy the author knew at school. **In that context we find the Master Code solutions**:

1. “I based *Moriarty* on Jonathan Wild” = 246
2. “*Moriarty:* a boy I knew at school” = 246
3. “*Moriarty* is schoolboy I knew” = 246

The Illustrious Client - although the identity of the client is not revealed explicitly, Watson finally realises that the secret illustrious client was royal – king Edward VII no less. In that context we recall the Master Code solution:

“Hid clue in: *The Illustrious Client*” = 246 which suggests the title is code

Applying *Skelton,* we find the contextually appropriate resonance equations:

1. “*The Illustrious Client*” = “a king’s name hidden by title” = 194
2. “*The Illustrious Client*” = “clue hides name: King Edward VII” = 194
3. “*The Illustrious Client*” = “is a hidden name: King Edward VII” = 194
4. “*The Illustrious Client*” = “is hint at King Edward VII” = 194
5. “*The Illustrious Client*” = “is the hidden king Edward VII” = 194
6. “*The Illustrious Client*” = “title hid a clue to a king’s name” = 194

The Blackmailer*: C. A. Milverton

Applying *Skelton*, gives the resonance equation: “*Milverton*” = “the blackmailer” = 102

And: “Named a blackmailer” = “*C. A. Milverton*” = 106

Also, the Master Code solution: “Clue is: *Milverton* based on Howell” = 246

**Charles Augustus Milverton* was based on the (alleged) blackmailer Charles Augustus Howell.

The Hound of The Baskervilles

We recall the Master Code solution: "*The Hound of The Baskervilles* hid code" = 246

Implying the title is a code; applying *Skelton*: "*The Hound of The Baskervilles*" = 218

Which gives the resonance equations:

1. "*The Hound of The Baskervilles*" = "title hid clue to the murderer" = 218
2. "*The Hound of The Baskervilles*" = "*Stapleton* was killer clue" = 218

Richard Cabell (? – 1677)

The squire of Buckfastleigh, one Richard Cabell of Brook Hall in Devon was reputedly a most wicked individual who supposedly sold his soul to the Devil. It was said that Cabell lived for hunting and that one stormy night he chased a maiden across the windswept moors, hunting her to death with his hounds. Cabell died in 1677. According to local legend, on certain special occasions a pack of phantom hounds is seen to stand at his grave. It is believed that Doyle used Cabell as his model for the evil *Hugo Baskerville* distant ancestor of *Henry Baskerville,* the young man *Holmes* and *Watson* are trying to protect.

In that context, we find the Master Code solutions:

1. "*Baskerville* was based on Richard Cabell" = 246
2. "*Hugo Baskerville* was Richard Cabell" = 246
3. "The phantom hounds of Richard Cabell" = 246

Hell-hounds at Crowsley Park

It seems that the real Henry Baskerville, owner of Crowsley Park in Oxfordshire, not only gave Doyle the name of the central character in his most famous story but also, in part, the idea of 'the hound from hell' - gateposts at the park's entrance are surmounted by a pair of 'hell-hound' statues.

In that context, we find the Master Code solution:

"Crowsley Park's hell-hounds" = 246

The Sign of (The) Four

We have seen the Master Code solution: "Secret code *hid* in: *The Sign of the Four*" = 246

Which suggests *The Sign of the Four* is a code. **Applying *Skelton,* we find the resonance equations:**

"The Sign of *The Four*" = "Sikh sign for death" = "A '4' is a Sikh death sign" = 141

Mycroft Holmes – Conan Doyle's super-brilliant 'alias'

In *The Adventure of the Greek Interpreter*, Watson is surprised to learn that Holmes has an older brother – having supposed that the brilliant eccentric must be a 'one-off'. Moreover, the doctor is astonished to discover that *Mycroft* is even cleverer than his younger sibling. Sherlock tells his friend that Mycroft's specialism is 'omniscience' and that he holds a singularly important position specially created for him at the centre of British government, the likes of which will probably never be seen again. Although Mycroft's abode is in Pall Mall, he is often to be found ensconced at the Diogenes Club - an institution for like-minded, reclusive gentlemen - which he co-founded. This raises the possibility that Mycroft is supremely knowledgeable because he represents the 'all-knowing' author. In order to write the stories - to devise the mysteries and their solutions - Doyle had to be at least as clever as his creation, the brilliant detective. Seen from that angle, Mycroft - rather than the 'obvious' candidate Doctor Watson - is the character that best represents the author.

The conjecture is tested using *Skelton* and the Master Code.

In this context we first note the Master Code solutions:

1. "*Doctor Watson* is Doyle's alias" = 246
2. "*Doctor Watson*: the alias of Doyle" = 246

As might be expected. However, applying *Skelton* in the context of Mycroft and Doyle, we find the resonance equation: "*Mycroft* is code for" = "Arthur Conan Doyle" = 146

Moreover, using Doyle's full name we find the resonance equations:

1. "Arthur Ignatius Conan Doyle" = "alias was *Mycroft Holmes*" = 215
2. "Arthur Ignatius Conan Doyle" = "hid by alias *Mycroft Holmes*" = 215
3. "Arthur Ignatius Conan Doyle" = "was hid as *Mycroft Holmes*" = 215
4. "*Mycroft Holmes* an alias for" = "Arthur Ignatius Conan Doyle" = 215
5. "*Mycroft Holmes'* name masked" = "Arthur Ignatius Conan Doyle" = 215

Applying the Master Code in this context:

1. "A. C. Doyle hiding as *Mycroft Holmes*" = 246
2. "A. I. C. Doyle hides as *Mycroft Holmes*" = 246
3. "A. I. C. Doyle hiding in *Mycroft Holmes*" = 246
4. "Conan Doyle hid by *Mycroft* mask" = 246
5. "Doyle hid by *Sherlock*'s brother" = 246
6. "Doyle is hidden by *Mycroft* guise" = 246
7. "Doyle is hidden in guise of *Mycroft*" = 246
8. "*Mycroft* hid Arthur Conan Doyle" = 246
9. "*Mycroft Holmes:* alias for Doyle" = 246
10. "*Mycroft* was an alias for Doyle" = 246
11. "*Mycroft* was cipher for Doyle" = 246
12. "*Mycroft:* secret name for Doyle" = 246

34. *Dracula* - Bram Stoker's Gothic Horror

Bram Stoker c 1906. Image attribution: unknown (Image: Wikipedia commons)

Irish writer Bram Stoker (1847-1912) was employed as a civil servant until he became the personal assistant to Sir Henry Irving (1838-1905) and manager of the Lyceum Theatre in London. Irving, the most famous Shakespearean actor of his day was idolised by Stoker and the two men developed an unusually close personal association. Indeed, some critics have discerned a homo-erotic strand in *Dracula,* a reflection perhaps of Irving and Stoker's private relationship.

Although Henry Irving was a Freemason, there is no record that Stoker was likewise a member of 'The Craft'. Nonetheless, code solutions very strongly indicate that Stoker knew *Skelton* (a Masonic cipher) and the Master Code; solutions indicate also that the author used Irving as the physical model for his vision of *Dracula,* concordant with critical opinion. The *historical character* on which the fictional Count was based - Vlad Tepes, a C15 Wallachian ruler - was a blood-thirsty, cruel tyrant appropriately nicknamed *Vlad the Impaler* for the barbaric method he used to dispatch thousands of enemy soldiers.

Bran Castle at Borgo Pass – inspiration for 'castle Dracula' (Wikipedia commons image)

Stoker got the idea for Dracula's ancestral residence from seeing an engraving of Bran Castle; however, it was while on holiday in the Yorkshire sea-side town of Whitby that the first hazy ideas for the novel began to form. It was to take another six years of research and writing before *Dracula* was finally published in 1897. The extensive use of the Master Code in *Sherlock Holmes* suggests the possibility that like Conan Doyle, Stoker too used the occult cipher in his supernatural gothic horror.

First, we note the resonance equations linking *Dracula* with *Skelton* and The Code:

"*Dracula*" = "The Code" = 42 &. "*Dracula* hides" = "*Skelton*" = 77

The conjecture is tested by applying the Master Code in the context of Stoker, *Skelton* and *Dracula*:

1. "A clue is: Bram Stoker used a code in *Dracula*" = 246
2. "A clue is: *Dracula* hides *Skelton's* codes" = 246
3. "A clue is: *Dracula* was Bram Stoker's" = 246
4. "A Masonic code in Bram Stoker's *Dracula*" = 246
5. "Abraham Stoker created *Count Dracula*" = 246
6. "Abraham Stoker: name of *Dracula* author" = 246
7. "Being called *Dracula* is supernatural" = 246
8. "Bram Stoker hid a Masonic code as *Dracula*" = 246
9. "Bram Stoker made use of *Skelton* code" = 246
10. "Bram Stoker: name of author of *Dracula*" = 246
11. "Bran Castle in Borgo Pass hid *Dracula*" = 246
12. "Bran Castle is the abode of *Count Dracula*" = 246
13. "Castle at Borgo pass is called Bran" = 246
14. "Castle at Borgo pass: *Dracula*'s home" = 246
15. "Clue is *Dracula:* a tale by Bram Stoker" = 246
16. "Clue is real name of *Dracula*: Vlad Tepes" = 246
17. "Clue is: *Skelton's* code hiding in *Dracula*" = 246
18. "Code is hidden in Bram Stoker's *Dracula*" = 246
19. "Codes *instructed* Abraham Stoker" = 246
20. "Codes used by Bram Stoker in *Dracula*" = 246
21. "*Count de Ville*: clue is the name hid a pun" = 246
22. "*Count Dracula* is a manifestation of a code" = 246
23. "*Count Dracula* is the name of a vampire" = 246
24. "*Count Dracula* named by Bram Stoker" = 246
25. "*Count Dracula* was a creature of The Code" = 246
26. "*Count Dracula:* thirsty for blood" = 246
27. "*Dracula* has hidden codes of Bram Stoker" = 246
28. "*Dracula* hides *Skelton*'s secret code" = 246
29. "*Dracula* is a name for *Vlad the Impaler*" = 246
30. "*Dracula* is Transylvanian name" = 246
31. "*Dracula* story hid a Freemason's code" = 246
32. "*Dracula* uses *Skelton*'s ciphers" = 246

33. "*Dracula* was hiding *Skelton* cipher" = 246
34. "*Dracula* was novel of Bram Stoker" = 246
35. "*Dracula*: a cipher for Henry Irving" = 246
36. "*Dracula:* a story of gothic horror" = 246
37. "*Dracula:* a tale in diaries and letters" = 246
38. "*Dracula:* title of Bram Stoker's book" = 246
39. "Freemason code hid as *Dracula* story" = 246
40. "Freemason's code in *Dracula* story" = 246
41. "Got the story of *Dracula* from a code" = 246
42. "Hid the Master Code in the *Dracula* tale" = 246
43. "Huge secret code in story of *Dracula*" = 246
44. "I dedicated *Dracula* to *little Tommy*" = 246*
45. "Irving: my model for *Count Dracula*" = 246
46. "*Nosferatu* is folk-name of vampire" = 246
47. "Real *Castle Dracula* called Bran Castle" = 246
48. "Stoker hid the secret code in *Dracula*" = 246
49. "Stoker uses a secret code in *Dracula*" = 246
50. "Story of *Dracula* hid a huge secret code" = 246
51. "Story of *Dracula* hides *Skelton*" = 246
52. "Story of *Dracula* hides the cipher" = 246
53. "Story of *Dracula* hiding secret code" = 246
54. "The clue is: Bram Stoker's *Dracula* code" = 246
55. "The code of Bram Stoker hidden in *Dracula*" = 246
56. "The name *Count de Ville*: pun on de-vil" = 246
57. "Very secret cipher hid in *Dracula*" = 246
58. "Vlad Tepes gave me the idea for *Dracula*" = 246
59. "Vlad Tepes inspired my *Dracula*" = 246
60. "Vlad the Impaler: *Dracula*'s real name" = 246
61. "You broke a code hidden as *Dracula.* Well done!" = 246
62. "You broke code hiding in *Dracula.* Well done!" = 246
63. "You cracked codes hid in *Dracula.* Well done!" = 246
64. "You discovered a secret hid in *Dracula*" = 246
65. "You found Bram Stoker's secret" = 246
66. "You found cypher of Bram Stoker" = 246
67. "You found secrets hidden by *Dracula*" = 246
68. "You have broken Bram Stoker's code" = 246
69. "You have cracked code by Bram Stoker" = 246
70. "You have found codes hid in *Dracula. Bravo!*" = 246
71. "You have found secret codes *Dracula* hid" = 246

*Stoker dedicated *Dracula* to 'Hommy-beg' - 'little Tommy' in Manx - nickname of his friend Hall Caine.

In the context of Caine and Harker, we note the Master Code solutions:

1. *"Jonathan Harker:* a cipher for Hall Caine" = 246
2. *"Jonathan Harker:* hiding name of Hall Caine" = 246
3. *"Jonathan Harker* is name for Hall Caine" = 246

The story is told in part through the diary of Jonathan Harker, the main protagonist.

The following synopsis is intended to facilitate an understanding of the ensuing code solutions. As always, it's necessary to read the book to gain fuller insight.

Jonathan Harker, a newly qualified solicitor in Exeter is sent by his superior, Peter Hawkins, to Transylvania to complete the transaction on Carfax Abbey a property in Purfleet, east of London. The purchaser - one Count Dracula, nobleman of the Szekely people - is in residence at the ancient family seat, an eerie castle perched high on a rocky out-crop in the remote Carpathian Mountains.

After a long and exhausting journey, Harker finally meets the Count and records details of his visit in a diary. The host, a tall thin pale figure with red lips and a scar on his forehead has noticeably sharp white teeth. A strange intimidating presence, Dracula never seems to eat and disappears during day-light hours. The Count is hell-bent on relocating to London, hence the property purchase and is attempting to learn all he can about England. However, it soon dawns on the hapless Harker that all is far from well, especially when he discovers that he is Dracula's prisoner - an evil being with superhuman powers. Furthermore, Harker makes the shocking discovery that three female inhabitants of the castle, weirdly seductive 'brides' of the Count, have no reflections and cast no shadows! Greatly alarmed by these nightmarish yet seemingly real phenomena and fearing for his life, Harker manages to escape Dracula's malevolent clutches and returns safely to England.

In the late nineteenth century, the wild Carpathian Mountains of Transylvania are sparsely populated lands. Count Dracula, a vampire of great antiquity, needs a regular supply of human blood for sustenance and regeneration. The dearth of suitable local prey is the reason he is so keen to emigrate to London - a city of millions where he has hidden fifty boxes of native soil, the earth on which he must periodically rest and recuperate. The milling throngs of the metropolis will be a limitless source of rejuvenating life-blood for Count de Ville, Dracula's alias in the capital. His plan is to take over the city by spawning a colony of ***nosferatu***; 'undead' zombies forced to perform their master's evil bidding - thralls held in the unrelenting grip of the vampire's supernatural power.

Having left Harker at the castle, Dracula sets sail for England in the ***Demeter*** a Russian schooner. Deep within the ship's hold, the resting vampire is stowed inside a strange chest along with many other curious boxes. The ***Demeter***'s crew, conscious of the highly unusual cargo, become increasingly ill-at-ease as unexplained events and mysterious sightings occur and... worse... as one-by-one they die. On reaching the Yorkshire coast a freak storm arises, blowing the ship towards the shore; miraculously, with no living crew left the schooner grounds in Whitby harbour and shortly thereafter a huge unearthly dog disembarks and races off into the night...

As strong as twenty men, the ancient supernatural being is able to influence animals and can transmogrify into animal form at will - sometimes appearing as a werewolf, sometimes as a huge bat and sometimes as a massive dog. Further, he has the ability to turn into mist, enabling him to pass through very narrow spaces around windows and under doors, so that few locations are beyond his reach – although a vampire must first be *invited* to enter a property.

Lucy Westenra, fiancée of Arthur Holmwood (Lord Godalming) is a habitual somnambulist. One night, on holiday at Whitby with her friend Mina Murray, she leaves the accommodation and while sleep-walking out-doors encounters Dracula. During the next few weeks, she develops a strange malady that gradually worsens and finally results in her death. Unknown to Lucy's friends, she has been transformed into a vampire by repeated nocturnal visitations of the blood-sucking Transylvanian Count. Eventually, the nature of her illness is recognised by a vampire expert from Amsterdam, Doctor van Helsing though he temporarily withholds the alarming diagnosis from the friends.

Shortly after Lucy's burial, children report seeing a weird 'bloofer lady' wandering at night in a graveyard. On learning of the strange sighting van Helsing, Harker and the Texan Quincey Morris set forth and discover the tomb. Whereupon Lucy's corpse is beheaded, a stake is driven through the heart and garlic flowers are placed in the mouth. By this gruesome ritual, the vampire curse is lifted and Lucy Westenra's soul achieves lasting peace; Van Helsing then reveals the terrifying truth about her illness and 'un-dead' condition.

Staying at Dr Seward's huge asylum, Lucy's friends set off in search of the diabolical Count. However, Dracula uses his supernatural power to communicate with an inmate of the asylum: Renfield - Harker's predecessor - a 'zoophagous' lunatic who eats insects and small animals in order to acquire their 'life-force'. Through Renfield, Dracula discovers the plot to destroy him and uses his power over the lunatic to enter the asylum and attack Mina, drinking her blood and forcing her to drink his. Now, like Lucy she is destined to become a vampire unless Dracula is destroyed first.

The friends discover all the Count's properties around London, finding boxes of soil hidden within; the sacrament is placed inside each of the boxes, making them useless for vampires. Dracula now has only one resting place left - 347 Piccadilly - and the friends nearly trap him there but he manages to escape. However, they soon discover that he is returning to the safety of his ancestral castle in Transylvania with the last remaining box of soil. Meanwhile, a psychic connection has developed linking Dracula and Mina - so van Helsing uses a hypnotic technique on her to track the Count's movements.

Eventually reaching Galaz in Romania the friends part company, van Helsing and Mina proceed directly to Dracula's castle where the professor destroys the three female vampires. At the same time Harker and Holmwood pursue the Count who, still resting inside the box, is travelling by river-boat to a rendezvous agreed with local men loyal to him. Simultaneously, Morris and Dr Seward track the boat by land. At the rendezvous, the box housing the supernatural creature is loaded on a wagon by the local men. The four friends in hot pursuit join forces and after a fight, overcome Dracula's helpers – though Morris is seriously wounded in the fray. Immediately, the box is flung open exposing its diabolical contents to the fading light of the sun. At once, Harker hacks through the vampire's neck as Morris stabs the abomination in the heart with a Bowie knife. The physical manifestation of evil that was Dracula crumbles to dust, Mina is free of the curse but Morris succumbs to his injury and dies.

Applying the Master Code in the context of the novel's details:

1. "**3-4-7**: the magical numbers of *Count Dracula*" = 246
2. "***347*** *Piccadilly* is London lair of *Dracula*" = 246
3. "***347*** *Piccadilly* was London address" = 246
4. "***347*** *Piccadilly:* a hide-out of *Count de Ville*" = 246
5. "***347*** *Piccadilly*: *Dracula*'s London hide-out" = 246
6. "A *bloofer lady* was *Lucy*'s nickname" = 246
7. "A lair of *Dracula* at ***347*** *Piccadilly, London*" = 246
8. "A sailing ship's name was *Demeter*" = 246
9. "A storm landed *Dracula* at Whitby" = 246
10. "*Berseker* was the wolf's name" = 246
11. "*Bilder* was a zoological garden keeper" = 246
12. "*Billington:* Whitby solicitor" = 246
13. "*Bloofer lady* is nickname of a vampire" = 246
14. "Called the un-dead vampire *nosferatu*" = 246
15. "Clue is: *Count de Ville* title of *Dracula*" = 246
16. "Clue is: *Dracula* can turn into mist" = 246
17. "Clue is: *Lucy*'s nickname *bloofer lady*" = 246
18. "Clue is: vampires cast no shadow" = 246
19. "Clue is: zoophagous lunatic *Renfield*" = 246
20. "*Count de Ville* was a title of *Dracula*" = 246
21. "*Count de Ville:* the alias *Dracula* uses" = 246
22. "*Count Dracula* had red eyes and red lips" = 246
23. "*Count Dracula* hid 50 boxes of soil" = 246
24. "*Count Dracula* is blood-sucking un-dead man" = 246
25. "*Count Dracula* is hidden as werewolf" = 246
26. "*Count Dracula* is the name of a vampire" = 246
27. "*Count Dracula* left the *Demeter* as a dog" = 246*
28. "*Count Dracula* returns to dust" = 246
29. "*Count Dracula* took the form of a huge bat" = 246
30. "*Count Dracula* travelled to London" = 246
31. "*Count Dracula* was *Count de Ville* in London" = 246
32. "*Count Dracula:* beheaded by *Jonathan Harker*" = 246
33. "*Count Dracula:* killed with Bowie knife" = 246
34. "*Count Dracula:* nobleman of Szekely" = 246
35. "Crucifix defends against a vampire" = 246
36. "*Demeter* was Russian ship name" = 246
37. "*Dr Seward* had huge lunatic asylum" = 246
38. "*Dr van Helsing:* an alias of Stoker" = 246*
39. "*Dr van Helsing: Dracula*'s nemesis" = 246
40. "*Dracula* grows younger from blood" = 246
41. "*Dracula* hid at the Borgo Pass castle" = 246

42. "*Dracula* hid his lair at **347** in Piccadilly" = 246
43. "*Dracula* landed at Whitby hid as huge dog" = 246
44. "*Dracula* made a special study of England" = 246
45. "*Dracula* rests on native soils" = 246
46. "*Dracula* rests until nightfall" = 246
47. "*Dracula* used ***347** Piccadilly* as address" = 246
48. "*Dracula* was a creature of darkness" = 246
49. "*Dracula* was as strong as 20 men" = 246
50. "*Dracula* was *Count de Ville* in London" = 246
51. "*Dracula:* blood-thirsty vampire" = 246
52. "*Dracula:* learning the English language" = 246
53. "*Dracula:* tall, thin and a scar on forehead" = 246
54. "*Dracula:* the vampire *and* werewolf" = 246
55. "*Dracula*: Transylvania's Count" = 246
56. "*Dracula:* twenty-men strong" = 246
57. "*Dracula*'s account in *Harker*'s diary" = 246
58. "*Dracula*'s plan is: take over London" = 246
59. "Exeter was *Jonathan* and *Mina*'s abode" = 246
60. "Fend off vampires with a crucifix" = 246
61. "Form of bat assumed by vampires" = 246
62. "Garlic is used to ward off vampire" = 246
63. "*Harker* told the *Dracula* story" = 246
64. "*Hawkins:* the Exeter lawyer" = 246
65. "*Holmwood* is titled *Lord Godalming*" = 246
66. "Jack Straw's Castle, Hampstead" = 246 a real place
67. "*Jonathan Harker* decapitates *Dracula*" = 246
68. "*Jonathan Harker:* a solicitor's name" = 246
69. "London lair of *Dracula* is ***347** Piccadilly*" = 246
70. "*Lucy* was a habitual sleep-walker" = 246
71. "*Lucy Westenra* is *Dracula*'s bride" = 246
72. "*Lucy Westenra:* fiancée of *Holmwood*" = 246
73. "*Lucy Westenra:* the bride of *Dracula*" = 246
74. "*Mina Murray*: name of *Harker*'s fiancée" = 246
75. "*Morris* stabbed at *Dracula*'s heart" = 246
76. "*Peter Hawkins:* name of a lawyer" = 246
77. "*Quincey Morris* came from the U.S." = 246
78. "*Quincey Morris*: he was Texan" = 246
79. "*Renfield* was a *zoophagous* lunatic" = 246
80. "*Renfield:* a servant of *Count Dracula*" = 246
81. "The Borgo pass castle hides *Dracula*" = 246
82. "The castle at Borgo pass hid *Dracula*" = 246

83. “*The Count de Ville:* an alias *Dracula* used” = 246
84. “The *Count Dracula* seduced *Lucy Westenra*” = 246
85. “The lair of Dracula is at ***347*** *Piccadilly*” = 246
86. “The madman *Renfield* eats insects” = 246
87. “The numerals **3-4-7** are *Count Dracula*’s” = 246
88. “The secret address: ***347*** *Piccadilly*” = 246
89. “The *three* vampire brides of *Dracula*” = 246
90. “The vampires have no reflection” = 246
91. “*Three Four Seven:* a code of *Count Dracula*” = 246
92. “Vampires assume the form of a bat” = 246
93. “*Van Helsing* is an alias of Stoker” = 246**
94. “*Van Helsing* is *Dracula*’s nemesis” = 246
95. “*Van Helsing* is name of Dutch doctor” = 246
96. “*Van Helsing:* home is in Amsterdam” = 246
97. “*Van Helsing*: vampire expert” = 246
98. “*Vanderpool* is herbalist of Haarlem” = 246
99. “Ward-off a vampire by using garlic” = 246
100. “Wound of *Morris* proved mortal” = 246

*Applying *Skelton,* we find: “big dog hid” = “Dracula” = 42 Dracula left the ship as a huge dog.

**It seems that just as Doyle was disguised as the super-genius Mycroft Holmes, Bram Stoker was concealed as the all-knowing ‘vampire expert’ van Helsing.

35. Sir Edward Elgar's Musical Enigma

Elgar c 1900 image attribution: unknown (Wikipedia commons)

Sir Edward William Elgar (1857-1934) the famous English composer was also an amateur cryptographer; his code-breaking ability demonstrated by his brilliant 6-page solution of a very difficult puzzle, said by its creator to be 'insoluble'. The composer solved the 'impossible' problem during a train journey and was the only person in Britain to succeed.

Variations on an original theme (Op 36) popularly known as the *Enigma Variations* or just *Enigma* was composed between October 1898 and February 1899. Dedicated by Elgar to 'my friends pictured within', the piece consists of 14 'sketches' representing in music each 'friend's' character and idiosyncrasies. The 'friends' consist of 13 people and a dog, alluded to in the score either by nicknames or initials - all bar one identified.

Work on opus 36 began at Elgar's home in Malvern on Friday 21st October 1898, following a hard-day teaching. After the evening meal the composer lit a cigar, sat at the piano and by way of relaxation started to tinkle the keys. On hearing the extemporisations his wife, Caroline, expressed a liking for a particular phrase; encouraged by her approval he continued to develop the tune and four months later '*variations on an original theme*' was complete.

As well as being a code-solver Elgar was an amateur code-maker and 'Enigma' is the musical cipher he bequeathed to posterity. The basic problem is to identify a well-known tune hidden as the first six bars of the 1st violin score, the part of the piece Elgar himself labelled 'Enigma'. By way of 'clues', he indicated that the hidden tune was 'popular' and a 'counterpoint' to the *Enigma* theme, adding that beyond it lay a 'larger theme' which is never heard – and so, there are *two* puzzles.

Although he gave a few obscure hints, Elgar said he would never reveal the secret of *Enigma* and the definitive solution died with him; however, he indicated that on finding the right tune the answer would be 'obvious' and '***a dark saying***' would be significant. The composer's close friend Dora Penny, driven by sheer frustration and desperate for the answer begged him to tell her the secret; giving little away, he said that 'of all people' he thought *she* would have identified the mystery tune...

Why *Dora* 'of all people'? Perhaps because, as has been suggested before, her name is a hint at the solution - specifically, 'Penny'. Does the mystery tune relate in some way to *money*?

If, as Elgar said *Enigma*'s hidden theme is a 'popular' tune it shouldn't be too difficult to identify. Yet, after more than 123 years an agreed answer remains elusive because there are so many possibilities, each based on the *subjective* interpretation of music. It seems, therefore, that there is little prospect of finding a definitive result through a purely 'musical' approach. By contrast, in light of the composer's proven expertise with ciphers and codes, cryptanalysis might offer a better chance of finding the answer. **The conjecture is that like some of his famous contemporaries, Elgar knew *Skelton*'s cipher and the Master Code and used it in opus 36 as the following solutions indicate:**

1. "Code of *Skelton* is solution of *Enigma*" = 246
2. "Elgar used *Skelton* cipher in *Enigma*" = 246
3. "Elgar used *Skelton* gematria for code" = 246
4. "*Enigma* puzzle hides *Skelton* code" = 246
5. "I used *Skelton's* code for *Enigma* riddle" = 246
6. "My *Enigma* uses the code of *Skelton*" = 246
7. "Need *Skelton*'s code to solve *Enigma*" = 246
8. "Numbers are clues to the code *Enigma* hid" = 246
9. "*Skelton* code is used for *Enigma* riddle" = 246
10. "*Skelton* code was Elgar's *Enigma* clue" = 246
11. "*Skelton* is Elgar's clue to a hidden code" = 246
12. "*Skelton* is Elgar's clue to cipher" = 246
13. "*Skelton* solves the code Elgar hid" = 246
14. "*Skelton* solves the code *Enigma* hid" = 246
15. "*Skelton*: Elgar's clue to cypher" = 246
16. "Solve a code *Enigma* hid using *Skelton*" = 246
17. "Solve code in *Enigma* using *Skelton*" = 246
18. "Solve *Enigma* with code of *Skelton*" = 246
19. "Use *Skelton* to crack Elgar's codes" = 246
20. "Use *Skelton* to crack *Enigma's* codes" = 246
21. "Use *Skelton* to crack my *Enigma* code" = 246
22. "Used *Skelton* gematria for *Enigma* code" = 246

Elgar's hint - a 'popular' tune

The fact that the composer called the mystery tune 'popular' suggests it's either a well-known folk tune or nursery rhyme *tune* – but not 'classical music' which (c 1900) had yet to be 'popularised' through recordings and other media. Nursery rhyme tunes are probably more widely known than folk tunes, as many of the former are sung at kindergartens across the land whereas the latter tend to be regional in character.

So - with the possible hint at Dora *Penny's* name - is the answer to the mystery a *nursery rhyme* featuring *money* – a nursery rhyme with a *tune*? Elgar had labelled the first 6 bars of the 1st violin score 'enigma' – a very significant clue from the composer. We see that there are 24 notes in the 6 bars. Is there a nursery rhyme *song* involving money which includes the numbers 6 and 24? The answer is – **yes** – 'Sing a *Song* of ***Six***pence' a pocket full of rye/**Four and twenty** blackbirds baked in a pie...

Enigma is a cipher whose secret is hidden in 'numbers'

So, the 'hidden' counterpoint to *Enigma* (first six bars of 1st violin score) is identified as the nursery rhyme tune ***Sing a song of sixpence*** **–** many code solutions (following) confirm the answer. However, identifying the hidden tune is only part of a much bigger problem because, as Elgar said, a larger theme which is never heard lies beyond - a hint perhaps at the code itself, which cannot be heard. In view of the code solutions above, further testing for the use of *Skelton* and the Master Code is appropriate.

Elgar's clue: applying *Skelton*, by trial and error we find the resonance equations:

"Elgar's clue" = "use the code of" = "*Skelton*" = 77

"*Enigma*" = "*hid* code of" = "Elgar" = 38

And: "Edward Elgar" = "*is* The Enigma" = 88

In the same context, applying the Master Code:

1. "Code *hidden* in Edward Elgar's *Enigma* tune" = 246
2. "Composer's name *hid* by *Enigma's* name" = 246*
3. "Edward Elgar's *Enigma* tune *hid* cipher" = 246
4. "Edward Elgar *hid Enigma*'s cipher tune" = 246
5. "Elgar *hid* secret code clue in *Enigma* score" = 246
6. "Elgar's *Enigma* tune *hid* the cipher clue" = 246
7. "Elgar's *Enigma* tune *hid* the cypher" = 246
8. "The code is *hidden* in Elgar's *Enigma* tune" = 246

***We note the resonance equations**: "*Enigma*" = "hiding" = "name of" = "Elgar" = 38

Applying *Skelton* to the title "Sing a song of sixpence" (gematria number 173) gives the following *contextually appropriate* resonance equations:

1. "A tune *hidden* as *Enigma:* clue is" = "sing a song of sixpence" = 173
2. "A tune *hiding* in *Enigma* was" = "sing a song of sixpence" = 173
3. "***Original theme***: the clue is" = "sing a song of sixpence" = 173
4. **"Sing a song of sixpence" = "a musical *enigma* is solved" = 173**
5. "Sing a song of sixpence" = "*Enigma*'s counterpoint" = 173
6. "Sing a song of sixpence" = "*hid* solution of *Enigma* as a code" = 173
7. "Sing a song of sixpence" = "*hid* the **digits** of a code number" = 173 **2, 4 & 6**
8. "Sing a song of sixpence" = "*hides* solution of *Enigma* code" = 173
9. "Sing a song of sixpence" = "tune *hides* as the *Enigma* code" = 173
10. "Sing a song of sixpence" = "tune *hiding* in the *Enigma* code" = 173
11. "Sing a song of sixpence" = "you found tune *hid* in *Enigma*" = 173
12. "Sing a song of sixpence" = "you found tune. Well done!" = 173
13. "Sing a song of sixpence" = "you solved the *Enigma* code" = 173
14. "Tune hiding in *Enigma*: clue is" = "sing a song of sixpence" = 173

Applying *Skelton* in the context of *Elgar*, *Enigma* and the Master Code:

1. "The Master Code" = "is the code of *Enigma*" = 111
2. "The Master Code" = "the clue to *Enigma*" = 111
3. "You discovered" = "the clue to *Enigma*" = 111

Reproduced by kind permission of Robert W. Padgett

The 1st violin score was labelled 'Enigma' by Elgar himself – the score is the key to the mystery.

Applying the Master Code to Elgar, Enigma etc. gives the following solutions:

1. "1st violin score *hides* code numeral" = 246 — 24 notes, 6 bars
2. "1st violin score *hides* secret code" = 246
3. "2 quavers and 2 crotchets *hide **code*** clue" = 246 — first 4 notes: "BG-CA" = 13 = "code"
4. "2 quavers and 2 crotchets *hiding **code***" = 246
5. "**24** notes are in **six** bars of *Enigma*" = 246
6. "4/4 time-signature to Elgar's *Enigma*" = 246
7. "13 friends and one dog are *hidden* by *Enigma*" = 246
8. "13 friends of Elgar and a dog *hidden* in *Enigma*" = 246
9. "14 variations on a theme *hide* in *Enigma*" = 246
10. "**84** *hides* in the *Enigma* score" = 246 — sum of 1st violin note-values using *Skelton*
11. "A clue to ***code*** is in first four notes" = 246 — first four notes: "BG CA" = 13 = "code"
12. "A clue to *Enigma:* ***6** pence* in title of song" = 246
13. "A ***code*** clue in 2 quavers and 2 crotchets" = 246 — "BG CA" = 13 = "code"
14. "A code clue is in the first six bars" = 246 — which Elgar labelled 'enigma'
15. "A code was *hidden* as *Enigma Variations*" = 246

16. "A key in first six bars of *Enigma*" = 246
17. "A key to *Enigma* is in the six bars" = 246
18. "A Masonic code hid by 1st violin score" = 246
19. "A Masonic code hid in score of 1st violin" = 246
20. "A nursery rhyme about money" = 246 'sixpence' & 'the king was in his counting house...'
21. "*A pocket full of rye:* hint at a song" = 246
22. "*A pocket full of rye* is song hint" = 246
23. "A *popular tune* is *hidden* in the *Enigma*" = 246
24. "A secret code *hid* as 1st violin score" = 246
25. "A song about 'blackbirds' *hides* clues" = 246
26. "A song of sixpence is a tune *Enigma hid*" = 246
27. "A tanner *hid* in *Enigma* tune's title" = 246 'tanner' is slang for sixpence
28. "A tune *Enigma hid* is very popular" = 246
29. "A well-known tune *hidden* by *Enigma*" = 246
30. "An unheard larger theme *hides* a cipher" = 246
31. "Augustus Jaeger: his code was *Nimrod*" = 246
32. "BGCA DBAC BDGA FGAB AGDB BGAG: test of your wit" = 246 notes for 1st violin in 'enigma'
33. "BGCA DBAC BDGA FGAB AGDB BGAG: the code tests wit" = 246
34. "Called opus thirty-six *Enigma*" = 246
35. "Clue in the first violin's score" = 246
36. "Clue is: Augustus Jaeger was *Nimrod*" = 246
37. "Clue is: count notes and bars of *Enigma*" = 246
38. "Clue is: *Enigma hid* the secret code of Elgar" = 246
39. "Clue is: *Enigma hiding* song about money" = 246
40. "Clue is: you have found Elgar's *Enigma* code" = 246
41. "Clue to a *hidden* code *hides* as *Enigma*'s score" = 246
42. "Clue to a hidden code *hiding* in *Enigma*'s score" = 246
43. "Clue to cipher *hides* as *Enigma*'s score" = 246
44. "Clue to cipher *hiding* in *Enigma*'s score" = 246
45. "Clue to *Enigma*'s cipher is *Skelton*" = 246
46. "Clue to *Enigma* tune: money in title" = 246
47. "Clues are in *song about blackbirds*" = 246
48. "Clues *hide* as *song about blackbirds*" = 246
49. "Clues *hide* in the first six bars" = 246
50. "Code clue: *Enigma* uses *Skelton*'s key" = 246
51. "Code Elgar *hid* in *Enigma* score is secret" = 246
52. "Code Elgar uses is *Skelton*'s key" = 246
53. "Code *Enigma Variations hid* is a test" = 246
54. "Code *hid* by Elgar in *Enigma Variations*" = 246
55. "Code *hid* by Elgar's composition *Enigma*" = 246

56. “Code in musical enigma composed by Elgar” = 246
57. “Code key *Enigma* uses is *Skelton*’s” = 246
58. “Code was *hiding* in *Enigma Variations*” = 246
59. “Code you have found is *Enigma* solution” = 246
60. “**Digits** 2-4-6 *hidden* by *Enigma* variation” = 246
61. “**Digits** *hide* in nursery rhyme” = 246
62. “**Digits** in 1st violin score *hide* a clue” = 246
63. “*Eating bread and honey* is song hint” = 246
64. “*Eating bread and honey:* hint at a song” = 246
65. “EDU nickname for Edward William Elgar” = 246
66. “Edward Elgar *hid* test as musical code” = 246
67. “Edward Elgar used the code of *Skelton*” = 246
68. “Edward William Elgar *hid* the *Enigma* code” = 246
69. “***Edward William Elgar:*** Elgar’s name” = 246
70. “Elgar composed *Enigma* using a cipher-code” = 246
71. “Elgar hid secret code clue in *Enigma* score” = 246
72. “Elgar used *Skelton* cipher in *Enigma*” = 246
73. “Elgar uses *Skelton* cipher for code” = 246
74. “Elgar’s *Enigma* uses *Skelton* as code” = 246
75. “Elgar’s *original theme* is the *Enigma*” = 246
76. “*Enigma* and song share same numbers” = 246
77. “*Enigma* code clue is: *a song about sixpence*” = 246
78. “*Enigma* code *hides* a nursery rhyme” = 246
79. “*Enigma* code *hides* initials of friends” = 246
80. “*Enigma* composition *hides* a secret code” = 246
81. “*Enigma hid* **6 pence** and **24 blackbirds** tune” = 246
82. “*Enigma hid* Elgar’s very difficult code” = 246
83. “*Enigma hid* initials of **C**aroline **A**lice **E**lgar” = 246
84. “*Enigma hid* musical cryptogram clue” = 246
85. “*Enigma hid* the same numbers as a song” = 246
86. “*Enigma hid* twenty-four and six” = 246
87. “*Enigma hides* 2-4-6 in first six bars” = 246
88. “*Enigma hides a* musical cryptogram” = 246
89. “*Enigma hides* extremely hard codes” = 246
90. “***Enigma hides Sing a song of sixpence***” = 246
91. “*Enigma hides* the initials of friends” = 246
92. “*Enigma hiding* my friends’ initials” = 246
93. “*Enigma* is twenty-four notes” = 246
94. “*Enigma* name is *hiding* composer’s name” = 246 “Enigma” = “Elgar” = 38
95. “*Enigma* tune hiding *song of sixpence*” = 246

96. "*Enigma* tune hint: the clue is *money*" = 246
97. "*Enigma* tune was song about money" = 246
98. "*Enigma* uses the Masonic cypher-code" = 246
99. "*Enigma* was a wit test by Elgar" = 246
100. "*Enigma* was Edward Elgar's secret" = 246
101. "*Enigma* was *hiding* a song about money" = 246
102. "*Enigma* was *hiding* the arithmetic code" = 246
103. "*Enigma:* a clue was in musical notation" = 246
104. "*Enigma*: big clue in nursery rhyme" = 246
105. "*Enigma:* counterpoint was the clue" = 246
106. "*Enigma*: gematria number **eighty-four**" = 246 see following
107. "*Enigma*: nursery rhyme *hid* a big clue" = 246
108. "*Enigma:* opening theme in G minor key" = 246
109. "*Enigma:* tune of nursery rhyme" = 246
110. "*Enigma' s hidden* counterpoint tune" = 246
111. "*Enigma*'s clues *hide* in song lyrics" = 246
112. "*Enigma*'s first four notes *hid* ***code*** clue" = 246
113. "*Enigma's* name was composer's name" = 246
114. "*Enigma*'s score *hides* clues to a cipher" = 246
115. "*Enigma's* theme in the key of G minor" = 246
116. "*Enigma's Variations hid* nicknames" = 246
117. "Few find **digits** in *Enigma* variation" = 246
118. "Few find Master Code **digits** in *Enigma*" = 246
119. "Find a secret number score of *Enigma hid*" = 246
120. "Find a secret numeral *Enigma* score *hid*" = 246
121. "Find *eating bread and honey* in a rhyme" = 246
122. "Find secret number in score of *Enigma*" = 246
123. "Find secret numeral in *Enigma* score" = 246
124. "First four notes are clues to ***code***" = 246
125. "First four notes *hid* ***code*** as cipher" = 246
126. "First six bars of *Enigma* hide key" = 246
127. "First-violin score *hid* Elgar's code" = 246
128. "First-violin score *hid* numbers" = 246
129. "First-violin score *hides* a cipher" = 246
130. "First-violin score *hides* my code" = 246
131. "First-violin score is hint at" = 246
132. "First-violin score: BGCA DBAC BDGA FGAB AGDB BGAG" = 246
133. "Friends initials are *hiding* in *Enigma*" = 246
134. "Friends of the composer *hid* in *Enigma*" = 246
135. "*Hid* a clue in first six bars of *Enigma*" = 246
136. "*Hid* clue as the first violin score" = 246

137. “*Hid* clues as *Sing a song of sixpence*” = 246
138. “*Hid* ***code*** as first four notes of *Enigma*” = 246 “BG CA” = 13 = “code”
139. “*Hid* code clues as a nursery rhyme” = 246
140. “*Hid* hint in score of first violin” = 246
141. “*Hidden* tune: *Sing a song of sixpence*” = 246
142. “I *hid* clue in the first violin score” = 246
143. “I *hid* ***code*** in first four notes of *Enigma*” = 246
144. “I *hid* secret number in *Enigma*’s score” = 246
145. “I use a nursery rhyme as tune” = 246
146. “I used tune in nursery rhyme” = 246
147. “Look at score to solve my *Enigma*” = 246
148. “Look for Master Code **digits** in *Enigma*” = 246
149. “Look for *the fall of the seventh*” = 246 one of Elgar’s obscure clues
150. “*Money* is a hint at the *Enigma* tune” = 246
151. “Monogram of Caroline Alice Elgar in *Enigma*” = 246
152. “Musical enigma composed by Elgar *hid* a code” = 246
153. “Musical enigma *hid* secret codes of Elgar” = 246
154. “Musical riddle left by Edward Elgar” = 246
155. “Nicknames *hide* in *Enigma Variations*” = 246
156. “Notes and bars in *Enigma hid* a code number” = 246
157. “Notes and bars in *Enigma* score hid clue” = 246
158. “Numbers hiding in *Enigma* score are clue” = 246
159. “Numbers in *Enigma* same as the song” = 246
160. “Nursery rhyme used as tune” = 246
161. “Nursery rhyme: clue for tune” = 246
162. “Nursery rhyme’s numbers” = 246 6 & 24
163. “Nursery song is tune of *Enigma*” = 246
164. “Nursery song: tune *hid* in *Enigma*” = 246
165. “*Parts* of song are clues in my code” = 246
166. “*Pocket full of rye* is clue to song” = 246
167. “Popular tune: the clues hide in *Enigma*” = 246
168. “*Same* numbers in *Enigma* as the song” = 246 6 & 24
169. “*Same* numerals are in *Enigma* and song” = 246
170. “Secret code **digits** are *hidden* in *Enigma*” = 246
171. “Secret codes *hidden* by Elgar’s *Enigma*” = 246
172. “Secret of *Enigma* discovered by you” = 246
173. “Secret theme is *contrapuntal*” = 246 theme is a counterpoint to the Enigma tune
174. “Secret tune in six bars of *Enigma*” = 246
175. “*Sing a song of sixpence* is *hiding* a code” = 246
176. “*Sing a song of sixpence:* an *Enigma* clue” = 246

177. "Six bars of *Enigma* hid a secret tune" = 246
178. "*Skelton* is clue to Elgar's cipher" = 246
179. "*Skelton* is clue to *Enigma*'s cipher" = 246
180. "*Skelton*: clue to Elgar's cypher" = 246
181. "*Skelton*: clue to *Enigma*'s cypher" = 246
182. **"Solution of *Enigma* is by secret code" = 246**
183. **"Solve *Enigma* with code of *Skelton*" = 246**
184. "*Song of sixpence* is big clue to *Enigma*" = 246
185. "Song's lyrics are *Enigma* code clues" = 246 for example 188 below
186. "Study *Enigma's* score: find the clue" = 246
187. "Tempo of the *Enigma* theme is *Andante*" = 246
188. "The code clue is: *the birds began to sing*" = 246
189. "The code *Enigma* uses is Masonic cipher" = 246
190. "***The dark saying*** refers to Death" = 246
191. "The *Enigma* code ends with the double bar" = 246 see 1st violin score
192. "The *Enigma* is Elgar's wit test" = 246
193. "The *Enigma* of Elgar hides 13 people and a dog" = 246
194. "The *Enigma* tune: a hint was money" = 246
195. "The *Enigma* tune is a hint at money" = 246
196. "The *Enigma Variations hide* a numeral" = 246
197. "The *Enigma Variations* of Elgar *hide* a code" = 246
198. "The first six bars are *hiding* a code" = 246
199. "The first violin score is code clue" = 246
200. "The first violin score was a code" = 246
201. "The first violin's score *hid* a clue" = 246
202. "*The hint is:* a song about *sixpence*" = 246
203. "The monograms of Elgar's friends" = 246
204. "The musical enigma composed by Elgar" = 246
205. "The musical riddle is left by Elgar" = 246
206. "The score of *Enigma hides* the numeral" = 246
207. "The score of *Enigma* is *hiding* **digits** 2-4-6" = 246
208. "The ***score*** of *Enigma* was **84**" = 246 (pun, see following)
209. "The score of *Enigma* was common time" = 246
210. "*Unheard larger theme* is the cipher" = 246
211. "Used a nursery rhyme's tune" = 246
212. "Used nursery rhyme as tune" = 246
213. "You cracked codes *Enigma hides*. Well done!" = 246
214. "You cracked Elgar's cipher. Well done!" = 246
215. "You cracked *Enigma*'s cipher. Well done!" = 246
216. "You discovered *Enigma's* secrets" = 246

217. "You discovered secret code by *Elgar*" = 246
218. "You have broken the *Enigma* code Elgar *hid*" = 246
219. "You have found key to the code of *Enigma*" = 246
220. "You have solved difficult code of *Enigma*" = 246
221. "You knew of the secret code *Enigma hid*" = 246
222. "You must have solved code in *Enigma*" = 246
223. "You must have solved *the Enigma*" = 246
224. "You passed Elgar's music test" = 246
225. "You passed *Enigma*'s music test" = 246
226. "You passed tests *hid* by Elgar" = 246
227. "You passed tests *hid* by *Enigma*" = 246
228. "You solved codes Elgar *hid*. Well done!" = 246
229. "You solved codes *Enigma hid*. Well done!" = 246
230. "You solved Edward Elgar's *hidden* code" = 246
231. "You understood a code Elgar's *Enigma hid*" = 246
232. "You understood code in Elgar's *Enigma*" = 246
233. "Your *Enigma* code guess was right" = 246
234. "Your guess at *Enigma* code is right" = 246

Reversed solutions:

- 246 = "a number *hid* as a nursery rhyme"
- 246 = "clue in the first violin's score"
- 246 = "*hid* as *Enigma* score's notes and bars"
- 246 = "in the nursery rhyme song"
- 246 = "is *hidden* in nursery rhyme"
- 246 = "is in the first violin's score"
- 246 = "is number nursery rhyme *hid*"
- 246 = "is the number the *Enigma* theme *hides*"
- 246 = "number a nursery rhyme *hides*"
- 246 = "number *hidden* in first six bars"
- 246 = "secret number *hid* as *Enigma*'s score"
- 246 = "was number *hiding* in *Enigma*'s score"

Applying *Skelton* to the notes in the first six bars of the 1st violin score, the part Elgar labelled 'Enigma', we find the resonance equation:

- "BGCA DBAC BDGA FGAB AGDB BGAG" = "*hid* Enigma's code" = **84**
- "BGCA DBAC BDGA FGAB AGDB BGAG" = "is the code clue" = **84**

So, **84** = "is the code clue"

Applying the Master Code in the context of the gematria number 84:

1. **"Eighty-four**: a clue *Enigma's* notes *hide***"** = 246
2. "Notes in *Enigma* add-up to **84"** = 246
3. "Notes of *Enigma* sum to **84"** = 246
4. "You have found **eighty-four** in *Enigma*" = 246

Inspection shows that there is no 'E'-note in the first six bars of the 1st violin score and in that context, we find the resonance equations:

1. "Very good indeed" = "you discovered" = "no **E**-note in *Enigma*" = 111
2. "Very good indeed" = "you discovered" = "the clue to *Enigma*" = 111

Applying the Master Code in the context of the 'missing' E note:

1. "'**E'**-note missing from 1st violin" = 246
2. "'**E'** is missing from the *Enigma* theme" = 246
3. "'**E'**-note is missing from the theme" = 246
4. "A clue spotted by you*:* *Enigma* has no '**E**'" = 246
5. "Clue is: there is no **'E'** in *Enigma*'s score" = 246
6. "Edward Elgar used no '**E'**-notes in *Enigma*" = 246
7. "*Enigma:* **'E'**-note is missing by design" = 246
8. "First violin score has no '**E**'-note" = 246
9. "Missing '**E'**-note was intentional" = 246
10. "Purposely left out the '**E**'-note" = 246
11. "The big clue: *Enigma* score has no **E**-notes" = 246
12. "The '**E**' is absent from *Enigma*'s score" = 246
13. "The clue was: no '**E**'-note in *Enigma* score" = 246
14. "The *Enigma* score is missing '**E'**-note" = 246
15. "The *Enigma* score left out the '**E**'-note" = 246
16. "You spotted clue: no '**E'**-note in *Enigma*" = 246
17. "You will find no '**E**'-note in the *Enigma*" = 246

A dark saying

The composer hinted that '*a dark saying*' would be significant when the correct solution was found. **Applying *Skelton* in that context gives the resonance equation**: **"A dark saying" = "Elgar's hint" = 99**

Applying the Master Code gives solutions that relate 'a dark saying' and Shugborough's Arcadia:

1. "*A dark saying:* a clue was *hidden* at Arcadia" = 246
2. "*A dark saying:* a clue was *hiding* in Arcadia" = 246
3. "*A dark saying:* clue is at Shugborough" = 246
4. "*A dark saying:* clue was *hiding* on Arcadia" = 246
5. "*A dark saying: hid* on Shugborough Arcadia" = 246
6. "*A dark saying:* in Arcadia in Shugborough" = 246

7. *"A dark saying:* is a code alluding to ***Death***" = 246
8. "Edward Elgar broke code O.U.O.S.V.A.V.V *hid*" = 246**
9. "Edward Elgar cracked code at Shugborough = 246
10. "Edward Elgar solved Shugborough code" = 246
11. "Edward Elgar used code *hid* in Shugborough" = 246
12. "Edward Elgar used Shugborough Hall code" = 246
13. "Elgar cracked the code clue at Shugborough" = 246
14. "Elgar found the code used at Shugborough" = 246
15. "Elgar knew about a code *hid* in Shugborough" = 246
16. "Elgar knew of codes *hid* at Shugborough" = 246
17. "Elgar knew of codes Shugborough *hides*" = 246
18. "Elgar knew of Shugborough's cipher" = 246
19. "Shugborough's codes broken by Elgar" = 246
20. "The code Elgar used is *hid* in Shugborough" = 246

Note: O.U.O.S.V.A.V.V inscribed on the base of Pan's shrine-folly has been identified as the acronym for the quotation: Orator Ut Omnia Sunt Vanitas Ait Vanitas Vanitatum - which translates as: *'Vanity of vanities, saith the preacher all is vanity'* and is taken to mean that life is ultimately pointless because everyone dies. The quotation is from Ecclesiastes (1:2). **Applying the Master Code in that context:**

"***Dark saying*** found in Ecclesiastes" = 246

**In view of his ability to crack very difficult cipher-puzzles and his evident knowledge of *Skelton* and the Master Code, it's plausible Elgar solved the cipher on Pan's shrine-folly at Shugborough (O.U.O.S.V.A.V.V) but if that *was* the case it seems he chose to keep the solution secret.

The dark saying on Pan's tomb: e*t in Arcadia ego* – 'and I am (also) in Arcadia' – where 'I' alludes to Death. Master Code solutions (above) imply that a clue to Elgar's 'dark saying' can be found in Arcadia at Shugborough.

Applying the Master Code in that context:

"Et in Arcadia ego is ***a dark saying*** in Arcadia" = 246

The composer's ominous hint that 'a *dark* saying' is significant alludes to the grim fact that death is everywhere and inescapable, as Arcadia's inscription implies. However, there is an alternative possibility consistent with another Master Code solution: it's possible Elgar was hinting at the Masonic oath's threat of a terrible fate awaiting those who reveal the Craft's secrets.

Applying the Master Code in that context:

"A Freemason's oath is ***a dark saying***" = 246

With either interpretation, we find the Master Code solutions:

1. *"Death is inescapable* is ***a dark saying***" = 246
2. *"The* ***dark saying*** refers to *Death*" = 246

Applying *Skelton*'s cipher to a popular title of the work: "*Enigma Variations"* (= 138) gives the following *contextually appropriate* resonance equations:

1. "Enigma Variations" = "a code *hides* as the music" = 138
2. "Enigma Variations" = "a very difficult code" = 138
3. "Enigma Variations" = "absent '**E**' note is a clue" = 138
4. "Enigma Variations" = "are a code *hid* as the music" = 138
5. "Enigma Variations" = "are a secret few find" = 138
6. "Enigma Variations" = "code clues in the music" = 138
7. "Enigma Variations" = "Elgar's *hidden* cipher" = 138
8. "Enigma Variations" = "few find code: well-done!" = 138
9. "Enigma Variations" = "few find secret clue" = 138
10. "Enigma Variations" = "*hid* a musical cypher" = 138
11. "Enigma Variations" = "*hid* clues of secret code" = 138
12. "Enigma Variations" = "*hid* code for the future" = 138
13. "Enigma Variations" = "*hid* Masonic cypher" = 138
14. "Enigma Variations" = "*hid* the code clue as music" = 138
15. "Enigma Variations" = "*hide* the secret codes" = 138
16. "Enigma Variations" = "*hides* a Masonic cipher" = 138
17. "Enigma Variations" = "*hiding* a code in the music" = 138
18. "Enigma Variations" = "*hiding* code of *Skelton*" = 138
19. "Enigma Variations" = "huge code Edward Elgar *hid*" = 138
20. "Enigma Variations" = "I *hid* code clue in the music" = 138
21. "Enigma Variations" = "is Elgar's secret" = 138
22. "Enigma Variations" = "is hiding a code you found" = 138
23. "Enigma Variations" = "is lacking the '**E**' note" = 138
24. "Enigma Variations" = "is secret few find" = 138
25. "Enigma Variations" = "is the Freemason code" = 138
26. "Enigma Variations" = "is the huge code Elgar hid" = 138
27. "Enigma Variations" = "*multum in parvo*" = 138
28. "Enigma Variations" = "music hid numeral clue" = 138 24, 6 clue to 246
29. "Enigma Variations" = "music hides a numeral" = 138
30. "Enigma Variations" = "no '**E**' is in *Enigma* score" = 138
31. "Enigma Variations" = "no '**E**': clue in *Enigma* score" = 138
32. "Enigma Variations" = "score's missing '**E**'" = 138
33. "Enigma Variations" = "secret code by Elgar" = 138
34. "Enigma Variations" = "secret code is true" = 138
35. "Enigma Variations" = "the code hid here is real" = 138
36. "Enigma Variations" = "the music is hidden code" = 138
37. "Enigma Variations" = "the secret of Elgar" = 138
38. "Enigma Variations" = "the tune is a cipher" = 138
39. "Enigma Variations" = "trust the codes" = 138
40. "Enigma Variations" = "used *Skelton* as code" = 138

41. “Enigma Variations” = “you found no ‘**E**’ in *Enigma*” = 138
42. “Enigma Variations” = “you guessed my code” = 138
43. “Enigma Variations” = “you have solved code” = 138

Reversed equations:

1. “Elgar *hid* ciphers as” = “Enigma Variations” = 138
2. “Elgar *hid* musical code as” = “Enigma Variations” = 138
3. “Elgar’s musical code in” = “Enigma Variations” = 138
4. “*Hid* secret cipher in” = “Enigma Variations” = 138
5. “I *hid* musical cipher as” = “Enigma Variations” = 138
6. “Musical code in Elgar’s” = “Enigma Variations” = 138
7. “***Popular*** tune *hid* in” = “Enigma Variations” = 138 Elgar said the tune was ‘popular’
8. “*This* is Elgar’s code” = “Enigma Variations” = 138
9. “You are right about” = “Enigma Variations” = 138
10. “You found code *hidden* by” = “Enigma Variations” = 138
11. “You found the clue to” = “Enigma Variations” = 138
12. “You found the code *hid* in” = “Enigma Variations” = 138

Applying *Skelton,* we find the resonance equation*:* “Enigma Variations” = “*multum in parvo*” = 138

An ‘unheard larger theme’

As indicated at the start, *Enigma* is *two* problems. Elgar said that in addition to the mystery counter-point tune there is a ‘larger theme’ which is never heard. **The conjecture is that the larger theme is the cipher itself. Applying *Skelton* in that context:**

1. “Larger theme” = “is *Skelton*” = 98
2. “Larger theme” = “is the cipher” = 98

Applying the Master Code in that context:

1. “The larger theme *is* the cypher” = 246
2. “The *unheard larger theme* is a hidden code” = 246
3. “*Unheard larger theme* is the cipher” = 246
4. “You have found *Enigma*’s unheard theme” = 246

It seems the answer to the second of Elgar’s ‘puzzles’ is that the unheard ‘larger theme’ is the cipher.

Applying *Skelton* to the title ‘The Enigma Variations’:

1. “*Bravo*! you solved code in” = “the Enigma Variations” = 167
2. “*Bravo*! you solved the” = “code in Enigma Variations” = 167
3. “The Enigma Variations” = “you cracked Elgar’s *Enigma*” = 167
4. “The Enigma Variations” = “you have solved the code” = 167
5. “The Enigma Variations” = “you solved secret code” = 167

Finally... the 1st violin score - the BIG clue...

The word 'enigma' implies something cryptic - like a cypher - and that suggests the musical puzzle might be solved through a cryptological approach. Elgar, a talented amateur cryptographer himself labelled the first six bars of the 1st violin score 'enigma', a highly significant clue from the composer and therefore a very strong hint that those six bars are the key to the mystery.

Applying the Master Code in the context of the 1st violin score:

1. "1st violin *hid* solution of *Enigma* code" = 246
2. "1st violin *hiding Enigma* solution" = 246
3. "1st violin score *hides* secret code" = 246
4. "1st violin score is *hiding* the clue" = 246
5. "A secret code *hid* as 1st violin score" = 246
6. "Clue in the first violin's score" = 246
7. "Crack *Enigma* code: read 1st violin score" = 246
8. "Digits in 1st violin score *hide* a clue" = 246
9. "*Enigma* code: clue is in 1st violin score" = 246
10. "*Enigma hid* a code: clue is 1st violin score" = 246
11. "*Enigma* is *hidden* in 1 st violin score" = 246
12. "*Enigma*: 1st violin score *hiding* big clue" = 246
13. "*Enigma*: 1st violin score is the clue" = 246
14. "*Enigma*: clue *hidden* in 1st violin score" = 246
15. "First-violin score *hid* cipher clue" = 246
16. "First-violin score *hid* cypher" = 246
17. "First-violin score *hid* Elgar's code" = 246
18. "First-violin score *hid Enigma*'s code" = 246
19. "First-violin score *hid* numbers" = 246
20. "First-violin score *hides* a cipher" = 246
21. "First-violin score *hides* my code" = 246
22. "First-violin score is hint at" = 246
23. "First violin score was hint" = 246
24. "First violin *score*: **84**" = 246 "BGCA DBAC BDGA FGAB AGDB BGAG" = **84** pun on 'score'
25. "First violin score: BGCA DBAC BDGA FGAB AGDB BGAG" = 246
26. "*Hid* clue as the first violin score" = 246
27. "*Hid* hint in score of first violin" = 246
28. "Key to *Enigma hid* in first violin" = 246
29. "Look for code first violin score *hid*" = 246
30. "The first violin score is code clue" = 246
31. "The first violin score was a code" = 246
32. "The first violin's score *hid* a clue" = 246
33. "You found code *hid* in 1st violin score" = 246

Reversed solutions:

- 246 = “is *hid* as the first violin score”
- 246 = “is in the first violin’s score”

Conclusion

Numbers are the common elements linking music and cryptography; in that context, we recall the Master Code solution:

“Numbers are clues to the code *Enigma* hid” = 246

It makes sense that numbers/digits connect *Enigma* and the mystery tune; the digits being the notes and bars in the 1st violin score - the same digits in *both* the nursery rhyme *and* the Master Code key.

This is not the first occasion that ***Sing a Song of Sixpence*** has been identified as the solution of the *Enigma* mystery tune; however, earlier suggestions were largely ‘guess-work’ unsupported by hard evidence. **This *is* the first time** that a great deal of evidence has been amassed which very strongly supports the assertion that the nursery rhyme’s tune is indeed *Enigma*’s ‘secret’ counterpoint and moreover, that Elgar’s ‘dark saying’ is concerned with death and that the larger ‘unheard’ theme is a secret cipher. Indeed, the foregoing plethora of solutions shows that the BIG secret hidden by *Enigma* was ‘*The Code*’ - not the mystery tune.

36. The 'magic' gematria number hidden as measurements

The Master Code's 'magic' gematria number 246, identified as special by the Master Code has been concealed at various locations and appears in both digit and numeral form – the purpose: to show that 246 has 'objective reality' and is not simply a figment of the solver's imagination.

In that context, we find the Master Code solutions:

1. "Clue is: find code key by measurement" = 246
2. "Find key to the code in measurement" = 246
3. "Hid *this* code number in measurement" = 246
4. "Key to code *hidden* as measurements" = 246
5. "Key to code is *hidden* in measurement" = 246
6. "Make measurements to find number" = 246
7. "Make measurements: find code numeral" = 246
8. "Measurement is clue to the code key" = 246
9. "Take measurements: find code's key" = 246
10. "You find code key *hid* as a measurement" = 246

The Master Code key is 'hidden' in/on buildings and monuments as the digits (2,4,6) and as a numeral (246). Examples include: Newton's tomb monument (digits), Shugborough estate's gate to Land's End direct distance (246 miles), Chiswick House garden-pool circumference (246 feet) obelisk-obelisk separation (246 yards) and *Andromeda* fountain's diameter at Osborne House (246 inches). So, the 'magic' gematria number appears as measurements in each of the old imperial units: inches, feet, yards and miles.

Applying the Master Code:

1. "A portrait of Queen *hides* code's key" = 246
2. "Code key *hidden* as a portrait of Queen" = 246
3. "Code key *hides* as portrait of Queen" = 246
4. "Code key *hiding* in portrait of Queen" = 246
5. "Key to code *hid* as *Andromeda*'s fountain" = 246 at Osborne House, I o W
6. "Key to code *hid* in portrait of Queen" = 246
7. "Key to code *hides* in a painting of Queen" = 246
8. "Key to code *hiding* at Shugborough Hall" = 246
9. "Key to code is *hid* in painting of Queen" = 246
10. "Key to the code *hid* in Chiswick Garden" = 246
11. "Key to the code in Margate's grotto" = 246*
12. "Key to the code on gate at *All Souls*" = 246
13. "Key to the code on Newton's tomb" = 246

*Location of the grotto's key is currently unknown.

37. Code solutions and resonance equations - why believe them?

Naming the cipher

The cipher was dignified with a name long ago (almost certainly) because it was deemed sufficiently important to warrant special recognition. Naming *Skelton* gave it a status that set it apart from a host of anonymous, unremarkable ciphers.

Correspondence

Many code solutions correspond exactly with known 'facts'; this happens hundreds of times because the solutions have been *arranged* to agree with the 'facts' by the code-makers.

'Correspondence' is especially evident in the works of authors that have made extensive use of *Skelton*, examples include: Benjamin Franklin, William Wordsworth, Charles Dickens, *George Eliot*, *Mark Twain*, *Lewis Carroll*, Arthur Conan Doyle, Bram Stoker, John Buchan, Agatha Christie, J. R. R. Tolkein, Graham Greene, Ian Fleming, *John le Carre*, Len Deighton, Kingsley Amis, Frederick Forsyth, Colin Dexter, Douglas Adams, J. K. Rowling/*Robert Galbraith*, Anthony Horowitz and Stella Rimington. It's very remarkable that so many well-known writers have used the *same* cipher with the *same* gematria number for the *same* purpose, that is: to link the names of characters to their respective roles. The consistency among many hundreds of examples is extremely strong evidence the solutions have been constructed intentionally.

Alternative number-letter substitution ciphers applied in the ***same*** contexts as *Skelton* and the Master Code, fail to achieve anything like a comparable degree of consistent, precise correspondence with established fact. In other words, if *Skelton* is replaced with an alternative cipher the huge set of *contextually appropriate* solutions is destroyed.

Deliberate mistakes

Intentional 'errors' have been left as 'hints' in/on various artefacts - texts, pictures, monuments etc - mistakes which 'make sense' only to those who know the cipher. By presenting deliberate 'errors' as clues the 'code-maker' shows the 'code-solver' they have the right cipher; moreover, 'mistakes' that appear as puns and jokes imply wit – so the 'errors' are far more likely the result of 'intentional human involvement' than random chance.

Information content of solutions

Among the works of C19 authors examined in the foregoing who have used *Skelton* extensively, we find large sets of solutions in which each solution contains verifiable information. In the case of Dickens' characters for example, there are (at least) 125 *non-repeating* solutions - the information content is therefore maximal, a state of affairs highly unlikely to have arisen by chance.

END OF PART 1

Acknowledgements

Kate Vereker

I will forever be indebted to Kate for her attentive reading of arcane occult texts – obscure material I would never have had either the inclination or patience to study myself. Above all, I want to thank her for bringing to my attention the gematria of *Skelton*, the crucial information that has proven absolutely essential and without which this book would not exist.

Joan Robinson

I owe an eternal debt of gratitude to Joan for providing the perfect 'five-star' environment in which to research, write and above all *think*. The 'multitudes' that know 'Joanie' personally would attest to her unbounded kindness, thoughtfulness and generosity. Without her unfailing encouragement and support for over twenty years, progress would have been impossible and *The Secret Code of Destiny* would never have seen the light of day.

The Author

Born in 1957, Robert Nield was raised in Saddleworth near Manchester. After attending Hulme Grammar Sch. Oldham, Bristol University & Manchester University he taught physics at SJD College in Cheshire (1980-2002) and mathematics & physics at Chengdu & Xinghua in China (2012-2015). In 2007 he published *Breaking the Shakespeare Codes* which identifies the secret author of the celebrated works for the first time.

His You Tube channel: ***Many Mysteries – One Secret Solution*** presents original work on the following:

- Building Giza's pyramids - the easy way
- Missing Malaysian flight MH 370 - evidence & reasoning identify a uniquely special location
- *Shake-speare*'s secret author - 'Mr W. H.'
- Sporadic Alzheimer's disease - cause, prevention & potential treatment
- Is 'natural' mathematics the foundation for a 'granular-holistic' cosmology?

Printed in Poland
by Amazon Fulfillment
Poland Sp. z o.o., Wrocław
06 September 2023

58248b02-194c-4d3f-9158-ea30a4947b1dR02